# Pop Goes the Decade

**Recent Titles in
Pop Goes the Decade**

Pop Goes the Decade: The Fifties
*Ralph G. Giordano*

Pop Goes the Decade: The Eighties
*Thomas Harrison*

Pop Goes the Decade: The Nineties
*Kevin L. Ferguson*

Pop Goes the Decade: The Seventies
*Richard A. Hall*

# Pop Goes the Decade

*The Sixties*

**MARTIN KICH AND AARON BARLOW**

BLOOMSBURY ACADEMIC
NEW YORK • LONDON • OXFORD • NEW DELHI • SYDNEY

BLOOMSBURY ACADEMIC
Bloomsbury Publishing Inc
1385 Broadway, New York, NY 10018, USA
50 Bedford Square, London, WC1B 3DP, UK
29 Earlsfort Terrace, Dublin 2, Ireland

BLOOMSBURY, BLOOMSBURY ACADEMIC and the Diana logo
are trademarks of Bloomsbury Publishing Plc

First published in the United States of America by ABC-CLIO 2020
Paperback edition published by Bloomsbury Academic 2025

Copyright © Bloomsbury Publishing Inc, 2025

COVER PHOTOS: Bob Dylan, ca. 1967. (Everett Collection Historical/Alamy Stock Photo);
Lyndon B. Johnson, ca. 1969. (Everett Collection Historical/Alamy Stock Photo);
Twiggy, ca.1960s. (Photofest); Infinite Flower. (LisaAFischer/iStockphoto)

All rights reserved. No part of this publication may be reproduced or
transmitted in any form or by any means, electronic or mechanical,
including photocopying, recording, or any information storage or retrieval
system, without prior permission in writing from the publishers.

Bloomsbury Publishing Inc does not have any control over, or responsibility for,
any third-party websites referred to or in this book. All internet addresses given
in this book were correct at the time of going to press. The author and publisher
regret any inconvenience caused if addresses have changed or sites have
ceased to exist, but can accept no responsibility for any such changes.

Library of Congress Cataloging-in-Publication Data
Names: Kich, Martin, author. | Barlow, Aaron, author.
Title: Pop goes the decade. The sixties / Martin Kich. Other titles: Sixties
Description: Santa Barbara : Greenwood, 2020. | Series: Pop goes the decade |
Includes bibliographical references and index.
Identifiers: LCCN 2019026592 (print) | LCCN 2019026593 (ebook) |
ISBN 9781440862847 (hardback) | ISBN 9781440862854 (ebook)
Subjects: LCSH: Popular culture—United States—History—20th century. |
United States—Civilization—1945- | United States—Social life and customs—1945–1970. |
United States—Intellectual life—20th century. | Nineteen sixties.
Classification: LCC E169.12 .K4624 2020 (print) | LCC E169.12 (ebook) | DDC 973.92—dc23
LC record available at https://lccn.loc.gov/2019026592
LC ebook record available at https://lccn.loc.gov/2019026593

ISBN: HB: 978-1-4408-6284-7
PB: 979-8-7651-4115-1
ePDF: 978-1-4408-6285-4
eBook: 979-8-2161-3040-6

Series: Pop Goes the Decade

To find out more about our authors and books visit www.bloomsbury.com
and sign up for our newsletters.

# Contents

*Timeline* vii
*Background and Introduction* xiii

**Exploring Popular Culture**

1 Film 3
2 Television 31
3 Music 60
4 Literature 87
5 Sports 151
6 Art 170
7 Fashion 187
8 Media and Advertising 194
9 Controversies 205
10 Game-Changers 249
11 Legacy 286

*Bibliography* 297
*Index* 301

# Timeline

**1960**   February 1: Sit-in protests against segregation begin in Greensboro, North Carolina, as four African American students remain at the lunch counter of a Woolworth's store that refuses to serve them.

March 23: Elvis Presley is discharged from the Army after two years' service as a draftee stationed in Germany.

May 1: Gary Powers, a pilot flying a U-2 reconnaissance jet for the Central Intelligence Agency, is shot down by the Soviet Union and captured alive.

June 23: The first birth control pill (after decades of development) is approved by the Federal Drug Administration, though "the pill" had already been in use, putatively for other purposes, for three years.

September 26: The first televised presidential debate, between Vice President Richard Nixon and Senator John Kennedy, takes place in Chicago. Three others would follow before the November election.

November 9: Senator John Kennedy beats Vice President Richard Nixon in a close presidential election.

**1961**   January 20: John Fitzgerald Kennedy is inaugurated as the 35th president of the United States, declaiming "Ask not what your country can do for you—ask what you can do for your country."

March 1: The Peace Corps is established through an executive order by President Kennedy, who named Sargent Shriver as director.

April 16: The invasion sponsored by the Central Intelligence Agency at Cuba's Bay of Pigs begins, the actual landing taking place during the early hours of April 17. The failing attempt, and its air support, would last until April 20.

May 4: The Congress of Racial Equality's first Freedom Ride leaves by bus from Washington, DC, for New Orleans, Louisiana. Others would follow throughout the rest of the year.

May 9: Newton Minow, chair of the Federal Communications Commission, gives a speech to the National Association of Broadcasters and calls television a "vast wasteland," sparking the first serious national conversation on the growing role of television in American culture.

May 25: In a speech to a joint session of Congress, President Kennedy proposes that "this nation should commit itself to achieving the goal, before this decade is out, of landing a man on the moon and returning him safely to the Earth."

**1962** August 5: Marilyn Monroe, the most famous American sex symbol since the early 1950s, dies by her own hand through a drug overdose at the age of 36.

September 29: James Meredith, accompanied by U.S. Marshals, becomes the first African American student to start the enrollment process at the University of Mississippi. Riots broke out, resulting in several deaths as well as burned cars.

October 15: President Kennedy is notified that U-2 aircraft reconnaissance has identified Soviet Union nuclear missiles in Cuba. The next day, Kennedy would convene his Executive Committee, starting a standoff that would last until October 29 with Nikita Khrushchev, leader of the Soviet Union, announcing the dismantling of the missiles.

**1963** August 29: During the March on Washington for Jobs and Freedom, Martin Luther King Jr. delivers his "I Have a Dream" speech to a crowd of a quarter of a million, asking Americans "to work together, to pray together, to struggle together, to go to jail together, to stand up for freedom together, knowing that we will be free one day."

November 22: President John Kennedy is assassinated in Dallas, Texas, by Lee Harvey Oswald. Vice President Lyndon Johnson is sworn in as the 36th president of the United States.

**1964** January 8: President Johnson declares a War on Poverty during his State of the Union address leading to the Economic Opportunity Act of 1964 along with a number of other initiatives.

January 11: The highest profile report to date detailing the dangers of tobacco is released by the Surgeon General's Advisory Committee on Smoking and Health. It established that cigarette smokers have an increased early mortality, that smoking is the primary cause of chronic bronchitis, that there is a correlation between smoking, emphysema, and heart disease, that smoking increases the chance of lung cancer, and that babies born to smoking mothers have a higher likelihood of being underweight.

February 7: The Beatles arrive for the first time in the United States, met by a huge crowd at New York's JFK International Airport, enhancing the "Beatlemania" that was already sweeping the youth of the country but that would reach new heights over the coming months.

May 7: In a speech at Ohio University, President Johnson proclaims that "We will build a Great Society. It is a society where no child will go unfed, and no youngster will go unschooled." "The Great Society" would become the first major catch phrase of his administration.

July 2: The first Civil Rights Act is enacted, prohibiting inequality in voter registration, schools, employment, and public accommodations.

August 2: The United States blames North Vietnam for firing on the USS *Maddox*, an American destroyer, in the Gulf of Tonkin incident on this day, though the claim would be made later, along with a claim of a second attack on August 4. These claims would lead to the passage of the Gulf of Tonkin Resolution on August 10 granting President Johnson power to conduct military operations in support of Southeast Asian countries under threat from "communist aggression."

October 1: The arrest of Jack Weinberg on the University of California campus at Berkeley sparks protests that continue for over a day before he is released in the first incident of what would come to be called the "Berkeley Free Speech Movement."

November 3: President Johnson wins election to a full term of his own by defeating conservative Republican Barry Goldwater in a popular-vote and electoral-college landslide.

**1965** February 21: Malcolm X is assassinated in the Audubon Ballroom in New York City by members of the Nation of Islam, the organization he had left to form a new Moslem group.

July 25: Bob Dylan appears at the annual Newport Folk Festival backed by an electric band to the consternation of some concertgoers but changing the boundaries within American popular music forever.

July 30: President Johnson signs into law the bill creating Medicare, universal health care for Americans over the age of 65.

August 6: After a long and difficult legislative process, President Johnson signs into law the Voting Rights Act of 1965.

August 11: Watts race riots in Los Angeles, California, begin on this day. Lasting until August 16, the riots were sparked by an incident in which an African American, Marquette Frye, was pulled over by police. A small altercation followed, blossoming into six days of violence.

**1966** October 15: Frustrated by what they saw as lack of success in the Civil Rights Movement, Huey P. Newton and Bobby Seale begin the process of establishing the Black Panther Party.

**1967** May 13: Scott Mackenzie's recording ("Be Sure to Wear Flowers in Your Hair") is released, heralding what would come to be called "the

Summer of Love," centering on San Francisco and bringing the image of the "hippie" to public consciousness.

June 16: The Monterey Pop Festival opens at the Monterey County Fairgrounds in California and lasts for three days. The festival and the subsequent movie brought acts like the Jimi Hendrix Experience and The Who to the attention of live American audiences for the first time and propelled Janis Joplin to stardom. It was the first major outdoor pop concert.

October 21: The March on the Pentagon of 50,000 protesters against the Vietnam War begins at the Lincoln Memorial and ends with the arrest of some 650 people for civil disobedience across the Potomac at the Pentagon.

**1968**

January 30: The Tet Offensive, which would become the defining series of events in the growing American realization that the Vietnam War was unwinnable, begins with attacks across South Vietnam.

February 27: Walter Cronkite urges the U.S. government to begin negotiations to end the war in Vietnam at the end of his weekday *CBS Evening News* program. He said, "the only rational way out . . . will be to negotiate, not as victors, but as an honorable people who lived up to their pledge to defend democracy, and did the best they could."

March 16: At My Lai, South Vietnam, American forces massacre hundreds of civilians, though news of the slaughter would not become public for a year and a half.

March 31: President Johnson speaks to the nation about the Vietnam War, ending with the bombshell announcement, "I shall not seek, and I will not accept, the nomination of my party for another term as your President."

April 4: In Memphis, Tennessee, Martin Luther King Jr., where he had gone to support striking sanitation workers, is assassinated by James Earl Ray.

April 23: Students at Columbia University in New York City occupy Hamilton Hall, starting a sequence of student protests against the Vietnam War and social injustice that would last throughout the remainder of the decade.

June 6: Senator Robert Kennedy, after winning the June 5 California primary, is assassinated by Sirhan Sirhan in the Ambassador Hotel in Los Angeles.

August 26: The Democratic National Convention opens at Chicago's International Amphitheatre. Almost immediately, antiwar protesters, some 10,000 of them, began to make their presence felt. They were met by brutal force on the part of the Chicago police in what is sometimes referred to as a "police riot."

November 5: Former vice president Richard Nixon defeats current vice president Hubert Humphrey for the presidency of the United States.

**1969**　　April 4: William Paley, head of CBS Television, cancels *The Smothers Brothers Comedy Hour*, allegedly for contract violations. The show had been controversial in its airing of political views outside of the conservative mainstream. The last episode would be aired on June 8, 1969.

June 27: When police attempt to arrest gay patrons of the Stonewall Inn in New York City's West Village, the gay community fights back, starting the movement toward gay rights.

July 20: Neil Armstrong sets foot on the moon in fulfillment of President Kennedy's promise to land a man on the moon by the end of the decade.

August 15: The three-day Woodstock Music and Arts Fair, which would attract a crowd nearing half a million, opens on this day. The event would prove to be a touchstone for members of the baby boom generation.

September 24: The trial of eight (reduced to seven when Bobby Seale was removed) men accused of crossing state lines with the intent to riot at the Democratic National Convention begins.

October 15: The Moratorium to End the War in Vietnam, a series of demonstrations and related events across the country, takes place as a prelude to the November 15 march in Washington, DC, that would draw approximately half a million protesters.

# Background and Introduction

Most commonly, historians and political, social, and cultural commentators have viewed the 1960s as a reaction against the 1950s. Certainly, there is much reason for doing so. After the unprecedented economic calamity of the Great Depression and the global devastation of the Second World War, the 1950s were a period in which America's economic and military power were singularly predominant. Previously, the nation's economic resources and its potential military power had been recognized. But the war made the United States into an economic powerhouse and an unquestionable military power.

In the aftermath of the Second World War, most of Europe and much of Asia lay in ruins, and millions of people had been displaced not only by the shifting battlefronts and the saturation bombing of major urban centers but also by forced labor, forced relocations, concentration camps, and detainment as prisoners of war. Not only were industrial plants and housing devastated, but the basic infrastructures of transportation, communications, and food production were wrecked. The United States was the only major power to emerge relatively unscathed from the war. Although large numbers of U.S. ships had been lost at sea and in just about every ocean, and although about 419,000 Americans had died in the war and another 670,000 had been wounded, the U.S. losses, even in manpower, paled in comparison to the losses suffered by other nations. The most striking contrast is with the Soviet losses. The Soviets not only had more than twice the number of people in uniform during the war (34.5 million to 16.3 million) but their forces had more killed and wounded than the total serving in the U.S. military (10.7 million killed and 14.9 million wounded). Including civilian deaths, the Soviet Union lost somewhere between 20 to 27 million people in the war. The United Kingdom, which had a population of 47.7 million compared to the total U.S. population of 131 million, lost more people in the war than the United States (about 451,000 to about 419,000). Even Yugoslavia, which had a prewar population of just 15.5 million, or not much more than a tenth of the U.S. population, lost almost as many military personnel as the United States (between 300,000 and 450,000) and, including civilians, lost somewhere between 1,025,000 and 1,700,000 people. U.S. deaths amounted to .32 percent of the population (or about one-third of 1 percent), whereas the Soviet Union lost between 8.26 and 8.86 percent of its population; the United Kingdom lost .94 percent (or almost 1 percent) of its population; and Yugoslavia lost between 6.63 and 10.97 percent of its population.

Beyond the comparatively light loss of American life, the only current U.S. states (both which were then still territories) that were directly attacked during the war were Hawaii and Alaska. (I am not including a fire started in the Oregon forests by a bomb carried across the Pacific on a high-altitude balloon or ships sunk off the Atlantic and Gulf Coasts in U.S. territorial waters.) Although the United States entered the war immediately after the shocking Japanese attack on the naval base at Pearl Harbor and although the army airfields on Oahu were also thoroughly strafed and bombed before most of the planes could even get off the ground, the attack actually did relatively little lasting damage to the U.S. war effort. As is often noted, the U.S. aircraft carriers were not in port at the time of the attack. Moreover, the third wave of Japanese planes, which was never launched, was supposed to target the naval oil storage and repair facilities on Oahu. That those facilities were left intact meant that the carriers and their support vessels could operate almost immediately against the Japanese. In addition, with the exception of the battleships *Arizona* and *Oklahoma*, as well as one lesser vessel, the rest of the ships damaged and even sunk at Pearl Harbor were eventually repaired and returned to service. In terms of their impact on the U.S. war effort, the seizure of the two most remote Aleutian islands, Attu and Kisku, was not only less consequential than the attack on Pearl Harbor, but it even very arguably enhanced the U.S. effort by prompting the construction of the Trans-Alaskan Highway and much other infrastructure in Alaska, especially in the ports along the southern coast and in the creation of airfields in previously largely inaccessible parts of the territory.

Because the U.S. mainland was not attacked during the war, the major issues were, first, how quickly existing U.S. manufacturing facilities could be shifted entirely to military production and then brought up to full production capacity and, second, how quickly new facilities could be constructed to meet new material and logistical needs. Even before air conditioning was available, the demands and logistics of war production opened the Sun Belt—and, in particular, Southern California and the Gulf Coast—to the manufacturing of durable goods that had previously been concentrated in the Northeast and Midwest. Likewise, the rapid expansion of aircraft production transformed—and did so, literally, almost overnight—many of the cities on the Central Plains and Great Plains into major new manufacturing centers. One of the lasting motifs of the Great Depression is the armies of unemployed men who "hit the road" in search of work. But, in actuality, the Great Depression stalled the large migrations of southern whites out of Appalachia and of African Americans out of the Deep South because the factories in which they had hoped to find jobs had either shuttered or were operating at much reduced capacity. It was actually the Second World War that greatly increased internal migration. Beyond the millions of military personnel who were being transported by train to training facilities and other bases, workers were encouraged to migrate to places where they were needed. In addition, the expansion of federal departments and the federal workforce during the New Deal was followed by a further expansion to coordinate the war effort and to meet the needs of both those serving in the military and their families.

Because of the Lend-Lease Act, American war production began to ramp up even before the United States became directly involved in the war. Even after the United States entered the war—and perhaps up to the final fifteen months of the war—its major contribution to the Allied effort remained the vast amounts of military material—vehicles, weapons, ammunition, and other supplies—that it provided to the Soviet Union, the United Kingdom, China, and other Allies. The role of the United States as a major supplier required, of course, that it rapidly expand its already sizable fleets of cargo ships and cargo planes. In total, the United States shipped almost 34 million tons of war material; the next highest total was, not surprisingly, by the United Kingdom, which shipped almost 13 million tons. Between 1941 and 1945, U.S. shipyards produced 2,710 Liberty ships, a no-frills type of cargo ship based on a British design. Indeed, there were very few categories of war production, either in the production of raw materials or the production of goods, in which the United States was not the leading producer. The United States produced 2,150 million tons of coal, more than any nation other than Germany (which was producing synthetic fuels from coal because it lacked any oil reserves beyond those available in Romania, one of its Allies for much of the war). The United States also produced 833 million tons of petroleum, about 80 percent of the 1,043 million tons produced by the Allies. The United States also produced 397 million tons of iron ore, or about two-thirds of the total Allied production and 165 percent of what Germany was able to produce. In terms of the trucks and other support vehicles, including the omnipresent jeeps, the U.S. produced almost 2.4 million of the approximately 4 million vehicles that the Allies produced—essentially freeing the Soviet Union from having to devote resources to the production of these vehicles. Of the 185 aircraft carriers produced during the war, 124 were in the U.S. Navy. To facilitate the European landings in North Africa, Sicily, Italy, and Normandy, as well as the "island-hopping" campaigns in the Pacific theater, U.S. naval yards produced 35,000 landing craft. The United States also produced 324,000 of the 537,000 planes produced by the Allies—with U.S. production in itself amounting to almost one and a half the total German production of 234,000 planes. Not surprisingly, the automobile, commercial aviation, and shipping industries would become major elements of the postwar economic boom in the United States.

Even a glance at the GDP figures over the course of the war highlights the degree to which the war expanded the U.S. economy and set the stage for postwar economic prosperity. In 1940, the U.S. GDP was $943 billion, and by 1945, it was $1,474 billion. This nearly 50 percent increase is extraordinary in itself but all the more extraordinary when compared to other major industrial nations. For instance, the United Kingdom's GDP had increased from $287 billion in 1939 to $361 billion in 1943 but, by 1945, it had declined to $331 billion. Every other major industrialized nation saw a decline in GDP. Even the Soviet Union's herculean and often ruthless efforts to relocate production east of the Urals and out of the reach of the Nazi invasion did not prevent a decline in GDP from $417 billion in 1940 to $343 billion in 1945. In the first two decades following the war, every other industrialized nation had to invest considerable resources into reconstructing basic transportation and communications infrastructure, housing, and industrial plants. In contrast, the United States experienced a brief recession in the first half-decade following the war as its industrial plants were shifted from military material to consumer goods. It then entered into an extended and sustained period of economic prosperity that has few, if any, parallels in human history.

At the end of the war, the U.S. economy not only had to make the transition from wartime to peacetime production but also had to absorb the more than 16 million Americans—almost all of whom were men—back into the workforce. During the war, the increased production had been possible only because racial minorities, women, and even prisoners of war were recruited to fill the labor shortages created by military enlistments and the draft. To ease the postwar transition, the federal government instituted the G.I. Bill of Rights, which provided returning veterans with funding that allowed them to attend colleges and trade schools, as well as with low-cost mortgages. The educational opportunities not only staggered the reabsorption of veterans into the workforce but also provided a workforce that allowed U.S. corporations to exploit commercially the technical advancements that had been made during the war for military purposes. The provision of affordable mortgages not only provided a major boost to the housing industry, but because much of the housing was constructed in the suburbs of major cities, it necessitated a great deal of infrastructure development, as well as new commercial real estate development. Urban expressways became the first step in the long-planned but long-delayed construction of an interstate highway system, and the realities of suburban life meant that automobiles became more of a necessity than a luxury, providing a major boost not only to the automobile manufacturers but also to all of the ancillary service industries related to the increased ownership of automobiles.

The broad-based material prosperity of the 1950s was also made possible by the increased rate of membership in labor unions. Even in the 1950s, two developments were starting to undermine the cohesion of the major industrial unions: the automation of manufacturing processes and the decentralization of production not just into the suburbs of major cities but also into smaller cities increasingly linked by interstate highways. But as rapid as those developments seem in retrospect, in the 1950s, their effects were not yet readily apparent and were eclipsed by the obvious economic and political power of the labor unions. Part of the New Deal response to the Great Depression, the Wagner Act, or National Labor Relations Act (1935), had formalized the right of all workers to unionize and to engage in collective bargaining. During the war, there had been a general prohibition against labor strikes, but, in the immediate aftermath of the war, there were so many labor strikes that legislation, most notably the Taft-Hartley Act, or Labor Management Relations Act (1947), was passed to limit the right to strike and to provide other mechanisms to resolve disputes that would be less disruptive to individual industries and to the economy as a whole. In allowing states to declare themselves "right to work," this act undermined unions fundamentally, though its impact would not become very evident until employment in the manufacturing sector began to erode in the 1970s and then decline more dramatically in the 1980s and 1990s. But, in the 1950s, the generation that had come of age during the Great Depression and had served in the military during the Second World War asserted its right to the American Dream, and it had enough collective political power and the United States held such singular advantages economically that employment became more secure and wages and benefits increased very steadily. Because between 35 and 40 percent of the workforce was unionized, the benefits secured by unionized workers extended to many, if not most, nonunionized workers, including white-collar workers. Within a relatively short time, many of the distinctions between the working class and the middle class began to diminish. A good job with an American corporation was idealized as lifetime employment. The ascendancy of "corporate culture" among returning war veterans who were still readapting to civilian life was memorialized in Sloan Wilson's novel *The Man in the Gray Flannel Suit* (1955), which was adapted into a popular and critically well-regarded film starring Gregory Peck (1956).

The 1950s became very firmly defined by acceptance with corporate culture, the contentment with material affluence, and the willingness to conform to the social mores of suburban American life. But, during that decade, American society had many layers of discontent. Most obviously, the period in which American economic and military power was predominant was also the period in which the Cold War and the proliferation of ever more powerful nuclear weapons threatened the basic survival of humanity and most life on earth. In some ways, the responses to the possibility of nuclear Armageddon seems, in retrospect, to have ranged from almost quaintly naïve to simply ridiculous. For instance, the civil defense shelters constructed under municipal buildings and other major urban structures, and filled with government-surplus supplies, may have been a somewhat effective defense against conventional bombing attacks, but in the event of nuclear attack, they would have been woefully inadequate. In fact, the shelters were so quickly neglected that within a relatively short time, they themselves became dank and vermin-ridden subterranean settings suggestive of dystopian possibilities. The family-sized backyard shelters that became somewhat popular in the suburbs were more an indication of the insularity of suburban culture than of the realities of nuclear devastation. And schoolchildren regularly practiced "duck and cover" drills in which they crawled under their desks and covered their heads with their arms—a practice that the comedian Lewis Black has described as "hiding under kindling."

Beyond those Cold War uncertainties, some of the veterans of the Second World War had no interest in pursuing the American Dream as it was conventionally defined, and they developed subcultures that would be described as forerunners of the broader Counterculture of the late 1960s. Some of the veterans of the war in the Pacific who had spent time in Australia, in Hawaii, and on some of the other tropical islands not devastated by the war were introduced to surfing and brought the sport back to the states, establishing the surfer culture that became very strongly identified with the coastal communities of Southern California in particular. Likewise, some of the soldiers who had served in Europe and had remained there during the postwar occupation of Germany had found it easy to "see Europe" from a motorcycle, and when they returned to the states, they formed motorcycle clubs. That some of these clubs catered to vets who felt alienated from mainstream American life is reflected in the fact that those clubs became increasingly associated with antisocial behavior and involvement in criminal activities. In the nightclubs in Paris and other major French cities, American jazz and African American jazz musicians had been very popular since the 1920s, and in the 1950s, the Beat Movement emerged from the jazz "scene," the jazz clubs in major American cities that were typically located on the margins of African American neighborhoods, and the Beats became a broader literary and artistic movement. The "beatnik" was a mainstream caricature of the Beat subculture that commonly blended into the mainstream caricature of the hippie that emerged in the late 1960s. Notably, although some Beats, most notably Allen Ginsberg, essentially became hippies, other Beats, most notably Jack Kerouac, adamantly rejected not just many of the ideas associated with the Counterculture but also the notion that the Beat Movement was a forerunner to it.

Between 1945 and 1965, about 65 million babies were born in the United States, and this "baby boom" had a profound effect on family structures and social mores. Births had declined during the Great Depression, and so the increase in the birthrate (which some commentators have argued began just before or during the Second World War) seemed especially dramatic by contrast. Although the popular culture celebrated the suburban family unit as the embodiment of American aspirations and ideals, the reality was not always defined by such contentment. For one thing, during the war, unprecedented numbers of women had not only entered the workplace but had assumed jobs that had previously been restricted to men, and in most instances, they demonstrated that they were every bit as capable as men in doing those jobs. After the war, the combination of the need to reabsorb 16 million veterans into the workforce and the increase in the average number of children per family during the baby boom relegated most women to being homemakers. Because there was no precedent for the baby boom, there were no alternatives in place for most women who would have liked to continue working after having children—no child care centers for preschoolers or after-school arrangements for somewhat older children. The migration to the suburbs also meant that extended families within the same household became less common. So, almost by default, the responsibility for child care fell largely, if not entirely, on mothers. When their children were almost grown, many women did return to the workforce, but in most cases, the only jobs available to them were relatively low-skilled and low-paid service jobs. At the one extreme were the women who were perfectly contented being wives and mothers, and at the other extreme were women who felt that their lives were very unfulfilling—that their potential had been sacrificed to conventional social expectations. In between those extremes, most women likely felt that although it was difficult to imagine how they might have managed to do more with their lives, it was at least somewhat disappointing that they had not been able to do more. Adding to the discontent was the largely unexamined strains on many marriages. Beyond the fact that men's professional lives were largely segregated from their wives' daily lives, the cultural celebration of the husband and father's role as the "provider" implicitly devalued, at least to some degree, the wife and mother's contributions. Worse, many couples married impulsively during and after the war and then stayed together "for the sake of the children" because divorce carried a significant social stigma, especially when children were involved. Beyond those "normal" strains, for many veterans, it was difficult to sustain the illusion that they had put the war behind them. The First World War's relatively narrow diagnoses of "shell shock" had given way to a somewhat looser recognition of "battle fatigue" during the Second World War and the more formally euphemistic diagnoses of "operational exhaustion" during the Korean War. But many of the symptoms of post-traumatic stress disorder (PTSD), including emotional withdrawal, erratic behavior, verbal and physical abuse, and substance abuse, very often went undiagnosed as such and were ineffectively treated, if they were treated at all. Given all of these strains, not surprisingly, as the first baby boomers began to reach adulthood, the divorce rate began to increase—in spite of all of the social constraints against divorce and even before the "sexual revolution" and other social changes made those constraints less formidable and less pervasive.

If many women were discontented with lives that the mainstream culture insistently suggested ought to provide complete contentment, the discontent of African Americans and other American minorities was much closer to the surface throughout the late 1940s and the 1950s. As it had for women, the war opened many economic opportunities for African Americans. Although many had migrated from the Deep South to the industrial centers of the Northeast and Midwest in search of decent jobs, those aspirations had generally been severely disappointed. Although it was typically not as formally codified as it was in the "Jim Crow" South, racial segregation was generally very strictly enforced in the cities of the Northeast and the Midwest, in both housing and employment. No matter how crowded the neighborhoods designated for African Americans became, it was almost impossible to expand them. Worse, overcrowding led to the deterioration of the available housing, but its artificially maintained scarcity increased the price of rents and, where individual homes were available, the purchase price. In the major industries, most better-paying jobs were reserved for whites, and because the jobs in support industries were generally secured through family or community connections, the segregation in housing directly reinforced the segregation in employment. During the war, the loss of manpower to military service opened many jobs to African Americans, but just as African Americans who served in the military returned home to be profoundly disenchanted by the lack of progress in basic civil rights, so, too, many African Americans who had found new jobs during the war were embittered when their new jobs were given back to returning white veterans and they were again relegated to lower-skilled, more physically demanding, and lower-paid positions. At the national level, the major labor unions did begin to advocate for civil rights—for equal opportunity and equal treatment regardless of race—but their stated policy positions were often at odds with the practices of locals. During the 1950s, judicial rulings gave the Civil Rights Movement enough impetus that the events of the 1960s could not have come as a great surprise to anyone who had actually been paying attention. Discontent among Hispanic Americans, Native Americans, and Asian Americans was less conspicuous but every bit as deeply felt, and it is not at all surprising that the Civil Rights Movement would lead to a broader demand for equal rights for a variety of marginalized groups for whom the material prosperity of the 1950s had been always kept out of reach.

In the early 1950s, America was preoccupied with the Korean War, the first of the "hot" conflicts within the Cold War. In many ways, the Korean War was predictive of what would occur in the Vietnam War in the 1960s. It was a much shorter conflict, but it involved a former colony—in this case, a colony seized by Japan well ahead of the Second World War, rather than a French colony occupied by Japan during the early stages of the war. In both cases, regimes in the northern halves of the new countries were supported by communist superpowers, and the regimes in the southern halves were supported by the United States and its Allies. In both instances, the regimes supported by the United States were ostensibly democratic but actually authoritarian, and the war aims were less genuinely to promote democracy and more simply to forestall the spread of communism and to accept any sustainable alternative to it. In Korea, the North Korean offensive against the South was launched suddenly in 1950 and caught the South Koreans and Americans completely by surprise. But although the Allied forces were backed into a precarious corner of the peninsula before American military power could be marshaled to prevent a catastrophe, once that power was brought to bear against the North Koreans, they were rather quickly driven back to the border with China at the Yalu River. The intervention of hundreds of thousands of communist Chinese troops and the restrictions on the use of U.S. airpower against targets across the Yalu River in China did bring the battle lines roughly back to the original dividing line between the two Koreas, and the "war," euphemistically termed a "police action" by President Truman, ended in a stalemate that persists to this day. Although it did not provide the satisfying and reassuring reinforcement of American military power that a clear-cut victory would have produced, the stalemate in Korea was seldom framed as a defeat. Indeed, the lesson of Korea seemed to be that the United States could win such a war if it needed to do so—if it was deemed to be worth the risk of provoking a broader war, which, it was widely believed, the United States would certainly have the resources to conduct and to win.

Even before the Korean War began in 1950, the United States had been supplying the French with the military equipment, including planes, tanks, and artillery, and the other supplies and the military intelligence that they needed to reestablish their control over French Indochina. Yet, less than a year after the truce ending the Korean War was signed in July 1953, the French forces were decisively defeated by the Viet Minh forces at Dien Bien Phu. It was one of the signal events in the decline of European colonial power, but it should not have been as shocking as it was. The French had been defeated by the Nazis, and in the years following the war, there were continuing reprisals against the tens of thousands of French men and women who were identified as having collaborated with the Nazis. That the French military needed to rely on American equipment and supplies was a reflection of the tenuous basis on which France was attempting to reassert itself as a major power. Under Ho Chi Minh, the Viet Minh had been fighting as insurgents against French imperialism and then against the Japanese occupation since the late 1920s. French Indochina was subsequently divided into three independent nations: Vietnam, Laos, and Cambodia. Even though, like Korea, Vietnam was further divided into North Vietnam and South Vietnam, with a never-to-be-fulfilled promise of elections aimed at unifying the two parts of the nation, the nature of the insurgency against the French made the subsequent Vietnam War very different than the Korean War.

Throughout the South, there were Vietnamese who had supported the Viet Minh against the French or who came to regard the American support of the South Vietnamese government as another imperial adventure. These issues related to the nation's fairly lengthy experience with European colonialism were complicated by the ostensible contest between Western and communist ideologies, and many disaffected South Vietnamese joined the insurgents commonly known as the Viet Cong. In effect, the South Vietnamese government was fighting a war against a significant segment of its own population, and although that situation certainly occurred in South Korea during that war, it did not occur there for the same reasons or with anything approaching the same scope. Worse, the initial regime in South Vietnam, led by President Diem, was as staunchly Catholic and anti-Buddhist as it was anticommunist. While the Viet Cong were attacking villages in the interior of South Vietnam, Buddhist monks were immolating themselves on the streets of South Vietnam's major cities. And although the assassination of Diem and a military coup against his government would defuse some of the anti-Buddhist focus of the regime, the government in the South could never formulate a convincing case for why its citizens should be loyal to it. Increasingly, it would be tied together by extensive corruption, and that self-interest did not translate into any viable, persistent sense of some national interest. The tragedy of the Vietnam War was that the Eisenhower administration recognized that it was unwinnable, and the Kennedy and Johnson administrations feared that it would be unwinnable, even as they escalated American involvement in it. The myths underlying the exercise of American power that were not changed by the stalemate at the end of the Korean War would be unraveled by the desperation for victory, and then for any settlement and extrication of U.S. forces that could be framed as a victory, in the Vietnam War.

The Korean War was the last American war that was not covered as it was occurring on American television. The rapidity with which televisions became commonplace in American homes in the early to mid-1950s is a testament to the transformative impact of the new medium on American society and culture. The new medium did not make either radio or film obsolete, as many feared it would, but it did significantly reshape those other media. It made the home a locus of entertainment much more than radio had done so, and in increments, it went from being regarded as the inferior stepchild of film to being one of the major sources of revenue for filmmakers, as videotapes, DVDs, and then live-streamed films have made the concept of a "home theater" more of a commonplace than extravagant possibility. The baby boom generation was the first to be raised on television programming—to have childhood memories that are attached to particular programs—and, not surprisingly, much of the network programming was aimed at children. Shows such as *The Mickey Mouse Club* and *Romper Room* were aimed at very young children and were forerunners of landmark programs such as *Sesame Street*. Situation comedies such as *The Adventures of Ozzie and Harriet, Dennis the Menace,* and *Leave It to Beaver* featured suburban families, focused on their daily lives and issues in a way that made them no less interesting because they were commonplace, and served to reinforce the mores of suburban, middle-class life. Other shows such as *Lassie, My Friend Flicka*, and *The Real McCoys* had more rural settings but reinforced the same mores, suggesting that there were adventures to be found beyond suburbia and that such adventures still had a distinctly American quality to them. In essence, such programming suggested an equivalency between the mores of middle-class suburban life and the values reinforced for a century or more through the American mythos. It was no accident that a staple of network television programming in the 1950s was the Western, or that shows such as *Bonanza* directly linked the family to such fundamental elements of the national mythos as manifest destiny and American exceptionalism. Given the thematic predictability and superficiality of much television programming, it is also not surprising that there would eventually be a backlash against it—criticism of the "unreality" of the images that it was presenting of American life, both in the United States and eventually, as television programs became a profitable export, abroad.

Because much popular music has always presented an idealized and even sentimentalized take on American life, it is not surprising that such music flourished during the 1950s. What was surprising, however, was the rather rapid emergence of rock and roll, a style of music that was often more jarring than soothing, more suggestive of rebellion than of contentment, and more erotic than romantic. That this new style of music was performed by and appealed to young people made it seem dangerous to those who saw themselves as the guardians of social mores and who were alarmed at the possibility of any uncontrolled social change. That rock and roll had its roots in African American music—blues, rhythm and blues, gospel, and even to some degree jazz—made it seem all the more subversive. Although mainstream American culture had long been appropriating from African American and other marginalized cultures, in most cases those appropriations were so diluted and homogenized that their impact was greatly mitigated. Some of the same sort of thing was attempted with rock and roll, with singers such as Pat Boone popularizing a very "white" facsimile of African American music. But other performers, most notably Elvis Presley, embraced their musical influences more directly, and within a decade, African American performers were being marketed to desegregated audiences—in clubs and other venues, on the radio and television, and in record stores. Music arguably would become the most significant cultural complement to the political advancements achieved by the Civil Rights Movement.

The youthful rebelliousness associated with rock and roll had a parallel in the film industry with the rise of such stars as Marlon Brando and James Dean. The anguished discontent projected in the screen personas of these actors stood in striking contrast with the public persona of President Eisenhower, whose two terms as president extended from the close of the Korean War through the end of the 1950s. Eisenhower was much admired because of his seemingly unflappable and consistently effective military leadership during the Second World War. As president, he continued to project the shrewd competence and the steady confidence that seemed likely to ensure continued American power and prosperity in spite of the underlying uncertainties created by the Cold War and the expanding American and Soviet nuclear arsenals. The faith in Eisenhower's imperturbable leadership ran so deep that even his heart problems never became the sort of issue, the cause of political uncertainty, that they might have become in many other presidencies.

But, by the 1960 presidential election, Eisenhower did seem old and tired, especially in contrast with John Kennedy whose public appearances were calculated to project youthful vitality (even though he had some very serious medical issues). One of the effects of Kennedy's very narrow election and his shocking assassination before he had finished his first term was that Eisenhower's presidency was subsequently undervalued by historians. In effect, Eisenhower became the face of a decade that, especially in contrast with the social, political, and cultural convulsions of the late 1960s, seems marked by social conformity, political moderation, and cultural blandness. Of course, historical perspective permits one to strike a more realistic balance between ready and striking contrasts between periods and a more nuanced sense of the continuities that link one period to the next. For all of its dramatic impact on American life and culture, the Counterculture Movement of the late 1960s did not prevent Richard Nixon's election in 1968 or his reelection by a landslide margin in 1972. Such movements are seldom majority movements, and the obverse is also more often true than not. Despite its enduring resonance in our national memory, the conformity of the 1950s was never quite as pervasive or as uniform as political and cultural nostalgia might lead some to wish it had been. Eisenhower, who once seemed to have been eclipsed by Kennedy, is now typically ranked with him at the bottom of the top tier of U.S. presidents or at the top of the second tier. And just as it was eventually revealed that Eisenhower had a much more complicated personal life than anyone watching him walk a gold course as president might have guessed, so, too, the period that he oversaw as president was much more socially, politically, and culturally complex than it is often remembered as being.

The 1960 election illustrated the political truism that each presidential election is inevitably a reaction to the preceding election or administration. It is just as natural that one decade's cultural tenor should be viewed as an inevitable reaction to the tenor of the preceding decade. But, as convenient as milestone years—the first or last years of each decade and each century—may be as historical markers, historical events and movements seldom conform to such neat divisions. Although understanding the 1950s in America is certainly important to understanding the defining events and movements of the 1960s, the roots of much of what occurred in the 1960s run much deeper than the previous decade.

For instance, the political events and movements of the 1960s can be seen as part of a process that began at the turn of the century. For the century following the Reconstruction period, the Republican Party generally carried the states in the Northeast, in the upper Midwest, and along the Pacific Coast; the Democratic Party consistently carried the former Confederate states and the so-called border states (the "slave" states that had remained in the Union during the war). The states of the Great Plains and the interior West were the battleground states, and Connecticut, New York, New Jersey, and Indiana were frequently "swing" states. Despite the fairly entrenched regional bases of the two parties, both parties were essentially pro-business, with the key issues being whether there should be high tariffs and a restrictive, anti-inflationary monetary policy, based on the "gold standard," to protect the rapidly expanding industries in the cities of the Northeast and Midwest, or there should be low tariffs and free trade, as well as a less restrictive or "free silver" monetary policy that favored the farmers and other commodity producers of the South, the Plains states, and the interior West. The progressivism advocated by Theodore Roosevelt was first push-back against corporate excesses, but with the election of William Howard Taft, the Republican Party became fairly consistently identified as pro-business. Thus, as the labor movement gathered strength, it became increasingly allied with the Democrats and a key part of the political machines that Democrats built in many northeastern and midwestern cities.

Woodrow Wilson took up the cause of progressivism, and although Wilson himself was hardly enlightened on racial issues, during his terms in office in the 1910s, large numbers of African Americans began to flee the "Jim Crow" segregation in the South and to migrate northward to the industrial centers of the Northeast and Midwest, seeking economic opportunity and some degree of civil rights. It would be decades before both of those aspirations would begin to be realized, but gradually African Americans became as important a Democratic constituency as the labor unions in the major cities. So, although Democrats carried few states outside of the Deep South in the presidential elections of 1920, 1924, and 1928, the Roosevelt New Deal coalition combined the traditional Democratic base in the South with a new labor-oriented base in the industrial centers of the Northeast and Midwest. This coalition was always tenuous, but in the midst of the cataclysms of the great Depression and the Second World War, it was held together, in large part by Roosevelt's great political acumen and stature. Ironically, in the 1950s and 1960s, the "liberal" Republicans who had had considerable power for more than a century in the northeastern and midwestern states, joined with northern Democrats in passing the important civil rights legislation of the 1960s. The southern dissatisfaction with the Democrats over their increasing support for civil rights led to Strom Thurmonds's Dixiecrat candidacy in the 1948 presidential election, led some of the states of the Deep South to vote for Goldwater in the midst of Johnson's landslide victory in the 1964 presidential election, and led to George Wallace's significant third-party candidacy in 1968 and 1972. As Democratic southerners, Jimmy Carter and Bill Clinton would carry some southern states, but starting with Ronald Reagan's election in 1980, the regional bases of the two major parties would essentially be flipped from what they were for the century between the

Civil War and the Civil Rights Movement. The events of the 1960s were the fulcrum on which one of the great pivots in American political history occurred.

Although the United States' emergence as a global superpower at the end of the Second World War places the Korean War and the Vietnam War in a different foreign-policy framework than previous American wars, it is nonetheless instructive to view these wars within a longer perspective on U.S. attitudes toward international affairs. Theodore Roosevelt had participated as a combatant in the Spanish-American War that had made the United States into an imperial power that could project its military strength across both the Atlantic and the Pacific Oceans. To demonstrate that reach, Roosevelt, as president, sent the Great White Fleet on a worldwide tour, demonstrating to potential allies and foes alike, that America was asserting itself beyond its own hemisphere and legitimately laying claim to being a world power. He inserted himself into world affairs, earning a Nobel Peace Prize by helping to negotiate the treaty ending the Russo-Japanese War. Americans responded enthusiastically to his "speak softly but carry a big stick" self-effacing jingoism. In effect, Americans were relishing being a world power equivalent to the British, French, Russian, and German empires, even as they were uncomfortable with the idea of having an empire. But in the early 1910s as the European powers teetered on the brink of conflict and then as cascading events led them somewhat impetuously into the First World War, which quickly proved to be much more of a cataclysm than almost anyone had anticipated, Americans were determined to remain neutral—to avoid a costly entanglement in a European war. In effect, Americans retreated to the notion that the oceans over which the nation had begun projecting national power could keep them safely removed from a conflict that had become worldwide in scope because the empires of the European powers extended across the other continents. The United States entered the war only when the Germans' engagement in unrestricted submarine warfare and their attempts to induce Mexico to attack the southwestern United States made further isolation seem as if it were an abdication of moral responsibility. The war against the "Hun" thus became a righteous cause, justified by Wilson's idealistic collection of postwar aims that became known as the "14 points" and, in effect, justifying the repression of dissent and civil liberties at home so that those liberties could be made available to all of the peoples of Europe who had been subjugated within the German, Austro-Hungarian, and Russian empires. Beyond the incoherence between the wartime policies and aims, Wilson proved physically and perhaps politically incapable of expediting the peace negotiations, and by the time that the very flawed Versailles Treaty was signed, sentiment in the United States had swung back to isolation and nativism. Both of those sentiments would be reinforced by the economic calamity of the Great Depression and the consequent rise of fascism in Europe. As the Second World War broke out in Europe, Franklin Roosevelt, who was seeking an unprecedented third term as president, had to reassure voters that he had no intention of sending their sons off to another European war. Only the "dastardly" Japanese attack on Pearl Harbor reversed the national mood. These historical patterns are important because they demonstrate that Americans have long had a great ambivalence about military commitments, especially when the military and political aims have not been very clearly defined or proven to be achievable within a seemingly reasonable period of time. Viewed from this longer perspective, the protests against the Vietnam War may be less surprising than the fact that the war extended for as long as it did despite the clear lack of effective military tactics and broader strategic goals.

One of the legitimate concerns about American involvement in the First World War was the degree to which the large population of recent European immigrants would support American involvement. According to the 1910 census, the total population of the United States was 92,228,531. Of that population, 13,515,886, or 14.7 percent, were foreign born. The first large surge of immigrants—from Ireland and Germany in the two decades before the Civil War—had led to a nativist backlash and even the creation of an anti-immigrant political party that became commonly known as the Know-Nothings. The second great surge—from central, eastern, and southern Europe in the three decades before the First World War—was not much larger than the first surge as a percentage of the total population, but it was five or six times as large in raw numbers. Worse, the immigrants seemed more exotic, more conspicuously foreign. During the First World War, there was a very deliberate and extensive—even fierce—suppression of the use of the German language and indications of German cultural heritage. The word "German" was often replaced with the word "American" in place names: for example, in many instances, "German Township" became "American Township." But, the general effect of the vilification of all things German was to reduce dramatically the number of all foreign-language newspapers and any cultural practices that were conspicuously "foreign." Beyond that forced assimilation during the war, the Bolshevik victory in the Russian Civil War (which included the largely ineffectual involvement of a sizable American Expeditionary Force dispatched to Asian Russia to help defeat the Bolsheviks) contributed to the postwar isolationist sentiment and led to a resurgence of nativism that became linked to institutionalized racism. Not only were strict constraints imposed on all immigration, but the Great Migration of African Americans from the Deep South to northeastern and midwestern cities led to a parallel racial backlash. The Klu Klux Klan, which had been formed in the Deep South to terrorize freed slaves during the Reconstruction period and the "Jim Crow" period that followed, suddenly became a national organization, with larger membership numbers in many midwestern states than in southern states. For much of the 1920s, it was treated, particularly in the Midwest, as if it were a civic or fraternal organization, with businessmen marching openly as Klansmen in municipal parades. It was only when several Klan leaders became involved in scandalous crimes that being a member of the Klan acquired a stigma. Three decades later, the resurgence of the Klan in the Deep South during the civil rights period would constitute another chapter not just in the nation's racial conflicts but in the tension between nativism and the "melting pot," and between the celebration of assimilation and the celebration of multiculturalism.

The Civil Rights Movement not only was complemented by a broader acceptance of and appreciation for African American music, but it also contributed, at least indirectly, to the development of the Black Arts Movement, which reasserted the value of African heritage and African American identity. It sought to provide meaningful support and outlets to writers and artists who were committed to exploring African American issues and themes through something other than established Western perspectives. The Blacks Arts Movement was often linked to radical political groups, in particular the Black Panthers, and it was committed to fostering a sense of racial pride, self-determination, and active engagement through the work of the writers and artists whom it encouraged and supported. Although the Black Arts Movement was clearly responsive to developments in the late 1960s, it was not without precedent. On the heels of the Great Migration, the Harlem Renaissance of the 1920s was clearly a forerunner, and despite the name, it was a national phenomenon, with writers, artists, and intellectuals in African American communities in cities across the northeastern and midwestern United States becoming galvanized to creatively express and define their racial heritage and identity. The Renaissance was given extra dimension by the involvement of Afro-Caribbean immigrants, some of whom came to cities such as New York after spending time in Paris. Occurring at a time when the Klan was achieving a certain social, political, and cultural legitimacy in states outside of the South, the Renaissance was a remarkable demonstration of racial self-assertion, and its impact extended across several decades and well into the postwar period.

Not coincidentally, the 1920s are most widely remembered as the Jazz Age. Like the 1950s, the 1920s were a decade in which the United States enjoyed an unprecedented postwar economic boom. But the resulting affluence was not as widely shared as in the 1950s. Because wealth became more concentrated, production of consumer goods, including automobiles, eventually outstripped demand, and that overproduction became a major contributing factor in the Great Depression. Although the United States had become a major producer of war materials, the scope of the production never approached what was achieved in the Second World War. As in the Second World War, the United States entered the First World War after it was well underway, but the U.S. involvement in the earlier war was much more abbreviated. Large numbers of American troops were engaged against the Germans only in the summer of 1918. Nonetheless, in less than six months, about 75,000 American soldiers were killed or declared missing in action, while another 194,000 were wounded. Despite the terrible losses suffered in frontal assaults on deep networks of entrenched troops, neither side had changed tactics very much since the first year of the war. The U.S. troops made a decisive difference in bringing the conflict to a close because the Germans had exhausted themselves in a last, major offensive, aimed at ending the war before American forces and material could be brought to bear against them. For all of the romanticizing of the "doughboys," most of the troops who experienced combat were psychologically scarred by the carnage. Worse, as American troops were being embarked by ship to Europe, the Spanish influenza became a worldwide epidemic. About 45,000 American military personnel died in the epidemic before they could return home after the war, and perhaps as many as two-thirds of them died in the epidemic even before they ever reached France.

After the war, there was something close to a cultural frenzy to enjoy the moment to the fullest. Gertrude Stein famously described Hemingway and other survivors of the World War as a "lost generation," and the description may have been even more true in France and the United Kingdom, where the losses in some university classes and in some towns were very grimly high. In those countries, as in the United States, there was a cultural tension between renewed piety and moral license, between a renewed faith in the Protestant work ethic and the conviction that the political, social, and economic institutions were morally bankrupt. Prohibition became the law of the land, but the related legislation outlawed the production and distribution of alcoholic beverages without outlawing the consumption of them. Especially in most large American cities, it was suddenly very respectable to engage in behaviors that were illicit on multiple levels.

People went to speakeasies not only to drink liquor but also to listen to African American jazz musicians. Many of the most popular speakeasies operated fairly openly on the edge of African American districts. Even racial taboos could be set aside, at least temporarily, for the sake of a good time.

In many ways, the 1920s were echoed in both the 1950s and the 1960s. There are clear parallels between the ebullient rejection of conventional mores both in the Prohibition period and in the Counterculture of the late 1960s. There are even parallels between the freewheeling consumption of bootleg alcohol in the 1920s and the unconstrained experimentation with hallucinogenic drugs in the 1960s. The Red Scare of the early 1920s was certainly echoed in the communist witch hunts of the early to mid-1950s. In both instances, the political excesses of the anticommunists led to an erosion of trust in government and the development of subversive political strategies and movements. In the cultural mythos, the artistic reactions to both World Wars reflected a loss of faith in conventions and a need to subvert them through experiments with subject, form, and style. As the First World War provided the impetus to modernism, so the Second World War gave rise to postmodernism. If the modernists seemed generally to have lost faith in everything but the nature and value of art, the postmodernists seemed to be questioning even what art is and why it has value. If the modernists seemed to be saying that the experiments were necessary because the essence of art had gotten lost beneath the conventions and needed to be recovered, the postmodernists seemed to be wondering if the essence of art that the modernists wished to recover had ever been there to begin with.

Among the least experimental literary works of both postwar periods were the American novels treating the wars. The major American novels about the First World War included John Dos Passos's *Three Soldiers* (1921), E. E. Cummings's *The Enormous Room* (1922), and Ernest Hemingway's *A Farewell to Arms* (1929). All were written within about a decade after the war and conveyed a sense of profound cynicism in response to its senseless brutality and waste. But none of them conveyed quite the vitriolic disenchantment that Dalton Trumbo expressed in *Johnny Got His Gun* (1938), which was published at the height of isolationist feeling against American involvement in the war that was clearly looming in Europe. Interestingly, the major American novels about the Second World War that were published in the decade following the war were profoundly cynical much in the manner of the novels by Dos Passos, Cummings, and Hemingway. Those novels included Norman Mailer's *The Naked and the Dead* (1948), Irwin Shaw's *The Young Lions* (1948), Herman Wouk's *The Caine*

*Mutiny* (1951), and James Jones's *From Here to Eternity* (1951). In the 1960s, those novels were somewhat eclipsed by several novels about the Second World War that were much more postmodern in subject, form, and style—Joseph Heller's *Catch-22* (1961) and Kurt Vonnegut's *Slaughterhouse Five* (1969)—both of which seemed to be saying much more about the Vietnam War than about the Second World War. Indeed, much the same could be said about Thomas Pynchon's *Gravity's Rainbow* (1973), which uses the German rocket program as one of its starting points and was published as American military involvement in Vietnam was ending.

Several of the major social movements in the 1960s not only developed in response to events and conditions during the 1950s but had much more remote sources in U.S. history. The Women's Movement, driven by second-wave feminism, was made possible by the Suffragette Movement. That incredibly sustained effort to secure women the right to vote began in the mid-nineteenth century and extended through the First World War. That effort also secured other basic individual rights for women. Previously, women had essentially given up many of their basic, individual rights when they married. For instance, they lost the right to own property at all, never mind separately from their husbands. It does not seem to be coincidental that the Suffragette and Abolitionist Movements had there start in roughly the same region and were linked in many ways. And, while it is true that some strain between the two movements began to show in the decades between Reconstruction and the First World War, when some advocates for a woman's right to vote balked at the idea that securing an African American man's right to vote might be given greater priority than ensuring that *any* woman had the right to vote, it is historically consistent that the two movements should have been linked again in the 1960s.

Although the Environmental Movement is generally thought to have begun in the 1960s, it is commonly linked to the Conservation Movement of the Progressive Era. The two main differences between the two movements are: first, the Conservation Movement was primarily aimed at preserving unspoiled landscapes, and often those with a particular visual interest, whereas the Environmental Movement was aimed more broadly at preventing pollution and rehabilitating sites that had become polluted; second, the Conservation Movement was primarily a top-down effort, led by government officials—including President Theodore Roosevelt—and by industrialists turned philanthropists, whereas the Environmental Movement would be much more of a grassroots effort, sometimes led by scientists and lawyers but sustained by citizen groups, often including those most directly affected by environmental degradation. In between the Conservation Movement and the Environmental Movement, an interest in preserving the environment both for sustainable development and for recreation was fostered by New Deal programs, such as the various efforts to mitigate the effects of the Dust Bowl conditions on the Great Plains and the projects undertaken by the Civil Conservation Corps (CCC), which recruited young men to work on public lands: to build or improve roads and trails, bridges, and service buildings; to provide flood control on streams and creeks, erosion control on hillsides and in floodways, and fire breaks in areas susceptible to forest fires; to develop some marginal lands for recreation and outdoor sports, to stock fisheries, and to eliminate infestations of insects and nuisance species. In the 1930s, the CCC camps provided meaningful work to more than 3 million young men, many of whom had grown up in cities and had a limited sense of the natural wonders of the country. It seems more than a coincidence that when many of those young men were in positions of influence in the 1960s, the Environmental Movement began to gain momentum.

During the Progressive Era, the vilification of the "Robber Barons," the industrialists and financiers who had used monopolistic practices to accumulate unprecedented wealth and power, led many of them and their children to seek to rehabilitate their images through philanthropy. Some focused on efforts such as the Conservation Movement, but others focused on improving social services, schools, and libraries and on supporting the arts, scientific research, and universities. Beyond simply making gifts, some of these industrialists and financiers employed marketing experts—early public relations or "P.R." men—to create photo opportunities and news stories that would humanize them and make them seem less remote and less sinister to ordinary Americans. These efforts are often cited as the beginning of celebrity culture. And although the lives of the wealthy and powerful would remain a staple of celebrity culture, with the Kennedys being a major illustration of somewhat deliberate marketing of wealth and style for political purposes, the development of the film industry and of professional sports greatly expanded the scope and impact of celebrity with American popular culture. Not only would newspapers and magazines devote space to stories about celebrities and columns devoted to reporting celebrity gossip, but whole magazines would be devoted exclusively to the topic. And as new media such as radio and television were introduced, attention to celebrities and the creation of celebrities became a staple part of their programming. As the studio system became entrenched in the film industry in the 1920s, "stars" became commodities, and they were marketed as professionally as any product sold in a store. In the 1950s, the studio system began to unravel because its monopolistic control of everything from film production to movie theater chains came under legal attack, but most of the major studios survived the upheaval, and because the development of television greatly expanded the pool of available celebrities, celebrity culture flourished, rather than perished, with the collapse of the studio system. Even in the 1920s, professional sports teams began to adapt the practices of the film studios and to market their "star" athletes. Indeed, at a time when team owners were still allowed to have tremendous control over players' salaries and mobility, the most popular athletes began themselves to supplement their incomes by endorsing products. By the late 1950s, when sporting events became not just a staple of television programming but one of the most reliably popular and profitable types of programming, the opportunities for endorsements became available to more than just the most extraordinary or celebrated athletes. Indeed, because film stars were no longer controlled by and protected by the studios, their private lives became fodder for "paparazzi," freelance reporters and photographers who are the parasites of celebrity culture. And as the "sexual revolution" began to radically alter the conception of sexual mores, the policies on what was "fit to print" also began to change quite dramatically. By the mid-1960s, Andy

Warhol could wryly observe that everyone gets fifteen minutes of fame, and that remark would generate countless commentaries on the implications of a culture in which fame and achievement were no longer necessarily related. But Warhol made that comment well ahead of the development of "reality television," the Internet, and digital media platforms would make his observation seem as quaint as it was prescient.

## FURTHER READING

Appell, Glenn, and David Hemphill. *American Popular Music: A Multicultural History.* Belmont, CA: Thomson Wadsworth, 2006.

Barkley, Elizabeth F. *Crossroads: The Multicultural Roots of America's Popular Music.* Upper Saddle River, NJ: Pearson Prentice Hall, 2007.

Baughman, James L. *The Republic of Mass Culture: Journalism, Flmmaking, and Broadcasting in America since 1941.* Baltimore: Johns Hopkins University Press, 2006.

Bigsby, Christopher, ed. *The Cambridge Companion to Modern American Culture.* New York: Cambridge University Press, 2006.

Boehm, Lisa Krissoff. *Popular Culture and the Enduring Myth of Chicago, 1871–1968.* New York: Routledge, 2004.

Boyd, Nan Alamilla. *Wide-Open Town: A History of Queer San Francisco to 1965.* Berkeley: University of California Press, 2003.

Cross, Mary, ed. *A Century of American Icons: 100 Products and Slogans from the 20th Century Consumer Culture.* Westport, CT: Greenwood, 2002.

Fried, Albert, ed. *McCarthyism: The Great American Red Scare: A Documentary History.* New York: Oxford University Press, 1997.

Glickman, Lawrence, ed. *Consumer Society in American History: A Reader.* Ithaca, NY: Cornell University Press, 1999.

Hall, Simon. *Peace and Freedom: The Civil Rights and Antiwar Movements of the 1960s.* Philadelphia: University of Pennsylvania Press, 2005.

Halttunen, Karen, ed. *A Companion to American Cultural History.* Malden, MA: Blackwell, 2008.

Heimann, Jim. *Car Hops and Curb Service: A History of American Drive-In Restaurants, 1920–1960.* San Francisco: Chronicle Books, 1996.

King, Richard H. *Race, Culture, and the Intellectuals, 1940–1970.* Baltimore: Johns Hopkins University Press, 2004.

Kotynek, Roy, and John Cohassey. *American Cultural Rebels: Avant-Garde and Bohemian Artists, Writers and Musicians from the 1850s through the 1960s.* Jefferson, NC: McFarland, 2008.

Lemann, Nicholas. *The Promised Land: The Great Black Migration and How It Changed America.* New York: Knopf, 1991.

Lichtenstein, Nelson. *State of the Union: A Century of American Labor.* Princeton, NJ: Princeton University Press, 2002.

McGrath, Patrick J. *Scientists, Business, and the State, 1890–1960.* Chapel Hill, NC: University of North Carolina Press, 2002.

Milkman, Ruth, ed. *Women, Work, and Protest: A Century of U.S. Women's Labor History.* New York: Routledge & Kegan Paul, 1985.

Musto, David F., ed. *Drugs in America: A Documentary History.* New York: New York University Press, 2002.

Patterson, James T. *Grand Expectations: The United States, 1945–1974.* New York: Oxford University Press, 1996.

Petigny, Alan Cecil. *The Permissive Society: America, 1941–1965.* New York: Cambridge University Press, 2009.

Rollin, Lucy. *Twentieth-Century Teen Culture by the Decades: A Reference Guide.* Westport, CT: Greenwood, 1999.

Sanders, Vivienne. *Civil Rights in the U.S.A. 1945–68.* London: Hodder Murray, 2008.

Scheurer, Timothy E. *Born in the U.S.A.: The Myth of America in Popular Music from Colonial Times to the Present.* Jackson: University Press of Mississippi, 1991.

Schultz, Nancy Lusignan, ed. *Fear Itself: Enemies Real and Imagined in American Culture.* West Lafayette, IN: Purdue University Press, 1999.

Scott, Allison M., and Christopher D. Geist, eds. *The Writing on the Cloud: American Culture Confronts the Atomic Bomb.* Lanham, MD: University Press of America, 1997.

Shannon, Christopher. *A World Made Safe for Differences: Cold War Intellectuals and the Politics of Identity.* Lanham, MD: Rowman & Littlefield, 2001.

Whitfield, Stephen J. *The Culture of the Cold War.* Baltimore: Johns Hopkins University Press, 1996.

Wood, Paul, ed. *Modernism in Dispute: Art since the Forties.* New Haven, CT: Yale University Press, 1993.

# Exploring Popular Culture

# CHAPTER 1

# Film

**BREAKFAST AT TIFFANY'S (1961)**

Holly Golightly became Audrey Hepburn's signature character almost as soon as this Blake Edwards film was released. Not only did the movie change the popular image of a major 5th Avenue jeweler but, at the other end of the cultural spectrum, it led to the casting of Buddy Ebsen in *The Beverly Hillbillies*. Part of a Broadway brother-and-sister dance act in the 1920s, Ebsen became part of the musical boom in 1930s Hollywood. In *Breakfast at Tiffany's*, he plays an aging rural veterinarian who arrives in New York to reclaim his wayward young bride. Today, the film is remembered, also, for Mickey Rooney's outrageously insensitive portrayal of a Japanese man.

**WEST SIDE STORY (1961)**

Neatly sidestepping black/white racial animosities, the Broadway musical on which this Robert Wise and Jerome Robbins movie is based does try to explore ethnic conflict among the urban young. It did more, however, to promote urban stereotypes among the vast suburban and rural American population than it did toward shedding light on the what had famously become known as "juvenile delinquency." The movie made Leonard Bernstein, already a top celebrity, a household name and promoted Stephen Sondheim into the first rank of American lyricists.

**THE MISFITS (1961)**

The last film featuring Clark Gable or Marilyn Monroe, and one of the last for Montgomery Clift, John Huston's movie was expected to be a blockbuster but proved a box office disappointment. Though its reputation has improved over the decades, in the 1960s it was seen as a sad ending to a career (Monroe's) that should have gone on for many more decades. More in keeping with film-noir–influenced dramas of the 1950s, the movie had little of the glitz normally associated with Monroe or even Gable. Because of the deaths of its stars, *The Misfits* was famous more as something too sad to watch than as a quality movie on its own.

### THE BOND FILMS (1962–1969)

Though British, the James Bond films had a huge impact on American culture. Created by British novelist Ian Fleming in the 1950s, James Bond hit the big screen in the campy *Dr. No* (Terence Young, 1962). Starring Sean Connery as Bond, it also featured Ursula Andress; it made both of them into major stars. Connery followed up as Bond in *From Russia with Love* (Terence Young, 1963), *Goldfinger* (Guy Hamilton, 1964), *Thunderball* (Terence Young, 1965), and *You Only Live Twice* (Lewis Gilbert, 1976). The last Bond film of the 1960s, *On Her Majesty's Secret Service* (Peter Hunt, 1969), saw George Lazenby replace Connery. Though the characters had been earlier created by Fleming, it was the movies that made Auric Goldfinger, Pussy Galore, and many other colorfully named characters even more famous. One of the most famous lines associated with Bond, "Shaken, not stirred" (referring to the creation of a martini), has remained common parlance ever since.

### *TO KILL A MOCKINGBIRD* (1962)

One of the only books to have a cocktail named for it ("Tequila Mockingbird"), the best-selling novel soon became a blockbuster movie directed by Robert Mulligan. Star Gregory Peck's performance impressed so many that his Atticus Finch became one of the iconic characters of the decade, showing what Americans could aspire toward, both professionally and in terms of personal relationships. The idealism of the movie affected younger views strikingly and had an impact on the growing youth movement of the next few years.

### *THE LONGEST DAY* (1962)

The Second World War loomed over the baby boom generation that was coming of age, for its parents had lived it. One of the clichés of the time was "What did you do in the war, Daddy?" (a question that would itself become the title for a 1966 Blake Edwards spoof). *The Longest Day*, almost three hours long, tried to answer that question seriously. The cast included one of the largest grouping of stars ever assembled and from a wide variety of genres. It included teen heartthrobs Fabian and Paul Anka and a number of actors who had actually served during the war, including Henry Fonda. Actors as different as John Wayne and Eddie Albert appeared, as did Richard Burton and even Sean Connery. This black-and-white epic presentation became the image of the war in Europe for an entire generation of Americans.

## CLEOPATRA (1963)

Though it was nominated for nine Academy Awards and actually won four, this Joseph Mankiewicz production quickly became a laughingstock, a prime example of the Hollywood studio system collapsing under its own weight. Though led by Elizabeth Taylor and Richard Burton and supported by an extremely experienced group of actors, the cast could not overcome the ponderous spectacles that ran the cost of making the movie to more than $30 million (about $250 million in today's dollars). Though its reputation has improved over the years, in the 1960s *Cleopatra* was seen as everything a movie shouldn't be.

## THE GREAT ESCAPE (1963)

Steve McQueen, already taking over from Marlon Brando and the ghost of James Dean as the coolest of movie stars, cemented his position in this John Sturges Second World War movie. His climactic scene, which ends when he jumps a motorcycle over a fence topped with barbed wire only to wind up ensnared in the next wire fence, also helped increase the popularity of motorcycle riding. McQueen's character, constantly assigned to punishment in the "cooler," never breaks but bounces a baseball against the wall over and over, doing so even after being returned to the prison camp after the escape. The goal of many young Americans in the 1960s was to face authority with the same unbreakable stamina.

## THE PINK PANTHER (1963)

Blake Edwards had made hit films before, but it was *The Pink Panther* that would define his career. Yes, the movie and its sequels also forever associated Peter Sellers with the bumbling Inspector Clouseau (no matter who would subsequently play the role), but it is the cartoon character introduced during the credits at the start of the film that most endures as the image of the franchise. Almost immediately, American children, many of whom had never seen the movie, became obsessed with the cartoon—and seeing the reaction, United Artists had a series of shorts built around the character, the first released in 1964. The first of these won an Academy Award, and the cartoon image of the pink panther has been a staple of American culture ever since.

## SERGIO LEONE'S TRILOGY AND *ONCE UPON A TIME IN THE WEST* (1964–1968)

They may have been Italian movies, but the trilogy of *A Fistful of Dollars* (1964), *For a Few Dollars More* (1965), and *The Good, the Bad and the Ugly* (1966) (in the internal time of the movies, the third precedes the other two) and then *Once Upon a Time in the West* (1968) were also quintessentially American. They created a persona that Clint Eastwood, star of the first three, would ride for decades and, in the fourth, showed American audiences that beloved Henry Fonda could play evil as well as he could good. The resilience and silence of "the man with no name" became goals of young Americans looking for a younger replacement for John Wayne.

### DR. STRANGELOVE OR: HOW I LEARNED TO STOP WORRYING AND LOVE THE BOMB (1964)

This Stanley Kubrick film made an icon of Slim Pickens, whose bronco ride on the atomic bomb climaxes the film. The movie was released not long after the Cuban Missile Crisis at the height of the Cold War. A black-humor look at the rationales that could lead to nuclear Armageddon, the film is anchored by Peter Sellers, who plays three significant roles in the movie: the title character, the president of the United States, and a British army captain on assignment to the United States. The movie fit well into the growing nihilist attitudes of many Americans who were coming to believe that nuclear war was not a possibility but a certainty and who were beginning to decide that living for today was the only option.

### THE SOUND OF MUSIC (1965)

One of the most enduring images of the 1960s is of Julie Andrews twirling in a dirndl in an Austrian mountain meadow at the start of one of the most beloved, and yet also reviled, movies of the decade—if not of all time. Though it is the film version of the musical that is best known today, during the 1960s, both were extremely popular, and the music had permeated almost every corner of American society almost as the musical opened on Broadway. "My Favorite Things," "Edelweiss," "Do-Re-Mi," "Sixteen Going on Seventeen," "Climb Ev'ry Mountain" and, of course, "The Sound of Music" itself were all instantly recognizable to almost everyone in the country even as early as the end of 1960, when the musical had only been running for less than a year and the movie was not yet even in the planning stages.

Though the movie premiered in 1965, the music had been first introduced to a national audience by Patti Page, who recorded the title song in late 1959 (though her version did not chart). The original-cast recording, recorded shortly after Page recorded the one song, had been released in 1960, quickly reaching the #1 spot on the *Billboard* chart for long-playing records where it remained for four months. By the time the movie came out, not surprisingly, there were few in America unfamiliar with its songs. If they didn't know them already, the popularity of the movie and its own soundtrack, which also reached #1 on the *Billboard* charts, made sure that they did.

*The Sound of Music*, in short, was an extraordinary phenomenon, and it colors our images of the 1960s even today.

The Broadway musical of *The Sound of Music*, with music by Richard Rodgers and lyrics by Oscar Hammerstein II, opened just six weeks before the 1960s began, on November 16, 1959. It was the last Rodgers and Hammerstein musical, and it changed their reputation from Broadway's prime innovators to panderers to sentimentality and purveyors of musical treacle—at least for the 1960s (opinion on the songs has changed a great deal since). Though the show and the 1965 film (directed by Robert Wise) that followed were extremely popular, they were not in keeping with the changing musical, theatrical, and cinematic trends of the decade.

The movie, in particular, ended up as the butt of jokes about the insipid nature of American popular culture, inspiring satires, including the one published in *Mad Magazine* (No. 108, January 1967) by Stan Hart and illustrated by Mort Drucker entitled "The Sound of Money." Hart calls the movie "Nothing but a collection of the same old dull clichés and boring tear-jerker gimmicks that you've been seeing in movie musicals for years." Another satire appeared in the song "I'm Bored," written in 1967 by Vivian Stanshall for the English novelty act The Bonzo Dog Doo Dah Band which, after the singer admits to hating every Julie Andrews film, includes this:

The Von Trapp children serenaded by Maria in the 1964 film *The Sound of Music*. (Michael Ochs Archives/Getty Images)

> I'm bored with it—men in spotty ties
> Who hum tiresome tunes like "Edelweiss."

"Edelweiss" was the last song with lyrics written by Hammerstein. Its subtext, a lament for his Austrian homeland by a man about to leave it because it has been overcome by Hitler's Germany, was lost on many Americans, particularly once the movie appeared based on the "quaintly old-fashioned book," as Bosley Crowther called it in his review in *The New York Times*. He goes on to say that its three-and-a-half-year Broadway run had been enough to convince director Wise "that what made it popular in the theater would make it equally popular on the screen." Wise was right: the movie won him an Academy Award as Best Direction and also pulled in Best Picture, Best Actress in a Leading Role (Julie Andres), Best Actress in a Supporting Role (Peggy Wood), and six other Oscars. It was, in other words, a blockbuster. Other reviewers agreed with Crowther, though the public generally seemed to feel otherwise—in fact, they loved it. In a famous tale, Pauline Kael who was on her way to becoming the dean of American film reviewers from a perch at *The New Yorker*, is claimed to have lost her position as film reviewer for *McCall's* because so many fans were appalled by her caustic review of the movie.

Strangely enough, Julie Andrews herself participated in one early spoof of the musical. For "Julie and Carol at Carnegie Hall," broadcast by CBS on June 11, 1962, she and Carol Burnett presented "The Pratt Family Singers" doing parodies of "My Favorite Things" ("The Things We Like Best") and "Do-Re-Mi" ("Ding Dong Yum Yum Yum"). Using pedestrian tunes with no similarity to the powerhouses of the show, this act, however, did not prove particularly memorable.

Anyone in the 1960s with any claim to taste or hipness, however, just hated the movie—or claimed to—and the damage done to the reputation of Broadway's greatest songwriting team was incalculable. True, it wasn't quite so simple, as Rodgers and Hammerstein biographer Todd Purdum writes, "A combination of factors was at play: the too often second-rate, middlebrow film versions [of Rodgers and Hammerstein shows] that minimized their shows' sophistication and maximized their schmaltz, the rise of 'concept' musicals that emphasized style over plot; and, of course, *The Sound of Music*" (314). But there would be no real recovery of the team's reputation, certainly not before the 1980s.

While the song "Edelweiss" was sometimes mistaken for a Tyrolian folk song and "Do-Re-Mi" was being forced on a generation of schoolchildren, another song from the musical was finding its way into jazz through the work of saxophonist John Coltrane. He recorded "My Favorite Things" for an album of the same name, creating what is now considered a jazz classic, one that, even to the Rodgers-and-Hammerstein hating sophisticates of the 1960s, was immediately cherished. Whatever one thought of the show, few could argue that the music itself was not superb.

The musical stems from a 1956 German film called *Die Trapp Familie*, which told a fanciful version of the true story of the von Trapp family who had established a ski lodge and music camp in Stowe, Vermont, after fleeing Austria soon after the Anschluss, the annexation of the country by Hitler's Germany in 1938. The team behind the musical tracked down Maria Augusta Kutschera von Trapp, who had written the book *The Story of the Trapp Family Singers*, which the movie was based on, but were told she had sold the rights to her story to the producers of the German film—who were then convinced to sell them for the Broadway production. The original Maria, however, did not fade completely from the scene but became an important supporter of the musical.

The story, as Maria von Trapp relates it in her book, tells of her leaving the abbey to teach an ailing von Trapp daughter. What follows is, essentially, what happens in the musical and movie, though the competition for the captain's love is somewhat different. There is greater lapse of time, however, and Maria gives birth to two children of her own. There are financial ups and downs and then recognition that the family has to flee the country after the Anschluss. Though Maria is pregnant with her third child, the family crosses over into Italy, finally ending up in the United States.

Playing Maria on Broadway would be Mary Martin, who had been an established Broadway presence since before the Second World War. That is, she would be playing a character about a quarter of a century younger than she was when the production opened. Martin, though, had star power and was an important backer of the show—but she clearly would not be appropriate for the movie, where she was replaced by Julie Andrews, twenty-two years her junior and star of the recent Disney film *Mary Poppins*. Andrews had earlier created the role of Eliza Doolittle for Frederick Loewe's and Alan Jay Lerner's 1956 musical *My Fair Lady* only to lose out to Audrey Hepburn for the 1964 film version of that hit show.

The book for the show was written by Howard Lindsay and Russel Crouse, longtime Broadway writers and producers. The story centers on Maria, a young postulant in Austria during the late 1930s who, not really ready for religious orders, becomes the governess for the seven children of a widowed naval captain. The first act concerns the conflicts engendered by this new personality in the household, the teaching of music to the children, and the unadmitted romance between the captain and Maria. Through it all, there is an undertone of unease due to the rise of fascism in neighboring Germany. At the end of the act, she returns to the monastery but is told she is denying her true feelings.

In the second act, the children become stage singers and their father has proposed to someone other than Maria. Maria, knowing nothing of this has decided to return. Learning of the situation, she decides once more to leave but stays on until another governess can be located. The captain and his fiancé soon fight over the coming unification with Germany. When she realizes he will never accept life under a Nazi regime, the fiancé breaks the engagement. The captain then recognizes his real love is for Maria and they marry.

The Anschluss, or unification with Germany, occurs and the children prepare for a performance at a festival but are told they must fly the flag of the Third Reich. At the same time, the captain is ordered to active service in the German navy. After the performance at the festival, however, the entire family slips away, leaving their now-fascist homeland.

The movie, with a screenplay by Ernest Lehman, sticks fairly closely to the book of the musical. Lehman, who had quite a good track record in Hollywood (among other things, he had adapted Rodgers and Hammerstein's *The King and I* for the screen). He cut out two songs in order to keep the focus on the family and another "An Ordinary Couple" that he felt unnecessary and switched placement of a few others. The scenes that he did invent were meant to enhance the story of the growing relationships within the family. Now, as Tom Santopietro writes, "Because Maria did not tell the captain that the children had put a frog in her pocket and forced her to sit on a pinecone, there now existed an actual reason for the childrens' capitulation to her" (56). Lehman also added a scene for the family taking place when Maria has returned to the monastery.

*The Sound of Music* has only been revived once on Broadway, in 1998 when it ran for thirteen months and 533 performances. Compare that with *Oklahoma!*, the first Rodgers and Hammerstein collaboration, which has been revived four times, most recently in 2002, for eleven months and 388 performances or the revival of *South Pacific*, which ran for two years starting in 2008 with 996 performances. More than any other of the enduring Rodgers and Hammerstein shows, however, *The Sound of Music* continues to be memorable, both for those who love it and those who hate it.

The movie, too, has endured. In 1998, the American Film Institute included it in fifty-fifth place on its list of the 100 best American movies. Other movies from the 1960s so honored include *Lawrence of Arabia, The Graduate, Psycho, 2001: A Space Odyssey, Dr. Strangelove, Bonnie and Clyde, To Kill a Mockingbird, Midnight Cowboy, West Side Story, Butch Cassidy and the Sundance Kid*, and more. That's august company for a movie that continues to be cordially hated by as many people as love it.

## *BLOW-UP* (1966)

The conceit of a murder accidentally captured on film is at the heart of this Michelangelo Antonioni film. But it was the post–Beatles British sound of The Yardbirds (with both Jeff Beck and Jimmy Page on guitar) and the destroying of guitars on stage that most resonated in American popular culture. Yes, The Who's Peter Townsend had already started making such actions part of his stage performance, but it was *Blow-Up* that first brought this to public attention as part of 1960s rock and roll. Significantly, a year after the release of *Blow-Up*, both Townend and Jimi Hendrix destroyed guitars during the Monterey Pop Festival.

## *WHO'S AFRAID OF VIRGINIA WOOLF?* (1966)

Perhaps the most famous couple in the world, Richard Burton and Elizabeth Taylor wanted to prove their worth in this Mike Nichols adaptation of Edward Albee's play. They did. The studio and Hollywood in general expected that the film would shock audiences with its profanity and sexual themes—but it did not. The American people had changed while Hollywood presumptions about them had not. Of course, the entire United States had changed a great deal since the establishment of the Motion Picture Production Code (MPPC) in 1930. By the mid-1960s, it was proving unenforceable; the producers of this film had much more latitude than did earlier filmmakers and could actually fight back against the censors. Within two years, the MPPC would be dead and movies would have more freedom than ever before under a new rating system meant to warn viewers but also to allow freedom of content to the moviemakers.

## *BONNIE AND CLYDE* (1967)

This Arthur Penn movie paved the way for new filmic depictions of sex and (especially) violence against the crumbling power of the MPPC. The climactic and final scene of the movie, in its bullet-laden depiction of the deaths of the title characters, immediately attained almost mythical status and set a standard for bloodiness that Hollywood had never before seen. It appalled more traditional film critics like Bosley Crowther who, writing for *The New York Times* on

August 14, 1967, said it was "a cheap piece of bald-faced slapstick comedy" (36), but it wowed audiences and changed the expectations of American moviegoers forever—and changed movies themselves.

## COOL HAND LUKE (1967)

Within weeks of the November release of Stuart Rosenberg's film, a high percentage had heard its iconic line, "What we've got here is a failure to communicate." Though the line refers to a recalcitrant prisoner in a Southern work camp, it was taken up by kids as their satiric image of the administrators of their schools and of adults in general. The older and more powerful world seemed to think that, if only they could get through to the younger generation, they could make them understand. No, the real problem, in the eyes of the young, wasn't communication but a perverted power structure unable to turn its eyes within.

## THE DIRTY DOZEN (1967)

Though it keeps to older stereotypes for Second World War films (people of every imaginable ethnic background coming together as a real team), this Robert Aldrich picture also feeds off of an antiauthoritarian attitude that was particularly part of the 1960s zeitgeist. Even the main character, not one of the convicts at the heart of the film but their commander, has a hard time with army discipline. This appealed to the independent streak in all Americans but particularly to the young, who were beginning to seriously rebel against what they saw as an overly regimented society.

## DON'T LOOK BACK (1967)

One of the first documentary concert-tour films, D. A. Pennebaker's *Don't Look Back* follows Bob Dylan's English tour in 1965 (with some other footage) and presents what would become one of the most influential song films (which became "music videos") of Dylan's "Subterranean Homesick Blues" as it opens. The black-and-white movie follows Dylan "behind the scenes," in front of the press, in concert, and in impromptu performance through handheld cinema-vérité–style camera work. Though it did not have a wide theater release, it was immediately sought after by Dylan fans who snapped up the paperback-illustrated transcript of the film that was published the next year.

## THE GRADUATE (1967)

College, in the late 1960s, was becoming a rite of passage for an increasingly large percentage of American youth. Graduation was becoming the gateway to adulthood. Part of this was due to simple economics: a college degree was believed to be redeemable in increased cash throughout one's career. Part of this was due to the draft: a student deferment could keep one out of the army for four years, allowing time to work out further exemptions. And part of it was cultural: the snob appeal of college graduation was quite real. Most young Americans actually looked forward to attending college. The problem lay in figuring out what came next—what to do after commencement.

And that, quite simply, was the question behind the phenomenal success of *The Graduate* (Mike Nichols). Earning $100,000,000 in its first release (about $725 million in today's dollars) it surprised Hollywood and even Embassy Pictures, its distributor, which did not open the movie widely, expecting success, but of a limited nature. After all, the critics did not love the movie, some seeing it as having a disconnect between halves and others considering it exploitative of youthful and naïve audiences. Certainly, it was in no way unusual and not particularly original.

*The Graduate* had two things going for it, however, that most of the critics didn't understand, things removed from the standard aspects of film that cineastes of an older generation appreciated most. The first was the soundtrack: finally, someone had made a movie using a score by musicians the young considered "serious" and not simply "pop." Simon & Garfunkel had already begun to turn away from concentration on the three-minute single for AM play, focusing more on music that might work with the new FM audience generally made

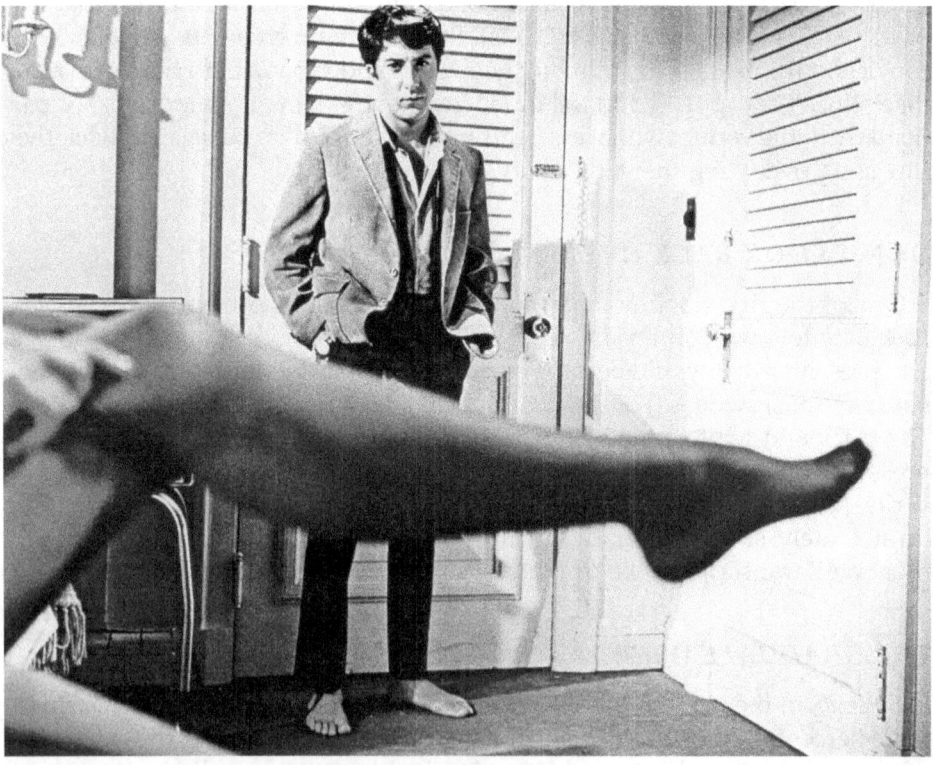

Mrs. Robinson (Anne Bancroft) pulling on a stocking in front of the much younger Benjamin Braddock (Dustin Hoffman) in the 1967 film *The Graduate*. (Embassy Pictures/Getty Images)

up of college students and the more musically aware of the young. Though Simon & Garfunkel had released a string of top 40 hits, Paul Simon was no longer simply writing for the medium of pop (and even commercial folk), changing his focus at just the same time college students were as they moved to LP collections and abandoned their old 45s. At the same time, the older Simon & Garfunkel songs, like "The Sound of Silence," remained nostalgic favorites from high school days for most college students in 1968 (the movie was released at the end of 1967). This, combined with the new "Mrs. Robinson," worked well for *The Graduate*, for students didn't feel they were being pandered to through the soundtrack, as so often happened, and approached the movie with positive curiosity of a sort that could easily have been lacking. The songs, after all, provided a sense of an era ending, too, providing memory of a slightly simpler time when the draft did not loom over young men and the split between generations was personal and not so broadly cultural. They also appreciated that the song "Mrs. Robinson" had been written specifically for the movie, giving the film the tacit endorsement of a respected musical favorite.

On the fortieth anniversary DVD of the movie in 2007, director Mike Nichols says that he chose to use the older songs because of an affinity he intuited between title character Benjamin Braddock and songwriter Paul Simon. He said that, at the time, Simon was searching as a songwriter in much the way Braddock was as a young man. This made Simon's songs the perfect expression of Braddock's inner spirit. Bosley Crowther, in reviewing the movie for *The New York Times* on December 31, 1967, wrote that "Especially subtle and appealing is the way background folk music is used to suggest moods and counterpoint fast humor with general wistfulness. The music . . . is especially appealing and appropriate to the strain of sadness that runs through the film" (D14). Unlike many of his contemporary reviewers, Crowther understood what was going on in *The Graduate* and loved it.

The second thing *The Graduate* had going for it that the critics could not understand was the ending. Not only is it genuinely funny, but it encapsulates the sense of frustration with American culture that many of the young in the late 1960s were feeling, frustration that their elders (including almost all film critics) couldn't quite share. It wasn't the angry faces that entranced young audiences as Braddock pounded on the glass from the balcony as the wedding ceremony reached its finality and Elaine Robinson looked up at him in anguish and hope, nor was it love triumphing over the absurdities of the plot. It was the leaving with nothing, not even in a car but on a public bus. It was the throwing of caution and common sense to the wind that so thrilled the young audiences. It encapsulated whatever cause there was to Braddock's angst in satisfying solution.

In a sense, all of the rest of the movie was simply window dressing, amusing and a good time, but essentially irrelevant to the decision by the young couple to give up all that their parents and society were offering them and head into the complete unknown. Not even Braddock's affair with Elaine's mother made any difference. What they did is what each young audience member secretly wanted to do, break out and break away. It was the logical extension of the philosophy of Ken Kesey and his Merry Pranksters, who also, of course, had a bus—a bus with the destination "Further" on its front.

It was also the opposite of so many other existential decisions depicted in the movies of the time in that it could be cheered, not just admired. Much like the ending of *Le Roi de cœur* (Philippe de Broca, 1966) where the protagonist strips off his uniform, rejecting the war-torn society of his day (the end of the First World War) in favor of that of a lunatic asylum, this ending celebrates rejection of standard assumptions about how life should be lived. However, where the soldier Charles Plumpick is exchanging one kind of confinement for another, Braddock and Elaine Robinson are dropping barriers completely. The fact that she is still in a wedding dress shows how insignificant the old cultural indicators have become for them. They really don't care, and they look back only briefly from the rear of the bus, turning to look forward, smiling, even at the gauntlet of confused and disapproving faces in front of them.

It is impossible to read too much into that final scene. The last spoken lines of the film are "It's too late" followed by "Not for me," spoken by Mrs. Robinson, who has orchestrated her daughter's marriage/capture, and Elaine. After all, just after those words, we see a Christian cross wielded as a club by Braddock and then used to latch the door out of the church. Not only are society's rituals being left behind, but religion, too.

However, even that can be taken too far. As Nichols told a group of Brandeis University students:

> I never meant Benjamin to look like Christ at the end. That drives me crazy, that Christ bit! Benjamin is terrifically lost, rebellious. He's always caught, behind a glass wall, under the water. At the end he is just as lost as he was at the beginning. People say the second half of the film is romantic. But it's not. It's setting up a trap. I think 10 minutes after the bus leaves, the girl will say to him, "My God, I have no clothes!" At least they're out of the terrible world they lived in, but they're not to be envied. I think Benjamin will end up like his parents. (*The New York Times*, February 18, 1968, D15)

The meaning, if there is any, lies in the act itself, not in its consequences.

Significantly, this positive image of throwing all caution to the wind is soon to be replaced by its darker side in two 1969 hit movies, *Butch Cassidy and the Sundance Kid* (George Roy Hill), which costars Katharine Ross who plays Elaine in *The Graduate*, and *The Wild Bunch* (Sam Peckinpah), where characters also cast aside all consideration but, do so in the face of immediate death. The year, 1968, which lay between the films changed American culture so significantly that the ending of *The Graduate*, instead of eliciting cheers, might have been scoffed at, had the movie been released a year later. As it is, the movie was seen, even on release, as almost a contemporary relic (in its presentation) of a more idealistic time, something that was needed as things started to worsen for America in 1968.

Though it may have been these two things, the music and the ending, that assured that *The Graduate* would be a hit, the movie is much more than that and has lasted in American popular culture for myriad reasons.

Looking back, it would seem that the movie had to be a hit. After all, it starred Dustin Hoffman. But he was an unknown when he got the part—Katharine

Ross, though she had an established film career, was only a bit more in the public eye. The rest of the cast, though, was quite experienced, and Ann Bancroft had already won an Academy Award for Best Actress, for *The Miracle Worker* (Arthur Penn, 1962). Other notable performers in *The Graduate* include William Daniels and Elizabeth Wilson as Braddock's parents, Murray Hamilton as Mr. Robinson, and even the seemingly ubiquitous Norman Fell. The director, Mike Nichols, had moved from comedy success (as half a duo with Elaine May) to the directing of Broadway plays to a directorial debut in film with *Who's Afraid of Virginia Woolf?* (1966). This rock-solid lineup (except for Hoffman) pretty much assured that the film would be at least a middling success, but nothing indicated just how well it would resonate with the viewing public.

And it did. Only *The Sound of Music* (Robert Wise, 1965), of all the films of the sixties, grossed more at the box office than did *The Graduate*.

Not that the movie was without controversy. In January 1968, the Transit Authority of New York City removed a subway ad for the movie showing Bancroft and Hoffman in bed together. A City Councilman had claimed that the ads were indecent, according to *The New York Times* for January 9 (35).

Almost immediately, *The Graduate* became a common touchstone for American college students everywhere, each one (the women as well as the men) seeing in Braddock reflections of their own angst. One of the genius moves of the film was an insistence on not giving reason to Braddock's feelings or actions and letting the audience project into the character their own feelings. In this way, the character becomes an Everyman, a stand-in for the frustrations of almost every person who watches the film—while they are young, that is. The movie's place in popular culture has been enduring, college students still finding much in Braddock with which to identify.

"I just want to say one word to you. Just one word," says a friend of Braddock's parents, a Mr. McGuire. "Yes, I am," replies Braddock. "Plastics" continues McGuire with a bit of advice that young America found as hilarious then as audiences do now. "Exactly how do you mean?" asks Braddock. "There's a great future in plastics. Think about it." This encapsulates the America Braddock, and those who identified with him so strongly, hoped to escape. As Nichols, not to mention co-screenwriter Buck Henry who penned those lines, knew, however, Braddock never would, his wonderful act of rebellion notwithstanding.

### *GUESS WHO'S COMING TO DINNER* (1967)

Something that white Americans, in particular, did not like to talk about was how race could affect their personal, family lives. Blacks did not either, as this movie shows. This Stanley Kramer film was released just six months after *Loving v. Virginia* established, through a Supreme Court ruling, that antimiscegenation laws were unconstitutional. Whites were only recently opening up to discussions of race in their personal lives and tentatively exploring the possibility of mixed-race families, especially their own. People would quickly point to this movie as indication that America was changing, that the country was becoming, at least, more open to the possibility of embracing difference.

## IN THE HEAT OF THE NIGHT (1967)

One of the most iconic lines from movies of the 1960s, the simple "They call me Mr. Tibbs," comes from this film. The chief of police of Sparta, Mississippi, is asking visiting Philadelphia detective, a black man, what they call him up there, asking spitefully and almost angrily with clear racial animosity toward a man he believes is acting above his station. It is the tone of Sidney Poitier's response that makes the line so iconic. Said calmly but firmly, yet clearly repressing real anger, it affirms the pride of a black man even in the face of belligerent racial aggression.

## THE PRODUCERS (1967)

At the time he made *The Producers*, Mel Brooks was best known for his act with Carl Reiner, "The 2000 Year Old Man," and the album of it that had been released in 1961. He had also cocreated (with Buck Henry) the popular sitcom *Get Smart*, but he was not in any way know as a filmmaker. Not only that, but when he first attempted to secure studio backing for *The Producers*, most walked quickly away, not willing to touch a satire built around a Hitler-centered musical comedy. The movie, as a result, did not get wide release, but the audiences who saw it, particularly college students, were wildly enthusiastic. Adding to that, Brooks managed to garner a nomination for the Academy Award for best screenplay, which he subsequently won, giving the film new momentum. With *The Producers*, Brooks gained a fan base that would never leave him.

## 2001: A SPACE ODYSSEY (1968)

The computer, the HAL 9000, from this Stanley Kubrick film quickly became emblematic of technology gone wild. Though the movie is long and, to some, quite ponderous, the red-camera/eye image of HAL quickly became identifiable by even those Americans who had never seen the movie. The deadpan voice of HAL, provided by Douglas Rain, became almost as identifiable. HAL (it stands for Heuristically programmed ALgorithmic computer) resists attempts to shut "him" down as he begins to malfunction, setting up the central conflict of the film.

## BULLITT (1968)

The car chase through the streets of San Francisco in this Peter Yates film was like none other American audiences had ever seen. It set the standard for all that would follow. Careful to keep to the actuality of the city behind its fiction, the ten-minute-long chase does, however, defy temporal possibility—that is, the ground covered could not be covered in the real time of the movie. Cameras showed parts of the chase from drivers' points of view, adding to the suspense. If asked about the movie at the time, few who had seen it could have explained the plot—but almost all of them could have described the chase.

## *PLANET OF THE APES* (1968)

The real point of this Franklin Schaffner picture is that we should be careful about what we think or do concerning others, for we might actually be doing it to ourselves. In our willingness to lay the blame on others, we actually continue the cycle of destruction. The more overt message about racism sometimes obscures this theme and, oddly enough, allows for a racist enthusiasm when, for example, Charlton Heston's character yells, "Take your stinking paws off me, you damn dirty ape." In this way, the movie was appreciated by both those who believe in racial divide and one-sided superiority and those who don't.

## *ROSEMARY'S BABY* (1968)

This Roman Polanski feature spawned a new horror subgenre of devil mumbo-jumbo films that base themselves loosely on Christian, particularly Catholic, iconography though few of them reached anywhere near the power of this spare film, almost the opposite, in presentation, of the gore-laden *Bonnie and Clyde* of the previous year. The film drew on the desire to find something more than what we normally experience in the world along with the titillation of the sexual unknown. It quickly became a touchstone and a dividing point.

## *BUTCH CASSIDY AND THE SUNDANCE KID* (1969)

Paul Newman had been a major heartthrob for more than a decade when he and rising star Robert Redford were paired in this George Roy Hill Western. The film might have been nothing more than another standard slightly goofy take on the genre, except for its ending, the other side of that of *The Graduate* but with an identical existential message: do what you need to and damn the consequences. The idea of fate following closely behind and, ultimately, unescapable is central to the movie and is reiterated through the repeated line, "Who are those guys?" This line quickly became a popular refrain used whenever something could not be shaken off.

## *EASY RIDER* (1969)

One of the first films to attempt an album-rock soundtrack, *Easy Rider* is the story of two Counterculture motorcyclist drug smugglers played by Henry Fonda and Dennis Hopper, who also directed. It was written by Terry Southern along with Fonda and Hopper and shows a great deal of what was popularly seen as the "hippie" Counterculture of the time. The filmmakers, especially for such an extremely low budget movie, did extremely well with the music they were able to afford (licensing was more than twice the cost of rest of the film), including recordings by Jimi Hendrix, The Band, Steppenwolf, and The Byrds. The film also brought Jack Nicholson to national attention for the first time.

## *MEDIUM COOL* (1969)

The events of 1968, particularly the "police riot" at the Democratic National Convention in Chicago in August, were not easily processed by American popular culture. Using a style combining fiction and documentary of the sort seen in *The Battle of Algiers* (Gillo Pontecorvo, 1966) and in *Z* (Costa-Gavras, 1969), which preceded *Medium Cool* by about six months, Haskell Wexler attempted to use the movies to come to terms with actual and traumatic political events. The title comes from Marshall McLuhan's distinction, in *Understanding Media*, between television as a "cool" medium, one that does not completely engage, and film as a "hot" medium that requires much more concentrated attention.

## *MIDNIGHT COWBOY* (1969)

Cementing Dustin Hoffman's position as a star and showing that he had a wide-ranging acting talent, this John Schlesinger movie also furthered 1960s myths about "the city," particularly New York City. What is perhaps most significant about the film, however, is its approach to sexuality. Though it does not embrace homosexuality or prostitution, it takes both in stride as part of American life, particularly urban life. A sad take on the lure-of-the-city theme, the movie quickly became an emblem for the way the United States ignores its downtrodden and lost.

## *THE WILD BUNCH* (1969)

The violence that Americans had been learning to live with through the Vietnam War, urban riots, and assassinations is reflected in this gruesome Sam Peckinpah tale that parallels, in some ways, the plot of *Butch Cassidy and the Sundance Kid*. Though the film also started a fascination with slow motion in action scenes and average shot length (ASL) much shorter than in the past, its main impact was in its almost loving depiction of violence and death. It showed that American culture embraced much more than platitudes about universal brotherhood and that Americans are as fixated on killing as they are on loving.

## TEEN MOVIES

Teenagers have always been on the forefront of popular culture. In the 1960s, movies tried hard to keep up with them and mostly failed. The teens did go to the movies directed at them, but often to laugh at them as much as to enjoy them. The stars weren't their real heroes and heartthrobs, and the music chosen for these movies was rarely of the best or even lasting favorites. There really was a generation gap; the people making decisions about the movies had very little real knowledge of the evolving youth culture they wanted to exploit as both subject and audience.

Though teen movies, as a genre, had gotten a start in the 1950s, it was the 1960s that brought the genre to its greatest level of success. Stars like Annette Funicello and Frankie Avalon propelled American International Pictures (AIP) to new heights, and even the large studios like Metro-Goldwyn-Mayer got into the act with movies like Henry Levin's 1960 success, *Where the Boys Are*. These movies drew on 1950s rock-and-roll movies and included Elvis Presley's continuing string of financial successes while also taking themes from films like *Rebel without a Cause* (Nicholas Ray, 1955), *The Wild One* (Lásló Benedek, 1953), and *Blackboard Jungle* (Richard Brooks, 1955). They generally included at least one new song intended as a hit single and made music and alienation part and parcel of their construction. Also important to the genre was the 1959 Paul Wendkos film *Gidget* starring Sandra Dee and James Darren.

The teen movies of the 1960s helped define a broader genre of "exploitation" films, movies generally produced quite quickly to take advantage of current trends in popular culture or specific, generally horrific, events. Though there have been exploitation films since the era of silent films, they became much more common and popular in the 1960s due to the relaxation of the film industry's self-censorship policies of the time. Among the many examples of teen-exploitation films is the William Shatner (pre–*Star Trek*) vehicle *The Explosive Generation* (Buzz Kulik, 1961).

There were, of course, releases from major studios aimed at teen audiences (at least in part). These include Universal Pictures' *Come September* (Robert Mulligan, 1961) starring Rock Hudson and Gina Lollobrigida but featuring teen idols Sandra Dee and Bobby Darin and including his song *Multiplication*, which became a minor hit. *Splendor in the Grass* (Elia Kazan, 1961), from Warner Brothers, focused on teenaged characters played by Warren Beatty and Natalie Wood, however, did not directly seek a teenaged audience. Its music, for example, was written by David Amram, a classical and jazz musician/composer, someone certainly not from the pop genre favored by most teen films. The same could be said of *West Side Story* (Robert Wise and Jerome Robbins, 1961) with music by Leonard Bernstein. Many films tried to cross the boundaries between adults and teens much the way *Come September* does. Among the more successful of these is *Bye Bye Birdie* (George Sidney, 1963), which parodies the crazes around pop music but includes teen favorites like Ann-Margret and Bobby Rydell.

Not included in the discussion here are the movies of Elvis Presley and The Beatles. Because of the unique natures of these performers, their films fit poorly into genres. For this reason, they are discussed in the entries devoted to the artists.

### Beach Movies

Lou Rusoff, son of a show business professional himself (something that would become a hallmark of AIP teen productions), started off the most iconic series of teen movies by producing the script for *Beach Party* (William Asher, 1963), the first of what would prove to be seven films. Influenced by *Gidget*, it starred Frankie Avalon, already an established teen idol perhaps best known for his hit single "Venus," and Annette Funicello, who was trying to break out of her child-star Disney mold (she was known to baby boomers primarily for her role as a Mouseketeer on *The Mickey Mouse Club*). They served the purpose

James Darren and Sandra Dee did in anchoring the earlier film. The movie is built on clichés about 1960s surfer youth, but that does not seem to have lessened the attraction. Though Bob Cummings (an established movie and television personality) headed the cast, it was Avalon and Funicello the young audiences flocked to see. Included was plenty of surfing, dancing, and bathing suits. There were farcical bad guys and well-meaning but clueless adults (like Cummings's Professor Sutwell).

The movie, though it had a putative connection to surfing and the growing subculture surrounding it—including use of the music of surfer-sound icon guitarist Dick Dale—had very little to do with actual surfing.

Based on the surprising success of *Beach Party*, AIP quickly got to work on a sequel, *Muscle Beach Party*, also directed by Asher and released in 1964 just ahead of *another* Asher sequel, *Bikini Beach*. These were followed by five other movies with related cast and characters (as well as a few others not so closely related) over the next two years: *Pajama Party, Beach Blanket Bingo, Ski Party, How to Stuff a Wild Bikini*, and *Dr. Goldfoot and the Bikini Machine*.

The surf-oriented beach movies weren't the only ones in the genre. The success of *Where the Boys Are* made sure that the new genre wasn't quite so specific. A much more expensive production than anything AIP could command, the movie featured a cast that, like that of *Beach Party*, featured both newcomers and experienced Hollywood actors like Chill Wills and Frank Gorshim and included TV regular George Hamilton, providing his breakthrough into the movies (though this was not his first movie role). Though the movie is sometimes called a comedy, it deals with much more serious issues than the determinedly light *Beach Party*. Singer Connie Francis, who has a role in the movie, also provides the theme song, which became a hit single. Furthermore, the teens in *Where the Boys Are*, unlike those of *Beach Party* (but like Moondoggie and Gidget by the end of *Gidget*), have plans and a sense of future: they are college students, not the nihilists on the beach in *Beach Party* and, aside from the main characters, in *Gidget*. *Where the Boys Are* ends positively but in the aftermath of rape and injury; *Gidget* ends with indication that the beach life is simply a way station; *Beach Party*, on the other hand, ends with more party. Still, the movies have so much in common that they define a genre that lasted throughout the decade.

Not surprisingly, the beach movies were not always confined to the ocean. *A Swingin' Summer* (Robert Sparr, 1965) moves the action to a lake. The movie is notable only because it included the first major film role played by Raquel Welch. Its musical element included appearances by Gary Lewis & the Playboys and The Righteous Brothers.

### Teen-Rebellion Movies

The successes of AIP's quickie horror and beach movies gave the studio funds for much more ambitious projects. Among these was one of the most successful teen-rebellion movies of the decade, *Wild in the Streets* (Barry Shear, 1968). Though quickly rejected by young leftists as preposterous, the movie struck a chord with many young people and was successful enough to gather an Academy Award nomination. The cast, which included Shelley Winters, Richard Pryor, and Hal Holbrook, sported more talent than most AIP pictures and included cameos by such luminaries as Ed Begley, Melvin Belli, Dick Clark, and Walter Winchell. As is true of most of the teen movies of the decade, music was an important part of the story, the main character being, at first, the leader of a band unnamed in the movie but called "Max Frost and the Troopers" with the release of a single from a song performed in the movie, "Shape of Things to Come." The song charted for nine weeks.

Another AIP film that fits into this category is *Riot on Sunset Strip* (Arthur Dreifuss, 1967). With music by the Standells, whose single for the movie "Riot on Sunset Strip" failed to break the top 100 Billboard chart. The inspiration for this exploitation film was a series of confrontations between youth and police in Los Angeles in late 1966 that also inspired Stephen Stills to write "For What It's Worth (Stop, Hey What's That Sound)," a song then recorded by his band Buffalo Springfield in 1967 and now considered one of the greatest of the era.

With a theme song by the light-pop band Harpers Bizarre (which had charted the previous year with "The 59th Street Bridge Song (Feelin' Groovy)" and "Come to the Sunshine"), Warner Brothers–Seven Arts tried to capitalize on drug-related "dropping out" in 1968 with *I Love You, Alice B. Toklas* (Hy Averback). Again, the studio didn't really understand what it was dealing with: Harpers Bizarre was not a favorite within the drug culture, and the depictions of drug use were wildly at odds with the experiences of the young. Only the presence of Peter Sellers, himself hardly young, redeems the movie.

Perhaps the most iconic of the films in this subgenre, however, did not use teens at all. Starring Peter Fonda and Dennis Hopper and introducing Jack Nicholson for the first time to a wide audience, *Easy Rider* (Dennis Hopper, 1969) built on the motorcycle tradition that goes back to *The Wild One*, the rock-and-roll movies also from the 1950s, and the growing "hippie" exploitation films. *Easy Rider* was far from the first biker film of the 1960s (Roger Corman's 1966 AIP film *The Wild Angels*, which also starred Peter Fonda, may hold that honor), but it is the one most sustained in American popular culture. Part of this due to timing, but part is due to the continuing successes of the cast, especially of Nicholson and Hopper. Part is also due to the soundtrack, which includes cuts by The Band, The Byrds, and Jimi Hendrix, all of whom have remained popular over the decades since the film's release.

Related to the biker films is *The Born Losers* (T. C. Frank, 1967), the first of the Billy Jack films (the other three of which appeared in the 1970s). Another AIP release, it also follows the tradition of the enigmatic loner that has roots deep in the Western genre.

At the heart of the teen movies of the 1960s was AIP, which was more interested in the quick buck from exploitation pictures than quality filmmaking. If a movie made money, the studio made another one like it. Generally at sea when it came to any sort of understanding of the young, the major studios often followed AIP's lead, making movies of poor quality and less sense. This can be seen most easily in the casting, which concentrated not on the real heroes of the young but on minor teen idols and the children of older stars (Peter Fonda, Nancy Sinatra, and Jody McRae, for example) and in the music which, until *Easy Rider* and with the exception of Dick Dale, contained almost nothing but treacly pop—which is strange, given the prevalence of rock-and-roll movies in the previous decade.

## ICONIC MOVIE STARS OF THE 1960S

### Ursula Andress

In her white bikini with white belt and sheath knife, a diving mask raised over her face, and carrying two large shells while singing "underneath a mango tree," she became a star in her first scene in *Dr. No* (Terence Young, 1962) and the model for all of the James Bond "girls" that were to follow. Though she had quite a bit of success as an actress throughout the 1960s, it was this one scene that established her place in the popular culture of the decade.

### Julie Andrews

What would Julie Andrews have become without *The Sound of Music* (Robert Wise, 1965)? Would the stardom stemming from *Mary Poppins* (Robert Stevenson, 1964) have been enough to sustain her new image as the all good, all positive, all pure nanny? Or would *The Americanization of Emily* (Arthur Hiller, 1964) have taken on more importance in her career, allowing her early on to move beyond the typecasting that so boxed her in. Starring in the top grossing film of the decade can't be all bad, but playing nannies in two hit films, and winning an Academy Award for Best Actress for her work in the lesser hit can certainly have an impact on the direction of a career.

Because of her two hit nannies, Andrews became identified in popular culture with all that wasn't hip but that was square and proper. Though she was immensely popular, not even her fans liked to admit they liked her—for doing so was a hoi polloi move, placing one well away from the hot and trendy.

### Ann-Margret

Though she started as a singer, Ann-Margret became famous for roles in *Bye Bye Birdie* (George Sidney, 1963) and *Viva Las Vegas* (George Sidney, 1964). In the 1960s, she also had a role in the serious drama *The Cincinnati Kid* (Norman Jewison, 1965), but it was her connection with Elvis (and the Elvis-inspired Conrad Birdie) that dominated her image. She became that sexy-but-pure stereotype that young people turned their noses up at, something she had to work hard to overcome—and wouldn't, really, until the 1970s.

Ann-Margret also quickly became the older generation's idea of what the kids "today" want. She was sultry but squeaky clean and went on tour with Bob Hope to entertain troops in Vietnam. Though she was associated with Elvis, well, even he, by 1968, was considered something of a has-been, a creature of the 1950s and not the hip modern day. In a way, she seemed more of a throwback to the 1950s than a real creature of the new decade.

### Bridget Bardot

Though few American moviegoers ever saw her in the movies, Bardot was well known through the press about her, where, by 1960, she had become the archetypal European "sex kitten." Hollywood tried to capitalize on this image with *Dear Brigitte* (Henry Koster, 1965), a James Stewart vehicle that features Bardot playing herself. Though she aspired to more than sex symbol status, that's about all she managed—in the United States in the 1960s, that is.

### Warren Beatty

In some ways, Beatty seemed to exemplify the Hollywood stud of the 1960s. After all, his first success was as a heartthrob in *Splendor in the Grass* (Elia Kazan, 1961) and a gigolo in *The Roman Spring of Mrs. Stone* (José Quintero, 1961), and he ended the decade riding the tremendous success of *Bonnie and Clyde* (Arthur Penn, 1967). In between, he was best known for playing the role of a star, womanizing and gallivanting his way across the tabloids.

### Richard Burton

He was a star in the 1950s, but in the 1960s he became Richard Burton. It began with the Broadway musical *Camelot* in 1960 and continued into the film *Cleopatra* (Joseph Mankiewicz, 1963) with the high publicity of his affair with co-star Elizabeth Taylor (they were both married to others, at the time) doing more to enhance his reputation than even *Camelot* had. The couple would be fodder for the tabloids even once they married in 1964.

"Liz and Dick" became one of the most famous couples in the world, making a number of films together, including *Who's Afraid of Virginia Woolf?* (Mike Nichols, 1966), which almost seemed a taunt to his own alcoholism, a disease that was debilitating him more and more as the decade wore on. Though he was an excellent and wide-ranging actor, he was best known to American popular culture for the tempestuous relationship he had with Taylor—through it, proving that a star could no longer be destroyed by extramarital affairs or even by rumors of drink.

### Sean Connery

No matter what else he might have accomplished, in the 1960s, Connery was nothing but James Bond. For many, it didn't seem possible that anyone else could play the role. In fact, only one Bond film of the 1960s, *On Her Majesty's Secret Service* (Peter Hunt, 1969) was released during the decade and less than two weeks before it was over. Connery became the personification of a certain type of cool—not hip, but decidedly cool—within a framework that was fast collapsing, where alcohol and not marihuana was the drug of choice and the life of the super-wealthy was the goal.

### Bobby Darin

Though his reputation as a pop singer was established in the 1950s, Bobby Darin was very much part of the popular American culture of the 1960s. He started the decade with a version of "Beyond the Sea" that charted well but ended it as something of a has-been, as someone who could not keep up with changing times—this even as he brought his leftist politics more to the forefront and abandoned his Sinatra-esque image for songs more in the folk tradition, even releasing a version of Tim Hardin's "If I Were a Carpenter" that sold well. Though he remained popular, Darin never was able to shake the pop image of his early years.

### Doris Day

All that was squeaky clean about the 1950s was wrapped in a bow and delivered to the next decade as Doris Day. Through her three films with Rock Hudson and vehicles such as *Please Don't Eat the Daisies* (Charles Walters, 1960) and *That Touch of Mink* (Delbert Mann, 1962), she became the exemplar of a coy attitude about sex that was fast disappearing in a decade where freedom, openness, and experimentation were replacing hints and winks and hidden sexuality. She became the symbol of coyness with no follow-through, a fake sensuality that many Americans were trying to shed.

### Sandra Dee

Already a star at the beginning of the 1960s, it was her role as *Gidget* (Paul Wendkos, 1959) that vaulted Dee into the iconosphere. The beach-movie genre that resulted from *Gidget* had a tremendous impact on American popular culture, not only furthering the popularity of surfing but promoting the idea that alternatives to the mainstream aren't as deviant as they may seem, providing at least a little comfort to parents of rebellious teenagers.

### Clint Eastwood

Perhaps the greatest of the antiheroes of the 1960s, Eastwood's Man With No Name from the Sergio Leone trilogy *A Fistful of Dollars* (1964), *For a Few Dollars More* (1965), and *The Good, the Bad and the Ugly* (1966) was as influential on American popular culture in general as he was on the Western. In a way, it was the mystery surrounding the character and his general silence that attracted fans: nothing was explained. Eastwood quickly parlayed his success in these movies into a number of films, including another Western, a police drama, and a World War III film—all of his characters played with his now trademark understated deadpan.

### Fabian

The manufacturing of teen idols predates Fabian and has continued unabated since, but this South Philadelphia boy thrust into stardom is one of the most pointed to. Never really comfortable as a singer, he turned to acting in the 1960s, performing credibly, if not all that well, in movies for major studios before turning to American International Pictures, the 1960s mainstay of second-string films. Fabian never overcame his built-up teen-idol status, however, and had faded in popularity by the end of the decade.

### Jane Fonda

*Barbarella* (Roger Vadim, 1968) and *Cat Ballou* (Elliot Silverstein, 1965), two title roles for Jane Fonda, cemented her position as a top star and not simply the daughter of a Hollywood legend. She topped off the decade, however, with a role much more serious than in any of her previous movies. Her performance in *They Shoot Horses, Don't They?* won her an Academy Award nomination as Best Actress, though she lost out to Maggie Smith, who won for *The Prime of Miss Jean Brodie* (Ronald Neame, 1969). After an incredibly productive decade, she had proved that she was no simple beauty hoisted to fame by family connection but a serious artist in her own right.

### Peter Fonda

Son of one of Hollywood's most famous actors and younger brother of one of the top actresses of the 1960s, Fonda turned away from mainstream film studios to get out of their shadows. His 1960s image was formed by the 1966 Roger Corman movie for American International Pictures, *The Wild Ones*. It was settled by *Easy Rider* (Dennis Hopper, 1969). Fonda was the rebel and hedonist, in public imagination, that so many dreamed of being. Though the characters he played suffered the consequences of their actions, he did not—or so it seemed.

### Annette Funicello

The former Mouseketeer parlayed her popularity on *The Mickey Mouse Club* into a career as a pop singer and, more significantly, as an actress. She was particularly associated with a series of beach movies made by American International Pictures that paired her most often with Frankie Avalon. She was the good girl who was still hip enough to run with the wild crowd without getting caught up in its dangers.

### Audrey Hepburn

Hepburn's character Holly Golightly in *Breakfast at Tiffany's* (Blake Edwards, 1961) became a 1960s stalwart, one of those few recognized by Americans everywhere, whether they had seen the movie or not. Though she was beaten out in the Academy Award for Best Actress by Sophia Loren, Hepburn, dressed as Golightly in a long, simple but sleek and chic black dress, her hair piled high, and a cigarette in a long, long holder, became part of the American national memory of the early 1960s. Though she had other film successes—indeed, she was one of the most popular actresses of the decade—it was as Golightly that others saw her. Even when she played Eliza Doolittle as the uneducated and filthy flower-seller she was at the start of the hit musical *My Fair Lady* (George Cukor, 1964), audiences knew that she would bloom.

### Dustin Hoffman

Though Hoffman's understated acting in his breakthrough role as the title character in *The Graduate* (Mike Nichols, 1967) didn't foretell to everyone the range of his talent, his 1969 portrayal of the dying con artist Ratso Rizzo in *Midnight Cowboy* (John Schlesinger) certainly did. *The Graduate* had made Hoffman one of the most popular actors in America, his Benjamin Braddock becoming a touchstone for young college graduates across the country. *Midnight Cowboy* showed that his performance wasn't simply a fluke, but that this actor, though only active in movies over the last years of the decade, was one of the greatest stars of the 1960s.

Holly Golightly (Audrey Hepburn) set the style for the early part of the decade with her little black dress in *Breakfast at Tiffany's* (1961). (George Rinhart/Corbis via Getty Images)

### Rock Hudson

The other half of an early-1960s romantic-comedy duo with Doris Day, Hudson turned the reputation he had earned through *Giant* (George Stevens, 1956) in a new direction, creating a new image for himself, one very popular early on but that could not survive the turmoil of the latter years of the decade. In *Pillow Talk* (Michael Gordon, 1959), *Lover Come Back* (Delbert Mann, 1961), and *Send Me No Flowers* (Norman Jewison, 1964), Hudson perfected an image of the slightly befuddled but lovable American male who constantly annoys and attracts his female counterpart.

### Jerry Lewis

Starting with *The Bellboy* (Jerry Lewis, 1960), Lewis took control of his own movies and comedy, his new success eclipsing anything he had achieved before. That his particular brand of slapstick and silliness didn't seem to impress many adults didn't matter: he drew at the box office and kids loved him. In the 1960s, however, his greatest fame came from his yearly telethon for the Muscular Dystrophy Association, which ran nationally on Labor Day starting in 1966.

### Sophia Loren

Loren's triumph in *Two Women* (Vittorio De Sica, 1960) made her more than simply the stereotypical Italian sexpot. Though she appeared in nineteen films during the 1960s, it was this movie that proved she could be both a beauty and a powerful actor. Throughout the decade, she was primarily seen as one of the most sensual women in the world, but she had earned a level of respect that few sex symbols have managed.

### Lee Marvin

Hardboiled? Yes, but he could be funny. The image of Marvin, no matter what else he did, remained that of the cold-blooded killer of the Western, an image solidified by *The Man Who Shot Liberty Valance* (John Ford, 1962). However, he was best loved in the 1960s for his roles as drunken Kid Shelleen in *Cat Ballou* (Elliot Silverstein, 1965) and Major John Reisman in *The Dirty Dozen* (Robert Aldritch, 1967), a Second World War officer with a rebellious streak and a sense of humor. In this way, Marvin was able to keep up with the spirit of the times, remaining popular even as the Western, for the moment, faded.

### Steve McQueen

No one, in the 1960s, exemplified "cool" as much as did McQueen. He parlayed stardom in the television Western *Wanted: Dead or Alive* into a film career placing him at the top of the Hollywood pantheon. Of all of his films, perhaps the most iconic is *Bullitt* (Peter Yates, 1968), a thriller presenting the most famous car-chase sequence of the decade. Always understated, ever persistent, McQueen's characters are often experts at cars and motorcycles and are fans of speed. No other actor in the 1960s quite so personified these aspects of the sixties character as it was popularly imagined.

### Paul Newman

Even before the start of the decade, Newman was a major star, known for steamy sensuality but with, perhaps, a bit more humor and all-American attitude than had James Dean and Marlon Brando, the two top sensual-male film icons of the 1950s. It wasn't until *Cool Hand Luke* (Stuart Rosenberg, 1967) that Newman began to show that he was of a somewhat different mold, something more than simply a sex symbol. This position was solidified two years later with *Butch Cassidy and the Sundance Kid* (George Roy Hill, 1969), elevating Newman to the absolute top of Hollywood stardom.

### Peter O'Toole

From the fame of his depiction of the title character in *Lawrence of Arabia* (David Lean, 1962), British stage actor O'Toole became emblematic of the person following one's own path, damn the consequences or even the morality of broader society. Even as a king, as in *Beckett* (Peter Glenville, 1964) and *The Lion in Winder* (Anthony Harvey, 1966), he was more concerned with himself than with the commonweal. Even in *Lord Jim* (Richard Brooks, 1965), he played the role of a man who, though he made mistakes, stayed true to himself. The existential nature of the characters made him a favorite throughout the decade.

### Gregory Peck

Though his career spanned decades, it was for one role that Peck became an icon of the 1960s: Atticus Finch in *To Kill a Mockingbird* (Robert Mulligan, 1962). So loved was Peck's character that even those who read the book without seeing the movie soon imagined his face as that of Finch. By 1962, many Americans were aching to see a better nature for their country, especially in the face of the exposures of racial hatred that had been buried for so long. Finch became the exemplar of what was best about the country and Peck his manifestation.

### Anthony Perkins

If any one character illustrated the dark side of the American psyche in the 1960s, it was Norman Bates, portrayed with chilling exactitude by Perkins in *Psycho* (Alfred Hitchcock, 1960). Quite quickly, Bates became a touchstone in popular culture, though this hampered his career in the United States throughout the decade. As a result, he turned to Europe, where he found success in a number of films there, where he was not quite so tied to the Bates image.

### Sidney Poitier

By the 1960s, Poitier was already the most prominent actor of African descent in the United States. His tour de force roles in *A Raisin in the Sun* (Daniel Petrie, 1961), *Lilies of the Field* (Ralph Nelson, 1963), *A Patch of Blue* (Guy Green, 1965), *In the Heat of the Night* (Norman Jewison, 1967), and *Guess Who's Coming to Dinner* (Stanley Kramer, 1967) kept him in the spotlight throughout the decade and provided inspiration for actors of all races as an exemplar of craft over stance. He became the ideal of the man of integrity standing tall, color notwithstanding.

### Peter Sellers

Though his comedy and talent were used much more broadly, Sellers was known in the 1960s primarily for two things: his role as Inspector Clouseau in *The Pink Panther* (Blake Edwards, 1963) and his multiple roles in *Dr. Strangelove or: How I Learned to Stop Worrying and Love the Bomb* (Stanley Kubrick, 1964). Mention of his name elicited immediate reference to one movie—or both. By the middle of the decade, millions of Americans could imitate the Clouseau accent or the half-salute of Dr. Strangelove—and no one would miss the reference.

### Omar Sharif

Two films create the iconography of Sharif in the 1960s, *Lawrence of Arabia* (David Lean, 1962) and *Doctor Zhivago* (David Lean, 1965). In both, he plays men with keen powers of observation but also with a certain passive positioning—men who are smart but who do not reach out and grab but who wait and then react to what others do. This makes them appear enigmatic, something that Sharif would play on his entire career, and always a little foreign to Americans, whose ideal is to shoot first and ask questions later.

### Frank Sinatra

By the 1960s, Sinatra had been a star for two decades. One of the biggest. But pop music had begun to move in directions he declined to follow, opening a rift between him and younger audiences, and his film roles could no longer be sustained by a boyish smile that wowed the bobby-soxers. Still, he remained a force to be reckoned with in popular culture. No matter that the baby boomers scoffed at him, his formal wear, and his outdated and over-orchestrated (to young ears) music, he remained one of the biggest draws in the country, on stage, on record, and on film. Two of his songs, "Strangers in the Night" in 1966 and 1967's "Something Stupid" (with his daughter Nancy), reached #1 on the pop charts, something that had not happened to a Sinatra single in over a decade. Though he continued to star in films, few of his movies of the 1960s, outside of *The Manchurian Candidate* (John Frankenheimer, 1962), became significant cultural markers, even though Sinatra remained one of the favorite film stars of Americans.

### Elizabeth Taylor

Though she had long been a star, Elizabeth Taylor became something more than that during the 1960s. Not only did she become half of that most famous couple in the world, "Liz and Dick," with Richard Burton, but she became both a laughingstock (for her title role in Joseph Mankiewicz's in 1963 disaster *Cleopatra*) and an exemplar of all an actress can be with her tour de force performance in *Who's Afraid of Virginia Woolf?* (Mike Nichols, 1966). She started the decade at the top of the Hollywood hierarchy, winning the Academy Award for Best Actress of 1960 for her role in *Butterfield 8* (Daniel Mann) and won a second for *Who's Afraid of Virginia Woolf?* By the end of the 1960s, however, though she was still in her thirties, her power as a Hollywood star had begun to wane, though she remained a popular figure in the media—as she would, for the rest of her life.

### John Wayne

By the start of the 1960s, John Wayne had been so successful for so long that he had started to become a parody of himself. During the decade, he both fought against that and used it, finally combining the two impulses in an Academy Award–winning performance in *True Grit* (Henry Hathaway, 1969). Through most of the 1960s, however, Wayne grew more and more unpopular with the baby boom generation that had grown up with his Westerns. His increasingly right-wing political views led him to be cordially reviled by his erstwhile fans, especially after release of his pro–Vietnam War film *The Green Berets* (John

Wayne and Ray Kellogg, 1968). Still, his distinctive voice and persona remained important and beloved to even those who most opposed him politically.

### Raquel Welsh

Raquel Welsh and her bikini became instantly famous (though she had already starred in one film, Richard Fleischer's 1966 *Fantastic Voyage*) in 1966 because of a publicity still and poster for her role in *One Million Years B.C.* (Don Chaffey, 1966). Aside from Welsh's eye-popping poses, the film gathered little positive reaction. After that worn by Ursula Andress as she rose from the sea in *Dr. No* (Terence Young, 1962) a few years earlier, this was the most famous bikini of the decade. Over the next few years, she took advantage of her notoriety, starring in a number of films, most of which were successful.

### Natalie Wood

Natalie Wood entered the 1960s an established star, but it was two musicals (in one of which she did not sing) and a story of youthful passion that, over the first years of the decade, cemented her position at the top of the Hollywood heap. The first of these was *West Side Story* (Robert Wise and Jerome Robbins, 1961), where she played Maria, her singing dubbed by Marnie Nixon. The other musical was *Gypsie* (Mervyn LeRoy, 1963), where she costarred with Rosalind Russell and did her own singing (though there was little called for). The third movie was *Splendor in the Grass* (Elia Kazan, 1961), which won her an Academy Award nomination for Best Actress. Though she continued to make hit films throughout the decade, it was these three that dominated her career throughout the 1960s.

### FURTHER READING

Crowther, Bosley. "'The Sound of Music' Opens at Rivoli." *The New York Times*, March 3, 1965, 34.
Gray, Beverly. *Seduced by Mrs. Robinson: How "The Graduate" Became the Touchstone of a Generation*. Chapel Hill, NC: Algonquin Books, 2017.
Hart, Stan, and Mort Drucker. "The Sound of Money." *Mad Magazine*, No. 108, January 1967.
Hirsch, Julia A. *The Making of "The Sound of Music."* Chicago: Chicago Review Press, 2018.
Hischak, Thomas S. *The Rodgers and Hammerstein Encyclopedia*. Westport, CT: Greenwood, 2007.
Maslon, Laurence. *The "Sound of Music" Companion*. New York: Simon & Schuster, 2007.
Purdum, Todd S. *Something Wonderful: Rodgers and Hammerstein's Broadway Revolution*. New York: Henry Holt, 2018.
Santopietro, Tom. *The "Sound of Music" Story: How a Beguiling Young Novice, a Handsome Austrian Captain, and Ten Singing Von Trapp Children Inspired the Most Beloved Film of All Time*. New York: St. Martin's Press, 2015.
Whitehead, J. W. *Appraising* The Graduate: *The Mike Nichols Classic and Its Impact on Hollywood*. Jefferson, NC: McFarland, 2011.

# CHAPTER 2

# Television

## VARIETY SHOWS

The 1960s can be viewed both as the heyday and the last gasp of the television variety show. Several of the most enduring of these variety shows began in the 1950s and lasted just past the beginning of the 1970s, when the form suddenly seemed to lose much of its appeal. In that sense, there is a striking historical parallel between the movie musical and the television variety show.

*The Ed Sullivan Show* was broadcast on Sunday evenings on CBS from 1948 to 1971. Although the show was originally called *The Toast of the Town,* it became widely known by the host's name before the network officially changed its name. Sullivan became one of the most beloved figures in the early history of American television—not simply because his show was popular but because viewers identified with his lack of pretention, with his remarkable, even mystifying ordinariness. Indeed, over the nearly quarter century that the show aired, television critics, social commentators, and comedians attracted notice with their creative attempts to explain the disparity between Sullivan's popularity and his lack of any discernible talent. It was often pointed out that even his introductions of the performers appearing on his show were often perfunctory, mechanical, or clumsy. But, often against the advice of the network's management and against the wishes of the show's sponsors, Sullivan introduced middle America not just to Elvis, The Beatles, The Rolling Stones, and other rock-and-roll performers, but also to jazz and blues musicians, to Motown groups, and to comedians who would reshape stand-up comedy. In addition, the show often featured pieces from Broadway musicals, as well as more "highbrow" performances of classical music, opera, ballet, and modern dance. Especially given the show's long run, it is understandable that some of these notable performers—such as the comedians Alan King, Shelley Berman, and Victor Borgia, the husband-and-wife comedy team Jerry Stiller and Ann Meara, the singers Connie Francis, Pearl Bailey, and The McGuire Sisters, and the opera singers Roberta Peters and Sergio Franchi—would make several dozen appearances on the show. What has always been more puzzling is why some of the more idiosyncratic or now obscure acts not only were invited to appear at all but became so popular that they became mainstays of the show. These idiosyncratic acts included the puppet mouse Topo Gigio, ventriloquist Rickie Layne and his dummy Velvel, and Senor Wences, a ventriloquist who drew his dummy's face on his own hand, which he moved to simulate a talking mouth. It is also noteworthy that the act with the most appearances on the show was Wayne and Schuster, Canadian comedians who specialized in sketch comedy. They appeared on the show sixty-seven times according to CBS but fifty-eight times according to them, and Sullivan routinely gave them 10–15 minutes of air time to perform their skits. But like the comedians Jack Carter and Myron Cohen, who are third and fifth on the list of those with the most appearances on the show, Wayne and Schuster are now largely forgotten. For all of the truly historical moments in the history of American popular culture that *The Ed Sullivan Show* provided, it was also very much a showcase of the moment's passing tastes and its host's own idiosyncratic preferences.

If Ed Sullivan was somewhat oddly at the forefront of dramatic changes in American entertainment, especially in terms of popular music and stand-up comedy, *The Red Skelton Show* and *The Lawrence Welk Show* harkened back with transparent nostalgia to seemingly "simpler" times. *The Red Skelton Show* was broadcast nationally from 1951 to 1971. After getting his start as a performer in burlesque, Skelton found some success in film comedies, especially in roles in which he could exploit his abilities as a clown. These roles would include the following: as Joseph Rivington Reynolds in *I Dood It* (1943), as J. Aubrey Piper in *The Show-Off* (1946), as Merton Gill in *Merton of the Movies* (1947), as Red Jones in *The Fuller Brush Man* (1948), as Aubrey Filmore in *A Southern Yankee* (1948), and as Dodo Delwyn in *The Clown* (1953). Drawing on his experience in burlesque, Skelton would begin each episode of his television variety show with a monologue into which he often interjected fanciful characters with distinctive voices and mannerisms. The rest of the show would alternate between performances by musical and other guests and comedy sketches largely featuring one of the characters that Skelton refined over the show's two-decade run. Two of the most popular of these characters were a hick named Clem Kadiddlehopper who hailed from Cornpone, Tennessee, and a panhandling bum named Freddie the Freeloader.

Although, like *The Red Skelton Show*, *The Lawrence Welk Show* aired from 1951 to 1971, it was local programming in Los Angeles from 1951 to 1955, when it was picked up for national broadcast. Likewise, although *The Lawrence Welk Show* is now also associated with rural America, it could not have been more different in tone from *The Red Skelton Show*. The show featured a stable of regularly appearing singers, dancers, and musicians, and although the segments featured Welk's schmaltzy arrangements of big-band tunes and numbers from Broadway and movie musicals, he would increasingly incorporate popular songs into the program, though the arrangements inevitably erased many of the differences in genre so that a pop tune, a folk song, and a rock song all ended up sounding strangely similar and similarly divorced from the source recording. The performers on the show typically wore matching outfits, and the colors became more vibrant but no less uniform seemingly in response to the more flamboyant clothing of the late 1960s. Like Ed Sullivan, Lawrence Welk developed a somewhat puzzling popularity as an emcee because, despite being on the air for more than two decades, he never lost his very pronounced German accent (which seemingly would have been a bigger liability for a performer when the show first began airing not much more than a half-decade after the end of the Second World War). Indeed, Welk ultimately made his inability to pronounce the "d" in "wonderful" something of a personal trademark.

Several other variety shows had long runs but have had less lasting cultural impact. *The Jackie Gleason Show* aired from 1952 to 1975, though in a variety of shifting formats. For the 1955–1956 television schedule, Gleason produced and starred in a half-hour situation comedy called *The Honeymooners*. The series lasted just thirty-nine episodes as a situation comedy, but the Kramdens and their neighbors, the Nortons, were the most popular among the recurring sets of characters featured in the sketches that were a major part of Gleason's variety shows. So there are hundreds of "Honeymooners" episodes, beyond the thirty-nine episodes aired as the situation comedy, that have been collected for syndication and released on DVD. But Jackie Gleason is now most remembered for playing Ralph Kramden than for hosting a variety show.

Two variety shows featuring crooners with affable personalities aired for most of the 1960s and into the early 1970s: *The Andy Williams Show* from 1962 to 1971 and *The Dean Martin Show* from 1965 to 1974. But, in the early to mid-1960s, there were also a fairly large number of more short-lived variety shows featuring well-known performers. Airing from 1961 to 1964, *Sing Along with Mitch* featured recording artist and record producer Mitch Miller and his orchestra; consistent with its title, the show featured a bottom-of-the-screen scroll of the lyrics of each song that Miller's band and his stable of regularly appearing singers performed. *The Judy Garland Show* lasted just one season in 1963–1964, and *The Danny Kaye Show* aired from 1963 to 1967.

The most successful and influential variety show of the late 1960s did not feature a very established performer but the comedian Carol Burnett. *The Carol Burnett Show*, which aired from 1967 to 1978, featured a core group of experienced sketch performers—Harvey Korman, Tim Conway, and Vicki Lawrence—whose talents were generously showcased and whose chemistry was readily apparent. One of the recurring pleasures of the show was watching Harvey Korman's futile attempts to keep a straight face as Tim Conway pushed a character to the limits of deadpanned plausibility. Although many of the sketches featured recurring characters, a roughly equal number drew inspiration from iconic films, other television series, and current cultural fads and odd news events. Some of these sketches—for instance, a parody of *Gone with the Wind* featuring Scarlett's creation of a ball gown from drapes—have become as much a part of the popular culture as the sources that inspired them.

Although it had a much more abbreviated run than *The Carol Burnett Show*, *The Smothers Brothers Comedy Hour*, which aired from 1967 to 1969, has had an enduring historical significance and cultural legacy. Starring the brothers Dickie and Tommy Smothers, the show featured them in low-key dialogues in which puns and non sequiturs were prominently featured, seemingly improvisational performances of folk music, and more standard comic sketches given a hip turn. The show also included an impressive list of guest performances by major folk and rock acts of the late 1960s, and its unsparing political satire became both a major source of the show's popularity and a major reason for its being taken off the air.

A spin-off of *The Smothers Brothers Comedy Hour* was the relatively short-lived and less memorable *Glen Campbell Goodtime Hour*, featuring the affable singer and former studio musician who was among the first country music performers to have a broad "crossover" appeal and a series of major hit records on the pop charts.

Like *The Jackie Gleason Show*, *The Jimmy Dean Show*, featuring another popular country music performer, was aired in various iterations from 1957 to 1975, though in several instances, *The Jimmy Dean Show* survived as local programming before it was aired again nationally. It is now most remembered as a forerunner to *Hee-Haw*, original episodes of which aired on network television only from 1969 to 1971, but which had a much more extended run as a syndicated program, from 1971 to 1993.

*Hee-Haw* appealed to viewers at the opposite end of the cultural spectrum, but it was nonetheless inspired by *Rowan and Martin's Laugh-In*. Airing from 1968 to 1973, *Laugh-In* featured a regular cast of performers who presented a rapid-fire series of mini-sketches and what can best be described as recurring vignettes, set pieces featuring characters doing variations on an action or a piece of dialogue. The musical accompaniment was straight from the pop charts, the sets featured pop-art designs, and the overall effect was an equal combination of hipness and silliness. Some of the performers—such as Arte Johnson, Ruth Buzzi, Judy Carne, and JoAnn Worley—received their peak exposure as performers on this show. Others, such as Goldie Hawn and Lily Tomlin, went on to much more notable accomplishments.

The attempt to reshape the more conventional variety show to appeal to younger viewers had limited success, at best, with *The Leslie Uggams Show*, which aired briefly in 1969, and with *This Is Tom Jones*, which aired from 1969 to 1971. *The Leslie Uggams Show* is notable for being just the second network variety show to feature an African American performer (the first being *The Nat King Cole Show*, which aired in the 1956–1957 television season). Uggams, who had come to national attention as a featured singer on *Sing Along with Mitch*, attempted to showcase mostly African American performers of her own variety show. In contrast to the abbreviated run of *The Leslie Uggams Show*, *This Is Tom Jones* was critically well received, with Jones himself receiving a Golden Globe; it attracted a broad variety of guest performers; and it has achieved something close to the status of a cult classic on DVD.

A type of variety show that originated in the 1950s did not include sketch comedy but, instead, featured musical performances—some live and others recorded, with the camera generally on teenagers doing the newest fad dances. The music was interspersed with interviews conducted by the host with both the performers and some of the teenaged dancers. The prototype of this type of show was, of course, *American Bandstand*, which aired nationally from 1956 to 1989, with Dick Clark hosting. Initially the show was broadcast on weekday afternoons for an hour and a half, but over the course of the 1960s, the length was reduced from 90 minutes to 60 minutes to 30 minutes. It was eventually moved to Saturday afternoons, as a 60-minute weekly show. It had a tremendous impact in shaping musical tastes and in promoting records and musical acts. Inevitably, it spawned much less successful primetime imitations, none of which attracted enough of the evening viewing audience to sustain them. The first of these shows was *Hootenanny*, which aired in 1963 and 1964 and featured folk music. It was followed by *Shindig!*, which aired from 1964 and 1966 and sought to exploit the popularity of the music associated with the British Invasion, although it did feature American pop and rock acts as well. And in 1965 and 1966, its competition included *Hullabaloo*, which, instead of having a regular host, had a different musical guest host for each show who performed his or her hit songs in between introducing other performers with current hits.

## SITUATION COMEDIES

One of the mainstays of television programming in the 1950s was the situation comedy focusing on the family. One of the longest-running series of this type was *The Adventures of Ozzie and Harriet* (1952–1966), which is now associated with the 1950s but had a run that extended well into the 1960s. Several similar series began airing in the late 1950s but ran for more seasons in the 1960s: *Leave It to Beaver* (1957–1963) and *Dennis the Menace* (1959–1963). The problem with series that feature mischievous young boys is that it is difficult to sustain their appeal as the characters age.

*My Three Sons* (1960–1972) got around that problem by featuring a widower (played by Fred MacMurray) raising boys with a considerable range in their ages. Similarly, in a sequel to *I Love Lucy* called simply *The Lucy Show* (1962–1968), Lucille Ball played a widow raising her adolescent son and daughter. In contrast to the situation comedies of the previous decade, which typically featured two-parent families, some of the most popular series of the 1960s featured single parents being added by household staff who, in effect, served as surrogate parents to the children. In addition to *My Three Sons,* in which the surrogate parenting was provided by Uncle Charlie, these series included *Family Affair* (1966–1971), which starred Brian Keith as an affluent bachelor who was raising his deceased brother's three children with the assistance of a butler, played by Sebastian Cabot, and *The Farmer's Daughter* (1963–1966), which starred Inger Stevens as the Swedish housekeeper for a widowed congressman and his two sons. One of the most enduring popular series of this type was, of course, *The Andy Griffith Show* (1960–1971), in which Opie Taylor, played by future film director Ron Howard, was being raised by a widower, Sheriff Andy Taylor, and his Aunt Bee. The series actually began airing in syndication in 1964, when the reruns being aired in the daytime hours were retitled as *Andy of Mayberry*, and it is still being seen by 4 to 5 million daily viewers.

*Hazel* (1961–1966), which starred Shirley Booth as the live-in maid of the Baxters, an upper-middle-class family, in effect combined the situations featuring two parents and surrogate parents.

Rob and Laura Petrie (Dick Van Dyke and Mary Tyler Moore) became one of America's favorite couples through *The Dick Van Dyke Show* (1960–1965). (CBS via Getty Images)

Two further series that had a family focus are worth mentioning: *Please Don't Eat the Daisies* (1965–1967) and *The Dick Van Dyke Show* (1961–1966), both of which featured a husband and father whose career involved the media. The latter series is considered one of the classic series of the decade because of the chemistry between the stars, Dick Van Dyke and Mary Tyler Moore, who played Rob and Laura Petrie—and because it was a series that was about smart television writing and actually featured very smart writing.

Although some of the other situation comedies already mentioned here include teenaged characters, for the first time in the 1960s, some television producers attempted to appeal very specifically to the teenaged baby boomers by creating shows that featured teenagers as the focal characters and that dealt primarily with their interests and concerns. Such shows included *The Many Loves of Dobie Gillis* (1959–1963), *The Patty Duke Show* (1963–1966), *Gidget* (1965–1966), and *Tammy* (1965–1966).

Beyond the attempt to appeal to a young audience, several situation comedies were notable for the ways in which they represented the changing social realities of the period. In *That Girl* (1966–1971), Marlo Thomas played Ann Marie, a young, single woman trying to navigate the sometimes competing demands of her work life—her pursuit of an acting career and the need to support herself with other work in the meantime—and her personal life. The series has been cited as one of the first television series to treat feminist themes, and the main character was so engaging that the series made feminism seem more a sign of inevitable progress than an existential threat to traditional gender roles and American values. Similarly, *Julia* (1968–1971) starred Diahann Carol as a single mother supporting herself and her son by working as a nurse. Not only was Julia the first African American female character to be the lead character in a television series, but the series was given an even more relevant backstory because she was a widow whose husband had been killed while serving as a pilot in Vietnam. Julia worked for a white physician at the health clinic of a large aerospace company, and the series dealt directly, if deftly, with issues of racial integration within the workplace and beyond. In a few instances, the racism was overt, but, in most instances, it was more subtle and nuanced. Given that the series aired shortly after the passage of the major civil rights legislation of the mid-1960s, this approach to the material was a credit to the series' creators and the actors, in particular Diahann Carol, and accounted for the series' popularity and broader cultural impact.

As a footnote to this discussion of socially relevant situation comedies, one very short-lived series *The Ugliest Girl in Town* (1968–1969) warrants mention for striking all of the wrong notes. It focused on a young man who was posing as a female model in order to pay for his pursuit of a young woman from Great Britain. If *Bosom Buddies* (1980–1982) would ultimately achieve a cult following because of its quirky treatment of transgenderism and related themes, it is worth noting that just about no one remembers *The Ugliest Girl in Town*.

If situation comedies such as *That Girl* and *Julia* were very forward looking and set in urban areas, another group focused on rural characters in a sort of lightly satiric manner that could be confused with nostalgia. *The Real McCoys* (1957–1963) was a sort of forerunner to this group of shows, but despite some very funny moments, it was closer in tone to *The Waltons* than to the show that literally succeeded it in its time slot, *The Beverly Hillbillies* (1962–1971). Likewise, *The Andy Griffith Show* is often placed in this group, but its central character distinguished it from the other shows. Although Andy Taylor was very much a product of his community, he was much more level-headed than some of his neighbors—most notably, Floyd the barber, Goober the gas station attendant, and Otis the town drunk. In situation comedies such as *The Beverly Hillbillies*, *Petticoat Junction* (1963–1970), and *Green Acres* (1965–1971), such largely one-dimensional characters would be the focus, rather than supporting characters. Even in *Green Acres*, in which Eddie Albert played Oliver Wendell Douglas, an urbane lawyer who chose to become an urban transplant to a rural community in which everyone else, including his own foreign-born wife, seemed at least slightly brain-damaged, the "normal" perspective and expectations that Oliver represented were fairly consistently undermined by the zaniness, rather than somehow redeemed in spite of it. Indeed, these series were sustained by the fact that although the characters were largely one-dimensional, they were not really stereotypes; instead, they were whimsical turns on stereotypes that made them both weirdly familiar and hilariously dumbfounding.

Given the continuing popularity of Western drama series in the 1960s, it is not surprising that several situation comedies would have Western settings.

*Here Come the Brides* (1968–1970) provided in some ways a historical parallel to *Petticoat Junction*. Much more heavy-handed was *F Troop* (1965–1967), in which comedic devices would be extended and exploited long past even the most tenuous suggestion of realism. The series may be the closest thing to Mel Brooks's *Blazing Saddles* (1974) ever produced for television.

The contemporary military was also a target for situation comedies of the 1960s, though the satire was generally lighter. *No Time for Sergeants* (1964–1965) was inspired by the film starring Andy Griffith. Other similar series included *McHale's Navy* (1962–1966), *Gomer Pyle, U.S.M.C.* (1964–1969), and *Hogan's Heroes* (1965–1971). All of these shows except *Gomer Pyle, U.S.M.C.*, were set during the Second World War, which in contrast to the Vietnam War was already being regarded as "the Good War." So, the satire, which was at least as often directed at the military as an institution as at the enemy, already had an element of gradually increasing nostalgia to it. It is worth noting that the most prominent antiwar novels of the 1960s—Joseph Heller's *Catch-22* (1961) and Kurt Vonnegut's *Slaughterhouse-Five* (1969)—were actually novels about the Second World War. But those novels were extended and unrelenting excursions into savage absurdity, and the intensifying skepticism about purpose and the cost of the Vietnam War doomed the more lightly satiric treatments of the military on television, where the often very graphic news coverage of the war's carnage was broadcast on a nightly, rather than a weekly, basis.

The military was not the only institution to become the subject of satire in the 1960s. As if the unintentionally comic, long-running drama series *Dragnet* (1951–1959) had not done enough to expose the satiric possibilities in law enforcement, *Car 54, Where Are You?* (1961–1963) followed the daily misadventures of two patrolmen in the Bronx: Gunther Toody, played by Joe E. Ross, and Francis Muldoon, played by Fred Gwynne. If the satire in *Car 54* was generally light, it was very broad and unrestrained in *Get Smart* (1965–1970). Written by Mel Brooks and Buck Henry, and starring Don Adams as Maxwell Smart, Agent 86, the series lampooned not just the intelligence services but also the fictional romanticizing of the intelligence services in the novels and films featuring James Bond—and all of the imitators that proliferated almost immediately in the wake of those novels and their film adaptations. *Get Smart* was full of ridiculous catchphrases and ridiculous gadgets, and Brooks and Henry were adept at repeating them relentlessly until the audience started laughing simply at the shameless recycling.

Unlike the situation comedies that focused on families, one of the most popular types of situation comedy in the 1960s did not have a lot of precedents in the 1950s. Just ahead of the most convulsive events of the late 1960s and early 1970s, there seemed to be a sudden and inordinate interest in situation comedies that can be broadly categorized as fantasies. In some of these situation comedies, the main characters simply have unusual powers. For instance, in *The Flying Nun* (1967–1970), Sally Field played a novice nun who discovered that she could fly, and in *Mister Ed* (1961–1966), the title character was a horse who could talk. In several of these situation comedies, the main characters were fantastical figures who attempted to assimilate into the lives of ordinary people. For instance, In *I Dream of Jeannie* (1965–1970), Barbara Eden played a genie who became the companion of an astronaut, played by Larry Hagman; in *My Favorite Martian* (1963–1966), Ray Walston played an extraterrestrial who lived with a single newspaper reporter, played by Bill Bixby, posing as the reporter's Uncle Martin; and in *Bewitched* (1964–1972), Elizabeth Montgomery played Samantha Stephens, a witch who married a businessman and wanted very much to be a "normal" housewife and mother—to avoid relying on her powers as a witch. Interestingly, in *Bewitched*, Samantha's husband Darren was originally played by Dick York, but when a debilitating back injury prevented him from continuing, he was simply replaced in the role by Dick Sargeant—without any explanation whatsoever being written into the show. *The Addams Family* (1964–1966) and *The Munsters* (1964–1966), which ran concurrently, flipped the premise of *Bewitched*, presenting families made up of banal versions of ghoulish creatures, who somehow failed to appreciate the impact of their appearances, mannerisms, and peculiar interests on the ordinary people among whom they lived. Carrying the occult premise one step farther were several other situation comedies of this decade in which the main characters communicated with the deceased. In *The Ghost and Mrs. Muir* (1968–1970), Hope Lange played a widow who rented a seaside cottage once owned by a sea captain whose ghost regularly interacted with her. In *The Smothers Brothers Show* (1965–1966)—not to be confused with its successor *The Smothers Brothers Comedy Hour* (1967–1969)—Tom Smothers returned from the dead as an apprentice angel whose attempts to "earn his wings" were consistently inept, requiring his mortal brother Dickie to resume straightening out the messes that he created. After *My Favorite Martian*, Bill Bixby starred in *My Mother the Car* (1965–1966), playing an attorney who purchased a jalopy from before the Great Depression and discovered that it was the reincarnation of his deceased mother. Widely panned as one of the worst shows ever made for network television, *My Mother the Car* nonetheless was an early effort of James L. Brooks, Allan Burns, and Chris Hayward, all of whom went on to create some of the most significant and popular situation comedies of the 1970s and 1980s, including *Barney Miller* (1975–1982), *The Mary Tyler Moore* Show (1970–1977), *Rhoda* (1974–1978), and *Taxi* (1978–1983).

For a long while, two of the more popular situation comedies of the 1960s were more often categorized as cartoons, but the unprecedented longevity and widely acknowledged significance of several animated series—from *The Simpsons* (1989–) to *South Park* (1997–), to *The Family Guy* (1999–)—have caused these forerunners to be reconsidered. Curiously, *The Flintstones* (1960–1966) focused on a Stone Age family, and *The Jetsons* (1962–1963) focused on a futuristic family.

Lastly, two very popular situation comedies from the 1960s are very difficult to categorize. *Gilligan's Island* (1964–1967) presented a loopy reworking of *Robinson Crusoe* involving a stranded group of eccentric characters, rather than a stranded individual, and *The Monkees* (1966–1968) focused on a rock-and-roll band that was created for the television series. Though widely panned as tripe, both shows have seemingly had an enduring influence. *The Monkees* has been followed by similar shows ranging from *The Partridge Family* (1974–1970) to *Hannah Montana* (2006–2011), but its influence can also be seen in the musical competition reality shows, in which the personalities and backstories of the participants have become almost as important as their performances. Likewise, although *Gilligan's Island* has remained something of an anomaly among situation comedies, its influence can arguably be seen in the reality genre as well—in particular in *The Survivor* franchise. Although this reality franchise has been imitated in a variety of wilderness survival shows, such as *Dual Survival* (2010–), *Naked and Afraid* (2013–), and *Alone* (2015–), it includes a large number of gimmicky elements that are not all that far removed from the schemes and props around which the episodes of *Gilligan's Island* were built. As with the reality shows about musical competitions, the emphasis in *The Survivor* franchise is on the mix of personalities among the contestants as much as it is on their survival skills per se.

## ACTION-ADVENTURE SERIES: DETECTIVE SERIES, LEGAL DRAMAS, MEDICAL DRAMAS, SELF-AWARE THRILLERS, AND MILITARY SERIES

This broad genre of series has been a staple of television programming across the nearly seventy-five years in which the medium has existed. One might have expected that the rise of the Counterculture would have dampened the interest in police dramas, and to some extent that was true. Series such as *Naked City* (1958–1963) and *The Untouchables* (1959–1963) were popular in the first half of the decade before the culture changes became pronounced. *The Naked City* was adapted quite faithfully from the film of the same name that had been released in 1948. The series was set in a police precinct in New York City and featured a broad cast of characters, some recurring but others not. The themes and the tone were gritty, especially for the period. Set in Chicago during the later years of Prohibition, *The Untouchables* starred Robert Stack as gangbuster Eliot Ness. It became the role for which Stack would most be remembered.

Those two police dramas were followed in 1966 by *The F.B.I* and in 1967 by *The Felony Squad*. *The F.B.I.*, which lasted nine seasons, was by far the more popular of these two series. It starred Efrem Zimbalist Jr. as F.B.I. Inspector Lewis Erskine, and Stephen Brooks, who initially played Erskine's assistant, Special Agent Jim Rhodes, was replaced after several seasons by William Reynolds who played Special Agent Tom Colby. The series was quite popular, even though it was on the air when the death of J. Edgar Hoover brought to a head the revelations about his abuses of power during his extraordinarily long tenure as F.B.I. director. *The Felony Squad*, which had a much shorter run from 1967 to 1969, starred Howard Duff as Sam Stone, a major-crimes detective with the police department of a large city that was never named but seemed clearly to be Los Angeles. Dennis Cole costarred as Stone's partner, Detective Jim Briggs.

Almost as short-lived as *The Felony Squad* was the revival of *Dragnet*, which starred Jack Webb as Joe Friday and Henry Morgan as his new partner Bill Gannon. Whereas the original series had had a nearly decade-long run from 1951 to 1959, this revival of the series had not quite half as long a run, airing from 1967 to 1970. The characters' woodenness was so out of sync with the late 1960s that it often seemed an exercise in self-parody, and the ill-timed revival certainly contributed to the series being generally regarded as the most parodied police series in television history. A series that seemed to have been conceived to provide as much of contrast with *Dragnet* as possible, *The Mod Squad* aired from 1968 to 1973. Starring Clarence Williams III, Michael Cole, and Peggy Lipton, who were described in advertising for the show as "one black, one white, and one blonde," were three culturally disaffected young people from diverse backgrounds who, after relatively minor brushes with the law, were recruited as an undercover police squad. Although the episodes focused on some of the more intractable urban problems and socioeconomic and cultural divisions of the period, often putting the main characters in some very rough environments and dangerous situations, they somehow managed to survive even though they were never armed. Beyond that unrealistic premise, the characters' use of Counterculture slang and their giving voice to Counterculture ideas helped to make the series seem socially relevant when it aired but ultimately made it ripe for parody. Even if it has not aged especially well, it got decent ratings and was critically fairly well received, receiving six Emmy Awards and four Golden Globe nominations.

The two most iconic police dramas of the 1960s were *Ironside*, which aired from 1967 to 1975, and *Hawaii Five-O*, which aired from 1968 to 1980. *Ironside* starred Raymond Burr in the title role, as former chief of detectives Robert Ironside. Confined to a wheelchair by a sniper's bullet that had made him a paraplegic, Ironside works as a consultant to the San Francisco Police Department. There are two detectives assigned to work with Ironside, played by Don Galloway as Sergeant Ed Brown and by Barbara Anderson as Officer Eve Whitfield. In addition, Don Mitchell played an AfricanAmerican former convict who becomes Ironside's personal assistant. So, although the detectives were not themselves defined by associations with the Counterculture, this series, like *The Mod Squad*, featured a black guy, a white guy, and a blonde, and because it was set in San Francisco in the difficult period after the "Summer of Love," it was able to treat issues related to the Counterculture in a fairly realistic way. But the series was carried by Raymond Burr, who was a gruffer version of his matter-of-fact, shrewd persona as the iconic defense attorney Perry Mason. For his portrayal of Ironside, Burr would receive six Emmy nominations and four Golden Globe nominations.

*Hawaii Five-O*'s twelve-year run distinguished it as the longest-running crime series not just up to its cancellation in the early 1980s but for two decades afterward. When it was displaced as the longest-running show, it was by several of the ongoing series within the ubiquitous crime-genre franchises of the 1990s and 2000s—*Law and Order*, *CSI*, and *NCIS*. *Hawaii Five-O* was filmed on location in the islands themselves, which, at the time that the series started airing, had been a state for not quite a decade. So, the setting was exotic, and the show's producers further emphasized the exoticism by including native Hawaiians not just in most of the background shots but also in the cast as detectives, criminals, victims, and witnesses. Moreover, the writers made an effort to interject, wherever possible, elements of the islands' history and culture into the story lines. Less believably, the plots often involved multiethnic criminal syndicates and conspiracies or sinister espionage being conducted by hostile foreign powers or criminal groups in their employ as mercenaries. Such story lines also serve to emphasize the islands' location and its convenience as a setting for international intrigue. But, the characterizations of the criminals were often so melodramatically focused on the menace that they represented that, in essence, the series reinforced some long-standing ethnic and racial stereotypes (in particular, the stereotypes related to the notion of the "Yellow Peril"), even as it was emphasizing multiculturalism.

*Hawaai Five-O* focused on a special state police task force headed by Steve McGarrett. Played by Jack Lord, McGarrett was the epitome of no-nonsense law enforcement—attentive to the details of police policy and procedure, demanding of but loyal to his subordinates, relentless in his pursuit of criminals and dedicated to the exposure and dismantling of their nefarious enterprises, and devoted to the administration of justice. In the Hawaiian sun, he almost always wore a dark suit and tie with a white shirt and yet never looked overheated. (In the few instances in which he put on a Hawaiian shirt, it always looked as if it had come straight out of a commercial presser.) Even when he stood on a dramatic escarpment, his neatly coiffed dark hair hardly moved in the strong ocean breezes. So, it was not just the show's longevity that made him seem somewhat cartoonish: it was his whole persona, accented by catchphrases— most notably the catchphrase with which he punctuated the end of almost every episode to his chief subordinate, "Book 'im (or, 'em), Danno!" It is noteworthy that the show's cancellation led to the development of another long-running series set in Hawaii, *Magnum P.I.* Although that series made cost-effective use of the production facilities created for *Hawaii Five-O*, its creators were motivated more pointedly by the obvious continuing appeal of the tropical setting. It is also noteworthy that *Hawaii Five-O* itself has been resurrected in the 2010s with a similar emphasis on the exotic elements of the setting but with less easily caricatured heroes and villains. And in the 2018–2019 television season, *Magnum P.I.* was also remade to appeal to a contemporary audience.

Although *Hawaii Five-O* was the first television show to be filmed on location in Hawaii, it was not the first television series to be set on the islands. The series *Hawaiian Eye*, which aired from 1959 to 1963, exploited the islands' statehood, though it was filmed on sets in Hollywood. It starred Anthony Eisley as private investigator Tracy Steele and a young and very tanned Robert Conrad as his half-Hawaiian junior partner, Tom Lopaka. Their detective agency not only provided the usual services to clients, but it also provided security services for the Hawaiian Village Hotel. Actual ethnic diversity and "local color" are provided by Pincie Ponce, who played a ukelele-strumming cab driver named Kim Quisado, as well as his seemingly endless number of family members, friends, and acquaintances.

Another show featuring a pair of private detectives was *77 Sunset Strip*, which aired almost concurrently with *Hawaiian Eye*, from 1958 to 1964. Starring Efrem Zimbalist Jr. and Roger Smith as former government operatives, the show also featured a cast of unusual supporting characters, most notably the hipster parking-lot attendant for the club next door to the detective agency, "Kookie" Kookson, played memorably by Edd Byrnes. Known for quoting rock-and-roll lyrics and rattling off inventive slang, Kookie eventually achieves his ambition and becomes a detective with the agency—though, in reality, Byrnes's popularity allowed him to demand publicly the bigger role. The series became a cult favorite for some gimmicky experiments. In one episode, "The Silent Caper," there was no dialogue, and in another, "Reserved for Mr. Bailey," Zimbalist's character visits a ghost town and is the only character seen on screen for the entire episode. More controversially, when the ratings began to decline, the entire cast except for Zimbalist was replaced, and in its final season, it became essentially a completely different series even though it was ostensibly the same series.

The rather limited popularity of the private-detective genre in the 1960s, especially in comparison to other genres, is evident in the only two other notable series. *Michael Shayne* lasted for only the 1960–1961 television season. The iconic hard-boiled detective created by Brett Halladay had been the subject of 77 novels published between 1939 and 1958, more than 300 short stories, and a dozen feature films, but the television series lasted only 32 episodes. At the other end of the decade, *Mannix* proved to be the exception that proved the rule about the genre. Starring Mike Connors in the title role, the series aired from 1967 to 1975. Interestingly, the series was originally conceived as a contemporary turn on the hard-boiled detective genre, with Mannix being an anachronistic old-school detective employed by an agency that employed the latest in computer technology. But after one season, it became clear that the technology was a gimmick that still had somewhat limited possibilities and that Mannix had considerable appeal as a character. So Mannix opened his own office, employing an African American office assistant named Peggy Fair, the widow of a police officer killed in the line of duty. Played by Gail Fisher, the character was one of the first major female African American characters in a television drama and provided an appealing counterpoint to Mannix's more brusque personality.

Like the series featuring hard-boiled private detectives, legal dramas were another genre that hit a lull in the 1960s. One of the most highly regarded legal dramas of all time, *Perry Mason*, starring Raymond Burr, had begun airing in 1957 and lasted a full decade to 1966, when Burr moved on to *Ironside*. The show was critically acclaimed as well as very popular, and although it created interest in other legal dramas, it quickly became apparent that it was difficult to replicate the chemistry among the characters and the story structure that had made it so successful. *The Defenders*, which aired from 1961 to 1965, starred E. G. Marshall and Robert Reed as a father and son team of defense attorneys. Although it focused on the defense of the accused, rather than on the police investigation and prosecution, the series anticipated the approach in the *Law and Order* franchise in the respect that it focused on crimes related to timely issues—to controversies that were receiving a great deal of media attention at the time. At the other end of the decade, *Judd for the Defense*, which starred Carl Betz as Clinton Judd, exploited the rise of attorneys whose flamboyant styles and willingness to take on cases pulled from the tabloid headlines was making them into celebrities. Ironically, the attempts to address controversial social issues in the series created as much backlash as interest, and it never found a consistent, substantial audience.

One of the most iconic television dramas of the 1960s focused on a doctor who was wrongly convicted of his wife's murder and on his way to death row when the train carrying him to prison derailed. *The Fugitive*, which aired from

1963 to 1967, starred David Janssen as Dr. Richard Kimble and Barry Morse as Police Lieutenant Philip Gerard, who doggedly pursued him. Beyond the framework provided by that pursuit and Kimble's search for clues to the identity of the real killer, a mysterious one-armed man, the series was a sort of picaresque, with Kimble briefly becoming involved with people whom he met in the course of his flight from the law and his pursuit of justice. The series was both critically acclaimed and popular, and its final episode, broadcast in two parts in successive weeks, became one of the first "events" in the history of major network programming—with the second part achieving the highest ratings of any regular programming to that date.

From 1965 to 1968, *Run for Your Life* starred Ben Gazzara as Paul Bryan, an ordinary man who was facing a different sort of death sentence. When his doctor informed him that he had a fatal form of leukemia and just twelve to eighteen months left to live, Bryan decided to squeeze as much living as possible into those remaining months. Like *The Fugitive*, he set out, in effect, on a trek across America, meeting all sorts of people who were grappling with issues in their own lives.

Both *The Fugitive* and *Run for Your Life* were preceded by and very clearly influenced by the popular series *Route 66*, which aired from 1960 to 1964. Inspired by Jack Kerouac's *On the Road*, the novel that gave the misadventures of the peripatetic Beats a permanent part in the American cultural mythos, this series focused on two young men played by Martin Milner and George Maharias. Disillusioned by the corporate vision of the American Dream and restless for adventure, they set out in a Corvette, traversing the continental United States and finding work along the way to pay their way. In the process, they discover a great deal about the country—about what America is and what it means to be American—and about themselves. In the era before the development of the interstate highway system, which was just beginning to be constructed in the period in which the series aired, Route 66 was, of course, the highway most associated with the transcontinental migration to the Pacific Coast. In the 1930s, that migration was undertaken largely by whole families and even communities of "Okies" fleeing the ruinous conditions of the Dust Bowl on the southern plains for the farms of California's Central Valley. By the early 1960s, the migration increasingly involved young people drawn to the beach and surfer culture of Southern California.

A very different sort of pursuit of adventure was showcased in a fairly new action-adventure subgenre on television: the spy thriller. Exploiting the international popularity of the James Bond novels and their film adaptations, these series featured glamorous "secret agents" who employed a mind-boggling arsenal of futuristic gadgets against memorably caricatured ideological opponents and criminal masterminds. These depictions of spy-craft were at the opposite end of the spectrum from the more dreary and almost banally vicious depictions of Cold War espionage in novels such as those by John Le Carre. The spy-thriller series of the 1960s included the following. *The Man from U.N.C.L.E.* (1964–1968) starred Robert Vaughn and David MacCallum as Napoleon Solo and Illya Kuryakin. The tremendous popularity of the series demonstrated the potential appeal of the spy thriller on television and led to the direct spin-off series, *The Girl from U.N.C.L.E.*, which starred Stephanie Powers as April Dancer. *I Spy* (1965–1966) starred Robert Culp and Bill Cosby as Kelly Robinson and Alexander "Scotty" Scott, spies posing as a tennis pro and his trainer. The series was very notable for featuring the first AfricanAmerican lead character in a television series, though it made almost no references to Cosby's character's race and avoided treatments of issues of race. But the longest-running of these series and the one with the most enduring cultural impact was *Mission Impossible* (1966–1973), which featured an ensemble cast that included Peter Graves as Jim Phelps, Barbara Bain as Cinnamon Carter, Martin Landau as Rollin Hand, Greg Morris as Barney Collier (another AfricanAmerican lead character), and Peter Lupus as Willy Armitage. Each member of the group had special skills that complemented the skills of the others, and each episode opened with the very distinctive theme music and Jim Phelps listening to a tape recording describing their next assignment—a tape recording that would self-destruct immediately after he finished listening to it. Of course, now that the series has been adapted into a tremendously successful film franchise starring Tom Cruise, it is very difficult to separate the legacy of the original television series from the impact of that series of films.

In many ways at the opposite end of the spectrum from *Mission Impossible*, *It Takes a Thief* (1968–1970) was a very loose television adaptation of the film starring Cary Grant. In the series, Robert Wagner played Alexander Mundy, a master thief who had nonetheless been imprisoned and who was released on the condition that he steal for the various intelligence agencies of the U.S. government. The series may now be most remembered for Fred Astaire's somewhat abbreviated role as Mundy's equally larcenous father.

Two other spy thrillers need also to be mentioned. Both were made in Great Britain and imported to American network television after they had already proved to be big hits in Great Britain. On the heels of the "British Invasion" of American popular music, these series had an almost ready-made audience in the United States and have remained cult favorites ever since. *The Saint* starred Roger Moore as Simon Templar, who like Alexander Mundy is a master thief. In Templar's case, he uses his criminal skills to help people caught up in predicaments involving police and/or intelligence agencies—both of whom inevitably target him as much as, if not more than, those whom he is trying to help. The character was created by the novelist Leslie Charteris in the 1920s, but Moore's suave portrayal seemed perfectly keyed to the 1960s—and led to Moore's eventually becoming the actor who would play James Bond most frequently on film. *The Avengers* starred Patrick Macnee as John Steed, a dapper private investigator with special skills who often worked for the intelligence services. Steed was paired with a series of female assistants, the most popular of whom were Dr. Cathy Gale, played by Honor Blackman, and Mrs. Emma Peel, played by Diana Rigg. Interestingly, although Honor Blackman created a sensation in Great Britain, because of the timing of when the series began to be aired in the United States, Diana Rigg became fixed in the American cultural memory as Steed's partner.

In the 1950s, in the relatively immediate aftermath of the Second World War, there were a number of series about the experience of GIs during that conflict.

In the early 1960s, two series about the war both premiered in 1962. *Combat!*, which aired from 1962 to 1967 and starred Rick Jason and Vic Morrow, followed a squadron of GIs fighting the Germans in France and, as much as was possible on network television at the time, depicted their experiences fairly realistically and with some complexity. In contrast, *The Gallant Men*, which starred William Reynolds and Robert McQueeney and focused on a squadron fighting in the Italian theater, lasted just the one season. Especially in comparison to *Combat!*, *The Gallant Men* relied much more on stock characters, stock situations, and even stock footage from films about the war, and, very unrealistically, the body count among the Germans was very high while the American squadron suffered very few casualties. The escalation of the Vietnam War made military series less popular, but *The Rat Patrol*, which aired from 1966 to 1968 and starred Christopher George as the leader of an Allied reconnaissance unit in the deserts of North Africa, had some singular appeal because it featured jeeps being driven over sand dunes at high speeds and often under enemy fire. So, beyond those interested in military stories, it also appealed to viewers who would have been interested in endurance races across deserts such as the Dakar Rally.

Finally, the medical drama remained a staple of television programming, with three noteworthy series airing in the 1960s. From 1961 to 1966, two of these series, *Ben Casey* and *Dr. Kildare*, featured young surgeons, played by Vince Edwards and Richard Chamberlain, who were in residencies at urban hospitals. Naturally, their work brought them into contact with all sorts of people in many kinds of circumstances, and both series explored their relationships with their peers and with their mentors, played by Sam Jaffe and Raymond Massey. Interestingly, although *Ben Casey* aired on ABC and *Dr. Kildare* on NBC, and although the latter series was moved around on the schedule, the two shows were never aired opposite of each other. In 1969, several years after both series went off the air, ABC introduced another medical drama, *Marcus Welby, M.D.*, in which Robert Young played a family doctor, with James Brolin playing the younger partner that he brought into his practice. So, although the setting was not as restricted to the hospital as in *Ben Casey* and *Dr. Kildare* and although the doctor played by Brolin was no longer a resident, the interplay between the older and younger doctors was maintained.

## WESTERNS ON TELEVISION

As network television developed during the 1950s, many of the categories of programming that are still being produced today became established. These persistent kinds of programming range from the evening news shows to the late-night talk shows and from situation comedies to medical and legal drama series. On the other hand, some of the staples of early television programming have either not survived at all or have become so infrequent as to seem novel or anomalous when they are reintroduced. These categories would include variety shows, prime-time game shows, and Westerns.

In the 1950s, many of the Westerns were short-lived, but the sheer number of the series produced during the decade attests to the broad popularity of the genre. In the 1960s, the number of series that were introduced declined somewhat, but a substantial number of series had such remarkable staying power that the Western is viewed as one of the dominant and most culturally significant types of television programming of the decade.

Some of the more iconic series began airing in the 1950s but had runs extending an equivalent length of time or longer into the 1960s. These series include: *Cheyenne* (1955–1963), starring Clint Walker as an itinerant cowboy; *Maverick* (1957–1962), starring James Garner as a gambler; *Tales of Wells Fargo* (1957–1962), starring Dale Robertson as a special agent of the company; *Have Gun—Will Travel* (1957–1963), starring Richard Boone as a gun for hire; *Wagon Train* (1957–1965), starring first Ward Bond and then John McIntire as wagon masters who guided settlers across the plains and the mountains to new settlements in Oregon and California; *Lawman* (1958–1962), starring John Russell as a marshal; *The Rifleman* (1958–1963), starring Chuck Connors as a rancher who preferred a repeating rifle to a pistol; *Laramie* (1959–1963), starring John Smith and Robert Fuller as brothers who ran a stagecoach shop; and *Rawhide* (1959–1966), starring Eric Fleming and Clint Eastwood as cattle drovers. All of these series were filmed in black-and-white, and although *Cheyenne* was the first hour-long Western television series, *Maverick*, *Laramie*, and *Rawhide* were also hour-long shows, and *Tales of Wells Fargo* was extended from a 30-minute to a 60-minute show.

Three other Western series that first aired in the 1950s endured into the 1970s, ranking them among the longest-running television programs of any kind. *Death Valley Days* (1952–1970) was a true-story anthology, now most commonly remembered for the hosts whose commentaries introduced and concluded each episode. These hosts included Robert Taylor and Dale Robertson—and, most notably, Ronald Reagan. Hosting this show was his last acting job before he began his political career as a candidate for governor of California. The series was also well known for its sponsorship by the Pacific Borax Company—and the promotion of its "20 Mule Team Borax." An even longer-running television series, *Gunsmoke* (1955–1975) featured James Arness as Marshal Matt Dillon of Dodge City, Kansas. Like *Death Valley Days*, *Gunsmoke* began as a radio series, but from 1955 to 1961, *Gunsmoke* aired as both a radio series and a television series, with another actor, William Conrad, playing Dillon on the radio show. Although it had a somewhat shorter run than both *Death Valley Days* and *Gunsmoke*, *Bonanza* (1959–1973) seems to have had the most enduring cultural impact. Focusing on the Cartwrights, a father and his three adult sons, who operated a sprawling ranch in northern Nevada called the Ponderosa, *Bonanza* appealed to younger as well as older viewers. Although it was hardly the first Western series to be heavily merchandized, it more singularly led to the development of both a theme park and a national chain of restaurants. Moreover, Michael Landon followed his role as Little Joe with leading roles in two other popular series, and his enduring appeal contributed to some extent to the enduring popularity of *Bonanza*.

Both *Gunsmoke* and *Bonanza* had runs that extended past 1971, outlasting the most popular series introduced in the 1960s and surviving beyond the rather abrupt end of the Western's period as one of the staples of network-television

Marshall Matt Dillon (James Arness) faces down a villain as he always did in *Gunsmoke* (1955–1975). (Michael Ochs Archives/Getty Images)

programming. The most popular series of the 1960s were filmed in color, rather than black-and-white, and several were 90-minute shows. These Western series included *The Virginian* (1962–1971), starring James Drury and Doug McClure as cowboys on a Wyoming ranch; *The Big Valley* (1965–1969), starring Barbara Stanwyck as the widowed matriarch of the Barkley family, who operated an immense ranch in California; and *The High Chaparral* (1967–1971), starring Leif Erickson as a larger-then-life rancher who established a ranch in Arizona well before the pacification of the Apache and other Native American tribes. Although not technically a Western, because it was set east of the Mississippi and included neither cattle drives nor wagon trains nor sprawling ranches, *Daniel Boone* (1964–1970) focused on the frontier experience, and it is usually included in discussions of the television Western for much the same reasons that the novels of James Fenimore Cooper are almost always included in critical surveys of fiction about the American West.

The demise of the Western can be attributed to the rise of the Counterculture, which questioned many of the cultural assumptions underlying the popularity of the genre. Several series of the 1960s anticipated some of the revisionist approaches that would come to characterize histories of the American West, as well as novels, films, and television series about the region, in the 1970s and 1980s. *F Troop* (1965–1967) was initially aired in the same season as *Hogan's Heroes* and treated life in Western forts with much the same mixture of farce and satire as Hogan's Heroes treated life in a German prisoner-of-war camp. Likewise, *The Wild Wild West* (1965–1969) focused with exuberant campiness on two government agents who operated against sinister frontier conspiracies with the same high style and technical gadgetry that James Bond brought to his contests with international villains.

Although some of the details in the preceding paragraphs may suggest that the television Western had completely exhausted its possibilities by the beginning of the 1970s, that was not entirely true. To cite just one example of a Western series that had many fresh elements—or at least presented a fresh combination of the genre's familiar elements—*The Guns of Will Sonnett* (1967–1969) starred Walter Brennan as a graying gunman and Dack Rambo as the grandson he had raised to adulthood. The two of them became preoccupied with finding their missing son and father, who had gained considerable notoriety as a gunfighter. Within the series' treatment of the archetypal quest for reconciliation, the episodes featured an unusual degree of dramatic and thematic subtlety, ambiguity, and complexity. Indeed, the show's transcendence of the usual conventions of the genre was reflected in the number of young but already important actors who agreed to do guest spots, including Jack Nicholson, Dennis Hopper, Cloris Leachman, and Charles Grodin. The series deserves to be considered one of the most underrated Westerns in television history. It had the misfortune of airing at a time when the American television audience was becoming increasingly skeptical about everything that the genre seemed to represent—or perhaps was simply losing interest in it because its conventions had become so familiar as to seem stale.

## FAMILY PROGRAMMING

Just as many of the sitcoms of the 1950s and 1960s were very clearly aimed at baby boomers, so, too, some of the dramas were designed to be "family programming" and scheduled in the earlier prime-time programming slots. On Sunday evenings, from 1954 to 2008, a Walt Disney anthology show was a prime-time staple. For almost half of those fifty-four years, it was aired early on Sunday evenings, but over its fifty-four-year run, the show had a half-dozen different names and was aired for some periods on all three major networks. During almost all of the 1960s, the show was called *Walt Disney's Wonderful World of Color*.

A group of these family-oriented shows featured animals that were either conventional pets or wild animals with whom their trainers had bonded. *Lassie*, which aired from 1954 to 1973, featured the collie who had become the star of a film franchise. Of course, the same dog and, since the television series almost always featured a young boy, not even the same human characters, starred during the entire run of the series. *Flipper*, which aired for just three seasons from 1964 to 1967 but was very popular and has remained so in syndication, was set on a marine preserve and featured the bond between the two sons of the game warden and the dolphin who gives the series its name. Like *Flipper*, *Gentle Ben*, which aired for two seasons from 1967 to 1969, was set on a Florida wildlife preserve. In this case, the focus is on the relationship between the son of the warden and a giant brown bear. Interestingly, the television series was based on a popular children's novel, which was set in the Alaskan wilderness—a setting almost diametrically opposite that in which the television series was set.

Two other series featured animals but were set in Africa. One was based on a long-running film franchise that had become a staple of matinee showing on Saturday afternoons, and the other was based on a popular feature film. *Tarzan*, which aired from 1966 to 1968, had a much shorter run on television than in the movie theaters. It was updated to take into account that most of Africa had become independent over the preceding decade, but since most of the characters were carried over from the film franchise, it had an anachronistic feel to it. *Daktari*, which aired from 1966 to 1969, was set on a game preserve in East Africa and featured the family of a wild-animal veterinarian. One of the main animal characters was Clarence the Cross-Eyed Lion, and although the series was based on a popular film named after the lion, it also benefited from the popularity of the film *Born Free* and of the very popular theme song from that film, which would not be adapted into a television series for another eight years. It is also possible that the show's producers were attempting to echo *Hatari!*, a John Wayne film of the early 1960s, which was itself a knockoff of the 1953 film *Magambo*, starring Clark Cable. Both of those films, however, featured former big-game hunters who were capturing live animals for zoos; so the attitude toward the animals was decidedly different than that presented in *Daktari*.

Another group of shows developed for family viewing went beyond exotic earthly locales. *Voyage to the Bottom of the Sea*, which aired from 1964 to 1968, was essentially an updated version of Jules Vernes's *Twenty Thousand Leagues under the Sea* featuring more advanced technologies, Cold War politics, and paranormal events. *Land of the Giants*, which aired from 1968 to the 1970s, was set in the near future (1983 to be exact). Its premise was that the crew of a suborbital spacecraft was sucked by a magnetic storm through a "space warp." Their space ship eventually crashes on a planet on which everything exists on a much larger scale than things exist on Earth. (In effect, it is a version of the sort of world that Jonathan Swift presents in the second book of *Gulliver's Travels*. Whereas Gulliver had been a giant in Lilliput, in Brobdingnag, he is a miniature figure.) *Lost in Space*, which aired from 1965 to 1968, was very pointedly an updated version of *The Swiss Family Robinson*, in which a family named Robinson is sent on a space mission to explore a planet orbiting the star nearest to our Sun, Alpha Centauri. Their spaceship, however, is deliberately directed off course by agents of a hostile power into a meteor shower, and their misadventures on other worlds begin.

## TELEVISION CARTOONS

Saturday morning cartoons had become a fixture of American television even before the 1960s, but it was during that decade that they became an immovable part of network schedules and a significant aspect of American popular culture. Some of the animated shows drew on earlier characters, as did *Popeye the Sailor*. Others, like *Mister Magoo* and *The Flintstones*, both of which premiered in 1960 quickly became notable in their own right. The list of others that quickly

Original host Monte Hall with audience contestants on *Let's Make a Deal* (1963–present). (NBC/NBCU Photo Bank via Getty Images)

became cultural touchstones includes *The Alvin Show* (premiering in 1961), *Top Cat* (1961), *The Yogi Bear Show* (1961), *Deputy Dawg* (1962), *The Jetsons* (1962), *Underdog* (1964), *Magilla Gorilla* (1964), *George of the Jungle* (1967), and *The Archie Show* (1968). The images of the characters were reproduced by kids across the country, on the notebooks and bedroom walls and anywhere else they could draw them.

## GAME SHOWS

In the 1950s, one of the staples of network programming were the game shows, in particular quiz shows in which contestants competed for prizes. But after it was revealed that programmers were rigging several of the shows—*The $64,000 Question*, *Twenty-One*, and *Dotto*—the viewing audiences lost interest in those types of shows. As a result, the game shows that continued to find an audience or that were introduced in the 1960s had considerably different formats. *The Price Is Right* aired, in its original rendition, from 1956 to 1965, though in 1963 it switched from NBC to ABC. Contestants tried to guess the prices of various products, and the winner was whoever came closest to the actual price without exceeding it. The show was resurrected in 1972 and has been airing ever since; so, it is somewhat hard to understand why it was taken off the air for the years between 1965 and 1972. *Let's Make a Deal*, which originally aired in 1963, has had a similarly enduring appeal—though after its initial run ended in 1977, there were several failed attempts to resurrect the show before one succeeded in 2009. Over its original run, the show was hosted by Monty Hall, one of its creators and producers, and in its current rendition, it is being hosted by Wayne Brady. But one of the failed attempted revivals of the show, as a prime-time show in 2003 that lasted for just three episodes, was hosted by Billy Bush, who in 2005 did the infamous *Access Hollywood* interview with Donald Trump.

Several other game shows asked contestants to guess the identities, occupations, or accomplishments of people of note who had not achieved enough celebrity to be readily recognizable. On *What's My Line?*, which aired from 1950 to 1975, a celebrity panel attempted to identify the guest's occupation. On *I've Got a Secret*, which aired from 1952 to 1967, the panelists attempted to identify what the contestant had done that had attracted attention. In some instances, the contestants had accomplished truly significant things, but in other cases, they had done something that had given them what Andy Warhol would describe as their "15 minutes of fame." On *Candid Camera*, which aired from 1948 to 1979 and was created by Allen Funt, ordinary people were put into unusual situations and their responses were filmed clandestinely. On *It Could Be You*, which aired for a much shorter period from 1956 to 1961, ordinary people were confronted on stage with accounts of embarrassing things that someone had seen them doing. The "fun" generated at the expense of these people was often less good-natured—much less spontaneous and even a little more deliberately belittling—than the responses caught on *Candid Camera*.

Two other game shows that premiered in the mid-1960s were very much a product of the rapidly changing sexual mores and the increasingly media-dominated culture that was breaking down the conventional boundaries between individuals' private and public lives. Both shows were produced by Chuck Barris. *The Dating Game* originally aired from 1965 to 1974, and, like other successful game shows, it has been periodically revived with very mixed results. On the show, a young woman or man would ask questions of three prospective dates who were seated out of the questioner's line of sight and could be heard but not seen by the questioner. *The Newlywed Game*, which originally aired from 1966 to 1974 and has been repeatedly revived, pitted four recently married couples against each other. First, the wives were taken offstage, their husbands were asked questions and their answers recorded on cards, and then the wives were brought back on stage and asked the same questions—with matching answers earning points. Then the process was reversed, with the husbands being taken offstage while their wives answered questions. Both of these shows were very popular for almost the entirety of their original runs, even though what was risqué in the mid-1960s had become corny by the early 1970s. For instance, the host Bob Eubanks often asked the contestants about their sex lives and made the phrase "making whoopee" something of a catchphrase that he continued using long after it had become an anachronistic euphemism, rather than a slang way around the network censors.

## SPORTS PROGRAMMING

Sports have been a major part of American popular culture since the middle of the nineteenth century. But the media coverage of sports did not become an industry until the celebrity culture emerged in the 1920s. Not only did the existing newspapers and magazines and then eventually radio programming begin to focus on news involving celebrities, but publishers also started magazines specifically devoted to coverage of celebrity news and gossip. For the first time, sports became a big business and began to be perceived as another type of entertainment business. As a result, star athletes such as Babe Ruth and Jack Dempsey became as widely recognized as film stars and popular singers. For the first time, newspapers had separate sections devoted entirely to sports news, and reporters were hired specifically to cover sports stories. Radio meant that sporting events could be covered as they occurred, rather than after the fact. Television then brought the audience right into the stadium or arena.

Even if the telecasts of games and matches were initially somewhat primitive, the novelty of the experience more than outweighed the obvious technical limitations. Because early televisions had small screens and the broadcast signal was not always consistent or picked up cleanly by the household antenna, sports that involved fast action or small balls were more difficult to broadcast effectively than those, such as boxing and wrestling, which took place in a relatively small space and did not involve large teams. In addition, sports such as boxing and wrestling usually took place in arenas where the ring was very well lit, and the quality of the broadcast was not further reduced by inadequate lighting. In the immediate postwar periods, baseball games were televised more often than football or basketball games not only because baseball was still unarguably the national pastime but also because much of the action occurred in the relatively short space between the pitcher, hitter, and catcher.

In the late 1940s, the television manufacturers and networks took note that every time a major sporting event was televised, the sale of television sets increased, sometimes very dramatically. Furthermore, sporting events were generally less expensive than other programming to produce, and as they became more of a fixture in television schedules, the professional leagues began to accommodate them in order to make the product more appealing and to provide more slots in which commercials could be aired. For instance, a shot clock was introduced in professional basketball in order to increase the pace of the games and to make them more exciting. And in professional football, time-outs were lengthened and regularly spaced "television time outs" were introduced into televised games to ensure that the maximum amount of advertising incomes could be generated. On the other hand, because sports teams still generated most of their revenue from ticket sales, concessions, and team paraphernalia, there was concern that televising games would reduce revenues for the teams, even as they were very profitable for the television networks. This concern led Ford Frick, who became the commissioner of Major League Baseball in 1951, to mandate that the view of the game provided by the television cameras not be better than that provided to a fan sitting in the worst seat in a stadium. Likewise, in the second half of the 1950s, major sports leagues began the practice of blacking out television coverage games to local audiences if the game being televised had not been sold out.

At the beginning of the 1960s, the paradigm began to shift as the networks started to bid against each other for the rights to broadcast the games of the major professional sports leagues. A 1962 decision by the U.S. Supreme Court allowed the teams within a league to bargain collectively for the national broadcast rights to their games. Previously, sports programming, like much other television programming, had been sponsored by particular corporations who thereby bought most, if not all, of the available commercial time. For instance, for more than a decade starting at the end of the 1940s, Gillette would sponsor the *Friday Night Fights* on NBC. But during the second half of the 1950s, most sports programming migrated from evening time slots to the weekend afternoons. The assumption was that women made up a larger percentage of the viewing audience in the evenings and would be less interested in sports. That assumption proved to be based more on gender stereotypes than on real differences in viewing interests, but the flip side of the assumption, that men could become conditioned to watching sports in the afternoon on their days off from work, proved to be accurate—and profitable. The contract rights to broadcast the major sports leagues suddenly became too expensive for individual corporate sponsors. So the networks bought the rights and found that they had little trouble selling the commercial time.

The effect of the networks' bidding against each other for the broadcast rights is especially evident in the case of professional football. The 1958 National Football League (NFL) championship game between the Baltimore Colts and the New York Giants would become known as the "Greatest Game Ever Played." The Colts won the game in sudden-death overtime. It was broadcast nationwide by NBC and watched by more than 45 million people nationwide—a total that was made even more impressive by the fact that the greater New York metro area had been blacked out. The game is viewed as a watershed moment in which the steadily growing popularity of professional football had suddenly reached a point at which it was credible to ask whether football might eventually compete with, if not overtake, baseball as the national pastime. In 1960, the American Football League was formed, and ABC, the smallest of the three major networks, legitimized the new league by offering it a four-year contract to broadcast its games. NBC had had the broadcast rights to NFL games through 1963, but when CBS successfully outbid NBC for the rights to those games, agreeing to pay the NFL $4.5 million per year, NBC outbid ABC for the broadcast rights to the AFL games, paying $42.5 million for a five-year contract starting in 1965. In that first year of the deal, Joe Namath was entering the league as a much-heralded rookie quarterback for the New York Jets, but the television contract, as much as the players that the AFL teams were drafting, made it clear that the AFL could eventually compete with the NFL, and it led to the creation of a Pro Football Championship Game between the winners of the two leagues. That game, which would soon become known as the Super Bowl, was almost immediately a ratings bonanza, very consistently drawing between a 40 percent and a 50 percent audience share. As of the end of 2018, Super Bowl broadcasts accounted for twenty of the twenty-five largest audiences in the history of American television. In 2015, a 30-second commercial aired during the Super Bowl cost $4.5 million, or $300,000 more than CBS paid for the broadcast rights to the entire 1964 NFL season.

As NBC and CBS secured the contract rights to televise Major League Baseball and professional football games, ABC managed to get the rights to broadcast professional basketball and college football games. Previously, only bowl games and special-interest games such as the annual Army-Navy game had been broadcast, but a young innovator named Roone Arledge introduced new elements into ABC's coverage that would change the way the other networks covered professional football games. Specifically, Arledge focused the cameras and focused the commentary on things beyond the plays on the field—on the coaches and others on the sidelines (including the cheerleaders) and on those in the crowd—giving the viewing audience a richer sense of what it was like to be at the game. He would encourage announcers to personalize the coaches and players by providing selective background details, and eventually he would promote the announcers as television personalities. These innovations would continue and even accelerate when, in 1970, ABC secured the rights to broadcast one NFL game per week—in prime time on Monday night. The tremendous popularity of Monday night football would begin the return of sports programming to the evening network schedules.

But Arledge's great laboratory was a weekly sports anthology show called *ABC's Wide World of Sports*. Each week this show would feature sports that seldom had received television coverage outside of perhaps the Olympic Games or in the case of sports such as tennis and golf, outside of the major tournaments. Because the broadcast rights for such sporting events were very low, Arledge was able to allocate more of the show's budget to travel costs and to technical upgrades and innovations. The show became as popular for the international locations from which it was broadcast as for the unusual sports and relatively unknown—at least to American viewers—athletes whom it showcased. A show that had begun as a low-cost alternative to the major sports programming of the other two networks became a landmark in the history of television, running for thirty-eight seasons and becoming outdated only with the proliferation of cable television networks that were specializing in sports programming and eventually competing to broadcast sporting events that would previously have been covered on American television only on *Wide World of Sports*—sporting events such as Australian rules football matches and ping pong championships. Even several decades after it stopped airing, the lead into *Wide World of Sports* has remained one of the most widely known pieces of sports promotion: "Spanning the globe to bring you the constant variety of sport. The thrill of victory, and the agony of defeat. The human drama of athletic competition. This is ABC's *Wide World of Sports*."

Throughout the 1960s, all of the major sports became increasingly integrated. It was not an entirely smooth movement toward social progress. One of the reasons that ABC was able to get the rights to broadcast the National Basketball Association (NBA) games was that as African American players increasingly began to dominate the league, there was a dip in the league's popularity. But for every setback, there were indications of progress. One of the most noteworthy of those indications of progress was the naming of Jackie Robinson as the first African American announcer on weekly nationally broadcast baseball games. Unfortunately, Robinson was hired in 1965, the last year in which ABC had the rights to broadcast Major League Baseball games. But his transition from the field to the broadcast booth demonstrated that sports were playing a part in the broader acceptance of racial integration, equal rights, and equal opportunities. Ironically over the subsequent half-century, no sport would do more to advance that cause than the NBA.

## MARSHALL McLUHAN (1911–1980)

Although much radio programming was adapted to television, television was not just a progressive advancement over radio. In many ways, the advent of television heralded a shift toward a completely new media-saturated and media-defined culture. Even before the introduction of the personal computer and the establishment of the earliest iterations of the Internet in the 1980s, the computer was having a significant impact on a broad range of elements of American life, from scientific and military research to data collection and analysis, to the development of related technologies and innovative reconceptions of communications. In a series of extremely influential books, Marshall McLuhan established himself as the preeminent commentator on the relationship between media, society, and culture in an increasingly media-dominated world. Even while he was alive, his views created controversy in various ways. First, critics emphasized that his analyses were often not as precise as they might have been, that they lacked some degree of academic rigor. Second, commentators have observed that the nonlinear structures of his books and his aphoristic style of writing meant that his insights sometimes resonated more strongly with readers than they held up to critical scrutiny. Lastly, especially in retrospective appraisals, critics have noted that those who have focused on his foresight have often ignored the ways in which his sometimes idiosyncratic views distorted his perceptions and undermined his arguments. Nonetheless, more than half a century after the publication of his most influential works, it is still difficult to discuss the impact of media on our society and culture without some reference to McLuhan's work. Like Freud's influence on psychology, McLuhan's influence on media and cultural studies has been controversial but enduring. More specifically, he remains a seminal figure in the legitimization of the academic study of popular culture.

In his first book, *The Mechanical Bride: Folklore of Industrial Man* (1951), McLuhan focused on the ways in which advertising's emergence as a major industry was shaping how people viewed themselves, the products that they used and consumed, their social relationships, and their cultural context. Of course, the impact of the advertising industry in the early 1950s was relatively limited even in comparison to its influence a decade of two later, when material prosperity was no longer just a happy consequence of the military victory in the Second World War but, instead, a defining assumption in discussions about the national character and American exceptionalism. In *The Gutenberg Galaxy: The Making of Typographic Man* (1962), McLuhan made the case that media not only affects how content is presented but also shapes how we view that content and, more broadly, the world around us. For instance, he points out that the invention of writing, of phonetic alphabets, and of mechanical printing presses have all influenced not only how we collect and transmit information but also how our social, economic, political, and cultural institutions have evolved—and have sometimes changed quite dramatically. He suggested that the development of visual media was creating a "Global Village" that could either reduce or accentuate tribalism, depending on how it developed.

McLuhan's next two books would be his most influential. In *Understanding Media: The Extensions of Man* (1964), he famously argued that "the medium is the message" and distinguished between "hot" and "cool" media: "hot" media are those that engage the audience most intensely and immediately but do not necessarily require any complex emotional or intellectual response from the audience; in contrast, "cool" media require much fuller and more variegated participation by the audience. Some critics have dismissed these categories as being simplistic, rather than insightful, but others have countered that McLuhan viewed media across a spectrum of possibilities, with these opposite categories suggesting the range of possibilities, rather than exclusive choices. In retrospect, it is interesting than McLuhan defined films as "hot" media but television programming as "cool" media because the rise of cable television and services such as Netflix have very much blurred the distinctions between the two media. It is also an open question what McLuhan would have made of a website such as YouTube, especially since television programmers are now counting subsequent web viewership in addition to viewership at time of broadcast. This calculation of the impact of programming is, of course, especially relevant for television programming that can be divided readily into segments, such as talk shows and variety shows. In *The Medium Is the Message: An Inventory of Effects* (1973), McLuhan pulls together elements of his previous books, making the case that media define us not only because they become extensions of ourselves but also because they actually change us at the most fundamental levels. If media has become one of our most significant products, we have also become products of those media. Likewise, if the differences in the media that have defined particular historical periods are visually apparent (and, as our media have become more sophisticated, apparent through other senses as well) then the differences in the people living within those historical periods should also be apparent.

McLuhan's final work published during the 1960s was *War and Peace in the Global Village* (1968). In this book, the idiosyncrasies in his intellectual interests come together in a way that can be described as astonishing, puzzling, or dubious without getting much of an argument over the choice of the descriptor. Although McLuhan was best known for his expertise in media and cultural studies, he was an English professor who regularly taught literature as well. In this book, he argues that the ten "thunders" in James Joyce's *Finnegan's Wake* provide a guide to the major stages of human history, each of which is defined by some sort of significant development in media. It is an ingenious proposition, but *Finnegan's Wake* is such a deliberately challenging and almost impenetrable work that proposing that it provides clarity on anything as complex as how we communicate and how our communications, in turn, not just define us but redefine us seems as audacious as any proposition that McLuhan dared to make.

## FURTHER READING

Austerlitz, Saul. *Sitcom: History in 24 Episodes from "I Love Lucy" to "Community."* Chicago: Chicago Review Press, 2014.

Baber, David. *Television Game Show Hosts: Biographies of 32 Stars.* Jefferson, NC: McFarland, 2008.

Benedetti, Paul, and Nancy DeHart, eds. *Forward through the Rearview Mirror: Reflections on and by Marshall McLuhan.* Cambridge, MA: MIT Press, 1997.

Billings, Andrew C. *Olympic Media: Inside the Biggest Show on Television.* New York: Routledge, 2008.

Bloom, Ken, and Frank Vlastnik. *Sitcoms: The 101 Greatest TV Comedies of All Time.* New York: Black Dog and Leventhal, 2007.

Britton, Wesley A. *Spy Television.* Westport, CT: Praeger, 2004.

Brook, Vincent. *Something Ain't Kosher Here: The Rise of the "Jewish" Sitcom.* New Brunswick, NJ: Rutgers University Press, 2003.

Burke, Timothy, and Kevin Burke. *Saturday Morning Fever.* New York: St. Martin's Griffin, 1999.

Davis, Jeffery. *Children's Television, 1947–1990: Over 200 Series, Game and Variety Shows, Cartoons, Educational Programs, and Specials.* Jefferson, NC: McFarland, 1995.

Deninger, Dennis. *Sports on Television: The How and Why behind What You See.* New York: Routledge, 2012.

Dunn, Mark. *Quizzing America: Television Game Shows and Popular Culture in the 1950s.* Jefferson, NC: McFarland, 2018.

Fagen, Herb. *White Hats and Silver Spurs: Interviews with 24 Stars of Film and Television Westerns of the Thirties through the Sixties.* Jefferson, NC: McFarland, 1996.

Gitlin, Marty. *The Greatest Sitcoms of All Time.* Lanham, MD: Scarecrow, 2014.

Gordon, W. Terrence. *Marshall McLuhan: Escape into Understanding: A Biography.* New York: Basic, 1997.

Ham, Eldon L. *Broadcasting Baseball: A History of the National Pastime on Radio and Television.* Jefferson, NC: McFarland, 2011.

Hodenberg, Christina von. *Television's Moment: Sitcom Audiences and the Sixties Cultural Revolution.* New York: Berghahn, 2015.

Hoerschelmann, Olaf. *Rules of the Game: Quiz Shows and American Culture.* Albany, NY: SUNY Press, 2006.

Hollis, Tim. *Hi There, Boys and Girls! America's Local Children's TV Programs.* Jackson: University Press of Mississippi, 2001.

Inman, David. *Television Variety Shows: Histories and Episode Guides to 57 Programs.* Jefferson, NC: McFarland, 2006.

Jenkins, Tricia. *The CIA in Hollywood: How the Agency Shapes Film and Television.* Austin: University of Texas Press, 2012.

Jones, Gerard. *Honey, I'm Home! Sitcoms, Selling the American Dream.* New York: Grove Weidenfeld, 1992.

Kackman, Michael. *Citizen Spy: Television, Espionage, and Cold War Culture.* Minneapolis: University of Minnesota Press, 2005.

Leszczak, Bob. *Single Season Sitcoms, 1948–1979: A Complete Guide.* Jefferson, NC: McFarland, 2012.

Levinson, Paul. *Digital McLuhan: A Guide to the Information Millennium.* New York: Routledge, 1999.
Marill, Alvin H. *Sports on Television.* Westport, CT: Praeger, 2009.
McKnight, Kirk. *The Voices of Baseball: The Game's Greatest Broadcasters Reflect on America's Pastime.* Lanham, MD: Rowman & Littlefield, 2015.
Miller, Jonathan. *Marshall McLuhan.* New York: Viking, 1971.
Miller, Lee O. *The Great Cowboy Stars of Movies and Television.* Westport, CT: Arlington House, 1979.
Miller, Toby. *Spyscreen: Espionage on Film and TV from the 1930s to the 1960s.* New York: Oxford University Press, 2003.
Milne, Mike. *Transformation of Television Sport: New Methods, New Rules.* New York: Palgrave Macmillan, 2016.
Nichols-Pethick, Jonathan. *TV Cops: The Contemporary American Television Police Drama.* New York: Routledge, 2012.
O'Dell, Cary. *June Cleaver Was a Feminist! Reconsidering the Female Characters of Early Television.* Jefferson, NC: McFarland, 2013.
Osgerby, Bill, and Anna Gough-Yates, eds. *Action TV: Tough Guys, Smooth Operators, and Foxy Chicks.* New York: Routledge, 2001.
Rosenthal, Raymond, ed. *McLuhan: Pro and Con.* New York: Funk & Wagnalls, 1968.
Sanderson, George, and Frank Macdonald, eds. *Marshall McLuhan: The Man and His Message.* Golden, CO: Fulcrum, 1989.
Schober, Adrian, and Debbie Olson, eds. *Children, Youth, and American Television.* New York: Routledge, 2018.
Schwartz, David, Steve Ryan, and Fred Wostbrock. *The Encyclopedia of TV Game Shows.* New York: Facts on File, 1999.
Slack, Trevor, ed. *The Commercialization of Sport.* New York: Routledge, 2004.
Strate, Lance, and Edward Wachtel, eds. *The Legacy of McLuhan.* Cresskill, NJ: Hampton, 2005.
Tahmahkera, Dustin. *Tribal Television: Viewing Native People in Sitcoms.* Chapel Hill: University of North Carolina Press, 2014.
Tucker, David C. *Lost Laughs of '50s and '60s Television: Thirty Sitcoms That Faded Off Screen.* Jefferson, NC: McFarland, 2010.
Tuohy, Brian. *The Fx Is In: The Showbiz Manipulations of the NFL, MLB, NBA, NHL and NASCAR.* Port Townsend, WA: Feral House, 2010.
Turnbull, Sue. *The TV Crime Drama.* Edinburgh, UK: Edinburgh University Press, 2014.
Vogan, Travis. *Keepers of the Fame: NFL Films and the Rise of Sports Media.* Urbana: University of Illinois Press, 2014.
Waldron, Vince. *Classic Sitcoms: A Celebration of the Best of Prime-Time Comedy.* New York: Macmillan, 1987.
West, Richard. *Television Westerns: Major and Minor Series, 1946–1978.* Jefferson, NC: McFarland, 1987.
Westengard, Laura, and Aaron Barlow, eds. *The 25 Sitcoms That Changed Television: Turning Points in American Culture.* Santa Barbara, CA: Praeger, 2018.

# CHAPTER 3

# Music

**ACID ROCK**

Closely associated with the San Francisco Sound, acid rock also arose as young musicians responded to The Beatles and the British Invasion as well as to the growing drug culture of the decade. Much more freeform than most popular genres, acid rock tried to pair itself with drug experiences, particularly with LSD. It is associated most generally with Jimi Hendrix, The Doors, The Grateful Dead and Jefferson Airplane (both also associated with the San Francisco Sound), Country Joe and the Fish, and Vanilla Fudge, though many bands more closely connected to other genres also contributed, including the rock band The Byrds (with "Eight Miles High") and even the surfer/hot rod band The Beach Boys (with "Good Vibrations").

The influence of Indian music on acid rock was high, either through The Beatles or directly from Ravi Shankar, particularly through his performance at the 1967 Monterey Pop Festival.

Jimi Hendrix's first single from his album *Are You Experienced*, "Purple Haze," though it broke into the Hot 100, was not quite the huge hit it is remembered as today. The single was not as important as the album, which was an immediate hit, but it has become one of the three songs most associated with Hendrix, the others being his version of Bob Dylan's "All Along the Watchtower" and his live rendition of "The Star-Spangled Banner" from Woodstock. With lines like "You got me blowing, blowing my mind/Is it tomorrow or just the end of time?" "Purple Haze" stabbed deeply to the hearts of the young Americans embracing drugs and wanting music that could accompany that experience.

Though The Doors, named for Aldous Huxley's drug exploration *The Doors of Perception*, came to popularity through the song "Light My Fire" from their first album, it was "The End," a trippy almost 12-minute song, that contributed most to acid rock. Its combination of recitation and music and willingness to follow paths taking it from the strictures of song as popular genres had long defined them made it a particularly good accompaniment to drug experiences.

## BLUES

The blues had been a major part of the race records of the 1920s and had experienced new appeal to white audiences in the 1930s through such artists as Lead Belly (Huddie Ledbetter), Big Bill Broonzy, Josh White, Brownie McGhee and Sonny Terry, and Bessie Smith, all of whom would be influential on white folk and blues artists in the 1960s. In Chicago, starting in the 1940s, the blues had gone electric, leaving behind the southern acoustic blues and creating one of the greatest influences on 1960s rock.

Two acoustic blues musicians, however, one from the Mississippi Delta and the other from the Carolina Piedmont became integral parts of the folk revival of the early 1960s. These were Mississippi John Hurt and Reverend Gary Davis, both of whose influence would be felt across the rock and folk genres. Hurt, who was born in 1892, died in 1966, a short three years after this race recording artist from the 1920s had been introduced to white audiences at the 1963 Newport Folk Festival. Reverend Gary Davis would also wow white audiences at Newport in 1965 and 1967. Davis, who was born in 1896, was still performing at the end of the decade.

Probably the most important Chicago blues musician of the 1960s was Muddy Waters, whose work was plumbed by rock musicians like The Rolling Stones throughout the decade. Though born in Mississippi in 1913, Muddy Waters, the stage name of McKinley Morganfield, made a name for himself recording for Chess Records in Chicago, his home since 1943. His fame had grown beyond Chicago by 1960, when he performed at the Newport Jazz Festival. But it would be in rock, and not jazz, where Muddy Waters would have the most influence in the 1960s outside of blues.

White American blues bands and musicians popular in the 1960s and influenced by Muddy Waters and the Chicago blues sound include The Paul Butterfield Blues Band, Canned Heat, The Allman Brothers Band, and Ry Cooder.

## BRITISH INVASION

A moribund rock-and-roll scene, one that had fallen back into pop, left an empty space in American youth music. The British bands that had grown up in response to local musical fads there offered a real alternative to the processed sounds the American music industry was producing, an alternative that would soon be identified, as it melded with new American sounds, as the rock music that would dominate the second half of the 1960s—and beyond.

Headed by The Beatles, the musical "British Invasion" of the 1960s was based in bands that had been created in response to Lonnie Donegan and the English Skiffle craze of the 1950s that was itself a recreation of African American music of the early part of the century. Donegan introduced British audiences to jug bands and to Lead Belly, leading to an "anyone can do it" mentality among young fans and a new interest in American blues.

Mick Jagger and Keith Richards of The Rolling Stones rehearsing for an appearance on *The Ed Sullivan Show* in 1969. (CBS via Getty Images)

The young fans and musicians scoured record stores for recordings by American black musicians and incorporated their songs into their own developing repertoires. The Beatles, The Rolling Stones, Cream, Led Zeppelin, and more used American blues and rock and roll as the heart of a sound they now reintroduced to the United States, this time to white audiences. Though the examples are numerous, one of the most famous of these is The Beatles' 1969 "Come Together," which opens with the line "Here come old Flattop, he come groovin' up slowly," a direct take from Chuck Berry's 1956 "You Can't Catch Me": "Here come a flattop, he was movin' up with me." "Flattop" probably referred to a Ford flathead V-8 engine.

Other British bands with lasting power who were part of the British Invasion were many, with The Kinks and The Who being particularly notable. Three of the top 20 songs for the decade were from the British Invasion. #2 was "Hey Jude" by The Beatles and #5 was their "I Want to Hold Your Hand." #18, appropriately enough, was by the other of the top two British Invasion bands, The Rolling Stones' "Honky Tonk Woman."

## BROADWAY AND OFF-BROADWAY

The 1960s experienced the continuation of the vibrancy of Broadway musicals that reached back at least to *Oklahoma!* in 1943. Richard Rodgers and Oscar Hammerstein's newest and final project *The Sound of Music* was packing the house as the 1960s began. New shows by composers and lyricists both experienced and just starting their careers continued to appear throughout the decade, some of them becoming instant classics.

The year 1960 saw the opening of *Camelot,* which became an emblem for the Kennedy administration, *Bye Bye Birdie,* about reaction to an Elvis-like pop star being drafted, and *The Unsinkable Molly Brown* about a survivor of the *Titanic* disaster. On Off-Broadway, *The Fantasticks* opened a run that would be among the longest in theater history. All of these would either become successful films or, in the last instance, would be shown on national television.

Not quite the year 1960 was, 1961 saw hits like *How to Succeed in Business without Really Trying* and *Stop the World—I Want to Get Off*. The year 1962's *I Can Get It for You Wholesale* introduced audiences to Barbra Streisand and *A Funny Thing Happened on the Way to the Forum*; Stephen Sondheim's first foray as both lyricist and composer also opened that year. In 1963, one of the major shows was the antiwar satire *Oh, What a Lovely War!* and another was an import from London's West End, *Oliver!*

The year 1964 was another banner year for Broadway, four musicals that have come to be considered classics opening: *Fiddler on the Roof*, *Funny Girl*, *Hello Dolly!*, and *Man of La Mancha*. Again, all of these musicals would become movies and Streisand firmly a star.

As though needing a breather from blockbuster shows, Broadway offered little in 1965 that had anywhere near the impact of the musicals of 1964.

In 1966, however, Broadway was back on track, with *Cabaret*, *Mame*, and *Sweet Charity*—all three of which, again, would become successful movies. The following year, 1967, saw *Hair* move to Broadway to become a tremendous hit and a major American icon. The year 1968 saw Andrew Lloyd Webber introduced to Broadway, through his *Joseph and the Amazing Technicolor Dream Coat* and also the debut year of *Promises, Promises*. In 1969, in a less than auspicious end to a brilliant decade, *1776* opened on Broadway and *Oh! Calcutta!* Off-Broadway.

The 1960s on Broadway began with the realization that there would be no more musicals from Rodgers and Hammerstein, that the decades of their dominance were over. Sondheim, however, was able to step into his mentor's shoes and others rushed in to fill the void, too. Bob Fosse, who had become one of the preeminent Broadway choreographers in the 1950s continued his successes, as did fellow choreographer Jerome Robbins, both of them helping maintain Broadway traditions going back to the end of the Second World War.

## CLASSICAL

Leontyne Price, Maria Callas, and Beverly Sills were perhaps the three most successful American (though Callas, born in the United States, was also Greek) opera stars of the 1960s. Price was a top soprano when the 1960s began while Callas's career was winding down and she was more famous for her scandals, her singing ending just as Sills was starting. Price, an African American, would further the normalization of integration that was occurring in all musical genres, but opera as a whole was not the major part of popular culture in the 1960s that it had been in earlier decades or would be again later.

Andre Previn, one of the more popular classical musicians of the decade, also worked in jazz and scored films. He came from a Jewish family who had left Germany for the United States on the eve of the Second World War when Previn was not yet a teenager. During the 1960s, after earlier successes in Hollywood, he moved more directly into the classical world, taking on the role of music director for the Houston Symphony Orchestra in 1967.

Leonard Bernstein, who had risen to media superstardom more than a decade before the 1960s, continued to be the most generally recognized figure of the classical world, serving as music director of the New York Philharmonic throughout most of the decade. A friend to the Kennedy family, he performed during John Kennedy's inaugural celebrations in 1961 and conducted a memorial concert the day after John Kennedy's assassination, a nationally televised performance featuring Gustav Mahler's "Ressurection Symphony." In 1968, he conducted the funeral mass for Robert Kennedy, again turning to Mahler, this time "Symphony #5."

Though it is hard to put John Cage in a genre, he is most often associated with a pushing of boundaries within the classical-music tradition. A forty-eight-year-old professor of music at Wesleyan University when the 1960s began, he attained notice with the publication of *Silence*, a collection of essays and lectures that sparked interest in his music. Soon, his older scores were being published and new work was in demand. His works, which did not always actually include music, were iconoclastic and questioning—and often demanded participation on the part of the audience. In fact, "happenings," a type of music and theater event meant to occur outside of traditional settings and with few boundaries between performers and artists, was an idea first put into action by Cage in the 1950s that gathered great popularity in the 1960s.

Another composer choosing not to work within the traditions of classical music but to challenge them was Philip Glass. A generation younger that Cage (he was born in 1937), Glass first achieved notice during the latter part of the decade, particularly with his work *Music in the Shape of a Square*, which was first performed in September 1968 at New York's Anthology Film Archives. Influenced by Cage, Glass had the musicians move from score to score, parts hanging on different walls of the room.

## COUNTRY

As the 1960s began, country music was concentrated around the Grand Ole Opry and Nashville, Tennessee, with a slicker, more pop-oriented style beginning to take control. Bluegrass, old timey, and even rockabilly and others were also beginning to coalesce there for a showcase at the Opry was the ticket to a successful career even in these subgenres. New stars whose shadows would be cast far beyond the 1960s began to join the Opry, including Patsy Cline (1960), who would be the first female country star to achieve crossover success in the pop market, Loretta Lynn (1962), whose 1960s success, like that of Willie Nelson (1965) and Dolly Parton (1969), would hold well into the next century. They joined Johnny Cash, who had been a member since the mid-1950s and a host of others in what was the nation's prime country showcase for all of the 1960s.

Nashville wasn't the only home to country music, however. In Bakersfield, California, a group of musicians led by Buck Owens and the Buckaroos were creating the "Bakersfield sound" that would produce, among others, Merle Haggard. Other country styles were beginning to flee Nashville and its highly polished production values, including bluegrass, which had been an integral part the Grand Ole Opry at least since Monroe had joined in 1939 but that was now finding its greatest successes outside of the Nashville industry. Monroe influenced bluegrass-related musicians, especially those of the old timey tradition, had also begun to find success within the folk music scene of the early years of the decade.

Bluegrass musicians Lester Flatt and Earl Scruggs and their Foggy Mountain Boys came to national attention twice during the 1960s. The first was for their "The Ballad of Jed Clampett," the theme song for the hit television show *The Beverly Hillbillies*, which reached #1 on the country charts and the top half of the Billboard Hot 100. The second resulted from the use of their 1949 "Foggy Mountain Breakdown" in the car-chase scenes of the 1967 film *Bonnie and Clyde*. The song ended up on the Hot 100 and Flatt and Scruggs were now familiar names across the country.

Only one country song made the list of the top 20 most popular songs of the decade, Jimmy Dean's "Big Bad John."

## DANCE

In the early part of the 1960s, dance crazes were a regular part of the American teenage experience. Dances like the twist, the frug, the hitch-hike, the locomotion, the shimmy, and the watusi came and went, with only the twist lasting throughout the decade. By 1967, in part in response to drugs and in part as a reaction to regimentation, most dancing by teens at their parties had moved to the free form that would be standard for the next few years.

There was a great deal more going on in the dance world, though. George Balanchine, who had moved to the United States in the 1930s, continued to set a high bar for American ballet, debuting his technically difficult "Jewels" in 1967. The American Ballet Theater, the only American company that could rival Balanchine's New York City Ballet, continued to emphasize more classical ballet throughout the 1960s under direction of Lucia Chase.

By 1960, the world of modern dance was dominated by Martha Graham and her Martha Graham Dance Company. Graham, though in her sixties when the decade began, continued to dance and choreograph through the decade, influencing other dancers and choreographers, both positively and as the colossus to avoid. Foremost among those she influenced includes Merce Cunningham whose own dance company, the Merce Cunningham Dance Company, established in 1953, had itself become quite influential and notable, especially in collaboration with composer John Cage. Paul Taylor, who had danced with both Graham and Cunningham, formed his own company, the Paul Taylor Dance Company, soon after Cunningham, was also an influential figure during the 1960s.

On the other hand, some dancers reacted against Graham and took their dancing in other directions. Notable among these was Alvin Ailey, who had established the Alvin Ailey Dance Theater in 1958. Ailey wanted to produce dance from a more expansive vision that includes jazz and blues and more, making for as full as possible an audience experience. His "Revelations," which premiered in 1960, incorporates, in addition, much of Ailey's own African American experience growing up in Texas in the 1930s and 1940s. By the end of the 1960s, Ailey had become one of the most recognizable choreographers in the United States.

## FOLK

An amalgamation of a number of American traditions, a new music scene centering on New York City's Greenwich Village and known vaguely as "folk" had arisen by 1960 and was beginning to have real commercial success. Arising from the work of John and Alan Lomax in recording Americans—most particularly African Americans—as they sang and played the music of their lives in the places where they lived and from the group of people surrounding singer/songwriter Woody Guthrie, the folk movement included jugs, spoons, washboards, washtub bases, four- and five-string banjos, harmonicas, dulcimers, autoharps, fiddles, and guitars—none of them electrified.

Among the musicians "rediscovered" as part of the folk movement were Mississippi John Hurt and Reverend Gary Davis. Hurt, from the Mississippi Delta, became a sensation following his performance at the 1963 Newport Folk Festival and an influence on a generation of folk guitarists. Davis, from the Carolina piedmont blues tradition, was also a Newport star, though in 1965. Other acoustic blues musicians, including Victoria Spivey, were also living influences on the movement, as was Sister Rosetta Tharpe, a gospel singer and guitarist who had first been popular in the 1940s.

Following in the footsteps of The Weavers (Pete Seeger, Lee Hayes, Ronnie Gilbert, and Fred Hellerman), who had been popular a decade earlier, the new folk musicians attempted to modernize classic American folk music but without the slick studio sounds of luscious strings and high production values. Following in the footsteps of Woody Guthrie, who had also had quite an influence on The Weavers, the new folk musicians also began to compose their own songs, setting an early conflict between traditionalists and those musicians more willing to experiment, a conflict that would erupt at the Newport Folk Festival in 1965 when Bob Dylan "went electric," effectively ending the folk music scene by melding it with rock.

Though Guthrie was ill with Huntington's disease throughout the 1960s to his death on October 3, 1967, his work was the single most important influence on folk music, combining political activism with his own brand of traditional music. "Woody's children," as Pete Seeger called them, changed the nature of the American popular song, giving it a breadth and depth it had never before had and bringing the singer/songwriter to the fore.

Among these was Bob Dylan, the single most influential songwriter and performer of the 1960s. His career took off with his second album *The Freewheelin' Bob Dylan*, promotion by Joan Baez, already a star, who featured him at her concerts and by performances and recordings of his "Blowin' in the Wind" and "Don't Think Twice, It's All Right" by another established folk act, Peter, Paul and Mary. Though his raspy voice and often mumbling delivery put off audiences conditioned to the smooth studio sounds of the postwar era and plenty of other artists recorded his songs, it was Dylan himself who had become, by 1964, the most important voice produced by the folk movement. His song "The Times They Are a-Changin,'" first performed in 1963, quickly became iconic not only for the folk movement but for protest movements throughout the decade.

Prior to the emergence of Dylan's less processed sound, folk music for pop radio had been sanitized and highly worked in music studios, acts like The Kingston Trio and Peter, Paul and Mary preferred by the record moguls for top 40 play. While popular, their hits were disparaged both by the traditionalists and the singer/songwriters for, on the one hand, destroying the purity of the original sounds and, on the other, for taking what were sometimes hard-hitting lyrics and reducing their power. Dylan walked away from The Ed Sullivan Show when told he could not perform his "John Birch Society Paranoid Blues," and Sylvia Tyson's words in her "You Were on My Mind," "I got drunk and I got sick" disappeared from the We Five pop version.

When future Nobel Prize winner Bob Dylan replaced his acoustic guitar with an electric one, the folk superstar almost instantly became one of rock's legends as well. (Library of Congress)

The folk movement included a wide range of musicians. The iconoclast Richie Havens, who would open the Woodstock festival in 1969 had little in common, for example, with the jug-band music of Jim Kweskin. Many of the acts of the folk movement, following the lead of Dylan and feeling the influence of The Beatles, would "leave the folk music behind," as John Phillips wrote in his 1967 song for The Mamas and the Papas, "Creeque Alley." Others who did included Jim McGuinn, who had played with the likes of The Chad Mitchell Trio and who (as Roger McGuinn) would found The Byrds; John Sebastian, who left The Mugwumps for The Lovin' Spoonful; and Simon and Garfunkel.

## GOSPEL

African American gospel music broke away from the churches starting in the late 1940s, some of its most talented musicians leaving the genre altogether and becoming founders of rhythm and blues and influencing everything from rock and roll to jazz and even classical music. Of those who stayed with the tradition, perhaps the most well known and influential in the 1960s was Mahalia Jackson, a New Orleans, Louisiana, native who sang at John F. Kennedy's inauguration, at the 1963 March on Washington, and even at the World's Fair in New York in 1964. For most white Americans, Jackson was all they knew about black gospel, though it was a thriving musical genre with recordings of it present in many African American households and experience of it every Sunday.

Perhaps the most influential black gospel musician of the 1960s was James Cleveland. His Cleveland Singers toured extensively during the 1960s and incorporated musical styles outside of the older gospel tradition. His 1964 live album (recorded in 1963) *Peace Be Still*, recorded with The Angelic Choir of the First Baptist Church of Nutley, New Jersey, became one of the best-selling gospel albums of all time.

White gospel and black gospel, though they share some of the same roots, had very little to do with each other during the 1960s, white gospel sticking mainly to its older traditions and its recordings falling mostly within the country genre, though rocker Elvis Presley recorded a successful gospel album *His Hand in Mine* in 1960, the first of an eventual three.

## JAZZ

For much of the 1960s, jazz seemed to have moved beyond the ken of the average American music fan, becoming technically sophisticated in ways audiences had a hard time following. At the same time, rock was beginning to find itself musically and technically, moving beyond the more simplistic rock and roll of the previous decade and beginning to pique the interest of jazz fans and even musicians. Starting in the second half of the decade, a few jazz musicians began to see the possibilities of a fusion, starting a revitalization and a new interest in jazz on the part of the baby boomer generation more accustomed to pop, folk, and rock and roll.

An early attempt at crossover was the jazz ensemble the Free Spirits led by guitarist Larry Coryell, who would later become one of the mainstays of the new jazz fusion. The group's success, however, was minimal, one album and a few live performances. Neither Coryell nor his bandmates abandoned the idea, however, and others took it up as well, most notably Miles Davis. Just as his 1959 *Kind of Blue* album set the standard for jazz in the 1960s, *In a Silent Way* (1969) would open the door for jazz fusion in the 1970s, highlighted by his own *Bitches Brew* the next year.

From the beginning of the 1960s, jazz was moving in new directions, many of them away from (yet also building on) the bebop that had dominated the 1950s. Ornette Coleman and John Coltrane were probably the most significant innovators of the early part of the decade in that they sparked work by a wide range of other jazz musicians. Coleman's 1960 album *Free Jazz: A Collective Improvisation*, though it was difficult listening even for some jazz fans (and critics), others found it intriguing and inspirational.

At the same time, John Coltrane was moving in the direction that would lead to what many consider his best and most influential recordings, 1965's *A Love Supreme* and, a year later, *Ascension*. Coltrane became the jazz musician Americans most wanted to like, but there were few who could follow from his rather astonishing but, in some ways conventional, rendition of Rodger's and Hammerstein's "My Favorite Things" to the much less traditionally structured work of his last years.

Another of the more "difficult" jazz musicians of the decade was Thelonious Monk who, along with groups like Sun Ra and his Intergalactic Arkestra, continue to push the boundaries of the genre. Most of the jazz recognized across America, however, was of the cool jazz of early Miles Davis and musicians like Dave Brubeck and Paul Desmond and Lee Konitz. This often understated approach to the genre, with its soothing tempos, often fooled people into thinking that it was not as complex as its bebop cousin. Though much older, it continued into the 1960s and became part of the "space-age modernism" of the early years of the decade.

Other, more traditional jazz musicians, such as Ella Fitzgerald and Louis Armstrong, continued to be popular into the decade, with Fitzgerald concentrating more and more on her "songbook" recordings of Broadway tunes and Tin Pan Alley stalwarts and Armstrong moving into the pop genre.

## LATIN

Antônio Carlos Jobim and Vinicius de Moraes's (English lyrics by Norman Gimbel) 1962 song "The Girl from Ipanema" brought the bossa nova to the United States in 1963. The Stan Getz recording with vocals by Astrud Gilberto became a top 10 hit and set off a bossa nova craze in the United States. Of course, there had been an off-and-on fascination with Latin music in the United States for decades, with Tito Puente, Desi Arnaz, and Carmen Miranda being but a sampling of Latin musicians popular with American audiences.

## LIVE MUSIC

In a good portion of the southern United States, as the 1960s began, live music venues had segregated seating for African Americans. By the end of the decade, this was not the case anywhere, a result of changing laws but also because of the musical acts themselves. Though most acts, in 1960, were still exclusively black or white, their audiences no longer were—not, at least, to the extent they once had been. Genres that had been almost exclusive to one race were beginning to open up more to the other (Charlie Pride in country music, for example, and Don Shirley in classical), and integrated bands were beginning to appear in many genres. Plus, the British bands playing all over the United States, many of whom had grown up with black musical heroes, were shocked to find segregated audiences and shied away from playing before them. The nationwide popularity of Motown, and the heavy presence of its acts on television, also contributed to the breaking down of barriers. As touring was a large part of the income for musicians at the time, this was a significant change, allowing musicians, who generally cared about the resolution of racial issues, to work in the South without qualm.

By 1960, the Newport Jazz Festival and its offshoot, the Newport Folk Festival, had both been successfully established as annual showcases for their respective genres, and both remained important parts of their respective scenes for the entire decade. Other annual festivals were also established, including, in California, the Monterey Jazz Festival and, some years later, the Big Sur Folk Festival, which Joan Baez established in 1964.

In 1967, the Monterey Fairgrounds also hosted the Monterey Pop Festival. Spearheaded by John Phillips of The Mamas and the Papas, the June 16–18 festival helped shoot Jimi Hendrix and Janis Joplin, among others, to fame. Twenty-six months later and in New York's Catskill Mountains, the greatest of all of the 1960s outdoor festivals, the Woodstock Music and Arts Fair, attracted an audience that may have been half-a-million strong.

Of the permanent indoor music venues that had become part of American popular culture, the clubs on the Las Vegas strip had become the most attractive, at least in terms of raw numbers, still featuring many of the acts that had come to prominence during the decade after the Second World War, including Frank Sinatra and the "rat pack" as well as stars like the pianist Liberace. Almost every genre, however, had its own mecca. For country music, it was the Grand Ole Opry. Housed at Nashville's Ryman Auditorium throughout the 1960s, the Opry was where every country musician wanted to play and every fan to see (and hear). For rock, in the late 1960s, it was the Fillmore Auditorium (later the Fillmore West) in San Francisco and the Fillmore East on New York's Lower East Side. For soul and rhythm and blues, it was the Apollo Theater, also in New York City, in Harlem. In Manhattan, the Copacabana, originally a showcase for Latin music, had shed its segregationist ways by the 1960s and hosted numerous Motown acts, its heyday being the early to mid-1960s.

## MOTOWN

One of the myths about early Motown—and there are many—is that it was royalties from The Beatles version of the early Berry Gordy and Janie Bradford song "Money" that made the real reach of Motown possible. No, what made Motown possible *was* Berry Gordy. Without his attention to every detail of the new business he was creating, the phenomenal success of the Detroit-based music behemoth would never have been possible. He imagined creating music on almost a factory model with careful attention to every step in the process—and he did so.

Through his dream, and Barry changed top 40 music and, as a consequence, blasted away the remaining cobwebs of the "race" music concept and the tactic of "covering" black artists for white consumption. Almost *all* young Americans loved Motown, which was unapologetically African American. Vocal groups like Smoky Robinson and the Miracles, Gladys Knight and the Pips, Stevie Wonder, The Temptations, The Four Tops and, of course, The Supremes and finally The Jackson Five. One Motown release, Marvin Gaye's version of "I Heard It through the Grapevine," cracked the top 10 list for the decade, ending up at #9.

Even before the arrival of the phenomenally successful Jackson Five, Motown had become a major part of American popular culture, its sound that of Saturday-night parties from coast to coast, from high school gymnasiums to college frat houses. Though people might have other favorite genres, when singles like The Supremes' "Baby Love" dropped onto the turntable, almost everyone wanted to get up and dance.

## NOVELTY

Frank Zappa, through his band The Mothers of Invention, used comedy as a vehicle for serious musicianship throughout the second half of the 1960s. Thousands of teenagers bought his records for the satire but became die-hard fans of the exquisite musicianship of the albums. His parody of the cover of The Beatles' 1967 *Sgt. Pepper's Lonely Hearts Club Band* on his own *We're Only in It for the Money* almost eclipsed the music itself which, while called rock, is really something much broader with hysterical lyrics of a sort never found in the genre. In many ways, Zappa's music really is a novelty—or a series of them—for it defies categorization.

Most of what are called "novelty songs" might better be called "comedy songs." The tradition of humor within American popular genres, however, goes back to the beginnings of almost every one of them, their separation into a "novelty" category really coming only after the Second World War. The 1950s had plenty of novelty songs of its own, and this putative "genre" continued at full steam through the 1960s.

One of the most successful of the early-1960s novelty acts was Allan Sherman, whose parodies on *My Son, the Folksinger* made it the fastest selling album ever, through 1962. His spoof "Hello Muddah, Hello Fadduh" broke into the top 10 during the summer of 1963, leaving kids laughing at his spot-on depiction of the summer-camp experience. While not as popular with radio audiences, another parodist, Tom Lehrer, one who had first made a name for himself in the 1950s, was providing songs for the American version of the British television show *That Was the Week That Was*. His work became increasingly political as the decade wore on, further precluding chances for success in the hidebound and controversy-averse radio universe.

Even classical music had its own novelty act. Starting in the mid-1960s, Peter Schickele started performing music of his fictional member of the Bach clan, P. D. Q. Bach. His shows quickly became a staple and continued long after the decade closed. Country music, which had a long tradition of humor, saw the rise, in the middle of the decade, of Roger Miller, whose "King of the Road" has become a classic but who also recorded songs like "You Can't Rollerskate in a Buffalo Herd" and "Dang Me." Another popular country novelty of the 1960s was the Statler Brothers' "Flowers on the Wall."

More squarely within the pop genre, the decade began with three versions of a song called "Alley Oop" inspired by a comic strip about a caveman, all of them charting in 1960. A mainstay of pop throughout the decade was Ray Stevens, who started the decade with a number of novelty songs including the hit "Ahab the Arab" in 1962. He ended the decade with another top 10 hit, "Gitarzan."

At least two novelty songs managed to get themselves into trouble during the 1960s. One of these, "The Monster Mash" by Bobby "Boris" Pickett, got itself banned by England's BBC for almost a decade while it had reached #1 on American charts in 1962, remaining popular throughout the decade and much beyond. The other controversial song was "They're Coming to Take Me Away, Ha-Haaa!" by Napoleon XIV (Jerry Samuels), which all but disappeared from the charts after complaints by mental health professionals caused it to be pulled from station playlists across the country.

## PAYOLA

After having spent the money to produce a record—a big investment—how do you protect it? How do you make your investment secure—and make a profit? If you have to, you shell out a little extra to radio stations to get the record on the air. You buy a hit.

Thing is, that's certainly unethical and possibly illegal. But it was once common practice even so. A hearing by Congress into this practice got under way in February 1960 with disc jockeys defending the practice as a legitimate quid pro quo that only got them to listen to the records, not to promise to put them on the air. This, members of Congress thought, might be a breach of the public trust because it involved the public airwaves.

Two careers of high-profile music-industry professionals, Dick Clark and Alan Freed, were threatened. Freed's career ended up being ruined while Clark managed to survive. Freed, it was shown, had done things like demand a share of the writing credit and, therefore, of the royalties from songs such as "Maybellene," which he then pushed heavily. He was ruined and ending up dying just a few years later, in 1965, a sad end for one of the early forces behind the success of rock and roll. Clark, on the other hand, was able to sidestep consequences by selling off his interests in recording companies and music publishers, allowing him to concentrate on his *American Bandstand* television show which, it turned out, was probably for the best, for Clark never again came under scrutiny.

## POP

When the 1960s began, the American popular song was being created, as much as anywhere, at 1619 Broadway, the Brill Building, in New York City. There, one could find music publishers, writers, producers and studios—and some of the names that would dominate popular music, especially top 40, over the decade. Gerry Goffin and Carole King, Barry Mann and Cynthia Weil, Sonny Bono, Don Kirschner, Phil Spector, Bert Bacharach and Hal David: these were just a few of the songwriters and producers who were headquartered, at least for a time, in the Brill Building.

Though there were other music centers across the country, the only other one as central to pop as New York was Los Angeles, where even more actual studio work was done. There, a group of musicians coalesced to become the go-to group for record producers. Now known as the "Wrecking Crew," they had no name in the 1960s, but they were among the most skillful musicians in the country and could be counted on to work quickly. They were first identified as a team during the development of Phil Spector's "wall of sound" at Gold Star Studios and were an integral part of The Beach Boys recording sessions, particularly in 1965 and 1966.

Associated with the Brill Building was Don Kirschner, who produced recordings of songs by King and Goffin, Mann and Weil, and others before moving to providing music (using his stable of writers and musicians) for the television shows *The Monkees*, which was monstrously successful both on television and on record, and then *The Archie Show*, a television cartoon that produced a number of "bubblegum" hits in the late 1960s.

Two significant figures in the pop music of the early part of the decade were Spector and Bobby Darin, both of whom also had Brill Building connections. Producer Spector is best remembered for "girl groups" like The Chrystals and The Ronettes, but he also produced the early hits of the extremely popular Righteous Brothers. Darin, who had risen to stardom with his version of "Mack the Knife," started the 1960s with the successful "Beyond the Sea." He was not happy with rock and roll and wanted to bring something of a Sinatra-esque sensibility to younger audiences.

Frank Sinatra had been a light jazz and pop star for two decades when the 1960s began, and his influence, like that of Elvis Presley, could not be denied even in the 1960s. A performing and recording dynamo, Sinatra began the 1960s at the top of the charts and ended it almost as well with "My Way," whose lyrics, though by Paul Anka, seemed tailor-made for Sinatra. His greatest years of the decade were 1966 and 1967, when he had #1 hits with "Strangers in the Night" and, with his daughter Nancy, "Somethin' Stupid." Sinatra's impact went far beyond his own shows and recordings. Of course, he was also a film star but, dissatisfied with the way musicians were treated by their record labels, he founded Reprise Records in 1960 so that he and other artists could have the creative control they often lacked when working for other labels.

After Elvis Presley was honorably discharged from the Army in 1960, his music became much more pop oriented than it had been before. Even so, he had three #1 hits that year and one each in 1961 and 1962, proving that he had lost little of his attractiveness to audiences. His popularity would decline, however, over the decade, with a resurgence in 1969 with "In the Ghetto" and "Suspicious Minds." For most of the 1960s, Elvis was popular less for who he was than who he had been in the 1950s. Signs of his influence were everywhere in American popular music, especially in the new rock genre where the stage sensuality that he had pioneered became a necessary part of the act.

For all of the attention paid to other genres in the 1960s, pop remained the central popular genre, often drawing on others as it evolved to meet popular demand. The pop songs on the list of the top-20 singles of the decade comprise a majority and are #1, "The Twist" by Chubby Checker; #3, "The Theme from 'A Summer Place'" by Percy Faith and His Orchestra; #6, "I'm a Believer" by The Monkees; #7, "Aquarius/Let the Sunshine In" by The 5th Dimension; #8, "Sugar, Sugar" by The Archies; #10, "Are You Lonesome Tonight?" by Elvis Presley with The Jordanaires; #11, "It's Now or Never" by Elvis Presley with The Jordanaires; #13, "I'm Sorry" by Brenda Lee; #14, "Love Is Blue (L'amour Est Bleu)" by Paul Mauriat and His Orchestra; #15, "Hello, Dolly!" by Louis Armstrong and the All Stars; #16, "Big Girls Don't Cry" by The Four Seasons; #17, "Sugar Shack" by Jimmy Gilmer and The Fireballs.

## PROTEST

Though Bob Dylan is the best remembered for protest songs in the 1960s, he wasn't the only one writing them and performing them—not by a long shot. The much older Pete Seeger, following the example set by Woody Guthrie, continued to write protest songs during the decade, climaxing with "Waist Deep in the Big Muddy," an antiwar song that he performed on the *Smothers Brothers Comedy Hour* after it was initially censored by the CBS network.

Perhaps foremost among the singer/songwriters of protest songs—after Dylan—was Phil Ochs, whose "Draft Dodger Rag," a satirical song about avoiding the draft, was also recorded by Seeger. His "There but for Fortune," a song about chance and class discrepancy, was recorded and sold well for Joan Baez. Throughout the decade, he could have been counted on to perform at protest marches and protests across the country.

One of the more successful protest songs was Barry McGuire's "Eve of Destruction," a Dylanesque catalog of reasons the world was nearing its end. It reached #1 in 1965. Another was Canadian Buffy Saint Marie's "Universal Soldier."

Quite a few other artists wrote and performed protest songs, some of them outside of the folk genre. From the rock genre, Country Joe and the Fish's "Feel Like I'm Fixin' to Die Rag" was one of these, as was Creedence Clearwater Revival's "Fortunate Son," both about service in Vietnam. Rhythm and blues artist Sam Cooke wrote the civil rights anthem "A Change Is Gonna Come," and Dion recorded the pop "Abraham, Martin and John."

## ROCK

Rock music began to appear as a separate genre in American popular music in the mid-1960s in response to The Beatles and the British Invasion and the move by a number of young folk musicians, led by Bob Dylan, into electrified music. It reached its height in the last half of the decade, starting with Dylan's "Like a Rolling Stone," which *Rolling Stone* places at the top of its list of the 500 greatest songs of all time.

Rock is quite a bit broader, stylistically, than its progenitor rock and roll but remains just as dependent on its rhythm section and guitar as the driving force. Rock songs tended to be longer than most pop releases, which made them less suitable for AM top 40 play or even release as singles. Most of the rock artists, however, were more interested in album production, play on the growing number of FM stations and live performances, freeing them from some of the constraints of popular radio—though an AM hit still certainly remained a goal, it was no longer the only one, though there were plenty of first-rate rock bands, like Creedence Clearwater Revival, who stuck with the singles-oriented formula.

Among the more influential American rock albums of the late 1960s were Dylan's *Highway 61 Revisited*, The Doors first album *The Doors*, *Are You Experienced* by The Jimi Hendrix Experience, The Band's *Music from Big Pink*, Frank Zappa's *Hot Rats*, *Cheap Thrills* by Big Brother and the Holding Company, the first Crosby, Stills & Nash album *Crosby, Stills & Nash*, and The Allman Brothers

Band's *The Allman Brothers Band*. There are many more from this period, which has come to be regarded as rock's classic era.

Rock was never simply an American genre. In fact, many more of its biggest acts were British than American, and it was the English who dominated rock's power guitar outside of a few American standouts like Duane Allman, Michael Bloomfield and, of course, Jimi Hendrix.

## ROCK AND ROLL

With the death in 1959 of Buddy Holly, something went out of rock and roll. The next few years showed a more pop-oriented rock and roll and the move of Elvis almost completely into pop. There were a few bright spots, Del Shannon's 1961 "Runaway" and the mega-hit (#4 for the decade) "Tossin' and Turnin'" by Bobby Lewis; there wasn't really much of the 1950s-style rock and roll produced any longer. Things were changing and, though the teenaged audiences still loved Little Richard and Chuck Berry, they were looking now for something other than the music of their older brothers and sisters.

One of the most significant features of 1960s rock and roll was the rise of the garage band, the do-it-yourself foursomes that imitated the relatively simple chord and rhythm structures of professional rock and roll. Some of the bands were themselves successful—such as The Kingsmen, whose version of "Louie, Louie" was a smash in 1963—spawning even more "why not we?" quartets.

## SAN FRANCISCO SOUND

Over the two years before the "Summer of Love" of 1967, a new rock sound began to build in San Francisco, California, centered around bands like The Great Society, Jefferson Airplane, The Grateful Dead, Big Brother and the Holding Company, Country Joe and the Fish, Moby Grape, The Steve Miller Band, Sly and the Family Stone, Mother Earth, and Quicksilver Messenger Service. Much looser in structure than earlier rock and roll or even the rock of the British Invasion, it was prone to free-form improvisation of a sort requiring either great talent in the frontperson to hold it all together or a high level of musicianship in the group as a whole. Grace Slick, for example, recognized this and jumped from her first band, The Great Society, to Jefferson Airplane. For general pop purposes, both bands were fine, but the skills of Jefferson Airplane took their work to a level of musicianship that, while rare in the pop world up to that time, was becoming necessary in the rock world. Just so, Janis Joplin would leave Big Brother and the Holding Company in 1968.

The bands of the San Francisco Sound were at least as interested in live performance as they were in working in the recording studio. They were inching toward a new ethos where the music and the lifestyle were more important than the money, though the inching stopped quite soon.

## SOUL/RHYTHM AND BLUES

The 1960s was a tremendous decade for soul and rhythm and blues. It was the time of James Brown, Aretha Franklin, Ray Charles, Otis Redding, and even

Sam Cooke, though he died in 1964. Two of the top 20 songs of the decade, "I Can't Stop Loving You" by Ray Charles (#12), and Otis Redding's "(Sittin' on) the Dock of the Bay" (#19), came out of these related genres. It was also the decade when this music finally broke with its gospel roots and smashed the racial barriers between audiences.

James Brown and Ray Charles led the way throughout the decade, both established stars within the black community when the decade began, superstars across the country when it ended. Brown could sing "I'm Black, I'm Proud" with many white people appreciating what he was doing, without causing racial strife. Charles could record country tunes and have a hit with Hoagy Carmichael's old "Georgia on My Mind."

With Cooke gone, it looked like rhythm and blues (R&B) might have a hard time of it, the genre's driving force gone from the scene. But two new voices, one of which, unfortunately, would not live out the decade, gave R&B a new force: Aretha Franklin and Otis Redding. Franklin had a power not heard since the days of Bessie Smith and the knowledge of life to contain it. Redding, who wrote the song "Respect" that Franklin had such a hit with, conveyed loss and pain with an emotional strength that he reached far across genre lines in his appeal.

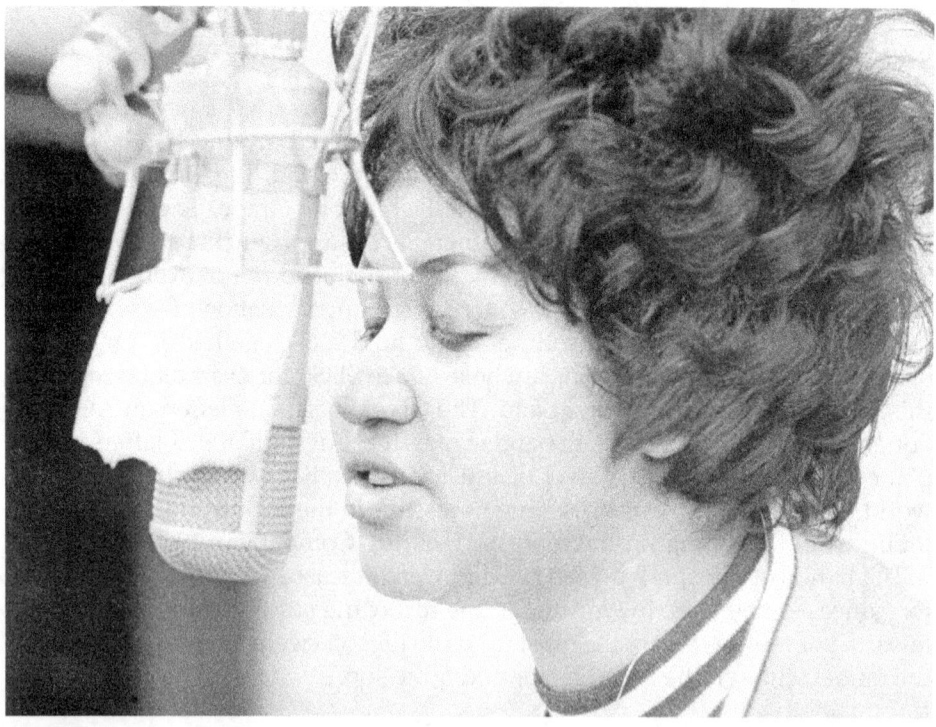

By the end of the 1960s, "The First Lady of Soul," Aretha Franklin, had shown that her talents rose above all genres. Here, she is recording her version of The Band's song "The Weight" in 1969. (Michael Ochs Archives/Getty Images)

## SURFER AND HOT ROD

Though The Beach Boys and Jan and Dean remain the best-known examples of surfer and hot rod music, guitarist Dick Dale, certainly the father of surfer music, probably had more influence on both than either of the more popular bands. It was to accommodate his sound that led to the combination of the Fender Stratocaster and large JBL speakers that underlay the power guitar of the 1960s.

The Beach Boys, behind the creative power of Brian Wilson, took surf music national and also contributed to the hot rod music craze. Songs like "Surfin' U.S.A." and "Surfin' Safari" promoted interest in surfer music even as far from the ocean as North Dakota while their "Little Deuce Coup" and "Fun, Fun, Fun" further emphasized the importance of the car to American youth culture everywhere. Wilson, unsatisfied with simple pop formulas, would eventually move the band elsewhere, but it is still for surfer and hot rod music that the band is best remembered.

Though they had been moderately successful for some years, Jan and Dean broke through to pop stardom with "Surf City," a song cowritten by Jan Berry and Brian Wilson in 1963, quickly followed by "Drag City," "Dead Man's Curve," and "The Little Old Lady from Pasadena."

The surfer and hot rod genre did not survive the British Invasion, but it was heavily influential on subsequent rock, from Dick Dale's guitar, and pop, from its close attention to vocal harmonies.

## TELEVISION MUSICAL AND VARIETY SHOWS

Though he had been on the air for more than a decade when the 1960s started, Ed Sullivan and his *The Ed Sullivan Show* became an important part of youth culture through promotion of acts like The Beatles and The Supremes, perhaps the two most important musical groups, in terms of enduring popularity, who performed principally in that decade. However, the young musicians were not always happy with Sullivan. Bob Dylan famously walked out when told he could not perform one of his songs, and Jim Morrison of The Doors, after agreeing to change a line in "Light My Fire" (something Sullivan asked bands to do when the lyrics were deemed too risqué) went on and sang the original words, much to Sullivan's displeasure. Even though they would tune in to watch their favorites, young people would not often stay to watch the rest of the show.

Like *The Ed Sullivan Show*, most of the musical variety shows of the decade focused on music for the older generation, with an occasional youth act thrown in. Among the most lasting of these were *The Andy Williams Show* (1962–1971), *The Danny Kaye Show* (1963–1967), *The Hollywood Palace* (1964–1970), and *The Dean Martin Show* (1965–1974). One of the most enduring musical variety shows was *The Lawrence Welk Show*, which ran from well before the 1960s started and for years afterward. Though the format was one of music performed by the show's "family" of acts and not guests, it remained a touchstone of American musical culture for decades.

The most enduring top 40 television showcase, *American Bandstand*, ran through the decade, its host Dick Clark becoming one of the most recognizable figures for the baby boom generation. Most of the performances were lip-synched, however, the purpose being to promote the records more than the performers.

*Hootenanny*, which ran on ABC in 1963 and 1964, tried to take advantage of the folk craze but featured the second tier of the stars in the genre after refusing to consider airing Pete Seeger due to his political associations. Neither Joan Baez nor Bob Dylan ever appeared, nor did Tom Paxton, Peter, Paul and Mary, Judy Collins, or Phil Ochs. The show was canceled, in part due to a dwindling pool of talent, and replaced by *Shindig!*, an attempt to cash in on the British Invasion and the changes going on in pop music.

*Shingdig!* ran for two seasons with broadcasts from both the United States and Great Britain. It featured some of the top acts from both countries (including The Beatles). The success of *Shindig!* led to a number of imitators, most notably *Hullabaloo*, which ran for two seasons in 1965 and 1966.

The musical variety show most influential on American popular culture in the late 1960s was *The Smothers Brothers Comedy Hour*, which ran from 1967 until it was canceled as a result of censorship disputes in 1969. Mixing music with satire and politics, the show appealed to 1960s youth as no musical variety show before had, not even *Shindig!* and *Hullabaloo*. The show reached further up into the pantheon of musical stars for the young even than *The Ed Sullivan Show* and *Shindig!* (if you discount The Beatles), featuring performers from a broad range of popular genres. Pete Seeger and Joan Baez both appeared, as did Buffalo Springfield, Ray Charles, Cream, Donovan, The Doors, Jefferson Airplane, Simon and Garfunkel, and The Who. No show up to that time so effectively reflected the tastes of baby boomer audiences.

## TEEN IDOLS

To be a teen idol in the 1960s did not necessarily mean being devoid of musical talent, though that sometimes seemed to be the case. Not all of them were even manufactured based on their looks, though many were. The best example, probably, is Ricky Nelson, son of Ozzie and Harriet Nelson and who grew up, so to speak, on their television show *The Adventures of Ozzie and Harriet*, which ran from 1952 to 1966. It was on the show, also, that he began his musical career as a seventeen-year-old in 1957. His biggest hit, "Travelin' Man," reached #1 in 1961, but he was on the top 100 charts often until 1964. Though his good looks and television pedigree did not hurt him, he was a legitimate musician and worked hard to overcome the "teen idol" label.

Perhaps the biggest teen idol of the early 1960s was Annette Funicello, who moved from 1950s fame on *The Mickey Mouse Club* to a series of beach movies for American International Pictures. With a small, almost reedy voice, she had little success as a singer but became a major hit in the movies.

Made popular by regular appearances on the television show *Shindig!*, Bobby Sherman served as a teen idol throughout much of the 1960s. In 1969, he scored his only real hit with "Little Woman."

Patterned after The Beatles, the four stars of the television show *The Monkees* (1966–1968) were the major teen idols of the late 1960s. Considering the members of the band were hired as actors, not musicians (though three of them did have musical experience, much of the music credited to the band was recorded by studio musicians), they had a surprising string of six top 10 hits in less than two years, starting with "Last Train to Clarksville" and ending with "Valleri."

## BOB DYLAN

There can be little doubt that Bob Dylan was the most influential musician of the 1960s, though his virtuosity lay neither in his voice nor in his guitar or harmonica. It was his songwriting and his innovation that drew people to him, along with his skill in recognizing the virtuosity of others. In 2016, he was awarded the Nobel Prize for Literature "for having created new poetic expressions within the great American song tradition." But he has done more than that; he has changed the American song, opening it up to possibilities never before imagined.

Often charged with musical and lyrical theft, and even plagiarism, Dylan is part of an American tradition that the shrinking of the commons (those things available for use by anyone) through copyright and the advent of recorded music has severely limited. Few songs, even into the twentieth century, could legitimately be claimed as "original" compositions, that is, as not being the direct descendants of other songs, sometimes close enough to be claimed as simply alternative versions. Songwriters, particularly those also performing their work, would simply take the song of another, give it their own twist, and perform it. As they moved it further and further from the original, they would claim it as their own.

Dylan did this, particularly in his early years, more concerned with the song and the performance than with the niceties of copyright—anyhow, most of what he was taking from was in the commons, the public domain. His "Girl from the North Country" was immediately identifiable as a descendant of the English ballad "Scarborough Fair" and "A Hard Rain's a-Gonna Fall" owes its chorus and structure to a ballad of the lowland Scots, "Lord Randall." Dylan modeled many of his early songs on those of Woody Guthrie and others of the earlier American folk tradition, drawing heavily on their tunes, images, and structures.

At the same time that he was learning and adapting from older music, Dylan was gaining skill and confidence in his own compositions. He soon began to chafe at limitations he felt imposed on him not only by tradition but by the music industry and the folk genre that had heretofore sustained him. As he wrote in "Maggie's Farm," "I try my best to be just like I am/But everybody wants me to be just like them." As his success grew, he had fewer and fewer reasons to listen, and so, he began to strike out in directions dictated by his inner interests and not by commercial considerations.

When he plugged in his guitar to an electric amplifier at the Newport Folk Festival, Dylan wasn't trying to shock or make any sort of statement; he was simply trying to play his music in the manner he saw fit. His inner imaginings of what he wanted led him to increased time in the studio and to a continual quest over the next few years for accompanying musicians who could express what he heard internally.

The 1960s roughly corresponded with Dylan's twenties, the decade of greatest creativity for most people, and Dylan used it well, going from the raw almost unnoticed interpreter of older songs (with one or two compositions of his own) on his 1961 debut album *Bob Dylan* to a sophisticated songwriter with an eye for talent who could circle back to an approximation to his self-appropriated "rustic" roots to a new type of simple-by-design that continued to present music a step ahead of his fans—as he had been doing since *Bringing It All Back Home* in 1965—but also stepping backward and letting others pass by.

It's hard to say where Dylan's peak in the 1960s lies. Possibly, it is with the frenetic *Highway 61 Revisited* that includes, as well as "Like a Rolling Stone," "Desolation Row," a somewhat encyclopedic examination of American culture in the tradition of his slightly earlier "It's All Right Ma, I'm Only Bleeding" and even "A Hard Rain's a-Gonna Fall." Listening to the album feels like a rush through musical styles and lyrical topics, a rush evoked by its very title, which refers to a highway down the Mississippi from Minnesota to Louisiana, passing through a bewildering variety of landscapes and even cultures on its way to the Gulf of Mexico. The feel of the album is like that of a road trip—one song, significantly, is titled "From a Buick 6." A listener can almost visualize its composition on a pad in the backseat of a Skylark, say, with a V6 engine as the car purrs through Arkansas toward the Mississippi Delta.

Possibly, Dylan's high point of creativity in the 1960s lies with his 1966 album *Blonde on Blonde* with lyricism that reminds some of John Keats. Lines like "The ghost of electricity howls in the bones of her face" from "Visions of Johanna" had never before been heard in any of the genres of the American popular song. "Sad Eyed Lady of the Lowlands," at more than 11 minutes, pushed the limits of the popular song to include spaces no one had ever expected, its desultory structure and unanswered questions. And the haunting "I Want You" is like no other love song ever recorded in an American studio.

Or maybe the pinnacle comes with *John Wesley Harding*, released at the end of 1967, with its return to a simpler sound and a reliance on allegory and story where Dylan himself may become "the little neighbor boy" with "his guilt so well concealed" of "The Ballad of Frankie Lee and Judas Priest." The album also contains "All Along the Watchtower," which would soon be turned into a classic by Jimi Hendrix, and "As I Walked Out One Morning," which in some ways seems like an abbreviated companion to W. H. Auden's "As I Walked Out One Evening."

Any way one looks at it, Dylan was the most important musical artist of the 1960s and its most distinctive voice. Without him, the decade would have sounded quite different from what it turned out to be.

## TRAGEDIES IN MUSIC

The 1960s decade was bracketed by deaths in popular music. The plane crash in 1959 that killed Buddy Holly, The Big Bopper, and Richie Valens presented its preamble, and the deaths from drugs of Janis Joplin and Jimi Hendrix in 1970 (with Jim Morrison following close behind in 1971) provided a tragic coda. It would continue to be vehicular accidents that claimed the lives of stars whose arcs were cut short by other than disease, with surprisingly few succumbing to drugs or alcohol. Others, like Nat King Cole, who died from lung cancer in 1965 at forty-five, and John Coltrane, felled by liver cancer at forty, were brought down by disease, and one major star died of gunshot wounds.

On March 5, 1963, the small Piper Comanche carrying thirty-year-old country and western superstar Patsy Cline crashed in bad weather, killing all on board. Almost two years earlier, she had barely survived an automobile crash and carried scars on her forehead from that. Her death stunned the Nashville country music scene and likely set back the integration of country into the broader American popular music scene, for Cline had been one of Nashville's first stars to attain real crossover success.

Sam Cooke, probably the most influential rhythm and blues musician of his time (only Ray Charles could perhaps match him), died after being shot in a motel office in Los Angeles, California, on December 11, 1964. The details of the incident remain murky, but alcohol and a possible prostitute were involved. His death was doubly tragic, for Cooke, who was only thirty-three when he died, had recently recorded the hopeful "A Change Is Gonna Come," which would become a civil rights anthem, melding protest and political activism into mainstream American music.

Perhaps the only songwriter within the folk movement who could match Dylan's talent, Richard Fariña was also a part of Dylan's inner circle. One of Dylan's first recordings was as a harmonica player on an album of Fariña's first wife, Carolyn Hester. Fariña's second wife was Mimi Baez, sister of Dylan's lover and passionate advocate, Joan Baez. Though he had only moderate success as a musician (teamed with his wife), Fariña's songs were gaining recognition when he died in a motorcycle accident on April 30, 1966, just two days after publication of his novel *Been Down So Long It Looks Like Up to Me*. He was twenty-nine years old.

Dave Lambert's greatest popularity was in the late 1950s and early 1960s when he teamed up with Annie Ross and Jon Hendricks to create Lambert, Hendricks & Ross, one of the premier jazz vocal groups of the time and one whose influence continues. He died when struck by a truck while changing a tire on a Connecticut Turnpike on October 3, 1966. He was forty-nine years old.

After his success at the 1967 Monterey Pop Festival, Otis Redding was beginning to have the kind of success with integrated and white audiences that he had already achieved with black ones. At the same time, Aretha Franklin's version of his "Respect" was charting at #1. The future looked bright with "Sittin' on the Dock of the Bay" ready for release when Redding's plane crashed into Lake Monona in Madison, Wisconsin, on December 10, 1967, killing all but one aboard, taking away one of the greatest talents of his generation. He was twenty-six years old.

Frankie Lymon's greatest success was in the 1950s when, with The Teenagers, he scored with "Why Do Fools Fall in Love." A heroin addict from a young age, he wasn't able to maintain his career and his habit. He was found dead of an overdose on February 27, 1968. Though he was only twenty-five when he died, he had been a star for over a decade.

## RECORDS AND CASSETTES

At the beginning of the 1960s, Americans could own recordings of music to play in their homes on records of three types: the old and no-longer-produced 78-rpm discs, 45-rpm singles, and 33-rpm long-playing (LP) albums of multiple songs that were beginning to be available in both monaural and the new stereo configuration. In addition, some people owned reel-to-reel 1/4-inch magnetic audiotape systems with 7-inch reels that could play prerecorded tapes (which were somewhat rare) or tapes recorded at home. At the time, these were the only vehicles for playback of recorded music available to the general public and, indeed, almost anyone. Yes, there was music offered on television and radio, but these lacked any sort of "on demand" system for listener playback control. The best one could do was call a radio station and request that a particular record be played.

Over the decade, with the development of superior home stereo players, the popularity of the 33-rpm album grew and the audiophile became more common and more sophisticated. Though the highest-quality sound came from the reel-to-reel tapes, the records were much easier to use and store, and cover art as well as commentary on the backs, as well as the technical quality of records themselves, improved dramatically, helping the record album become the heart of home music collection. By the end of the decade, almost every baby boomer had a collection of at least some dozens of albums, sometimes numbering well into the hundreds. By that time, too, the 45-rpm single (which had been the mainstay of youth home-listening in the 1950s) was beginning its decline, and the reel-to-reel machine was also disappearing, replaced by the lower quality but much cheaper compact cassette tape and the 8-track tape system, both of which came on the American market in the mid-1960s.

Though prerecorded compact cassettes and 8-tracks were available in growing numbers over the years after the systems' introduction, especially after car players were introduced, they remained secondary in popularity to vinyl records. The 8-track players for cars were immediately popular (automobile compact cassette players came a little later), but a clunk when tracks were changed could interrupt songs; tapes, like those of compact cassettes, were prone to breaks and snarls, these last being particularly difficult to straighten in cassettes. The quality of compact cassette players and of the tapes themselves was fairly low throughout the 1960s, keeping them from reaching the popularity they would find in later decades.

Cassettes and the small machines that played them did have advantages, however. They were portable and easy to use. Designed originally as recorders as much as playback machines (unlike the 8-tracks, which only did the latter), the cassette recorder could capture live music, political speeches, and many other sounds. Andy Warhol quickly saw the possibilities of this easy-to-use technology and began carrying and using a cassette recorder along with his omnipresent camera in 1965. His 1968 book *a, A Novel* is comprised of transcriptions of cassette recordings he made with actor Ondine (Robert Olivio) in 1965, 1966, and 1967.

Still, it was that the vinyl record album that remained dominant throughout the 1960s, with record stores selling both new and used LPs becoming common to just about every American city and town by the end of the decade, replacing the record aisles that had expanded to the point of near domination in stores like Kresge's and its 1960s offshoot Kmart.

In most genres, before 1960, LPs were simply collections of songs built (often) around what was hoped would be a hit single with pictures of performers on the cover and track lists on back. In the 1950s, in jazz, however, musicians had started to see the new LP format as a single canvas rather than simply an anthology and, for musical shows, the album (as it had done in the days of the 78) followed the progression of the live production, making the listening experience one whole rather than just a compendium of separate songs. In the 1960s, musicians in other genres began to follow suit, especially folk artists and, by the middle of the decade, rock artists. By the end of the decade, the LP had become a total package, song progressions carefully crafted (sometimes into "concept" albums where the songs form a sort of narration) and coordinated with covers that sometimes folded out, containing the artwork, lyrics, and commentary that were part of the package and increasingly valued by young fans. Covers also served as identifiers for young people, the records in their collections giving immediate indication of their tastes and predilections. Although the cover of The Beatles' *Sgt. Pepper's Lonely Hearts Club Band* remains one of the two most famous of the decade, along with R. Crumb's artwork for Big Brother and the Holding Company's *Cheap Thrills*, others were almost as stunning. Among the most memorable album artwork is the parody of *Sgt. Pepper's* that was meant for the cover of The Mothers of Invention's *We're Only in It for the Money*, but that the record company forced inside, and Andy Warhol's banana cover for *The Velvet Underground and Nico*.

Though singles taken from the albums remained extremely important, by the late 1960s, it was clearly the albums as a whole that were becoming the works of art in almost every genre (with country coming behind), certainly after the success of *Sgt. Pepper's Lonely Hearts Club Band* in 1967. For artists, there was now added flexibility in song length, the basic 3-minute standard of the 45 disappearing, allowing artists to record songs, such as Bob Dylan's "Sad Eyed Lady of the Lowlands" for his 1966 *Blonde on Blonde*, that could even take up one entire album side.

If any particular type of work of art can be said to have been emblematic of the 1960s, it was the LP, especially when considered as a whole, with artwork and liner notes included. It grew in all respects over the decade during which the baby boomers who bought them so eagerly also grew up. What had once been simply another medium for making money from the popular song had become the art of a generation from its music to its images.

## RADIO

Though the higher-quality and often stereophonic sound of FM radio began to make inroads during the 1960s, radio broadcasting during the decade was still dominated by the AM band. Though the decade did see the start of news radio and talk radio, music programming was the most important part of American radio. And most of that was directed at youth and dominated by *Billboard* magazine's Hot 100.

In 1963, FM was first offered as an option for automobile radios. FM would become more popular for both cars and homes over the decade though a simple AM radio was still the standard equipment offered in most cars, and the transistor radios that had been introduced in the 1950s and dominated radio had come to dominate the decision making of radio programmers. One reason for this was that the transistor radio had become almost ubiquitous even though the sound, at the time, was tinny, at best. Though FM sound was superior (especially once FM stereo was introduced), few portable radios received it. There was no point; the increased broadcast quality would be lost by the inadequate reception of the small radios. At the start of the decade, as a result, most FM stations were simply simulcasts of sister AM stations for the minority of listeners using state-of-the-art home (and not portable) equipment. This lasted until a Federal Communications Commission ruling against the practice went into effect at the start of 1967. From that time on, FM quickly built a new and separate audience and style of programming from its AM ancestors.

### AM

Television had changed radio extensively during the 1950s. Narrative entertainment—particularly the soap operas and situation comedies that had become radio mainstays—had abandoned radio for the new small screen. Radio turned to music programming, particularly programming aimed at the young, to fill what would otherwise have been empty air. Still, those changes brought about by television aside, the 1960s did not start off well for radio. The payola scandal, investigated by Congress in 1960, uncovered a system of paying disc jockeys for airing records, spawned distrust in the accuracy of top 40 rankings but had little impact on the teen listeners who were now dominating the radio audience.

Talk radio, which would come to dominate the AM dial, was in its infancy during the 1960s, leaving the music programming formats of earlier decades in a dominant position. That would change over the 1960s as new sorts of programming, including all-news, the glimmering of oldies rock, expanded sports broadcasting (including sports talk) and talk formats, began to appear.

Although the all-news format had been around since the start of the 1960s, it was not an immediate hit. Soon, however, a successful pattern did evolve of major hourly national/international news broadcasts with recaps sometimes as often as every 15 minutes along with local, business and sports news, and the weather. By the start of the 1970s, along with the hourly news roundups on almost all stations, news would become a mainstay of American radio. The broadcasts were not enhanced by the technical advantages of FM, so the all-news format remained primarily on the AM dial.

### FM

By 1967, baby boomers were tiring of radio that did not reflect their changed record-buying tastes and new listening habits. In San Francisco, just in time for the Summer of Love, a small FM station, KMPX, initiated what would become a new format, "freedom rock," which quickly became "progressive rock." Playing album cuts from an expansive collection of genres, the station quickly grew in popularity, the new format catching on with FM stations as far away as New York by the end of the year. This would prove the real breakout for FM, something that AM stations, with their lower sound quality, were unable to match.

## RADIO PERSONALITIES

The 1960s were not dominated quite as much by on-air personalities as the 1950s had been, but there were still a number who stood out:

### Dick Biondi

Already a successful over-the-top (screaming) radio personality when the 1960s began, Biondi gained national recognition as a disc jockey for Chicago's WLS, a 50,000-watt clear channel station where he anchored the nighttime programming until he was fired for telling an off-color joke on air. In the mid-1960s, he hosted a syndicated top 40 show for the Mutual Broadcasting System after moving to Los Angeles. He returned to Chicago in 1967 to work at WLS rival WCFL.

### Murray Kaufman (Murray the K)

"Murray the K" was a New York City radio host in the 1960s who managed to work his way into The Beatles entourage during the band's first visit to the United States in early 1964. He accompanied them during their tour, broadcasting live from their stops. By 1967, he had moved to FM on WNEW where he became one of the first progressive-rock DJs.

### Joe Pyne

There were talk shows in the 1960s, but few were of the in-your-face variety that would become popular several decades later—except for *The Joe Pyne Show*. Though it was on television as well, the show was syndicated to well over two hundred radio stations by the late 1960s, making radio Pyne's primary medium. Very conservative (though iconoclastic) Pyne loved confrontation, which bought listener loyalty even from those who didn't always agree with him. He pioneered what would become a mainstay of AM radio over future decades but was almost alone in the format in the 1960s.

American radio, at the end of the 1960s, was quite different from what it had been at the start. The genres, except for oldies, that have become the foundations of radio's continued success throughout the century, were all in place by the end of the decade while, at the start, radio had been dominated by only two of them, top 40 and country.

### Robert Weston Smith (Wolfman Jack)

"Wolfman Jack" was the on-air personality created by Smith in the early 1960s who broadcast via tape out of Ciudad Acuña, Mexico, on a signal higher in power than was allowed in the United States, so powerful that it could cover much of the country. His gravelly voice made him into an instantly recognizable personality that he began to trade on outside of radio, keeping him in the public eye throughout the decade.

## FURTHER READING

Banes, Sally. *Reinventing Dance in the 1960s: Everything Was Possible*. Madison: University of Wisconsin Press, 2003.
Baraka, Amiri. *Blues People: Negro Music in White America*. New York: Perennial, 2002.
Bernstein, David W., and Christopher Hatch, eds. *Writings through John Cage's Music, Poetry, and Art*. Chicago: University of Chicago Press, 2001.
Blaine, Hal, and David Goggin. *Hal Blaine and the Wrecking Crew*. Emeryville, CA: Mix Books, 1990.
Duckworth, William. *Talking Music: Conversations with John Cage, Philip Glass, Laurie Anderson, and Five Generations of American Experimental Composers*. New York: Da Capo Press, 1999.
Frith, Simon. *The Sociology of Rock*. London: Constable, 1978.
Goldstein, Richard. *Goldstein's Greatest Hits: A Book Mostly about Rock 'n' Roll*. New York: Tower Publications, 1970.
Ladd, Jim. *Radio Waves: Life and Revolution on the FM Dial*. New York: St. Martin's Press, 1991.
Lejeunne, Denis. *The Radical Use of Chance in 20th Century Art*. Amsterdam: Rodopi Press, 2012.
Nicholls, David, ed. *The Cambridge Companion to John Cage*. Cambridge: Cambridge University Press, 2002.
Perrone, James E. *Music of the Counterculture Era*. Westport, CT: Greenwood Publishing Group, 2004.
Ratcliffe, Philip R. *Mississippi John Hurt: His Life, His Times, His Blues*. Jackson: University Press of Mississippi, 2011.

# CHAPTER 4

# Literature

## BEST SELLERS: FICTION

The annual lists of best-selling fiction included a fairly large number of titles that not only would be categorized as "serious" or "literary" fiction but that are regarded as major novels of the period. These titles would include: J. D. Salinger's *Franny and Zooey* (1961–1962) and *Raise High the Roofbeams, Carpenters, and Seymour—An Introduction* (1963), Harper Lee's *To Kill a Mockingbird* (1961), Henry Miller's *Tropic of Cancer* (1961), John Steinbeck's *The Winter of Our Discontent* (1961), William Faulkner's *The Reivers* (1962), Katherine Ann Porter's *Ship of Fools* (1962), John Rechy's *City of Night* (1963), Mary McCarthy's *The Group* (1963), Terry Southern and Mason Hoffenberg's *Candy* (1964), Saul Bellow's *Herzog* (1964–1965), Bernard Malamud's *The Fixer* (1966), William Styron's *The Confessions of Nat Turner* (1967), Thornton Wilder's *The Eighth Day* (1967), Gore Vidal's *Myra Breckinridge* (1968), John Updike's *Couples* (1968), and Philip Roth's *Portnoy's Complaint* (1969). (Note the years in parentheses refer not to the year of publication but to the year or years on the best seller list.)

Several other authors clearly had serious literary ambitions, but their critical reputations have been fading with time. Louis Auchincloss, whose career extended from the late 1940s to the 2000s, focused primarily on the professional and business classes of New York and, in the 1960s, produced the best sellers *The Rector of Justin* (1964) and *The Embezzler* (1966). John O'Hara focused similarly on the professional and business classes of southeastern Pennsylvania. O'Hara came to national attention in the 1930s with *Appointment in Samarra* (1934) and *Butterfield 8* (1935); his novels of the 1960s extended a string of much more expansive, best-selling works that began in the late 1940s: *Ourselves to Know* (1960), *Sermons and Soda-Water* (1960), and *Elizabeth Appleton* (1963).

Three of the best-selling novels of the 1960s had a major cultural and literary impact that extended well beyond the decade. James Clavell's *Tai-Pan* (1966) resurrected the interest in Western fictions about Asia, which had peaked with Pearl Buck's novels of the 1930s but then declined dramatically after the Second World War, with the exception of novels treating the war itself. Ira Levin's *Rosemary's Baby* (1967) moved the horror genre into the mainstream. And Mario Puzo's *The Godfather* (1969) transformed the Mafia from a topic of investigative nonfiction into a major subject of not just fiction but film.

It should not be surprising that a decade that included charismatic political figures, closely contested elections, political assassinations, and political and cultural mass movements would produce a large number of best-selling novels on very timely political, historical, and culturally timely topics. Allen Drury focused on insiders' views of political machinations in such best sellers as *Advise and Consent* (1960), *A Shade of Difference* (1962), *Capable of Honor* (1966), and *Preserve and Protect* (1968). Fletcher Knebel and Charles W. Bailey II collaborated on the political thrillers *Seven Days in May* (1962) and *Convention* (1964), and Knebel was the sole author of *Vanished* (1968). Arthur Hailey specialized in focusing on major industries in moments of crisis, with *Hotel* (1965) and *Airport* (1968) being just the first novels in a string of best sellers. Elia Kazan, the critically lauded but politically controversial film director, began writing novels. *The Arrangement* (1967) was a huge best seller and provided a sort of 1960s update on *The Man in the Gray Flannel Suit*, charting the psychological cost of focusing ruthlessly on professional success. Edwin O'Connor's fiction provided an insider's view of politicians and others typically on a somewhat more local scale. His most remembered novel, *The Last Hurrah* (1956) had focused on the political career of a mayor and the challenges to the political machine that he leads. *The Edge of Sadness* (1961), a portrait of a priest, won the Pulitzer Prize as well as being a best seller, and *All in the Family* (1966) focuses on a political family very clearly modeled on the Kennedys. For the most part, Leon Uris focused on political intrigue of historical importance, producing the best sellers *Mila 18* (1961) about the Warsaw ghetto uprising, *Armageddon* (1964) about life in Berlin from the Soviet assault on the city through the Berlin airlift, and *Topaz* (1967), about Cold War espionage. Largely forgotten today, Irving Wallace produced best-selling novels that had many of the characteristics of journalistic exposés—in particular, detailed research and intimate revelations: *The Chapman Report* (1960), *The Prize* (1962), *The Man* (1964), *The Plot* (1967), and *The Seven Minutes* (1969). The Australian novelist Morris L. West focused primarily on international politics and, in particular, on the role of the Roman Catholic Church in international politics in such best sellers as *Daughter of Silence* (1961), *The Shoes of the Fisherman* (1963), *The Ambassador* (1965), and *The Tower of Babel* (1968). Herman Wouk is most remembered for novels about the Second World War, the very narrowly focused *The Caine Mutiny* (1951) and the much more expansive *The Winds of War* (1971). But, in between, he wrote the best sellers *Youngblood Hawke* (1962) and *Don't Stop the Carnival* (1965).

If Irving Wallace exploited the sexual elements of the timely topics that he treated in his novels, several other novelists made sexuality the salient feature of their fictions. Harold Robbins gave the hard-boiled fiction of the 1940s and 1950s a more casually vulgar turn in novels such as *The Carpetbaggers* (1961), *The*

*Adventurers* (1966), and *The Inheritors* (1969), and Jacqueline Susann explored changing sexual mores in a sensationalized way in *The Valley of the Dolls* (1966) and *The Love Machine* (1969).

Appealing in more conventional ways to a largely female leadership, several novelists who had established themselves decades earlier continued to work within the traditions of popular genres. Taylor Caldwell was primarily a writer of historical romances, producing the best sellers *The Listener* (1960), *Grandmother and the Priests* (1963), and *Testimony of Two Men* (1968). Mary Stewart specialized in romantic mysteries, often with Gothic elements, such as *The Rough Magic* (1964) and *The Gabriel Hounds* (1967). And Daphne Du Maurier wrote novels of romantic suspense such as *The Glass Blowers* (1963) and *The House on the Strand* (1969).

Bridging the romantic suspense and suspense-espionage genres, Helen MacInnes's career extended from the beginning of the 1940s to the middle of the 1980s. In the 1960s, her output included the best sellers such as *The Double Image* (1966) and *The Salzburg Connection* (1968). The suspense-espionage genre did not, of course, begin in the 1960s, but the careers of the two novelists most associated with it overlapped in the decade. John LeCarre published his first five novels, including the best sellers *The Spy Who Came in from the Cold* (1964), *The Looking Glass War* (1965), and *A Small Town in Germany* (1968). LeCarre's work in the genre has had a thematic seriousness and a literary style and sensibility that has led many critics to assert that it transcends the genre. In contrast, Ian Fleming began writing the James Bond novels in the 1950s, but they did not become best sellers in the United States until after they began to be adapted to films in the early 1960s. In fact, the first two Bond novels to become best sellers in the United States did so after Fleming's death—*You Only Live Twice* (1964) and *The Man with the Golden Gun* (1965). In contrast to LeCarre's novels, Fleming's novels feature satiric exaggeration—a somewhat cartoonish hero with very identifiable traits and catchphrases, who is equipped with somewhat futuristic gadgets to combat even more cartoonish villains, whose flamboyant eccentricities are matched by their grandiose schemes. It is difficult to imagine someone extending one of LeCarre's novels, but a series of novelists have extended the Bond series, turning the character into one of the most identifiable heroes of the Cold War era, and even beyond.

Two very popular novelists of the 1960s relied more on extensive historical research than on agile imaginations. James Michener's novels are typically set in the present but explore matters with deep and often arcane historical roots; indeed, many of his novels focus on histories of specific geographical settings that for some reason or another are of special current interest. His best sellers in the 1960s included *Hawaii* (1960), *Caravans* (1963), and *The Source* (1965). Irving Stone was more strictly a historical novelist, specializing in fictionalized biographies, as in the best sellers *The Agony and the Ecstasy* (1961–1962) and *Those Who Love* (1965).

In recent decades, multicultural fiction has become a staple of the best seller lists. But in the 1960s, one of the few multicultural novelists to achieve wide popularity was Chaim Potok, whose novels about Orthodox and Hasidic Jews included the best sellers *The Chosen* (1967) and *The Promise* (1969).

Two other best-selling authors of the decade are of historical and cultural interest. Though hardly a household name today, Catherine Marshall was the author of thirty books that sold more than 16 million copies. She came to national attention with *A Man Called Peter* (1951), her biography of her late husband, a prominent minister. In the 1960s, her novel *Christy* (1967–1968) spent two years on the best seller list. Based on her mother's experiences teaching in the isolated, poverty-stricken communities of Appalachia, the novel was turned into a television series. It stands today as one of the first works of "Christian fiction" to achieve a much broader popularity.

At the opposite end of the spectrum were Henry Sutton's string of best-selling novels, which began with *The Exhibitionist* (1967), which sold more than 4 million copies, and was followed by *The Voyeur*. Henry Sutton is a pseudonym of the highly regarded poet David R. Slavitt, who has written fiction in other popular genres under several other pseudonyms as well. He wrote *The Exhibitionist* under a pseudonym because it was very deliberately written to exploit the relaxed obscenity laws and the growing obsession with celebrity, and he rightly was concerned about the impact of the certain notoriety on his academic career and standing as a serious poet. Like most "racy" novels of the period, *The Exhibitionist* seems relatively tame today, and in our age of reality television and social media "stars," Slavitt's concerns about notoriety seem rather quaint.

## BEST SELLERS: NONFICTION

Of the one hundred titles in the nonfiction best seller lists for 1960 to 1969, twenty-six titles were related to cooking, homemaking, child care, diet, and health. Interestingly, seventeen of those twenty-six titles appeared on the lists from 1960 to 1963, and none from 1964 to 1966.

The nonfiction best seller lists for 1964 to 1967 included eleven titles related to President John F. Kennedy, two of which appeared on two of the annual lists. Kennedy's own book, *Profiles in Courage* (1955), appeared on the list in both 1963 and 1964, and in the three years immediately following his assassination, the following histories of his presidency were published: Bill Adler's *The Kennedy Wit* (1964), Jim Bishop's *A Day in the Life of President Kennedy* (1964), William F. Manchester's *Death of a President* (1967), Arthur M. Schlesinger Jr.'s *A Thousand Days*, which appeared on both the 1965 and the 1966 lists, Mark Shaw's *The John F. Kennedys* (1964), Theodore C. Sorensen's *Kennedy* (1965), and Theodore H. White's *The Making of the President* (1964). The Manchester, Schlesinger, Sorensen, and White books are still cited today, as is White's earlier book on Kennedy's election, *The Making of a President, 1960* (1961). In 1964, the number 1 best-selling nonfiction title was the American Heritage and United Press International's commemorative photo-book, *Four Days*. And although it was published only in December 1963, Victor Lasky's *J.F.K.: The Man and the Myth* was the number 3 nonfiction best seller for that year. Mark Lane's *Rush to Judgment* (1966), a critique of the findings of the Warren Commission on the Kennedy assassination, was the first in an ever-lengthening list of best-selling books suggesting that Lee Harvey Oswald was either part of a conspiracy to assassinate the president or one of several actual shooters.

The nonfiction best sellers for the decade also included several other political titles, including the following: Barry Goldwater's *The Conscience of a Conservative* (1960); William Lederer's *A Nation of Sheep* (1961), about the widespread ignorance of foreign policy among the American public; and Joe McGinness's *The Selling of the President 1968* (1969). Beyond these books on current politics, the best sellers included some titles on historical topics—William L. Shirer's landmark volume *The Rise and Fall of the Third Reich*, which remained on the list from 1960 to 1961, Frederic Morton's *The Rothschilds* (1962), about the family that amassed one of the world's great fortunes through international banking, Cornelius Ryan's *The Last Battle* (1994), about the cataclysmic battle for Berlin that closed the Second World War in the European theater, as well as such memoirs as General Douglas MacArthur's *Reminiscences* (1964).

Several memoirs by notable novelists also made the best seller lists in the 1960s. John Steinbeck's *Travels with Charley* (1962) recounted the novelist's travels by car around the United States with his dog. Ernest Hemingway's *A Moveable Feast* (1964), a memoir of his early years in Paris with his first wife Hadley, was published posthumously. Truman Capote's "nonfiction novel" *In Cold Blood* (1966), about the brutal and senseless murder of a Kansas farm family, and Rumer Godden's autobiographical novel about an extramarital affair interrupted by adolescent children, *The Battle of the Villa Fiorita* (1966), were included on the nonfiction lists.

A number of celebrities produced books that were anecdotal, part autobiography and part social observation, and generally humorous: late-night talk show host Johnny Carson's *Happiness Is a Dry Martini* (1965) and *Misery Is a Blind Date* (1967), comedienne Phyllis Diller's *Phyllis Diller's Housekeeping Hints* (1966) and *Phyllis Diller's Marriage Manual* (1967), Bob Hope's *I Owe Russia $1200* (1963), raconteur Alexander King's *May This House Be Safe from Tigers* (1960), Beatle John Lennon's *In His Own Write* (1964), and late-night talk show host Jack Paar's *I Kid You Not* (1960).

Several best sellers became focal points in the intensifying debate over conventional social mores. The "sexual revolution" was addressed in such best sellers as Helen Gurley Brown's *Sex and the Single Girl* (1963) and William Howard Masters and Virginia E. Johnston's *Human Sexual Response* (1966). Eric Berne more broadly explored the transactional nature of human relationships in *Games People Play*, which remained on the best seller list from 1965 to 1967. And Laurence J. Peter and Raymond Hull explained why people rise within organizations to the level of their incompetence in their best seller *The Peter Principle* (1969), which of course added another idiomatic expression to the language.

Books on spirituality have always been staple genre among nonfiction best sellers but especially when the sense of uncertainty is heightened by convulsive political events and natural disasters. *The New English Bible: The New Testament* was a best seller in 1961 and 1962. Other titles related to spirituality addressed topics from the state of formal religions to states of spiritual rapture to what we now classify as "new age" spirituality: Father James Kavanaugh's *A Modern Priest Looks at His Outdated Church* (1966), evangelist Billy Graham's *World Aflame*, Ruth Montgomery's *A Gift of Prophecy* (1965), Jess Stearn's *Edgar Cayce—The Sleeping Prophet* (1967), Jeane Dixon's *My Life and Prophecies* (1969), coauthored with Rene Noorbergen, and Linda Goodman's *Linda Goodman's Sun Signs* (1969), the first astrology book to make an annual best seller list.

Five years after the secretary general of the United Nations, Dag Hammarskjöld, died in a plane crash in central Africa while attempting to broker a peace agreement to end the civil war in the newly independent Congo, an English translation of his book, *Markings*, reached the U.S. best seller list in 1966. Drawn from the diaries that Hammarskjold had kept from his youth, the book was acclaimed as a profound record of his spiritual struggles and his deepening faith. Other inspirational best sellers of the 1960s included: Pat Boone's *Between You, Me, and the Bedpost* (1960), a paean to traditional values; Virginia Cary Hudson's *O Ye Jigs and Juleps!*, a fixture on the best seller list in 1962 and 1963, in which the author offered reflections on nineteenth-century values with an emphasis on family and community; and Sam Levinson's *Everything but Money* (1966), a reminiscence on how families not just survived the Great Depression but grew closer because of it. Louis Nizer's *My Life in Court* (1963) provided insights into the notable legal cases in which he was involved over his long and distinguished career as an attorney, and Bill Sands's *My Shadow Ran Fast* (1965) documents his transformation from a young man serving three life terms in the prison at San Quentin to a successful businessman and inspirational speaker and author.

There were other groups of best-selling nonfiction that might be described as a cross between inspirational and entertaining. The poet Rod McKuen was extraordinarily popular, even though his readership far exceeded his gifts as a poet. His books of best-selling poems included *Stanyan Street and Other Sorrows* (a best seller in both 1967 and 1968), *Listen to the Warm* (1968), *Lonesome Cities* (1968), *In Someone's Shadow* (1969), and *Twelve Years of Christmas* (1969). So, in the last two years of the decade, McKuen accounted for 25 percent of the twenty titles on the nonfiction best seller list. Likewise, Charles Schulz's *Peanuts* books were extremely popular, including the best sellers *Happiness Is a Warm Puppy* (the number 5 best seller in 1962 and the number 1 best seller in 1963), *Security Is a Thumb and a Blanket* (1963), *I Need All of the Friends That I Can Get* (1964), and *Christmas Is Together Time* (1964).

## COMICS AND CARTOONS

American children of the postwar generation, the baby boomers, were engrossed by comics, in the newspapers, in comic books, and as cartoons on television. Cartoon shorts at the movies, once a regular part of the packing of a film showing, had all but disappeared. Animated feature films were dominated by Disney but Hannah-Barbera Productions, the most successful creator of Saturday-morning cartoons, had started expanding its franchises into full-length movies.

This new generation grew up with comic books that were quite different from those of their parents and even older siblings due to the imposition of the Comics Code Authority (CCA) in the mid-1950s. This fundamentally changed comic books and would alter other cartoon genres as the influence of the new sort of comic book grew. Another unintended consequence of the CCA was the death of EC Comics and the rise of EC's *Mad Magazine*, which spun into Harvey Kurtzman's *Playboy* strips and, in the mid-1960s, the birth of underground comix.

Some of the 1950s comic books, ones with CCA approval and never coming close to controversy, did survive through the 1960s and beyond, and even most of the new cartoons of the decade were relatively benign. But work in cartoons and animation in the 1960s did lay the foundation for the diverse and expansive types of cartoons and animation we have today.

### DC and Marvel

Probably the single most important figure to superhero comics, a subgenre dominated by DC and Marvel, was Jack Kirby. He worked for both DC and the predecessors of Marvel in the late 1950s. In the 1960s, he returned to what was now called Marvel Comics and, working with Stan Lee, soon created *The Fantastic Four*. Quickly, Kirby became the dominant artistic force at Marvel, creating its look as well as its philosophy of art and story. In fact, through *The Fantastic Four* and the other new titles that followed on its heels, Kirby changed the superhero comic far beyond Marvel's pages. Even arch-rival DC began to show influence of his new style and thinking.

Though Marvel set the bar for 1960s superhero comic books, it was DC Comics that was pacing the genre when the decade started. Here again, though, Kirby had been at the center of things. Before his return to Marvel, Kirby had created *Challengers of the Unknown* for DC Comics' *Showcase Comics*, part of a late-1950s response to the repressive CCA and the vacuum that the death of EC's line of comic books had left. At first, it looked like DC Comics would be the only one filling it. In addition to the *Challengers of the Unknown* books, DC revitalized its older superheroes Superman, Batman, and Wonder Woman, updating the look of the comics and adding characters and spin-offs as well as detective and fantasy elements.

With Kirby again at Marvel, that brand shot ahead. Kirby and Lee, though never comfortable with each other, proved a good team, though Lee chose another artist, Steve Ditko, for *The Adventures of Spider-Man*, which would prove the most successful Marvel creation of the decade. However, even Ditko operated under Kirby's influence at Marvel and on American superhero comics in general.

### Preteen

One of the most successful comics of the 1960s was the *Archie* franchise. Though it had been around for almost two decades when the 1960s began, *Archie* continued to be strong, even spawning an animated TV show that made the main characters into a band—which produced a number of top 40 hits. Other comics were also aimed at preteens, including the Dell Comics titles from Disney, *Mickey Mouse* and *Donald Duck*. Another comic book aimed at this age group was *Richie Rich*, with the character appearing in his own book for the first time in 1960.

### MAD

Technically a magazine and not a comic book for all but its first few years in the 1950s (it changed format to avoid the CCA code), *MAD*'s first editor was Harvey Kurtzman, but a dispute over finances led publisher William Gaines to replace Kurtzman with Al Feldstein, who edited the magazine from 1956 until 1985. Kurtzman would go on to found another magazine of satire, *Help!* In 1960 he was hired to write the long-running strip *Little Annie Fannie* for *Playboy*, premiering in 1962. By the time he left, Kurtzman and Feldstein had made *MAD* into one of the most important publications for the baby boom generation—and had helped establish a milieu allowing for the rise of underground comix.

*MAD* spawned a number of other magazines of satire that included a substantial percentage of cartoons, including *Help!*, *Sick* (also founded in 1960), and *Cracked*, which preceded these other two by a couple of years and was the most closely imitative of *MAD*.

### Newspaper Strips, the Sunday Funny Pages, and Single-Panel Comics

The Sunday funnies in color, a pullout section in most newspapers, had been an American tradition for a generation by the time the 1960s began. The daily smaller black-and-white strips, though quite popular, never were associated with the same sense of family and routine and, even in the 1960s, nostalgia for simpler times. The most popular of the newspaper comic strips was *Peanuts*, which began to spin off into television and even popular song. Almost everyone in the country, by the start of the decade, could identify the characters and their primary traits. Baby boomers often had particular ones they identified with. *Li'l Abner* and *Pogo* remained quite popular, though Al Capp's right-wing politics, becoming more and more evident in the strip, alienated many of his younger readers. Walt Kelly, on the other hand, who long had worn his liberal beliefs on the sleeve of his strip, so to speak, gained followers. *Dennis the Menace* and the newcomer *B.C.* (the former sparking a television show and the latter a popular song) were also popular throughout the decade. Though it never appeared in newspapers, *Bazooka Joe* was known to all baby boomers, for it came wrapped about pieces of penny bubblegum.

Jules Feiffer and Charles Addams were two of the most popular cartoonists for magazines and weekly newspapers of the decade, Feiffer working for *The Village Voice* and winning an Academy Award in 1961 for writing the short animated film *Munro* and Addams contributing regularly to *The New Yorker*. His single-panel cartoons there spawned the mid-1960s *Addams Family* television show.

### Animated Movies

In the 1960s, American animated movies continued to be dominated by Disney, including *101 Dalmatians* (1961), *The Sword and the Stone* (1963), and *The*

*Jungle Book* (1967), but the television giant Hanna-Barbera Productions was beginning to make inroads with films from its TV shows. Probably the most significant animated movie of the decade, however, was *The Beatles: Yellow Submarine*. Even though it was not an American production, the chief animators were American, it brought Milton Glaser's "look" to the movie screen for the first time, and it had an immediate impact on American popular culture.

### Underground

Satire in comics arrived in strength in the 1950s with the creation of *MAD* magazine and its first editor's subsequent creation *Help!* In a number of ways, that editor, Harvey Kurtzman, along with artist Will Elder, could be said to be the father of the American underground comix movement of the 1960s. *Help!* published early work by Robert Crumb and Gilbert Shelton, two of the foundational artists of the underground-comix movement.

The year 1968 was critical for the formation of underground comix as a distinct genre and not simply a creature of college humor magazines and offbeat newspapers. Not only did *Zap Comix* #1 appear (with Crumb listed as "R. Crumb") but Shelton's *The Fabulous Furry Freak Brothers* was born, albeit for a college human magazine. *Zap*, which Sheldon would soon join, became the premier publication within what would prove to be a fast-growing (though small, in industry terms) and influential genre. In addition to Crumb and Shelton, S. Clay Wilson and a number of others contributed to *Zap* after its first Crumb-only issue.

### TRUMAN CAPOTE (1924–1984)

In terms of his public persona, Truman Capote was in most ways at the opposite end of the spectrum from Ernest Hemingway. Capote's early stories, published in such prestigious periodicals as *The Atlantic Monthly*, *Harper's*, *The New Yorker*, and *Story*, established him as a writer of considerable promise. But, although his first novel, *Other Voices, Other Rooms* (1948), was critically well received, it attracted considerable notoriety because the photo of Capote that appeared on the back of the dust jacket was perceived as homoerotically suggestive. Throughout the 1950s, Capote worked in various genres—short stories, film scripts, essays, travel writing, and other reportage. But he did not come to national attention again until *Breakfast at Tiffany's: A Novel and Three Short Stories* was published in 1958. The central character of *Breakfast at Tiffany's*, Holly Golightly, would become one of the most compelling female characters in American fiction published in the two decades following the Second World War. The sales of the book were again boosted by notoriety. In this case, Capote had arranged to have the novella published in *Harper's Bazaar* before the book was released. But when the magazine's publisher balked at publishing it out of concern that its subject matter would alienate Tiffany's, a major advertiser, *Esquire* agreed to publish the novella. The media attention to the controversy not only increased the sales of the magazine issue but also provided intensive and free prepublication promotion of the book, increasing its sales and making it a hot property for film adaptation. Moreover, despite the concerns of the publisher of *Harper's Bazaar*, the book and its film adaptation have also provided decades of free advertising for Tiffany's, making the luxury jewelry retailer a point of cultural reference in households throughout the country, regardless of whether the occupants have the means to shop there.

In 1959, as Capote was looking for a follow-up to *Breakfast at Tiffany's*, he came across a brief article in *The New York Times* about the murder of an entire family on their farm in rural Kansas. He decided to go to Kansas to investigate the story, even though at that point no one had any idea who the murderers might be and, therefore, what directions the story might take. Capote ended up inserting himself into the community and getting a very intimate sense of the impact of the crime on it. But, for him, the story really took shape when the murderers were arrested and awaiting trial. Getting access to both Dick Hickock and Perry Smith, Capote became especially close to Perry Smith, and the resulting book, *In Cold Blood*, derives much of its power from Capote's portrait of Smith's background and the psychological factors that led to his participation in the murders.

Truman Capote's novella *Breakfast at Tiffany's* became an iconic film in 1962, but his fame was cemented by his "non-fiction novel" *In Cold Blood* in 1966. (Library of Congress)

First serialized in *The New Yorker*, the book was an immediate sensation and best seller, and it has remained continuously in print since its publication in 1966. Several issues surrounding Capote's writing of the book have never been settled. First, the book's copyright date is 1965, but its publication date is 1966 because it was clear that Capote wanted to include an account of Hickock and Smith's executions, which were delayed. So, despite Capote's expressed empathy for them, and especially for Perry Smith, he clearly had material reasons for wanting to see them executed. Second, Capote claimed to have a photographic memory, and so he never took notes during interviews but, instead, waited until sometime later to compile those notes. Although there is no dispute that he took voluminous notes over the more than half-decade that he was following this story, journalists have been able to identify a number of instances in which Capote seemed to misquote his sources, to attribute quotations to sources that they did not make, or to invent details.

Lastly, the rise of the New Journalism both enhanced the reputation and further increased sales of the book and brought into question how it ought to be classified. In contrast to traditional reportage, the New Journalism was predicated on the immersion of the journalist into the stories that they were researching and writing about; it stressed the supremacy of "truth" over "facts" and therefore acknowledged and permitted the subjective perspective of the journalist; and it permitted a literary style—the adaptation of fictional techniques—to long-form nonfiction. *In Cold Blood* seemed to meet all of these requirements—to provide a masterful illustration of them in the opinion of many reviewers. But, quite soon after its publication, literary critics created a new classification for the book—the nonfiction novel. No one can argue that *In Cold Blood* did not become a model for many subsequent books in what is now a firmly established genre or that the fact that critics have sought to retroactively apply the label to works preceding Capote's book only reinforces, rather than undermines, the significance of *In Cold Blood*. However, both novelists and journalists acknowledge that there is a distinction between the New Journalism—or its more recent iteration, creative nonfiction—and the nonfiction novel. And the dispute over which of these categories best accommodates *In Cold Blood* has still not been definitively settled. In fact, the issue of Capote's veracity was resurrected when journalists were unable to identify the murder described in "Handcarved Coffins," described as a true crime story in the collection *Music for Chameleons* (1980).

After *In Cold Blood*, Capote never published another full-length book over the two remaining decades of his life. He became a celebrity, a fixture on talk shows and in magazine profiles, and his very idiosyncratic appearance, manner, and speech became as much a part of the popular culture as the defining characteristics of film stars, musical entertainers, and prominent political and social commentators. In effect, Capote reduced himself to a self-caricature, and worse, he began to cannibalize his celebrity in his work. Before they degenerated into self-caricature, Capote's idiosyncrasies, in combination with his obvious talent, had made him an intimate to a broadening circle of affluent and famous people, including many middle-aged women. These social connections reached their culmination in the Black and White Ball, a masked ball held in the Grand Ballroom of New York's Plaza Hotel that Capote organized to honor Katharine Graham, the publisher of *The Washington Post*. Because of the prominence of those who were invited to attend, the event received extensive coverage in all sorts of publications beyond the usual sources of celebrity gossip. Indeed, on anniversaries of the event, the media coverage is still resurrected, attesting to the event's cultural impact. While he was first investigating the crimes that were the basis of *In Cold Blood*, Capote conceived of a series of novels modeled on Marcel Proust's *Remembrance of Things Past* or, to use its more recent and literal title, *In Search of Lost Time*. The never fully realized and fragmentary work that resulted from that ambitious conception was a single book eventually called *Answered Prayers*. Capote may have initially planned to focus on the complexities and ambiguities of his own interior life, but the work evolved into a sort of gossipy insider's look at the lives of his prominent intimates. Although he publicly discussed the work in the late 1960s, none of it appeared in print until the mid-1970s, when several sections were published in *Esquire*. One of those pieces, titled "La Cote Basque 1965," provided intimate details of the private lives of William and Babe Paley. It not only outraged the Paleys but led to Capote's being ostracized by most of his affluent and famous intimates, who naturally were appalled that their secrets would be exposed as well. In the end, the posthumously published book, *Answered Prayers* (1986), was advertised as an "Unfinished Novel," and it had the impact of stale gossip.

Capote will be remembered for *In Cold Blood*. Indeed, because the increasing frequency of mass murders has made it impossible to keep up with the carnage—to culturally come to terms with its meaning—Capote's book, in focusing on an equally gratuitous crime with a much smaller body count offers readers a perspective on such crimes that is more comprehensible and still relevant. Not surprisingly, Capote himself has remained a figure of interest, though two recent, critically acclaimed biopics have focused on his life during the period that he was working on *In Cold Blood*. In *Capote* (2005), based on Gerald Clarke's biography published in 1988, Philip Seymour Hoffman portrayed the author, earning an Academy Award and four other major awards for his performance. Catherine Keener was also nominated for an Academy Award for her portrayal of Harper Lee, the author of *To Kill a Mockingbird*, who was one of Capote's closest, lifelong friends. In the following year, another Capote biopic, *Infamous*, was released. Starring Toby Jones as Capote and Sandra Bullock as Harper Lee, this film was based on George Plimpton's book *Truman Capote: In Which Various Friends, Enemies, Acquaintances and Detractors Recall His Turbulent Career* (1997). Although the film was critically well received, it generally suffered in comparisons to *Capote*, and although it was honored with some major award nominations, it did not win many of them.

## NORMAN MAILER (1923–2007)

If Truman Capote's public persona was at the opposite end of the spectrum from Ernest Hemingway's, Norman Mailer often appeared to be very deliberately cultivating a public persona as Hemingway's successor. Mailer came to immediate national attention with his first novel, *The Naked and the Dead* (1948). An exploration of the political and cultural divides between senior and junior officers and between all officers and ordinary soldiers, the novel was set on an island in the Pacific theater of the Second World War. An instant best seller that has remained continuously in print since its publication, *The Naked and the Dead* remains one of the most notable novels about the Second World War. Unfortunately for Mailer's long-term literary standing, it is also, arguably, his best novel—with the only other contender for that designation being *The Executioner's Song* (1979), which is a nonfiction novel about a murder and an execution that almost automatically invites comparisons to Capote's *In Cold Blood* but that is written in an entirely different style and has a much more ambitious thematic reach.

In the 1950s, Mailer struggled to replicate the success that he had achieved with *The Naked and the Dead*. His entire output of published books for the 1950s consisted of two lightly regarded novels and one collection of miscellaneous writing. The first of the novels, *Barbary Shore* (1951) focuses on a veteran of the Second World War, an amnesiac whose memories of his wartime experiences are just starting to return, in fragments. He is attempting to write a novel, but does not have much more success with bringing it to life than Mailer has with this novel. The main character lives in a Brooklyn boarding house where his neighbors of various stripes and backgrounds and undercover federal agents attempt to root out communists and their fellow travelers. Although Mailer's third novel, *The Deer Park* (1955), would be more successful commercially than *Barbary Shore*, it nonetheless reinforced the notion, both to critics and to Mailer himself, that he might be incapable of replicating the achievement of *The Naked and the Dead*. *The Deer Park* was drawn from Mailer's experiences as a screenwriter, but although a few prominent critics asserted that it had a place among the best novels written about Hollywood, it has not generally been included in that group of novels.

Coming after the failure of *Barbary Shore* and the modest success of *The Deer Park*, *Advertisements for Myself* (1959) was not only strange for its haphazardly gathered contents—essentially all of the writing that Mailer had done to that point that had not been collected into a book or was unlikely ever to see publication—but also for its persistent aim of supporting the author's promotion of himself as one of the greatest literary voices of his generation. The book heralded the dramatic change in Mailer's public persona and in his literary style that would extend through the 1960s and into the subsequent decades. Mailer presented himself as an antiestablishment voice—a formative voice in what would become the Counterculture of the 1960s, with its emphasis on the following: racial equality and a normalization of relations between the races; sexual liberation and the rejection of conformity to Puritan moral virtues, social mores, and social institutions that suddenly seemed anachronistic; a new sort of political radicalism that was based on a rejection of the military-industrial state and a reconnection with the foundational political principles of the American experiment; and a new interest in self-realization, in alternative religious paths to personal enlightenment and in the use of drugs to alter consciousness and access states of mind generally unreachable by other means. In retrospect, like many countercultural figures of the 1960s, Mailer remained anachronistically attached to the values of the old political Left and to restrictive notions about gender. With his pugnacious style, he sometimes came across as a Hemingwayesque figure in mod dress. It is important to note that, in the mid-1950s, as part of Mailer's increasing forays into extraliterary activities and his cultivation of an extraliterary level of celebrity, he cofounded, with Dan Wolf and Ed Fancher, the alternative weekly newspaper, *The Village Voice*. Although Mailer was initially intended to be a "silent partner" in the venture, he soon began contributing essays to the newspaper. One of his essays of this period, "The White Negro" (1957), which was originally published in *Dissent*, became a sort of manifesto of the hipster movement that bridged the Beat Movement of the 1950s and the Hippie Movement of the late 1960s.

For Mailer, the 1960s began with his being focused on organizing a campaign to get him elected as the mayor of New York in the 1961 election. In November 1960, Mailer and his wife, the painter Adele Morales, hosted a party in their apartment for about 200 guests—a mixture of potential campaign contributors and street people, ranging from young hipsters to actual homeless people—whom Mailer had the cockeyed notion of bringing together in that very crowded space to form a new political coalition. The affair quickly degenerated, with Mailer himself eventually becoming completely intoxicated and ranging outside to pick fights with passersby. At about four in the morning, Mailer and Morales got into an argument and he stabbed her twice with a penknife, once in the neck and once very close to her heart, inflicting a life-threatening wound. After she was taken to a neighbor's apartment and then rushed to the hospital for emergency surgery, Mailer's behavior was appalling—even if one makes allowances for his being very inebriated. After initially claiming that she had fallen on broken glass, Morales admitted that Mailer had stabbed her. He was taken before a judge, who committed him involuntarily to Bellevue Hospital for psychological evaluation. The main concern that Mailer expressed at that point was the potential long-term impact on his literary reputation. Although Morales refused to press charges, Mailer eventually was charged with felony assault, pled guilty to a reduced charge, and was given a suspended sentence and placed on probation. Not surprisingly, this incident marked the end of Mailer's first marriage, and because of the tremendous media coverage that it received, it should have also marked the end of his political aspirations.

Because of its basic subject matter and its themes, Mailer's first published novel in a decade, *An American Dream* (1965) is either an audacious or an exploitative work. The focal event of the novel is Stephen Rojack's murder of his estranged wife, the daughter of a wealthy and powerful businessman known for his ruthlessness. The novel is clearly intended as a response to Theodore Dreiser's *An American Tragedy*, in which Clyde Griffiths is convicted of the murder of his working-class girlfriend who is pregnant with their child because he learned of her pregnancy just as all of his social and economic aspirations were about to be fulfilled. In Mailer's novel, Stephen Rojack has acquired everything that Clyde Griffiths has yearned for, and yet Rojack's life is just as frustratingly unfulfilling as Griffiths's—perhaps more so because whereas Griffiths's dreams remain just beyond his grasp, Rojack has discovered that the dream—in particular, the American Dream—is not what it is supposed to be and, worse, will never be what everyone has supposed it to be. A veteran of the Second World War, Rojack has been, in turn, a successful political candidate, a successful academic, a popular author and media figure, and, through his marriage, has had access to powerful business interests, personal wealth, and social privilege. He discovers, however, that it is all, in some way or another, image-making. After he murders his wife, he makes decisions that complicate his escape, but he manages to stay just ahead of the law, the underworld, and political forces aligned with his father-in-law. Ultimately, he heads toward Mexico, but, although it is very clear what he is escaping from, it is less clear what sort of life he is seeking or will find. The novel was very controversial because unlike most serious novelists who have written about such a crime and have tried to transcend the material, Mailer fully exploits the melodramatic possibilities of the crime and its consequences, creating a tour de force beyond anything typically found in the genre of crime novels. In this sense, the novel anticipates both the very highly regarded nonfiction novel *The Executioner's Song* and the generally dismissed novel *Tough Guys Don't Dance*. Given that *An American Dream* was Mailer's first novel following his stabbing of his wife, feminist critics, in particular Kate Millett, has a field day highlighting the blatant misogyny in Mailer's portrait of Rojack's wife and in the luridly detailed way in which her murder is described.

Mailer's other novel of the 1960s, *Why Are We in Vietnam?* (1967), is similar to Michael Cimino's film *The Deerhunter* in that both feature extended hunting trips and link the hypermasculine values that pervaded American culture with the way in which Americans, in general, viewed the war and with the ways in which those who served in Vietnam fought the war—especially before it became widely regarded as unwinnable and thus widely unpopular. Mailer's novel is different from Cimino's film, however, in two very important respects. First, while Cimino's film focuses on a working-class community in a western Pennsylvania steel town, Mailer's novel focuses on a more upper-class group of characters—people who have the means to fly to Alaska for a hunt and to exert some political influence on public policy. Second, while Cimino's film depicts the characters' experiences in Vietnam and their attempt to readjust after they return home, Mailer's novel never extends beyond a going-away party held on the night before the two central characters are to depart for Vietnam. Of course, Mailer's title rhetorically asks simply the reasons for the U.S. involvement in Vietnam, and the novel suggests that that involvement really has next to nothing to do with international relations, domino theories, or even the politics behind the long-standing conflict within Vietnam itself. In that sense, Mailer's novel was both radical for the immediate time period in which it was published and prescient about how American involvement in the war would be reevaluated over subsequent decades. What Mailer probes in the novel is the mindset that allowed socially liberal political leaders to embrace a war that served conservative political principles.

Despite the mixed critical response to the two novels, Mailer became much more of a public figure because of his provocative political writing and expanding public role as a political activist. In 1963, Mailer's early political essays were collected in *The Presidential Papers*. Within three years, he had enough additional essays to collect them in *Cannibals and Christians* (1966), though in this collection Mailer ranged beyond politics to social, economic, environmental, and cultural issues. In 1967, Mailer participated in the March on the Pentagon, and he wrote about the experience in *The Armies of the Night* (1968), which first provided a journalistic report on the event in which Mailer was the reporter and then retold the event as a fiction in which Mailer was one of several major characters. This hybrid form seems as strange today as it did in the late 1960s, but the book won both a Pulitzer Prize and a National Book Award and it remains a fascinating read. In 1968, Mailer attended both political conventions and reported on them in the very well received book *Miami and the Siege of Chicago: An Informal History of the Republican and Democratic Conventions of 1968*, and in that same year, he collected his political writings on the Kennedy and Johnson administrations in *The Idol and the Octopus*. These books so set the direction of the middle years of Mailer's career that in the 1970s, he published seven books of nonfiction and just two novels, both at the very end of the decade—in 1978, the almost completely forgotten *A Transit to Narcissus* and, in 1979, the nonfiction novel *The Executioner's Song*, which won a Pulitzer Prize and was a finalist for a National Book Award.

In the 1960s, Mailer published the collection of poems *Deaths for the Ladies (and Other Disasters)* (1962), the collection of short stories *The Short Fiction of Norman Mailer* (1967), and a stage adaptation of his third novel *The Deer Park: A Play* (1967). None of these works are noteworthy except for the fact that he wrote them, and none of them have contributed to his standing as a major writer. In another extended diversion from writing novels, Mailer made several improvisational films in the late 1960s: *Wild 90* (1968), *Beyond the Law* (1968), and *Maidstone* (1970).

For Mailer, the 1960s ended as they had begun, with him attempting to enter politics as a mayoral candidate in New York. In 1969, he entered the Democratic primary, paired with the columnist Jimmy Breslin who was a candidate for City Council President. Mailer's main campaign proposal was that the New York metro area should secede from the state of New York and petition to become the fifty-first state. As odd as that may sound today, his campaign was actually praised for the reasoned approach to governance and the thoughtful solutions to the city's escalating social and economic problems that Mailer was advocating. Still in the end, Mailer received just 41,288 votes, or 5 percent of the total votes cast, and the press coverage that Mailer's campaign received far exceeded its actual political impact.

## GORE VIDAL (1925–2012)

In some ways, Gore Vidal's career paralleled the careers of both Truman Capote and Norman Mailer. Like Mailer, Vidal drew on his experiences during the Second World War in writing his first novel. But in Vidal's case, the novel was *Williwaw* (1946), a novel about the crew of a naval vessel in the Aleutian Islands who, as they are preparing to ride out a major storm, also have to deal with a murder. Although the novel received some critical praise, it never had the impact of Mailer's *The Naked and the Dead*. If the suggestive photo on the dust jacket of Capote's first novel had raised eyebrows, Vidal's third novel, *The City and the Pillar* (1948), caused open outrage because it focused on a homosexual relationship while avoiding any suggestion that it was aberrant, a shocking thing at the time. Although Vidal published four more novels under his own name over the next four years, none of them received much notice. For the rest of the 1950s, Vidal began to write screenplays and teleplays, as well as more mainstream novels that he wrote under several pseudonyms. These included a commercially successful series of detective novels that he wrote under the name Edgar Box.

Vidal could count several prominent political figures among his immediate ancestors, and like Mailer, he sought political office in the 1960s, running for a seat in the U.S. House of Representatives in 1960. Although Vidal did better than any Democratic candidate had ever done in what was a solidly Republican district in upstate New York, he still lost by 14 percentage points. Vidal was tenuously related to the Kennedy family through one of his stepfathers, and he knew most of the Kennedys personally. Those connections and the essays collected in *Rocking the Boat* (1963) got him onto talk shows, where his wryly acerbic observations turned him into something of a celebrity. In 1968, he was hired by ABC News to provide commentary at the Republican and Democratic National Conventions, with the conservative William F. Buckley providing the contrasting view. During the Democratic National Convention, the two were asked to address the protests that were degenerating into mayhem outside the convention hall, and as both Buckley and Vidal began to interrupt each other, Vidal ended up calling Buckley a "crypto-Nazi," and Buckley retorted that Vidal was a "queer" and threatened to "sock him in the goddamned face and you'll stay plastered." It remains one of the most memorable moments in the coverage of any political convention, and their feud would continue until Buckley's death and involve several lawsuits along the way. Vidal would cement his position as an acute critic of American imperialism and as a perceptive commentator on the decline of American power and influence, politics, and culture with the collection of essays *Reflections upon a Sinking Ship* (1969).

During this period, William F. Buckley was not the only person with whom Vidal engaged in very public feuds. On an episode of Dick Cavett's talk show, Vidal and Norman Mailer exchanged personal insults, and Mailer reportedly head-butted Vidal when they were just offstage. Mailer apparently was holding a grudge over something Vidal had written about his stabbing of his second wife, Adele Morales, and he began the heated exchange by remarking, "I have had to smell your works from time to time." In the mid-1970s, Vidal and Truman Capote exchanged much-publicized insults after Vidal sued Capote for slander over Capote's assertions that an inebriated Vidal had once behaved very boorishly in the Kennedy White House. Vidal won the suit, but Capote may have had the last word when he said, "I'm always sad about Gore—very sad that he has to breathe every day."

In the 1960s, Vidal published only three novels, the third of which earned him at least as much notoriety as his political commentary and public feuds. In subsequent decades, his output of novels would increase significantly, but the three novels published in the 1960s would set the categories into which almost all of his subsequent work would fit. In *Julian* (1964), Vidal would focus on the Roman emperor who, while allowing religious tolerance, attempted to revitalize the traditional Roman religion in order to offset the growing influence of Christianity and to reverse what he saw as the deterioration of the cultural and the political unity of the empire. Although he did not persecute Christians, he was given the name Julian the Apostate by later Christian historians. This novel extends Vidal's fictional use of ancient history, mythology, and religion first evident in *The Judgment of Paris* (1952) and later extended in the novels *Creation* (1981) and *Live from Golgotha* (1992). In *Washington, D.C.* (1967), Vidal focused on the period between the beginning of Franklin Roosevelt's second term and the beginning of the Cold War. This novel is the first published novel in what would become the seven-novel series, *Narratives of Empire*, though chronologically it is the sixth of the seven novels.

Both *Julian* and *Washington, D.C.* were commercially successful and critically well received, but neither attracted the notice that *Myra Breckinridge* (1968) provoked. In fact, one could argue that none of Vidal's other novels were as provocative either in their moment or in the longer term. Myra Breckinridge is a transgender woman who runs an acting academy in Hollywood, with a side interest in teaching her male students lessons in female dominance, bondage, and sadomasochism. Although this novel was far more explicit and outrageous than *The City and the Pillar*, times had changed so dramatically and the tone of the novel was so campy, that the moral outrage was balanced, if not actually drowned out, by the sheer audacity in a major author's daring to produce such a work. That the novel has become part of the literary canon is a testament to its originality and its still very relevant critique of sexual repression, gender bias, and sexual imposition. The novel was adapted to a film starring Raquel Welch and Mae West that has been included in many lists of the worst films ever made because the filmmakers could not approximate the novel's tone, and so what was campy in the novel became simply tasteless in the film. Although the film adaptation initially seemed to damage the novel's reputation, it has been subsequently seen as a demonstration, by contrast, of the novel's strengths and of Vidal's achievement in striking and sustaining an approach to the materials that remains shocking because it does not simply aim to shock.

## J. D. SALINGER (1919–2010)

J. D. Salinger is known for one novel, *The Catcher in the Rye*, which was published in 1951. The book is narrated by its central character, Holden Caulfield, a sixteen-year-old who has gone to New York City after being expelled for the fourth time from an elite school. The novel was an immediate best seller, and it has remained continuously in print since its initial publication. In the 1950s, it suggested the adolescent discomfort with the increasing conformity that seemed to be a social by-product of the increasing corporatization and expanding prosperity of postwar American society. Specifically, Holden Caulfield's contemporaries had been born in the middle of the Great Depression, had been in elementary grades during the Second World War, and were coming of age just as the Cold War escalated. Even for the product of a fairly privileged background such as Holden Caulfield, the surface optimism of the postwar world very clearly had very tenuous underpinnings. By the time that the baby boomers began to reach Holden Caulfield's age in the 1960s, his narrative seemed to resonate all the more because at the height of the postwar economic prosperity, nuclear confrontation became a reality, rather than a nonspecific threat, during the Cuban Missile Crisis; multiple progressive political leaders with a special appeal to young adults were assassinated; American cities were convulsed by very destructive race riots; and the escalation of U.S. involvement and the reliance of the draft brought young Americans into the streets to protest a war about which the government seemed to be disseminating misinformation, for which the military seemed to have no strategy that would lead to victory; and which seemed increasingly a pointless waste of their contemporaries', if not their own, lives. During this period, Salinger's novel became standard reading in high school English curricula, and even though it has to some degree acquired as much historical significance as current relevance, its annual sales have consistently ranged between one-quarter-million to one-half-million copies per year. In short, that one novel provided Salinger with an extended source of substantial income while also sustaining his name recognition.

Salinger published a collection of short stories, *Nine Stories*, in 1953, and then *Franny and Zooey*, a novella and a short story, in 1961, and two novellas *Raise High the Roof Beam, Carpenters* and *Seymour: An Introduction* in 1963. In 1965, his novella *Hapworth 16, 1924* appeared in *The New Yorker*. And then, for literally the second half of his long life he published nothing. In fact, over the last thirty years, he became increasingly reclusive, giving his last interview in 1980. Fans trekked to his New Hampshire retreat, but they very seldom got more than a glimpse of him, and when a former lover, Joyce Maynard, and his daughter, Margaret, published memoirs, the interest that the books generated was all out of proportion to the revelations that they provided. Likewise, when Ian Hamilton attempted to publish a biography using letters from Salinger obtained from some of his correspondents, Salinger successfully sued to stop the book from being published. Hamilton ended up writing a biography that was less about Salinger's life and more about Hamilton's struggles to write the biography.

## THOMAS PYNCHON (1937–)

In the 1980s, literary critics started to take stock of postwar American fiction, and many of the most influential critics focused on the experimental novelists who not only manipulated the conventions of fiction as the modernists had done but actively sought to undermine those conventions. As a group, these novelists were called postmodernists, metafictionists, and antinovelists. They included such writers as John Hawkes, William Gaddis, John Barth, Donald Barthelme, Joseph McElroy, and William Gass, among others. Although their novels and short stories were often considered to be almost unreadable, they provoked massive outpourings of literary criticism—in particular, intensive applications of literary theory—that far exceeded the length and the density of many of their most expansive works. Some three decades later, the interest in many of these writers seems to have diminished, at least to the degree that their work has more of a historical interest than a continuing relevance. There are exceptions, of course, and one of the most significant exceptions has been Thomas Pynchon.

Pynchon's first novel, *V*, was published in 1963 and was nominated for a National Book Award, bringing him immediately to public notice. Pynchon was twenty-six years old, and the basic facts of his family background, education, military service, and job history to that date quickly became known. But from 1963 onward, the author has taken great pains to keep his personal life private and to maintain a public anonymity. Searches of public records have confirmed that he has lived in various locations in the New York metro area and in California and that he has married and he and his wife have a child. But, for a writer who would produce *Gravity's Rainbow* (1973), widely regarded as one of the most important novels of the second half of the twentieth century, as well as substantial novels at regular intervals over the past three decades, the anonymity that Pynchon has maintained has been so determined and sustained as to be extraordinary. Indeed, the fact that seventeen years elapsed between the publication of *Gravity's Rainbow* and that of Pynchon's fourth novel, *Vineland* (1990), simply fueled public curiosity and provoked elaborate speculations about what had happened to him. In an article for *New York* magazine titled "Meet Your Neighbor, Thomas Pynchon," Jo Ann Sales links the publication of *Vineland*, as the long-awaited follow-up to *Gravity's Rainbow*, to a chronicle of the repeated and often consuming searches that had produced what little was known about the preceding quarter-century of Pynchon's life. She illustrates how the dearth of verifiable facts fueled speculations that stand as the closest contemporary literary equivalent to the theories about who assassinated John F. Kennedy. One of the most sustained of those theories was, ironically but not altogether surprisingly, that Thomas Pynchon was a pseudonym being used by J. D. Salinger.

Pynchon's first novel, *V*, might have suggested to readers the mystery that he would allow others—and the simple passage of time—to create about him. The novel focuses on a ragtag group of people, known as the Whole Sick Crew, scratching out a tenuous day-to-day existence in New York City. The novel's ostensible protagonist, a recently discharged seaman named Benny Profane, earns his living for a while hunting alligators in the sewers underneath Manhattan. So, even at this gritty, surface level, the novel synthesizes fact and fabulation. Benny Profane becomes acquainted with Herbert Stencil, whose psychological issues are reflected in his fixation on his father's mysterious death in the years immediately following the First World War on the island of Malta—and, more specifically, his conviction that uncovering the identity of a woman named V, who is mentioned in his father's journal, is somehow the key to understanding how and why his father was killed. Through the introduction of this mystery, the novel ranges across considerable time and space, but in almost all instances, the temporal and spatial settings are on the historical margins—pointedly removed from anything that has—or at least would seem to have—any actual historical significance. Indeed, characters, places, and things whose names begin with the letter "V" begin to proliferate in the novel, suggesting that the quest is, at best, hopelessly complicated and ambiguously focused. Although these characters' lives cannot be separated from the historical currents shaping the world in which they are living, they also seem of marginal historical importance, even though the narrative keeps suggesting that such a judgment may be premature—that in some still unrevealed and unlikely way they may turn out to be historically significant.

Pynchon's second novel, *The Crying of Lot 49* (1966), seemed a major change in direction from *V* because it is much shorter and much more like conventional speculative fiction. The main character, a middle-class housewife named Oedipa Maas, is more materially comfortable and emotionally contented than Benny Profane and the rest of the Whole Sick Crew. But when a former lover dies and she discovers that he has designated her as an executor of his estate, she is gradually drawn into a historical mystery. It is at this point that Oedipa's quest becomes very similar to Herbert Stencil's quest for V. The premise is that

Thurn and Taxis, the first private company to contract to deliver the mail (historically, throughout the Holy Roman Empire over much of the nineteenth century), had forced its main rival, Trystero (or Tristero), out of business but that Trystero may have survived as a mysterious underground network, which uses stamps as a sort of secret currency. The pursuit of a particular set of these stamps, ultimately available at an auction as Lot 49, leads Oedipa up and down the California coast. Along the way, she meets a very strange assortment of characters that seem the realization of every dismissive characterization of California as a magnet for eccentrics and kooks, ranging from innocuous oddballs to more sinister figures. The novel seems, in sums, to capture the obsession with conspiracy theories and suppressed and subverted history that became prevalent after the assassination of John Kennedy—and, of course, prefigures all of the strange theorizing about Pynchon's identity and life as well.

## FREDERICK EXLEY (1929-1992)

In contrast with J. D. Salinger and Thomas Pynchon, Frederick Exley never wrote a best-selling book and never made a conscious decision to escape or to avoid the limelight. Throughout his adult life, Exley struggled with alcoholism, schizophrenia, and other psychological disorders, and during much of the 1950s and some of the three subsequent decades, he was institutionalized in mental health facilities. His personal issues made it difficult for him to maintain employment and to sustain his personal relationships. As a result, he held a remarkable variety of jobs, and his marriages followed a similarly short arc from unlikely infatuation to complete exasperation. In the mid-1960s, Exley turned his personal obsessions and travails into a "fictional memoir" that was titled *A Fan's Notes* because one of the constant elements of Exley's experience had been his devotion to the *New York Giants* pro-football team and his admiration for the Hall of Famer Frank Gifford. Because the book was so unusual, it is not surprising that it took some time for Exley to find an agent and the agent to find a publisher. After it was published in 1968, it received very positive critical notice, eventually becoming a finalist for a National Book Award, but even for a first book, its sales were disappointing. Very gradually, the book did gain a sort of cult following, but when Exley attempted two follow-up volumes, published as *Pages from a Cold Island* (1975) and *Last Notes from Home* (1988), neither book made much of a mark either critically or commercially.

When Exley died four years later in 1992, his passing did not attract a great deal of notice, and no one would have anticipated that, over the next quarter of a century, *A Fan's Notes* would not only gain many new readers but more readers than it had initially attracted. Moreover, the form of the book, the "fictional memoir," would become more commonplace—in some cases, unintentionally, as with James Frey's *A Million Little Pieces* (2003) and *My Friend Leonard* (2005)—and Exley's book would be regarded increasingly as a prototypical work and even as a sort of landmark work. Despite its extended resonance, Exley's book is now seen as a very characteristic work of the 1960s because, for the first time, life of the social margins began to be treated as something other than an aberration or a regrettable anomaly. In part, this shift was due to the choice that many people were making to "drop out" of the "rat race" and to live in unconventional ways. But this undermining of the acceptance of—and even outright rejection of—conformity also meant that some degree of personal dysfunction was increasingly regarded as a condition to be accommodated, rather than as an abnormality to be shunned or isolated and thereby largely ignored. In fact, because the conformity to a corporatized social order was being actively challenged, personal dysfunction began to be seen less often as a personal failure to succeed and more often as social consequence of distorted measures of personal fulfillment.

## JOHN KENNEDY TOOLE (1937–1969)

John Kennedy Toole spent much of the last half-decade of his life in his hometown in New Orleans, living with his mother, teaching at a local Catholic college, and trying to get a publisher to accept his novel *A Confederacy of Dunces*. Although his friends and students enjoyed his dry, acerbic wit, his abilities as both a raconteur and impersonator, and his public persona as someone meticulous about his personal appearance and indefatigably self-possessed, in the last year of his life he became sloppy about his appearance and increasingly prone to rants and exhibitions of paranoia. In 1969, he left New Orleans, driving in a wide loop to California and then to Georgia, where he visited Flannery O'Connor's former home, and finally back toward New Orleans. In Biloxi, Mississippi, he committed suicide by running a hose from the exhaust pipe of his care into the passenger compartment.

After Toole's death, his mother basically made it her life's mission to find a publisher for *A Confederacy of Dunces*. Eventually, after she badgered the novelist Walker Percy into reading it, he also began to advocate for its publication. In 1980, it was published in a limited edition of 2,500 copies by Louisiana State University Press. Despite that very modest beginning, it would become a literary sensation—undoubtedly in part because of its back story—winning a Pulitzer Prize in 1981 and ultimately selling more than 1.5 million copies.

The novel is a cross between the picaresque narrative of Cervantes's *Don Quixote* and the digressive satiric essays of Jonathan Swift, and it contains almost as much discussion of the medieval philosopher Boethius as very vivid and intimate descriptions of its New Orleans setting. Its main character and narrator, Ignatius J. Reilly, really has very little to recommend him except for his relentless gift of gab and his equally relentless critique of just about every aspect of modern life. Reilly is much more eccentric in his views, but "listening" to him is comparable to reading Gore Vidal in that one does not have to agree with him to find him amusing and even insightful. Like Holden Caulfield, Benny Profane, and Frederick Exley's fictional alter ego, Ignatius J. Reilly is a voice of the 1960s. A decade earlier most people might have dismissed his wildly careening narrative out of hand, wondering, as one fairly sympathetic book editor repeatedly did, if there is any point to his story that makes it worth reading. But, Reilly simply demands to be heard, and by the time Toole's book finally was published more than a decade after his suicide, there was not only a clearer sense of how the tumult of the 1960s had changed in not only American politics and social mores but also in literary and cultural expectations. That is, the 1960s were acquiring their first layer of nostalgia.

## JOSEPH HELLER (1923–1999)

Joseph Heller spent about eight years working on *Catch-22*, which was published in 1961. It would be the only novel that he would produce over the 1960s. In fact, *Something Happened*, his second novel, would not be published until 1974. It was so different than *Catch-22* in almost every way that it appeared that Heller had had difficulty conceiving and executing a follow-up to his first novel. Over the next twenty-five years, he would produce five additional novels, including a sequel to *Catch-22*, titled *Closing Time* and published in 1994. None of these other novels were critically or commercially as successful as *Catch-22* has proven to be. In fact, it is fair to ask if Heller would be remembered for any of the other novels had he not written *Catch-22*.

*Catch-22* was not, however, any sort of immediate success, critically or commercially. It received very mixed reviews, and even given that it was a first novel, its sales were modest and concentrated in the Northeast. During the decade after the end of the Second World War—the period in which Heller conceived the novel—most of the major American novels about the war were being written: Norman Mailer's *The Naked and the Dead* (1948), Irwin Shaw's *The Young Lions* (1948), James Gould Cozzens's *Guard of Honor* (1948), Herman Wouk's *The Caine Mutiny* (1951), James Jones's *From Here to Eternity* (1951), and Leon Uris's *Battle Cry* (1953). By the time that Heller's novel was published, the interest in the war was already taking on a nostalgic tone, as in the film *The Longest Day* and in the television series *Combat* (1962–1967), which follows a platoon of GIs from D-Day onward. (Interestingly, another series, *The Gallant Men*, which like Heller's novel was set in the Italian theater, ran for only one season, 1962–1963.) There was not a natural audience for a satire on the way in which that war, which within two decades would be labeled "The Good War," was fought. Most of the enthused early responses to the novel were from readers who recognized that although the novel was set during the Second World War, it was very much a response to some of the most unsettling aspects of the Cold War: the development of the military-industrial complex, the increasingly bureaucratic military leadership, the impulse to waste material and lives on military commitments that had no defining goal or strategy that justified their cost, and the increasingly convoluted, jargon-filled, and self-referential rhetoric that made enemies out of anyone who had the temerity to question what any of it actually meant.

The popularity of *Catch-22* broadened and intensified as the American involvement in the Vietnam War and then the opposition to the war escalated. The novel's absurdist tone, which had put off many early reviewers and readers, now seemed very much in sync with the irreverence toward institutions that defined the Counterculture and the increasing bewilderment about the war itself. As young men were struggling with the decision of whether to accept being drafted and then deployed to Vietnam or to resist the draft by either accepting a prison term or fleeing the country, the concept of Catch-22 seemed very pointedly relevant. In the novel, the central character, a bombardier named

Yossarian, asserts that he should be excused from flying more missions because he is becoming mentally unbalanced by the certainty that he will not survive enough bombing missions to be discharged. He is told, however, that his acute anxiety is actually a sign that he is sane and therefore fit to fly more missions. Worse, each time that he flies a mission, he is demonstrating that he is insane and should not have been allowed onto the plane, but once the plane is in the air, his state of mind is beside the point. Likewise, although an airman is assured that he will be discharged after flying a specified number of missions, there is nothing to prevent that number of missions from being increased, even retroactively. So, in one instance, Yossarian comes back from what he believes has been his final mission only to learn that he has a substantial number of missions left to fly. The convoluted logic of the military rhetoric is reflected at every level of the novel, including its structure. The sections of the novel are related entirely by free association but, like the circular reasoning that seemingly entraps almost everyone in the military, the events of the novel loop back over each other with enough frequency that the convolution becomes a structural device—paradoxically, a mechanism for bringing order to the disordered narrative about the chaos and insanity of war.

Heller's novel includes some very memorable characters. The most ridiculous character in a novel full of ridiculous characters is probably Major Major Major Major, whose father perversely named him Major Major Major and who has risen inexplicably to the rank of Major by scrupulously avoiding his subordinates and most of the decisions that someone in command would typically make. Major Major represents the ways in which bureaucracy, even in the so-called crucible of war, often advances those who do nothing to warrant advancement beyond avoiding everything that has any potential to impede their advancement.

Milo Milobender is a caricature of the military "scrounger" who graduates to involvement in the black market trade in military material. But in Milo's case, the capitalist impulse becomes preposterously magnified. He not only becomes centrally involved in a syndicate that brings a corporate approach to the black market profiteering, but soon the profits generated by the syndicate become more important to its principles and investors than the war itself. It no longer matters to the syndicate to whom it is selling weapons or supplies. Milo personally is responsible for the sale of missiles to the Germans, and in one battle, he switches sides repeatedly, bombing both sides in an effort to maximize the syndicate's potential profits.

Less grandiose in his ambitions but equally repulsive is Captain Aardvaark, the navigator in Yossarian's bomber. Nicknamed Aarfy, he is an incredibly inept navigator, but he is also seemingly impervious to flak. Aarfy cultivates a friendship with Nately simply because he hopes to secure a position with Nately's father's firm after the war. Likewise, although Aarfy presents himself as a person of moral conscience and, more specifically, as a defender of women who are abused by GIs, he commits one of the most shocking acts of violence in the novel, raping and murdering the maid Michaela. Appalled by what has occurred, Yossarian asks him why he had not simply found a prostitute, and Aarfy responds with the lame male boast that he has never "paid for it." Aarfy's reflexive, unthinking self-justification makes the brutal, impulsive crime all the more appalling, and it provides, in microcosm, a suggestive parallel to most of the essentially self-perpetuating violence of the war.

As despicable as Aarfy turns out to be, the most terrifying character in Catch-22 is Nately's whore. Although she is an apathetic prostitute, for a long while she remains completely unmoved by Nately's passionate infatuation with her. Then, very shortly after she finally becomes responsive to his romantic appeals, Nately perishes in a bombing mission. Yossarian feels obligated to let her know what has happened to his friend, but when he delivers the news, she inexplicably blames him for Nately's death. For the rest of the novel, she becomes a truly haunting presence—pursuing Yossarian, stalking him, and attempting to ambush him. After several close calls, she succeeds in stabbing him, causing a serious enough wound that he has to be hospitalized. Nately's whore seems to represent the deep feelings of aggrievement that are not necessarily entirely rational and that often persist long beyond the conclusion of any war. In contrast, the "kid sister" of Nately's whore has no ambition other than to be a prostitute like her older sister, and yet Yossarian becomes determined to locate her and to "save" her by taking her to Sweden with him, even though at that point he has absolutely no idea what has become of her.

## KURT VONNEGUT (1922–2007)

Previous to the publication of *Slaughterhouse-Five* in 1969, Kurt Vonnegut had managed to make a living as a writer, though not as a fiction writer. He supplemented the income from his novels and short stories with stints as technical writer, an advertising copy writer, a freelance contributor to magazines—and with several well-timed grants from arts foundations. His first five books included *Player Piano* (1952), *The Sirens of Titan* (1959), *Mother Night* (1961), *Cat's Cradle* (1963), and *God Bless You, Mr. Rosewater* (1965). Most of these novels present speculative, futuristic situations to a satiric purpose. Although they received generally favorable, if sometimes somewhat guarded, reviews, they produced modest sales. After *Slaughterhouse-Five* became a best seller and, just as importantly, after it became a "cult classic" that was frequently on the reading lists for literature courses, all of Vonnegut's previous novels were rereleased and sold better than they had sold when initially published. But out of those first five novels, only *Cat's Cradle* has gained some stature as an important American novel of the second half of the twentieth century.

*Cat's Cradle* is an important forerunner to *Slaughterhouse-Five* for three reasons. First, *Cat's Cradle* presents a warning about the ultimately unpredictable consequences of rapidly developed technologies—in particular, those that are developed within the military-industrial complex to address a specific military need and that are then commercialized in ways unimagined by their developers. The character in the novel that sets all of the subsequent events into motion is Felix Hoenniker, one of the scientists who developed the atomic bomb. When the first bomb was dropped, he was playing the string game from which the novel derives its title. He also developed a substance called "ice-nine," which when added to water at room temperature, turns it into a solid. Although it was originally developed to make the swamps in the Pacific and Southeast Asian theaters of the Second World War more passable for Allied troops, it has evolved into a potential superweapon.

Second, *Cat's Cradle* incorporates or, more precisely, works from the history of places that have received media attention but remain exotically unfamiliar. In this case, one of the major settings is the Caribbean island of San Lorenzo, which is ruled by a ruthless dictator named "Papa" Monzano who maintains power with open exhibitions of brutality. The terrorized and deeply impoverished population engages in the rituals of an officially outlawed but generally permitted cult religion of Bokononism. The island is obviously modeled on Haiti, which during the 1960s was still ruled by Francois "Papa Doc" Duvalier, whose secret police, known as the Tonton Macoute, routinely tortured suspected political opponents and committed many extrajudicial killings. And Bokononism is just as clearly a postmodern turn on the widespread practice of voodoo in Haiti—not much removed from Duvalier's attempt to redirect some of the rituals and appeal of voodoo into a "cult of personality" around himself.

Lastly, *Cat's Cradle* presents an apocalyptic scenario that has an element of the ridiculous to it but serves to highlight the absurdity of scientific and technical developments that bring us ever closer to self-destruction—while very clearly echoing contemporary events. Beneath the diplomatic reassurances about the paradoxical advantages of "mutually assured destruction," there has been a consistent anxiety about an accidental triggering of an apocalypse. Such scenarios have been treated very suspensefully in novels and films such as *Fail-Safe* (1964) and very satirically in novels and films such as *Dr. Stangelove* (1964), both of which gained much extra resonance after the Cuban Missile Crisis. In its tone and effect, Vonnegut's novel is much closer to the Kubrick film. After Monzano commits suicide by ingesting "ice-nine," attempts are made to isolate everything that came into any contact with his corpse, which became, in effect, a large chunk of "ice-nine." But while the corpse is being transported by helicopter, it falls into the sea, triggering a global apocalypse, as most of the Earth's water becomes a solid substance.

Like *Catch-22*, *Slaughterhouse-Five* is associated with the Vietnam War though a major portion of the novel is actually set during the Second World War. Like Vonnegut himself, the central character, Billy Pilgrim, is captured by the Germans during the last year of the war and ends up in Dresden just before the city is firebombed in a massive Allied air attack. He survives in the underground cooler of the slaughterhouse from which the novel's title is derived, and after the raid, he is put to work, with his fellow prisoners of war, pulling some of the thousands of corpses from the rubble. It is important to remember that between March of 1965 and November of 1968, the U.S. military conducted a massive and sustained bombing campaign against sites in North Vietnam. Known as Operation Rolling Thunder, this bombing campaign was just one of a dozen bombing campaigns conducted against groups of targets in Vietnam, Laos, and Cambodia, during which the U.S. military dropped more ordinance than it had during the combined strategic bombing operations against both Germany and Japan during the Second World War. But Operation Rolling Thunder became particularly controversial because it became as closely associated in the public mind with the futility of U.S. military strategy as the attention to body counts and the Tet Offensive.

A second major portion of *Slaughterhouse-Five* involves Billy Pilgrim's abduction by aliens from the planet Tralfamadore, light years away from Earth. On Tralfamadore, Billy is exhibited in a zoo, in an enclosure designed to look like the interior of a suburban house. Eventually, the Tralfamadorians also abduct a film actress named Montana Wildhack so that Billy will have a female of his species with whom to mate. Like the sections about the bombing of Dresden, these sections of the novel especially resonated with readers in the 1960s because although there had previously been reports of alien abductions, the account of the alien abduction of Barney and Betty Hill in 1961 was the first one to receive widespread media attention. Its impact is reflected in the fact that it provided a template for most subsequent abduction narratives. The phenomenon even got some measure of academic legitimacy when a psychologist at the University of Wyoming, Dr. R. Leo Sprinkle, became the first to research it in depth. Sprinkle's work always received much more attention from nonacademics than from academics, and among scholars, it was definitively dismissed some two decades later, after Sprinkle began to claim that he himself had been abducted by aliens.

One of the major effects of Billy Pilgrim's time among the Tralfamadorians is that he acquires the ability to move backward and forward in time. The structure of the novel is very nonchronological to reflect Billy's nonlinear existence. Likewise, Counterculture catchphrases such as "turn on, tune in, and drop out" are echoed in the Tralfamadorians' fatalistic acceptance of life's unpredictability and their nonchalance about death—both of which are reflected in their catchphrase "so it goes." Billy also is introduced to and fascinated by the works of an obscure, radical novelist named Kilgore Trout, and he ultimately is targeted for assassination as part of an elaborate conspiracy several decades in the making. So, all sorts of elements of the novel had a particular cultural relevancy for readers in late 1960s America. In fact, juxtaposed among Billy's intergalactic adventures in Talfamadore are set pieces from his middle-class family life, and like most families of the period, his family's contentment is undermined by both the ordinary tragedies of modern life and more extraordinary misfortune.

Beyond all of these considerations, Vonnegut's novel resonated because he freely borrowed characters from his earlier novels—and then recycled characters from *Slaughterhouse-Five* in later novels. Although this strategy may seem somewhat contrived and haphazard from a historical distance, it not only drove curiosity about and sales of his earlier novels, but it also created something of a cult of readership around his body of work. Indeed, although some readers will find the rather haphazard recycling of characters less satisfying than what typically occurs in a series of novels, many readers in the 1960s—in particular, young readers—found the unconventionality of Vonnegut's approach refreshingly inventive. For a time, critics who have focused on the American novel in the second half of the twentieth century have attempted to group Vonnegut with the metafictionists such as William Gaddis, Joseph McElroy, John Barth, Donald Barthelme, and Thomas Pynchon. But, like Barthelme's short fictions,

Vonnegut's novels have always been closer in sensibility to *National Lampoon* than to *Tristram Shandy* or *Ulysses*.

## PHILIP ROTH (1933–2018)

Philip Roth's first book, *Goodbye, Columbus*, was published in 1959, and it immediately placed him among the expanding group of notable writers who were making Jewish American fiction a prominent subcategory of post–Second World War American fiction. The book includes the novella *Goodbye, Columbus*, as well as five short stories, three of which—"The Conversion of the Jews," "Defender of the Faith," and "Eli, the Fanatic"—have been frequently anthologized. The novella and the stories explore the tensions in Jewish American identity from a variety of intersecting angles: the immediate aftermath of the Holocaust and the establishment of the state of Israel; the expanding prosperity created by the postwar American economic boom; the social, political, and cultural unease that was just beginning to surface as a counterpoint to the mainstream cultural emphases on the interrelationships between affluence, contentment, and conformity; and the increasing impatience of marginalized, non-WASP segments of the American population who were demanding equal treatment without entirely embracing assimilation. The novella was adapted in 1969 to a critically well received and commercially successful film starring Richard Benjamin and Ali MacGraw. But although elements of the novella seemed daring in 1959, there was little in the film that seemed especially shocking by the time that the film was released a decade later.

In the 1960s, three of Roth's novels were published. The first two, *Letting Go* (1962) and *When She Was Good* (1967) attracted some attention when they were published but have since received considerably less critical attention than a significant number of Roth's subsequent novels. *Letting Go* focuses on Gabe Wallach, a graduate student in literature at the University of Iowa who is an admirer of the novels of Henry James. In a very Jamesian manner, the novel focuses on the tensions in Gabe's relationships with his parents, his acquaintances, and his lovers—delineating the ways in which issues of class, ethnicity, religion, and gender complexly intersect in his experience and gradually shape his awareness and expectations. In *When She Was Good*, Roth seems determined in every possible way to do something strikingly different than what he did in his first two books. It is Roth's only novel with a female central character. That character, Lucy Nelson, also comes from an entirely WASP and decidedly non-Jewish background and lives in a nondiverse community. Whereas *Goodbye, Columbus* pointed to the Midwest as a sort of suggestive point of cultural reference, *When She Was Good* is actually set in a small town in the Midwest. The title highlights Lucy Nelson's core dilemma—the failure of the important men in her life to live up to her expectations, which in her mind are equivocated with moral standards. In her frustration at their failure to be "good" enough, she testifies against her father and ensures that he will be imprisoned. Later, in what is, in effect, the other bookend, melodramatic moment framing the novel, she kills herself and her unborn child to make it clear to her husband how severely and thoroughly he has failed to measure up to what seem to her to be reasonable expectations of a spouse and a prospective father. The novel's style has been compared to the family sagas and social chronicles of such novelists as John O'Hara, Louis Auchincloss, and Louis Bromfield. But in the focus on Lucy Nelson's skewed morality and disturbed psyche, comparisons to Sherwood Anderson's *Winesburg, Ohio* are inevitable.

Reportedly, Roth was still working on *When She Was Good* when he also began to work on his third novel, *Portnoy's Complaint* (1969). This revelation is surprising because the two novels could not be more different. In *Portnoy's Complaint*, he returns to the cultural milieu and thematic concerns of his first two books with something of a vengeance. This novel is written as a transcription of Alexander Portnoy's sessions with his psychoanalyst, sessions in which Portnoy provides an unsparing and often very vulgar account of his sexual experiences and emotional issues and connects them not only to his Jewishness but also to the increasingly conflicting social and sexual mores of the period. Some of the vulgarity of this novel is prefigured in sections of *Letting Go*, but, in this novel, Roth so completely lets go (pun intended) that readers were both riveted and shocked—and, at the extremes, amused and appalled—by the frankness of the narrative. This paradoxical reader response had a ready parallel in Portnoy's descriptions of himself as both sexually promiscuous and sexually unsatisfied. The most shocking episode in the novel remains Portnoy's masturbating into a piece of liver that is later cooked and served by his mother. At the time of its publication, the novel exploited the dramatic relaxation of obscenity standards, and it reflected the proliferation of both sexually provocative novels and nonfiction treatments of sexuality that were often packaged as scholarly studies. A synthesis of these two publishing phenomena was achieved in the best-selling novel *The Harrod Experiment*, by Robert Rimmer (which may sound like a campy, sexually suggestive pseudonym but was actually his name). The novel treats a study of sexuality being conducted at an American university that involves considerable direct experimentation.

Despite the ways in which *Portnoy's Complaint* was very much a product of the convulsive, Counterculture-dominated period in which it was published, it has maintained its standing as not only a major novel of the 1960s but also a major work of postwar American fiction and even of twentieth-century American literature. It 1998, when Modern Library asked critics to produce a list of the one hundred most important novels written in English in the twentieth century, Roth's novel was ranked fifty-second on that list. Likewise, in 2005, when *Time* magazine produced a list of the one hundred best novels in English published from the 1920s onward, *Portnoy's Complaint* was again included. The continuing appeal of the novel is, in part, due to its being a tour de force expression of unsparing and unapologetic self-revelation—an exercise in self-examination that produces some increased self-awareness even if it does not result in any sort of facile self-improvement, never mind substantive personal transformation. In addition, the continuing resonance of the novel may be a testament to the continuing relevance of the political, social, and cultural convulsions of the 1960s in contemporary American life. In many ways, digital technologies and social media have only exacerbated the personal and sexual dilemmas that preoccupy Portnoy, even if his articulation of those dilemmas and the circumstances that illustrate them sometimes seem dated.

## JOHN UPDIKE (1932–2009)

Like Philip Roth, John Updike published his first book-length fiction in 1959. Unlike *Goodbye, Columbus*, Updike's first short-story collection, *The Same Door*, and his first novel, *The Poorhouse Fair*, garnered some positive critical notice but did not bring Updike to any sort of national notice. *The Poorhouse Fair* is set in a county home for the elderly and focuses on the annual fair at which the residents sell their crafts and garden produce to people from the surrounding rural communities. Although it provides some perceptive character studies and shrewd observations about the social distinctions that exist even in small communities, neither the subject matter nor the stylistic treatment of it is especially remarkable.

Updike did come to national notice, however, with his second and third novels, *Rabbit, Run* (1960) and *The Centaur* (1963). Although *Rabbit, Run* was critically and commercially successful, it is difficult to separate it now from the widely acclaimed subsequent series of novels focusing on Rabbit Angstrom, whose life story provides a sort of chronicle of the transformation of American society from the 1950s through the 1980s. In *Rabbit, Run*, Rabbit is introduced as a star high school basketball player who has married the daughter of a local car dealer and impulsively tries to run away from a life that has absolutely none of the thrill that he felt on the court and that made him feel that his life had some sort of promise.

For *The Centaur*, Updike won the National Book Award. The novel focuses on the relationship between a disenchanted small-town school teacher and his physically and socially self-conscious, but quietly imaginative son. Although the material might not seem any more promising—or any less mundane—than that treated in *The Poorhouse Fair*, in this novel Updike exhibits the richly literate style that would become something of a defining characteristic of his work— to the great gratification of some critics and the annoyance of others. In *The Centaur*, the main character's mother is a well-defined character but clearly in a more subordinate role than the father. In his next novel, *Of the Farm* (1967), Updike would invert that emphasis. This short novel focuses on a man's visit to the family farm to which his mother is emotionally bound. He wants to convince her to move away and live with him, his wife, and their son. But his mother's resistance to the idea of leaving the farm strains her relationship not only with him but with his generally agreeable wife. Like *The Poorhouse Fair*, this novel has become something of a footnote work in critical discussions of Updike's prolific output.

Although the early editions of *Rabbit, Run* were edited by the publisher to tone down some of the novel's sexually oriented material, none of Updike's first four novels could have prepared readers for his fifth, *Couples* (1968). The novel focuses quite explicitly on the sex lives and the sexual experimentation of ten upper-middle-class couples living in the seaside town of Tarbox, Massachusetts. Most provocatively, the novel treats the "swapping" among the couples, a sexual phenomenon that would lead, almost a decade later, to the establishment of so-called swingers' clubs, the most notorious of which was Plato's Retreat in New York. These clubs would also be treated in Gay Talese's *Thy Neighbor's Wife* (1981), a nonfictional exploration of the very dramatic ways in which sexual mores evolved between the 1950s and the 1970s. But the heyday of these clubs would be relatively short-lived, a minor casualty of the growing awareness of the AIDs epidemic.

The prepublication word of mouth surrounding Updike's novel led to *Time* magazine's decision to feature Updike in its cover story—a decision that the magazine's editorial board began to second-guess as it became clearer just how provocative the novel would actually be. But all of the media attention to the qualms about the cover story simply ensured that the issue of *Time* would sell out and that Updike's novel would almost certainly be a best seller. Indeed, although the initial reviews of the novel were generally positive and cited Updike's skill in writing in an explicit and yet literary way about what was still widely viewed as aberrant sexuality, the commercial success of the novel led to some second-guessing of Updike's "seriousness" as a novelist. Such doubts were not entirely unfounded. A year earlier, the poet David Slavitt had assumed the pseudonym Henry Sutton because he suspected that his sexually explicit novel, *The Exhibitionist* (1967), would severely damage his reputation as a poet. But when *The Exhibitionist* sold more than 4,000,000 copies, Slavitt, as Sutton, quickly produced a sequel, *The Voyeur* (1968). And in 1980, a year ahead of Talese's book, he produced, again as Sutton, *The Proposal*, a novel on "swinging" (a slang euphemism for a more casual and even random selection of sexual partners than what was typically involved in "swapping"). Indeed, in the longer term, the "lyricism" of Updike's style in *Couples* began to be seen by some critics less as a saving grace of his treatment of explicit sexual material than as a sort of cloying mismatch with that material. So, although Updike's novel is often mentioned with *Portnoy's Complaint*, the linkage is largely an acknowledgment of the immediate sensation caused by both novels at almost the same historical moment. *Couples* has simply not had the same enduring critical stature of Roth's novel, though Updike's substantial output would largely put to rest any misgivings about his seriousness as a novelist.

## SUE KAUFMAN (1926–1977)

The emergence of the Feminist Movement as a major political, socioeconomic, and cultural force in the1960s was signaled and impelled by some very influential works of nonfiction. These included Betty Friedan's *The Feminine Mystique* (1963), Andrea Dworkin's *Child* (1966) and *Morning Hair* (1968), Valerie Solanos's *SCUM Manifesto* (1968), and Kate Millett's *Sexual Politics* (1968), as well as the Statement of Purpose of the National Organization for Women (NOW) (1966) and the National Organization for Women's Bill of Rights (1968), as well as innumerable, influential periodical articles, some published in new journals devoted to the Women's Movement.

But an equal outpouring of significant feminist fiction did not occur until the 1970s. One of the major exceptions was Sue Kaufman's *Diary of a Mad*

*Housewife* (1967). The novel focuses on Tina Balser, a woman who superficially seems to be living the suburban American Dream. She is married to a successful lawyer in a prestigious New York law firm, and they live with their two daughters in an affluent suburb. But one does not have to look very deeply beneath the surface of her daily life to see that it is far from ideal. Her husband takes every opportunity to criticize her appearance, her behavior, her housekeeping, and her parenting, and their daughters take their cue from him and treat her with an almost casual disrespect. Tina attempts to escape her marriage through an affair, but her lover treats her as badly as her husband does, and she enters a therapy group only to have the others in her group rather unsparingly critique her attitudes and actions when she attempts to share her frustrations with them. Events come to a head when her husband confesses that he has lost most of their savings on risky financial speculations, that he has been involved in an extramarital affair, and that his position in the law firm is now at risk because in focusing on his schemes and mistress, he has been neglecting his work there. Tina responds in a relatively restrained and even somewhat sympathetic way to these revelations, but when she relates these events to her therapy group and reveals that she did not reveal to her husband that she herself has been having an extramarital affair, the group predictably turns on her yet again. At this climactic moment, Tina is described as staring silently in a very detached way. Very pointedly, she comes to the recognition that the only viable response to her "madness"—her failure to live up to the very skewed standards of middle-class American life—is anger.

Kaufman wrote four other novels—two before *Diary of a Mad Housewife* and two afterward—as well as a collection of short fiction. None of her other works are much remembered, but because she died at age fifty, it is impossible to say whether she might have produced other significant work.

## JAMES BALDWIN (1924–1987)

In the 1950s, James Baldwin came to national attention with two well-received novels, *Go Tell It to the Mountain* (1953) and *Giovanni's Room* (1956), a successful play, *The Amen Corner* (1954), and the very influential collection of essays, *Notes of a Native Son* (1955). Although his novels were overshadowed by Ralph Ellison's *Invisible Man*, Baldwin's consistent output and the attention that it provoked stood in contrast with Ellison's long periods of public silence and made Baldwin seem the successor to W. E. B. DuBois and Richard Wright as a leading voice in African American letters.

In the 1960s, Baldwin produced two collections of essays, *Nobody Knows My Name: More Notes on a Native Son* (1961) and *The Fire Next Time* (1963), which became central texts to the intensifying Civil Rights Movement. In these essays, Baldwin very directly but eloquently addresses the impact of race and racism in American history, in contemporary American life and politics, and in American culture and the conceptions of American identity. Baldwin also highlights the role of religion in shaping African American identity and in providing much of the moral force behind the Civil Rights Movement. In addition to these profoundly influential essays, Baldwin's second play, *Blues for Mister*

*Charlie* (1964), and his first collection of short stories, *Going to Meet the Man* (1965), were critically acclaimed and reverberated through the broader culture. Although *Blues for Mister Charlie* is not a structurally accomplished play and although most of the white characters are little more that common caricatures, it includes some very powerful scenes that not only expose the ugly contradictions of racism but very powerfully convey the costs of racism to white Americans. Likewise, the stories collected in *Going to Meet the Man* look at the African American experience from a variety of perspectives and treat the issues of race and racism with considerable emotional intensity and with very perceptive, nuanced complexity. The most important story in the collection is "Sonny's Blues," which as the fifth story among the eight in the collection, is literally its centerpiece. The story, which is almost the length of a novella, has nonetheless been widely anthologized because in focusing on the strained relationship between two brothers, it explores issues of responsibility and self-indulgence, and self-abuse through the prisms of African American family life, family histories and secrets, military service and civilian opportunities, justice and incarceration, drug use, jazz, and religion.

In pointed contrast with those essays, stories, and play, Baldwin's novels of the 1960s, *Another Country* (1962) and *Tell Me How Long the Train's Been Gone* (1968), received at best a very mixed critical response. In both novels, Baldwin attempts to treat interracial sexual relationships along with bisexuality and homosexuality, and to highlight through those complicated and often very conflicted relationships some of the central truths about the causes and effects of deeply entrenched racism. The first novel has been hailed by some critics, in particular those from outside the United States, as a seminal work. For instance, the British novelist and critic Anthony Burgess included *Another Country* in his book-length survey of the most significant novels in English since 1939, *Ninety-Nine Novels* (1984). At the other end of the spectrum, the novel seems to have permanently antagonized the American writer Norman Mailer, who seems rightly to have perceived it as a critique of his very influential essay "The White Negro." If *Another Country* has had a mixed reception, *Tell Me How Long the Train's Been Gone* has generally been regarded as a very flawed novel in which Baldwin seems to be more concerned with delineating his themes—and, in the process, reducing them to simplistic messages—than in developing multidimensional situations and characters. The criticism of this novel dovetailed with the criticism of Baldwin's views by younger and more radicalized African American activists, most notably Eldridge Cleaver. In the space of half a decade, Baldwin went from being acclaimed as a leading—if not *the* leading—intellectual voice of the Civil Rights Movement to being derided for holding anachronistic views on race and racism. Although his most vocal critics have themselves been subject to considerable reappraisal, Baldwin's literary reputation has never really recovered from those sometimes very personalized attacks.

## MAYA ANGELOU (1928–2014)

James Baldwin's influence can be seen in the career of Maya Angelou, whom he encouraged to write about her life as an African American woman who had

Though poet and activist Maya Angelou's greatest fame would come after the 1960s, her iconic memoir *I Know Why the Caged Bird Sings* first appeared in 1969. (National Archives)

grown up poor in the South and who had subsequently traveled extensively in the United States, Europe, and Africa. Through those travels, Angelou had begun to acquire a deep understanding of the intersections of American racism and European colonialism and of the American Civil Rights Movement and the postcolonial movements in Africa and the Caribbean.

By necessity, Angelou worked in a broad variety of occupations before she began to write with earnestness. But, even after she established herself as a writer and throughout her long life, she continued to pursue a number of nonliterary and extraliterary interests. Likewise, although Angelou rather quickly earned a reputation as an accomplished poet and essayist, her work in those genres has been at least somewhat overshadowed by her series of seven autobiographical books. The earliest of these books were written before the term "creative nonfiction" came into vogue. The emergence of the "New Journalism" and the success of Truman Capote's and Norman Mailer's "nonfiction novels" were, however, bringing a legitimacy to a bridging or a blurring of categories that had previously been regarded as very definitively exclusive. Some critics have regarded Angelou's autobiographical books as autobiographical novels since she very clearly shapes the materials using techniques commonly employed by novelists and her observations very clearly move beyond the sort of verifiable fact that is required in reportage, histories, and biographies and that is expected in memoirs and autobiographies. But other critics have treated the books as meta-autobiographies, regarding them as Angelou's attempt to record and to explore the salient elements of her experience and to suggest how her experience may be representative of the broader experience of African Americans across the tumultuous decades of the twentieth century. But beyond those aims, these critics argue that Angelou is testing the conventions of the genre of autobiography—demonstrating, in effect, that a genre largely developed to accommodate the experience of white Europeans, almost certainly cannot accommodate the very different cultural experiences and perspectives of those of African descent—or those of other racial and cultural backgrounds.

The first of the seven books in Angelou's autobiographical series has remained her most well-known, widely read, and controversial work. *I Know Why the Caged Bird Sings* (1969) was an immediate best seller and an immediate source of contention for librarians and high school English teachers who chose to include it in their collections or in their curricula. The book provides a very vivid and sensitive account of Angelou's often difficult upbringing, but much of the power of the book derives from Angelou's decision to deal with troubling topics very directly—to suggest that being anything but direct is to convey less than the full truth about the kinds of experiences that either can be transcended or can be ruinous. Those outraged that young people should be assigned or even exposed to the book have typically pointed to Angelou's account of her sexual molestation at a very young age, confusing the directness of her account with a graphic appeal to prurient interest or a calculated manipulation of such material for its shock value. Astonishingly, given how frequently the merits of the book have been debated and litigated, it has remained on the annual list of the ten most frequently censored books in just about every year in the almost half-century since its initial publication.

*I Know Why the Caged Bird Sings* was initially published at a historical moment in which both the Civil Rights and the Women's Liberation Movements had emerged as the most dynamic forces in American politics, in social and economic debates, and in cultural studies. It is very important to emphasize that Angelou's gender did not simply compound the impact that her book had because of her race. Rather, Angelou emphasized that being black and female was something quite apart from being either black or female—that being black and female demanded its own radical reshaping of literary form and voice because neither the Civil Rights nor the Women's Liberation Movements—nor even the predominant concerns of postcolonial studies—were adequately accommodating the experiences of women of color.

## WILLIAM S. BURROUGHS (1914–1997)

When people mention the Beat writers of the 1950s, William S. Burroughs is almost always included as one of the three most important writers in the group—after Jack Kerouac and Allen Ginsberg. Ironically, Burroughs was the oldest of the three, and although he struggled throughout his life with addictions to various illicit drugs, he outlived both Kerouac and Ginsberg. More ironically, although almost every undergraduate English major has read Kerouac's *On the Road* and Ginsberg's *Howl* and although relatively few of them have probably read any novel by Burroughs, Burroughs very arguably has had a broader and more extended influence, especially among other types of artists and across the broader popular culture. *On the Road* was galvanizing because of the free-flowing manner in which it describes a lifestyle devoted to following one's impulses. The novel's style is as accessible as its content was radical, especially for the 1950s and early 1960s when conformity was a major expectation across suburban, middle-class American society. Much the same can be said of *Howl*. Although Ginsberg employed the long, unrestrained poetic line associated with Whitman's poetry and employed it to make shocking proclamations about the underside of American society, and in particular about the marginalized youth in that society, the poem was not only easy to read, but it also became widely known in part because of Ginsberg's powerful public readings of it.

In contrast, Burroughs is one of the most experimental and arguably unreadable novelists that America has ever produced. He came to attention in the mid-1950s with *Junky*, an autobiographical novel on addiction that was originally published under a pen name. Written in the style that the hard-boiled writers of the 1930s and 1940s had borrowed from Hemingway, the novel unsparingly explores the causes, effects, and daily realities of drug addiction. If, like most of Nelson Algren's novels, *The Man with the Golden Arm* (1949) treats the dark topic of addiction with a certain lyricism (the sort of paradoxical, if not oxymoronic, synthesis of subject and style suggested by the title of another one of his books, the collection of short fiction titled *The Neon Wilderness* [1947]), then Burroughs's novel doubles down on the hard-boiled elements and emphasizes by subtraction the very truncated lyrical possibilities in the sordid world that his characters inhabit.

During the 1950s, Burroughs accumulated a sizable number of unpublished manuscripts in various stages of completion, which he called his "Word Hoard." Some of these manuscripts would be published individually and in full at later dates. For instance, the novel *Queer*, which was written as a companion work to *Junky*, was not published until 1985. (Notably, in *Junky*, Burroughs had treated the homosexuality of the major character, but his "aberrant" sexuality could be written off as an element of his more broadly aberrant lifestyle. But focusing more pointedly and exclusively on homosexuality, as Burroughs does in *Queer*, made it almost impossible to find a publisher in the 1950s.) The "Word Hoard" would be put to use in creating Burroughs's most notable works of the late 1950s and 1960s.

In the late 1940s and 1950s, Burroughs's drug use and personal associations kept him on the verge of serious legal problems. His impulse was to relocate ahead of arrest or conviction. In 1952, he was living in Mexico with a woman named Joan Vollmer, with whom he had begun a relationship almost a decade earlier. Vollmer was also a drug addict and their relationship was volatile. In Mexico, Burroughs supposedly tried to shoot a highball glass off her head in some sort of narcotically clouded reenactment of the tale of William Tell. The result of the stunt was that Vollmer took a bullet through the head that killed her instantly, and Burroughs was arrested and had to bribe his way out of jail and then flee Mexico. He would spend most of the late 1950s and 1960s living abroad, most notably in Tangiers and in Paris. Much of the writing that he produced and that found its way into the "Word Hoard" would become the novels with which he is now most associated, *Naked Lunch* and *The Nova Trilogy*.

It is almost impossible to provide a plot summary of any of these four novels because to describe them as nonlinear is an understatement. While he was in Paris, Burroughs met the British artist Brion Gysin whose paintings went a step beyond the experiments of the Dadaists and the Cubists in juxtaposing cutouts of images not just to suggest motion or three-dimensionality in new and provocative ways but to challenge the whole notion of the integrity of the image.

Gysin extended his experiments with cut-up techniques to audio and multimedia projects, some of which were collaborative, and to his poetry. Burroughs was fascinated by Gysin's experiments and began attempting to apply them to fiction in order to challenge the whole notion not only of the linearity of narrative and, more fundamentally, to any units of text, but also the concept of the self-contained literary work. Unlike the antinovels and metanovels of postmodernists such as William Gaddis, John Barth, Donald Barthelme, Thomas Pynchon, and Joseph McElroy, Burroughs went well beyond creating maze-like narrative structures, undermining reader expectations about such basic fictional elements as setting, plot, and character, and manipulating tone, style, and point of view to disorient readers and to remind them of the artificiality of narrative in relation to experience. Burroughs would literally cut up existing narratives in completely random pieces, mix up the pieces, and reassemble them. So one piece of narrative can merge into another not just in juxtaposed narrative sections or from paragraph to paragraphs but in midsentence. Moreover, he suggested that pieces of the work of different types of works and multiple authors might be run together in this manner, challenging the concepts of genre and authorship.

The first of Burroughs's "cut-up" novel is *Naked Lunch* (1959). Kerouac and Ginsberg helped Burroughs to edit the text to the version that was ultimately published, and Burroughs himself initially pointed to the precedents in the cut-up technique employed by T. S. Eliot in *The Waste Land*, which was much accentuated by Ezra Pound's editing, and John Dos Passos's editing of the short "nonfiction" sections of *The U.S.A. Trilogy* that were inserted between the narrative sections much as Ernest Hemingway inserted reportorial vignettes between the stories of *In Our Time*. But, as much as there are modernist precedents for what Burroughs was doing, *Naked Lunch* is much more postmodern in its structure, style, and themes. Like *Junky*, *Naked Lunch* features a main character who is a drug addict and who devotes much of his time and energy eluding the police. Unlike *Junky*, however, *Naked Lunch* is set in a more overtly dystopian "alternative" reality in which there are all sorts of agencies beyond the police that are conducting surveillance in the service of an indecipherable web of political, social, economic, and cultural conspiracies. The result in a sort of repressive chaos in which authority is deeply entrenched but opaque and arbitrarily exerted and in which predatory behavior is largely permitted as long as it does not challenge the controls that those in authority do wish to exert. Within this dystopian world, national boundaries continue to exist but only because they serve the propaganda of those in authority who clearly have international reach, who can use nationalism as a political distraction with which to keep the masses preoccupied. So the cut-up form of the novel on many levels is perfectly reflective of the themes that the novel presents. Moreover, in his emphasis on the impact and grotesque possibilities of mass media, digital technologies, and medical experimentation, Burroughs anticipates some of the major technological forces that will increasingly define and dominate life in the last decades of the twentieth century and into the twenty-first century. On the most basic level, his cut-up narrative anticipates the possibilities in hypertexts.

Although *Naked Lunch* was originally published in Paris in 1959, it was not published in the United States until 1962 and in the United Kingdom until 1964 because Burroughs's freewheeling use of vulgarities and his frank treatment of predatory heterosexual and homosexual behavior led to the novel's being banned and its then becoming the subject of extended litigation. Thus, it is truly a novel of the 1960s not only in its structure, style, and themes, but in its actual impact on the Counterculture Movements emerging in the mid-1960s.

The impact of *Naked Lunch* was reinforced by the publication of *The Nova Trilogy* across the first half of the 1960s and with significant revisions of the first two of the novels being issued in the second half of the decade, to bring those novels into line with the refinement of the conception of the trilogy that Burroughs came to in working on the third novel. The three novels are *The Soft Machine* (1961, with a revised edition published in 1966), *The Ticket That Exploded* (1962, with the revised edition published in 1967), and *Nova Express* (1964). Although this trilogy has often been described, even by Burroughs himself, as an extension of *Naked Lunch*, it moves as much beyond *Naked Lunch* as that novel moves beyond *Junky*. Burroughs has asserted that in the trilogy, he is attempting to provide a new mythology for the space age. Accordingly, the world of the trilogy is the product of an ancient alien invasion: that is, the aliens gave human beings the "gift" of language, which they and their descendants have used to control humanity by distorting the way in which human beings perceive their own experience. In this world, the only way for humanity to liberate itself is to break free from the constraints of language. So, again, the cut-up form of the novels in itself reinforces the theme that nonlinear narrative is the mechanism for escaping self-limiting and self-destructive mythologies expressed through conventional narratives that reinforce archetypes and other expressions of thought derived from those mythologies. In effect, Burroughs is using the patterns and conventions of speculative fiction to suggest how speculative fiction needs to be transcended because the worlds it presents are too rooted in the fraudulent assumptions of literary fiction and conventional narrative traditions.

As in *Junky* and even more than in *Naked Lunch*, Burroughs also exploits the conventions and the style of hard-boiled crime and detective fiction. The alien authorities who police the world of the trilogy are known as the Nova Mob. The name itself blurs the conventional distinctions between law enforcement and criminal organizations, and it reinforces the notion that authoritarianism is based on values that are arbitrary in inverse proportion to how stridently they are proclaimed and how aggressively they are ostensibly enforced. As in *Naked Lunch* and in the hard-boiled genre, there are conspiracies to be uncovered and real reasons for paranoia, but in Burroughs's trilogy, these challenges are too innumerable to be addressed, never mind surmounted or resolved. And instead of the knight-errant detective who straddles the lawful and illicit realities of his society, Burroughs presents us with the "partisans" whose aim is to make nonsense, rather than sense, of it all.

Although *The Nova Trilogy* has sometimes been compared to linguistic experiments such as Gertrude Stein's *Tender Buttons*, James Joyce's *Finnegan's Wake*, and William Gaddis's *JR*, each of those novels seems to be intended to reinvent language or, perhaps more accurately, to reinvest readers in the process of developing a more acute awareness of language as language, of language as a signifier rather than on the thing signified. In contrast, Burroughs seems to assert a complete loss of faith in language and to propose that, paradoxically, guttural noise has more meaning than words.

Burroughs went so far in *The Nova Trilogy* that even he might have supposed that he had boxed himself in at a dead end. But in his last work published in the 1960s, *The Last Words of Dutch Schultz* (1969), Burroughs basically turns his approach in the trilogy on its head. After the gangster Dutch Schultz had been gunned down, he lingered in a semiconscious state before finally succumbing to his wounds. As he passed in and out of consciousness, he made rambling comments that law enforcement thought might implicate some of his associates or competitors. So they tasked a stenographer with taking down everything that Schultz uttered in his extended delirium. The transcript was no more revealing or coherent than a cut-up text, but Burroughs supposedly uses selected parts of the transcript to provide a structure to a fictional reimagining of Schultz's career. Some of the events and characters are based on what is generally supposed to be fact, but other parts of the novel are to some degree, if not completely, invented.

## ALLEN GINSBERG (1926–1997)

Allen Ginsberg was born and grew up in northern New Jersey. While enrolled at Columbia University, he became closely acquainted with Jack Kerouac and William S. Burroughs. The three writers would become central figures in what became known as the Beat Movement, a loose association of young people rebelling against conformity, materialism, and nationalism that was increasingly characterizing the increasingly suburban mainstream American culture of the decade. The Beats offered an alternative to the conventionalized social mores, heterosexual norms, and racial segregation reinforced by the rapid development of television and the broader rise of mass media.

But Ginsberg did not come to national attention until he moved to San Francisco, where he became acquainted with another group of poets, most notably Kenneth Rexroth and Robert Duncan. In October 1955, Ginsberg gave a dramatic reading of his poem *Howl* at the Six Gallery, an event that became one of the seminal events in the history of the Beat Movement. In the following year, *Howl and Other Poems* was published by City Lights Bookstore. Shortly thereafter, the book was seized because it was deemed to be obscene, and its publisher (the manager of City Lights Bookstore) was charged criminally for producing and distributing it. The resulting obscenity trial received national attention, and when a judge finally ruled that the colloquial and often crude language of the poem seemed essential to both its force and its meaning, the book had gained so much notoriety that it became a best seller. Indeed, although the poem was undoubtedly more shocking to most readers of the 1950s—because of the directness of its language, the ferocity of its tone, and the rejection of materialism and its institutional supports—it has retained a good deal of its force and relevance for several subsequent generations of readers. *Howl and Other Poems* has not only remained continuously in print to this day, but it has become one of the best-selling books of poetry of the past century.

In the 1960s, unlike Burroughs and Kerouac, Ginsberg became a significant figure in the Counterculture that is often viewed as a successor to the Beat Movement. Like Burroughs, Ginsberg spent a significant portion of the 1960s overseas, but, unlike Burroughs who became a somewhat mysterious cult figure, Ginsberg spoke out on issues from wherever he happened to be, and when he was in the United States, he was a very visible activist on behalf of the causes and values associated with the Counterculture. In this respect, Ginsberg became a striking contrast to Jack Kerouac, who became a reactionary figure, outspokenly critical of the Counterculture and asserting that it represented more a bastardization than an extension of the Beat Movement. In 1965, Ginsberg was a focal figure in the International Poetry Incarnation, a reading featuring more than a dozen poets from the United States and the United Kingdom that was held at the Royal Albert Hall in London and attracted an audience of 7,000. When he returned to the United States, Ginsberg began to incorporate music and Buddhist and Krishna mantras and chants into his readings. In a number of high-profile public events, including the Human Be-In in San Francisco in 1967 and the Democratic National Convention in Chicago in 1968, he repeated the mantra "Om" for hours on end. He even convinced conservative icon William F. Buckley to permit him to perform a Krishna chant on *Firing Line,* the widely watched weekly television program hosted by Buckley.

In 1961, City Lights Bookstore published *Kaddish and Other Poems 1958–1960,* which is generally regarded as Ginsberg's most significant book of poetry other than *Howl.* When Ginsberg's mother died in 1956, Ginsberg, who had not been a practicing Jew for quite some time, asked the rabbi to allow the Kaddish to be read with Ginsberg's non-Jewish friends in attendance. When the rabbi refused to permit it, Ginsberg's sense of alienation from his birth religion was exacerbated. He decided to compose his own version of the Kaddish in memory of his mother, and over the next three years, he worked on drafts of the poem. The published version has two sections, both of which are highly anecdotal and impressionistic but neither of which presents a conventionally structured narrative. The first section provides a personalized depiction of his mother's experiences as a radicalized Russian-Jewish immigrant to the United States who lived through the socioeconomic and political upheaval of both the Great Depression and the Second World War. The second section presents an intimate account of her serious psychological problems, which manifested themselves in an often acute and debilitating paranoia. Much of this section focuses on Ginsberg's own efforts as a child and especially as an adolescent to try to meet his mother's needs while also gradually coming to terms with the impact of her illness in shaping his view of the world. Although his mother's paranoia was not the direct result of any single traumatic experience, it can easily be seen as a psychological response to the extremely violent and frightening historical events through which she and her generation lived—if they were fortunate enough to survive them. Moreover, in reflecting on his mother's life and death, Ginsberg openly extends those reflections to considerations of the meaning of his own existence and of his own mortality—and, by extension, the core truths of the broader human condition. The title poem constitutes almost a third of the book. The other poems included in it are: "Poem Rocket," "Europe! Europe!," "To Lindsay," "Message," "To Aunt Rose," "At Apollinaire's Grave," "The Lion Is for Real," "Ignu," "Death to Van Gogh's Ear," "Laughing Gas," "Mescaline," "Lysergic Acid," "Magic Psalm," "The Reply," and "The End." The poems generally complement the title poem of the collection thematically, though the collection, like the title poem, does not have a very clear, conventional structure.

*Kaddish and Other Poems* was followed two years later, in 1963, by the collection *Reality Sandwiches*. The title comes from the poem "On Burroughs' Work," specifically from these lines: "A naked lunch is natural to us, / we eat reality sandwiches." Despite the nod to Burroughs in the title, the collection is dedicated to the Beat poet Gregory Corso. The collection features poems that Ginsberg wrote from 1953 to 1960 as he was traveling overseas—in locations from Paris to Havanna and from Mexico to Peru—and in the United States—from Times Square in New York City to the plains of Kansas to Berkeley and the Bay Area. Taken together, the poems convey his maturing sensibility as a poet and a spiritual seeker, but, again, there is not a clearly cohesive structure to the collection as a whole. In addition to "On Burroughs' Work," the collection includes the following poems: "My Alba," "The Green Automobile," "Siesta in Xbalba," "Love Poem on Theme by Whitman," "Malest Cornifici Tuo Catullo," "Dream Record: June 8, 1955," "A Strange New Cottage in Berkeley," "My Sad Self," "I Beg You Come Back & Be Cheerful," "To An Old Poet In Perú," and "Aether."

In 1968, *Planet News* became the third collection of Ginsberg's poetry published in the decade. The collection includes poems written between 1961 and 1967, again while Ginsberg was traveling widely—indeed, even more widely than he had traveled in the previous decade. In addition to moving between the two coasts across the United States, Ginsberg spent considerable time not only in Europe and Latin America but also in Africa and Asia. Indeed, some of the most memorable poems in this collection and some of the most profound influences on his work resulted from his extended trips to India and Japan. *Planet News* includes the following poems (the unconventional capitalization of words in the titles is Ginsberg's): "Television was a Baby Crawling Toward that Deathchamber," "This form of Life needs Sex," "Stotras to Kali Destroyer of Illusions," "Describe: The Rain on Dasaswamedh," "Death News," "The Change: Kyoto-Tokyo Express," "Why is God Love, Jack?," "After Yeats," "I am a Victim of Telephone," "Kral Majales," "Who Be Kind To," "First Party at Ken Kesey's with Hell's Angels," "Wichita Vortex Sutra," "City Midnight Junk Strains," and "Wales Visitation." "Death News" is a response to the news that William Carlos Williams, one of Ginsberg's early mentors, had passed away, and it and "After Yeats" show Ginsberg reflecting on how a poet's influence and his or her place in literary history is determined.

Ginsberg's poetry treated themes that would emerge as central preoccupations of the Counterculture: the spiritual antidotes to rampant, all-consuming materialism and corporatism; the interest in Eastern and indigenous "alternatives" to institutionalized Western religions; the advocacy of a new type of grassroots political radicalism that focused more purposefully on the issues of marginalized groups, extending the Civil Rights and Women's Movements to LBGTQ individuals, indigenous peoples, and economically and socially displaced people such as impoverished rural communities, the homeless populations of major metropolitan areas, and the incarcerated, in particular those imprisoned for nonviolent drug offenses and sexual behavior that was increasingly being viewed as nonconformist rather than clinically aberrant; and, lastly, an increasingly cosmopolitan attitude toward other cultures and a rejection of more parochial definitions of what it means to be a "true" American. Like many others in those who shaped both the Beat Movement and the Counterculture, Ginsberg was a restless figure whose peripatetic travels reflected his spiritual and artistic searching.

A major feature of the Counterculture was, of course, the experimentation with various types of drugs to achieve altered states of consciousness, which could mean anything from an escape from the grinding inanities or hardships of everyday life to a path to enhanced spiritual enlightenment. Although the book's contents were actually produced during the 1950s and although it is largely forgotten today, *The Yage Letters* attracted considerable attention when it was published in 1963 and for the rest of the decade. At its simplest level, the book is a collection of the correspondence between William S. Burroughs and Ginsberg, starting with Burroughs's trip to the Amazon rainforest to locate the "yage" of the title, the ayahuasca plant that has hallucinogenic properties and that is said to invest at least some of its users with paranormal powers such as clarifying visions and telepathy. The correspondence extends to Ginsberg's own later experimenting with yage. Because the book also includes some other writings by the two authors (writings that have varied somewhat from edition to edition), it has also been treated as a miscellany. And the publisher, City Lights Bookstore, has even classified it as a novel, which given Burroughs's radical experiments with the novel form is not at all a preposterous proposition. So, at a minimum, this volume illustrates the effects of the Counterculture in further eroding the distinctions of genre that had first been challenged in the experiments of the modernists. More broadly, through his interest in combining poetry readings and musical performances, Ginsberg contributed to the increasing erosion of the distinctions between high art and popular culture, especially as topics worthy of serious consideration and study. The rise of musicians who not just composed their own songs but also created "concept" albums caused an increasing number of critics and scholars to consider lyrics with much the same seriousness with which they analyzed poetry. And, from the opposite direction, the work of obviously significant but decidedly nonformalist poets such as Ginsberg began to force a gradual reappraisal of the "literary canon."

### CARLOS CASTANEDA (1925–1998)

Trained as an anthropologist, Carlos Castaneda came to worldwide attention in 1968 with the publication of the first of his twelve books treating his firsthand experiences with shamanism. *The Teachings of Don Juan: The Yaqui Way of Knowledge* was written while Castaneda was doing fieldwork among the Yaqui

Indians in northern Mexico from 1960 to 1965. It was accepted as his master's thesis from the School of Anthropology at UCLA, was originally published by the University of California Press, and included a foreword by noted anthropologist Walter Goldschmidt who was a faculty member at UCLA at that time. In an introduction to the twenty-fifth anniversary edition of the book, Castaneda describes, however, the role of his mentor, Dr. Clement Meaghan, in encouraging him to continue the fieldwork and complete the resulting thesis despite the general lack of enthusiasm for the project among most of the other faculty in the School of Anthropology. Indeed, during this fieldwork, Castaneda completed the manuscript for not only *The Teachings of Don Juan* but also of the two follow-up books on the topic, *A Separate Reality* (1970) and *A Journey to Ixtlan* (1971). On the basis of this work, Castaneda would earn his PhD in anthropology.

The publication of these books was very timely. The opposition to the Vietnam War was producing a broader reappraisal of the commonly accepted truths about American history and American exceptionalism. Specifically, in conjunction with the Civil Rights Movement and the efforts to eliminate both open and implicit racial segregation, among Native Americans there was resurgent interest in their cultural heritage and identity, in revisionist histories of their resistance to their subjugation by white Americans, and in assertions of their political rights. The interest in preserving indigenous cultures that had been pushed to the edge of extinction dovetailed with the interests in investigating alternatives to institutionalized Western religions and in environmentalism. Moreover, indigenous spiritual practices and rituals often involved the use of mind-altering substances available in their natural environments, and so the experimentation with these substances appealed to those who were already experimenting with synthetically produced comparable substances and were looking for more "natural" alternatives. Finally, the books were also appealing because they were written in the first person, providing a narrative account of and guide to self-exploration, in addition to a compendium of a spiritual seer's wisdom.

There was a counterpoint to the fascination with Castaneda's books that was also very much a product of the 1960s. In 1973, *Time* magazine would publish a major profile of the author that famously described him as "an enigma wrapped in a mystery wrapped in a tortilla." This playful but nonetheless very pointedly flippant appraisal expressed the skepticism about Castaneda's books that had stretched beyond the discouragement of his fieldwork by most of the faculty in UCLA's School of Anthropology. To varying degrees, anthropologists who reviewed the books raised concerns about the accuracy of Castaneda's depiction of Yaqui culture. One very unsparing critique of *The Teachings of Don Juan*, written by Weston La Barre for the *New York Times Book Review*, was never published because it seemed gratuitously out of step with the general enthusiasm for the book, which, after all, had the benefit of considerable, prestigious academic endorsement. As the backlash against the Counterculture intensified in the Reagan era, it was inevitable that works such as Castaneda's would be challenged for being fraudulent on multiple levels. Richard de Mille made something of a personal scholarly industry out of thoroughly analyzing

Castaneda's work and amassing ever-increasing evidence of its illegitimacy. But despite the sense that de Mille had turned his critique into something of a vendetta, other anthropologists also began to provide further, detailed critiques questioning Castaneda's credibility. The problem with popularizing a very specialized niche in an academic discipline is, of course, that the attention to the work inevitably exposes differences that can be attributed to some degree to the requirements in writing for a very specialized, scholarly readership and for a general reader. A simplification intended to heighten the appeal of the material to the general reader can become a major point for a scholar, especially one with a stringent sense of professional standards or with a strong sense of competitiveness. Furthermore, the popularity of the work almost always also increases scholarly attention to the subject of the work, exposing the limits to what the writer was able to ascertain from more limited previous fieldwork and his own fieldwork. Even the most transparent and most publicly available scholars can find such attention extremely challenging and damaging. And Castaneda was neither transparent nor publicly available.

Following the publication of his third book and the profile in *Time*, Castaneda disappeared from public view for about two decades. Then, when he did reemerge from his reclusion in the mid-1990s, to promote a commercial enterprise called Cleargreen through which he was attempting to market a new path to spiritual enlightenment that he called Tensegrity, he passed away less than five years later. Indeed, Castaneda's reclusiveness not only included a great guardedness about the details of his personal life but also extended beyond extreme privacy to a somewhat bewildering ambiguity. For instance, his date of birth has been given as both 1925 and 1935, and although it is known that he emigrated to the United States in 1950, his country of origin has been identified as both Peru and Brazil. Although he was said to have married Margaret Runyon in Mexico in 1960 and then to have divorced her either in 1960 or 1973 (or both), his death certificate indicated that he had never been married. Likewise, he is listed as the father of Runyon's son, C. J. Castaneda, even though there is evidence that he was almost certainly not the biological father. Then, when Castaneda died, his death was not announced until two weeks after it reportedly occurred, and C. J. Castaneda challenged Castaneda's will because he appeared to have signed it a day after a medical report indicated that his terminal illness had rendered him incapable of making such a decision. To make matters even more bizarre, in the decade following Castaneda's death, several of his closest associates mysteriously wandered off into the wilderness and disappeared. When their remains were eventually discovered, very little about their last days was clarified except for the fact that they had indeed died.

All of these circumstances taken together have reinforced the sense that there was something both spurious and calculated in the way that Castaneda created and promoted the works that made him an international figure. The books have sold almost 30 million copies and have been translated from English into at least a dozen and a half other languages. But they are now considered by most anthropologists to be fiction. Ironically, the general professional skepticism about their veracity has only reinforced some enthusiasts' conviction that they present a vision so radical that it is incapable of being embraced by institutionalized scholars and the mainstream culture. Finally, it is also worth noting that the issue of whether Castaneda's books are factual or fictional has been complicated by the rise of the New Journalism and the acceptance of new genres such as faction, creative nonfiction, and the nonfiction novel. Indeed, despite their initially having academic endorsement, Castaneda's books are, like most spiritual works—especially seminal religious works—accepted as factual by believers and as myth or worse by nonbelievers.

## RICHARD FARINA (1937–1966)

When Richard Farina died in 1966 at the age of twenty-nine, he had already established himself as a folk singer and musician, performing and recording with his wife Mimi, the sister of Joan Baez. He and Bob Dylan had met very early in their careers in the early 1960s and had become close friends, and like Dylan, Farina had begun to focus increasingly on protest songs in the music that he wrote and performed.

Two days before his death while riding as a passenger on the back of a friend's motorcycle, Farina's first book, the loosely autobiographical novel, *Been Down So Long It Looks Like Up to Me*, had been published by Random House. The novel has often been described as the picaresque chronicle of a young American's coming of age, following him from his formative experiences in the American West, to his experiences in Cuba during the Cuban Revolution that brought Fidel Castro to power, to his college education at a prestigious private university, identified in the novel as Mentor University but quite clearly based on Cornell University, which Farina had attended on a scholarship, studying first engineering and then English, though he left shortly before he would have graduated.

Farina had been writing fiction almost as long as he had been writing songs. While he was at Cornell, he had placed stories with both highly regarded literary journals such as *The Transatlantic Review* and popular magazines such as *Mademoiselle*. Indeed, at Cornell, Farina had met and became close friends with Thomas Pynchon, who would serve as the best man at Farina and Mimi's wedding. Pynchon would describe Farina's novel as "coming on like the Hallelujah Chorus done by 200 kazoo players with perfect pitch . . . hilarious, chilling, sexy, profound, maniacal, beautiful, and outrageous all at the same time." Pynchon would later dedicate his third novel *Gravity's Rainbow* to his deceased friend.

In a retrospective article published in the London *Guardian* in March 2016, David Barnett has described Farina as a transitional figure between the Beat Movement and the Counterculture. The protagonist of Farina's novel is named Gnossos Pappadopoulis to suggest his comical parallels to that most famous of Greek wanderers and misadventurers, Odysseus. Certainly, Gnossos has a great deal of the wanderlust—the impulse to seek new experiences in off-the-beaten-track, sometimes exotic, sometimes mundanely dreadful, and occasionally very dangerous places—that characterizes the most prominent of the Beats. On the other hand, Gnossos exhibits the political radicalism that is more closely associated with the Counterculture than the Beats. But his interests in underground music, in offbeat and especially locally popular alcoholic drinks, in regional and indigenous cuisines, in both spiritual seeking and sexual pursuits, all make him a figure that could be associated equally with both the original hipsters and the hippies. Although viewing him in this way, as a transitional figure, is thought-provoking, the designation does depend a great deal on Farina's tragically shortened life and the impossibility of placing his only novel and other shorter works within any larger body of work.

## RICHARD BRAUTIGAN (1935–1984)

Richard Brautigan was born into poverty, to a working-class, single mother who had a succession of marriages to men who were neglectful, struggling with alcoholism or other psychological issues, and, in several instances, emotionally and physically abusive. Nonetheless, Brautigan managed to do well in high school and developed an interest in writing creatively while contributing to school publications. His formative experiences would continue to provide much of the material on which he would focus throughout his writing career, whether he was addressing his experiences straightforwardly or metaphorically. Yet, his work never quite became a mechanism for accommodating, if not moving beyond, the psychological trauma of his childhood and adolescence. When he was still quite young, he was arrested for throwing a rock through the window of a police station. Although he supposedly committed this act of brazen vandalism simply because he was desperately hungry and knew that he would get regular meals in jail, his behavior while in custody was so unusual that he ended up being committed to a mental hospital, where he was diagnosed with and treated for severe depression, acute paranoia, and schizophrenia. Throughout his life, Brautigan would be prone to emotional volatility and would struggle with alcoholism. And, ultimately, he would commit suicide—the emotional isolation of his existence being reflected in the fact that his corpse would remain undiscovered for about a month.

One of the truisms about the Hippie Movement has been that young people from relatively affluent families became disenchanted with the values associated with middle-class suburban life and idealistically or naively decided to "drop out," believing that a materially comfortable life had become antithetical to a spiritually fulfilling life. The perversion of this search for an alternative way to live came to be represented in the Manson "family." There was great consternation not just that hippies would commit such savage crimes but also that young women from very "comfortable" backgrounds could somehow be turned into cold-blooded murderers. As an author, Richard Brautigan, who came from a background much more similar to Charles Manson's than to that of many of the young women in Manson's "family," somehow became the literary voice of the most idealistic, whimsical, and transcendently naïve impulses of the Hippie Movement.

The existential problem for Brautigan was that when the Counterculture lost its momentum and focus, being absorbed in various ways into the mainstream of American culture and in other ways being rejected as unsustainable or misguided, the whole attitude underlying his work became anachronistic. Although he was only in midlife and barely a decade removed from his greatest success as a writer, most new readers were now coming to his "old" work with a pronounced sense of nostalgia, and his new work went largely unnoticed because it no longer seemed especially relevant. Analogously, although some critics have argued that the thematic complexity of Brautigan's work has been very underappreciated, the consensus has been that while Brautigan was able to convey the ways in which the main currents of American culture and the core elements of American identity were being exposed as fractured in the maelstrom of the 1960s, he was not able to explore those themes and those core elements of American identity in any sort of coherent way: that is, arguing otherwise is tantamount to finding in Brautigan's work a complexity of intention and thought that simply is not there; what power the works do have rests in their more visceral, imaginative energy and in the considerable surface tension in Brautigan's seemingly buoyant voice serving up descriptions of a quite thoroughly wrecked America.

*Trout Fishing in America* (1967) was Brautigan's second published novel. Most biographical profiles note that it was the first novel that he wrote, but it and his first published novel, *A Confederate General from Big Sur* (1964), were both written in the summer of 1961 during an extended camping trip in Idaho. *A Confederate General from Big Sur* was largely ignored, and the bulk of its sale followed its being reissued after *Trout Fishing in America* became a best seller and a sort of Counterculture phenomenon. Viewed against most of the other best-selling novels of the period, which tended to be big, thick books that often featured sprawling narratives—that were often literally blockbusters—*Trout Fishing in America* was physically a very obvious anomaly. A very thin book for a novel, it was only 112 pages long in its original edition. Moreover, those 112 pages included a considerable amount of white space because the novel includes more than forty sections, some as short as a single paragraph. Indeed, not only does the novel not have any conventional structure, stringing together anecdotal sections with an apparently deliberate randomness, but many of the sections are not even primarily anecdotal or narrative. Instead, they are more like fragments of essays, of casual reportage, of off-the-cuff commentary, of journal entries, or of prose poems. Taken all together, these elements have the feel of inspired improvisation, of something sustainable over a book of this length but not much longer.

The antinovelistic quality of *Trout Fishing in America* encouraged critics to categorize it as a metafictional postmodern work. Ironically, most of the works in this classification are, like the best-selling novels of the decade, big, sprawling books. Notable exceptions would be many of John Hawkes's novels and the short stories of Donald Barthelme, but the works of both of those authors feature an intensity of purpose and a compression of execution that are not present in Brautigan's work. Even Kurt Vonnegut's novels, which owe as much to the popular genres of fiction as to postmodern metafictional experiments, exhibit a deliberate manipulation of forms that is not evident, or at least as evident, in Brautigan's work.

These sorts of contrasts are evident in a consideration of even some of the superficial elements of the novel. For instance, the title *Trout Fishing in America* is also a character, of sorts, in the novel, the name given to a voice that comments primarily on the historical heritage and natural bounty of America as it is typically idealized. This voice is so ambiguous that at times it seems undifferentiated from the nameless protagonist and first-person narrator. And another character, a legless, cantankerous, panhandling wino in San Francisco is called Trout Fishing in America Shorty. When one compares this ambiguous differentiation of or overlap among Brautigan's characters to what Pynchon does structurally, dramatically, and thematically with the multiple characters named V in his first novel named for those multivariously connected characters, the differences in the complexity of intention and of execution should be very strikingly apparent.

All of this is not to deny the great appeal of *Trout Fishing in America*, especially for readers of the period in which it was initially published. As a result of its deliberate formlessness, one can open it to almost any page and find a passage that seems almost to compel one to read it out loud. Brautigan had a very fine ear for aphoristic observations—or, perhaps more accurately, near-aphoristic expressions in which the observation goes in an unexpected direction, becoming either directly metaphoric or suggestively metaphoric because it is literally incongruous or even ridiculous. What follows are several randomly selected examples: "Now it was close to sunset and the earth was beginning to cool off in the manner of eternity and office girls were returning like penguins from Montgomery Street"; "One spring afternoon as a child in the strange town of Portland, I walked down to a different street corner, and saw a row of old houses, huddled together like seals on a rock"; "I walked home past the glass whiskers of the houses, reflecting the downward rushing waterfalls of night"; and "The bookstore was a parking lot for used graveyards. Thousands of graveyards were parked in rows like cars. Most of the books were out of print, and no one wanted to read them anymore and the people who had read the books had died or forgotten about them, but through the organic process of music the books had become virgins again."

Some of the sentences are very characteristic of the period in being both straightforward and not quite explicable: "You're not fooling anyone by taking your clothes off when you go to bed"; "I thought about it for a while, hiding it from the rest of my mind. But I didn't ruin my birthday by secretly thinking about it too hard"; "He looked ninety years old for thirty years and then he got the notion that he would die, and did so"; and "It only made sense that drinking intelligent blood would make intelligent fleas." Others are built around quirky references to the material artifacts of the popular culture: "We were all silent except for blink, blink, blink, blink, blink," and "He created his own Kool Aid reality and was able to illuminate himself by it." The most often cited examples of this sort of wordplay may be the very last line of the novel, which is "I always wanted to write a book that ended with the word Mayonnaise."

For those with more background in literature, there are obvious echoes of Hemingway and the hard-boiled writers who were influenced by his direct, spare style: "I drank coffee and read old books and waited for the year to end," and "He learned about life at sixteen, first from Dostoevsky and then from the whores of New Orleans." There are also some hipster-style allusions to literary movements: "After he graduated from college, he went to Paris and became an Existentialist. He had a photograph taken of Existentialism and himself sitting at a sidewalk cafe. Pard was wearing a beard and he looked as if he had a huge soul, with barely enough room in his body to contain it."

And there are consistent references to trout fishing and trout streams that seem to tie the work together organically, even if trying to link them analytically seems like a very quixotic undertaking. Some of the allusions are whimsical: "Excuse me, I said. I thought you were a trout stream. I'm not, she said," and "I remember mistaking an old woman for a trout stream in Vermont, and I had to beg her pardon." Some have the sound of folk wisdom: "You had to be a plumber to fish that creek." And some are just amusing wordplay: "The fish was a twelve-inch rainbow trout with a huge hump on its back. A hunchback trout," and "Truth is stranger than fishin.'" What follows is just a selection of the more substantial of those allusions: "The girl was very pretty and her body was like a clear mountain river of skin and muscle flowing over rocks of bone and hidden nerves"; "The old drunk told me about trout fishing. When he could talk, he had a way of describing trout as if they were a precious and intelligent metal"; and "My sperm came out into the water, unaccustomed to the light, and instantly it became a misty, stringy kind of thing and swirled out like a falling star, and I saw a dead fish come forward and float into my sperm, bending it in the middle."

Brautigan's first publications were actually small chapbooks of poetry. When he was still in the mental hospital, he wrote and briefly shopped around the manuscript for a book called *The God of the Martians*. The manuscript fit onto two pages, and although it was only 600 words in total, it was divided into twenty sections. It anticipates not just the brevity, aphoristic style, and improvisational structure of *Trout Fishing in America*, but also the salient qualities of Brautigan's poetry. Most of his output from the 1960s would be collected in *The Pill versus the Springhill Mine Disaster*. Typically identified as Brautigan's seventh published book of poetry, this collection includes ninety-eight poems, sixty of which appeared in previous collections, in a total of just 108 pages.

In addition to *Trout Fishing in America*, Brautigan produced two other published novels in the 1960s, *A Confederate General from Big Sur* (1964), mentioned previously in this article, and *In Watermelon Sugar* (1968). Both novels were more formally structured and somewhat longer, but not dramatically longer than *Trout Fishing in America*. In its original edition, *A Confederate General in Big Sur* is 158 pages long, and *In Watermelon Sugar*, 138 pages.

*A Confederate General from Big Sur* is essentially a quixotic quest novel. The protagonist, Lee Mellon, believes that he is a descendant of the title character, though there is no historical record indicating that such a person ever existed. But Mellon's quest is given renewed purpose and direction when he meets a man who has heard stories about such a general. The novel basically is premised on an underlying parallel between the noble "lost cause" of the Confederacy and the contemporary efforts of those in the Counterculture to resist the conventional politics, the social conformity, the corporatism, and the rampant materialism of mainstream contemporary American culture. If such a premise did not especially resonate in the 1960s, more than half-century later, with the renewed emphasis on the racism inherent in the memorializing of the confederate cause, such a premise seems very ill-conceived.

*In Watermelon Sugar* is a post-apocalyptic narrative set on a hippie commune whose focal landmark is a building called iDEATH. Those ostracized from the commune include the narrator's former lover Margaret and a critic of iDEATH named inBOIL. The group that has formed around inBOIL lives near the Forgotten Works, which is basically a scrap heap of the material remnants of the society that existed before the apocalypse destroyed it. A central but ambiguous event in this post-apocalyptic world is the extermination of the tigers. The tigers represented a dramatic threat to the survival of the commune, but it is never clear whether they were beasts, anthropomorphic creatures, or other human beings, perhaps altered in some terrible way by the apocalypse. The title of the novel comes from the central role of watermelon sugar as an element in much of what the commune produces, uses, and consumes. The novel is interesting for all of the reasons that most of Brautigan's work is of interest, but it is not especially notable as a work of post-apocalyptic fiction.

## LAWRENCE FERLINGHETTI (1919–)

Among poets, Lawrence Ferlinghetti may be the figure most associated with the 1960s and the Counterculture. This association is somewhat puzzling in certain respects. For one thing, Ferlinghetti was older than most of the major figures in the Beat Movement, almost all of whom have predeceased him. Although he has been associated with the Beats, who were perhaps the major "alternative" literary movement of the late 1950s and the early 1960s, and although his City Lights Bookshop small press published many works by the Beats, most notably Allen Ginsberg's *Howl* and *Kaddish*, Ferlinghetti seemed from the beginning of his career as a poet to be anticipating and then embodying the political, social, economic, and environmental activism associated with the late 1960s. But, as much as any of the Beats, Ferlinghetti also seemed the embodiment of the beatnik poet. He not only dressed like a beatnik, but he also had the affect—all of the mannerisms—of a beatnik. Like Allen Ginsberg, Ferlinghetti often included music in his public readings, but unlike Ginsberg who mixed music and chants into his readings generally as interludes or as bridges between the poems, Ferlinghetti often had live jazz music accompanying his readings and accentuating the rhythm and meaning of the poems. In a period in which the unconventional was given every chance to subvert the conventional, even such a seemingly anachronistic approach to performance could be accepted on its own terms as both genuine and genuinely hip.

Ferlinghetti's most well-known book of poetry, *A Coney Island of the Mind*, was published in 1958 by New Directions. Although it became the highest selling book of contemporary American poetry and had a tremendous influence of other writers and a whole generation of readers, his many publications throughout the 1960s were largely with small presses, in more ephemeral forms such as broadsides and chapbooks, and in other genres (including the novel *Her* and several produced plays). The one notable exception in terms of his poetry is the collection *Starting from San Francisco*, which was published by New Directions in 1961. It is also noteworthy that a poem from this period, "Two Scavengers in a Truck, Two Beautiful People in a Mercedes," was included for four decades in the anthology selected by the Assessment and Qualifications Alliance for students preparing for the General Certificate of Secondary Education (GCSE) in Great Britain. The poem has been praised for the way in which it illustrates, by coincidental juxtaposition, the continuing issue of income inequality in the United States and other affluent Western societies.

Allen Ginsberg's poetry owes a clear considerable debt to Walt Whitman's: in its reliance on long lines; in its expansive effort to catalogue the details of the American experience, giving almost equal emphasis to both the ideas and actions of major historical figures and the mundane details of the daily lives of seemingly insignificant, ordinary people; in its challenge to the conventional hesitancy to address issues of radical individualism and sexuality; and in its projection of the poet, paradoxically, as both a witness and a seer, as both an unapologetic radical and a moral conscience, and as both an insistent individualist and a depersonalized voice of the mass of humanity. Although Ferlinghetti's poetry also clearly owes a debt to Whitman's, his poetry seems to owe a greater direct debt to the influence of William Carlos Williams's work. In striking contrast to the unrestrained length of the Whitmanesque line, Williams's poems typically have short lines. Indeed, especially for those used to reading poetry by the line in order to emphasize meter and end rhymes, Williams's lines will seem very awkwardly fractured, deliberately arranged to make them difficult to read. Because the lines sometimes include a single word or end with a preposition or even an article, the sense that they are fractured is not just auditory but visual as well. The effect is heightened even further by Williams's emphasis on colloquial and even conversational syntax and diction—so that a reader of a poem such as "This Is Just to Say"—especially at the time when the poem was written—might be provoked to wonder why it is regarded as a poem at all. Of course, what Williams is doing is forcing the reader to experiment with how the poem might be read, even if that exercise seems to make irrelevant the issue of how it ought to be read. With his interest in jazz music, Ferlinghetti adds a layer of complexity to the process, reemphasizing that what the poem is saying is linked very viscerally to how it is read. The poem becomes, in effect, a formal corollary to ordinary conversation, in which only a certain amount of the meaning is in what is said and much more of the meaning can be contained in how it is said. So, in subverting the surface conventions of "traditional" poetry, Ferlinghetti is actually reinvesting those conventions with meaning—emphasizing that while regular meter and rhyme are generally no longer assumed to convey the meaning of the poem, conveying meaning through the sound of the poem does remain an essential element of poetry.

Another linkage between Williams's and Ferlinghetti's work is the mutual interest in the visual arts and in salient moments in the literary and cultural history of the West. In emphasizing the contrasts between the more formalist poetry written by and influenced by T. S. Eliot and Ezra Pound and the more colloquial poetry written by and influenced by Williams, critics have often described Eliot's and Pound's poetry as being much more dense with allusions. The footnoting of Eliot's *The Waste Land* has, in itself, made this sort of characterization almost inevitable and inescapable. But, just as Eliot's poetry is more colloquial in its syntax and diction than is sometimes acknowledged, Williams's poetry is more rooted in a sense of literary and cultural traditions and more invested in revitalizing those traditions through subverting and reinventing them than is sometimes acknowledged. Like Williams, Ferlinghetti includes many direct allusions to literary and artistic works in many of his poems. But, as critics such as John Alspaugh and Leslie Allen Jones have illustrated, even more than Williams, Ferlinghetti has been very fond of "repurposing" lines from literary works—for effect, rephrasing them slightly, placing them in an unlikely context, or juxtaposing them against a competing idea or sentiment or against an expression or an image that in any other context would seem to have very little poetic potential. So, paradoxically, in making his poetry very accessible and at the risk of making it seem simplistic, Ferlinghetti is actually investing it with all of the layers of meaning that are associated with "serious" poetry.

Although Ferlinghetti grounds his poems in his own personal experiences, they are almost always, in one way or another, about broader public issues. A self-identified "philosophical anarchist," he advocated positions that would now generally be defined as progressive or characteristic of democratic socialism. His concerns ranged from politics at every level, from the local to national and even international disputes, to a broad range of social and economic issues that today would largely be grouped under the phrase "social-justice issues," to humanitarian and environmental concerns. His 1961 collection, *Starting from San Francisco*, which includes fourteen poems, is most remembered for the political poems "Tentative Description of a Dinner to Promote the Impeachment of President Eisenhower" (which is very much in the style of Whitman and Ginsberg) and "One Thousand Fearful Words for Fidel Castro."

Of course, Ferlinghetti is not just a poet who has been willing to address issues of current public interest. He has insisted on the necessity of the poet's assuming a very public role in addressing issues affecting the communities of which he or she is a part. In the 1960s, few, if any, literary figures stood more consistently and visibly at the forefront of the sometimes tumultuous and contentious intersection of the arts and public life. In 1965, he read the poem "Kyrie Eleison Kerista or the Situation in the West, Followed by a Holy Proposal" at the Albert Hall Festival in London. The poem provoked considerable controversy in suggesting a relation between uninhibited sexuality and spiritual enlightenment. Given the rapidity with which the Countercultures subverted mainstream sexual mores, it was difficult, even a decade later, to appreciate the stir created by Ferlinghetti's poem, which, at least in the moment, seemed somewhat comparable to the furor created by the publication of Ginsberg's *Howl* a decade earlier. In 1967, Ferlinghetti was the featured "performer" at the "Human Be-In," which is often identified as the event that initiated the "Summer of Love" in the Bay Area.

In 1966, Ferlinghetti began publicly challenging the morality of the war in Vietnam, introducing the poem "Where Is Vietnam?" in a reading at Reed College that received widespread media coverage. Then, after Ferlinghetti had been arrested several times while participating in antiwar protests, he began to feature the poems "Salute" and "Santa Rita Blues," both of which treat those experiences of being jailed, regularly in his readings, encouraging his listeners to engage in and accept the consequences of their own similar acts of civil disobedience. In 1968, Ferlinghetti was among the prominent figures who signed the Writers and Editors War Tax Protest, pledging to withhold his federal taxes because they might be used to fund the war. In response to the assassinations of Martin Luther King Jr. and Robert M. Kennedy, he wrote the very moving poem "Assassination Raga." At the decade that had begun with a poem mulling the impeachment of Dwight D. Eisenhower, Ferlinghetti produced one of his most jubilantly caustic political pieces, "Tyrannus Rex," on the election of Richard M. Nixon, who had previously served as Eisenhower's vice president, to the presidency.

## GARY SNYDER (1930–)

Unlike most of the Beats and Counterculture writers who came from very urban backgrounds and brought a very urban perspective to their treatments of their experiences, Snyder spent much of youth doing manual labor in the rural Northwest, including working with logging crews. These jobs, as well as his academic studies, brought him into contact with the Native American tribes in the region, and given his own sense of connection to the wilderness, he developed a deep appreciation for the reverence for the natural world that, even after the conquest of the West by Europeans, continues to inform Native American life and culture. Despite his rural focus, Snyder's literary output has been anything but parochial. Rather, it has been informed by a broad and multicultural perspective. Like Allen Ginsberg, Snyder has become an increasingly devout Buddhist, and his religious beliefs are integral to understanding his poetic critique of the unthinking materialism that often distorts mainstream American culture and skews political, economic, and moral priorities at all levels of American government and society. Although Snyder has continued to be most at home in rural America and although he never became quite the public activist that Ginsberg and Ferlinghetti became, he has pointedly supported many of the same progressive and even radical causes that animated their activism and their literary work. In the end, however, his work is distinguished from theirs by its strong focus on issues related to humanity's relationship to the natural environment and, in particular, Western culture's destructive—and ultimately self-destructive—reduction of natural resources to commodities whose value is measured almost entirely by the immediate profits that they generate. Although Snyder was not the first writer or poet to have a very marked ecological focus, his work very much helped to shape the environmental movement that gained a great deal of momentum in the 1960s, and he is rightly regarded as a major literary voice for that movement whose literary influence has been considerable and more enduring than that of many other Counterculture writers.

Snyder published about a dozen books of poetry in the 1960s. These include *Myths and Texts* (1960), *Hop, Skip, and Jump* (1964), *Nanao Knows* (1964), *The Firing* (1964), *Riprap, and Cold Mountain Poems* (1965), *Six Sections from Mountains and*

*Rivers without End* (1965), *A Range of Poems* (1966), *Three Worlds, Three Realms, Six Roads* (1966), *The Back Country* (1968), *Sours of the Hills* (1969), *The Blue Sky* (1969), and *Regarding Wave* (1969). In 1955, Snyder participated in the reading at Six Gallery that is remembered for Ginsberg's first public reading of *Howl*. Snyder read "A Berry Feast," which would become one of his best known and most often anthologized poems. But despite his growing reputation as a poet, Snyder's first book, *Riprap,* was not published until 1959. It was in short order followed by *Myths and Texts*, published in 1960. Although *Myths and Texts* includes work that Snyder wrote throughout the 1950s, he would revise the poems in the collection multiple times over the next two decades, and it would eventually be republished in 1978. The book is divided into three sections. In the first, "Logging," Snyder draws on his work experience and focuses on the destructive effects of the industrialized harvesting of the resources of the wilderness. Although the basic themes are more commonplace now than they were in 1960, the poems remain striking because the themes are grounded in Snyder's intimate knowledge of the work that logging crews do. The second section, "Hunting," explores the ways in which the hunt metaphorically has served to shape our broader notions of the wilderness, especially since hunting has shifted from being necessary to subsistence to being a recreational diversion. And the third section, "Burning," attempts to connect the more concrete experiences described in the first two sections to the conceptions of human experience central to Native American spiritual beliefs and Buddhist thought.

If *Myths and Texts* would be gradually revised over the two decades after it was originally published, *Six Sections from Mountains and Rivers without End* (1965) is, as its title suggests, selections from a much broader work in progress. Snyder conceived of *Mountains and Rivers without End* as an expansive work comparable to Ezra Pound's *Cantos* and William Carlos Williams's *Paterson*. Conceiving the book as a work that would evolve over his career, he would spend much of the next four decades revising the individual sections and expanding the scope of the work as a whole. The structure of the poem is largely spatial, rather than chronological, emphasizing location over event. The sections are connected primarily through metaphors, most of which are geological or architectural, though most are also linked to metaphors used to elucidate concepts fundamental to Buddhist beliefs. So instead of the layers that characterization and conflict add to a narration, the poem works through the literal and metaphoric layers of physical spaces that have accumulated historical, mythic, and/or spiritual layers of meaning. In this way, the personal symbolism that accrues to the poet's and any other individual's experience is shown to merge into the symbolism recognizable to various populations or universally. The work emphasizes the process of living over the results of life choices, and it sets the insights and truths captured within works of art and available within moments of spiritual clarity against the inherent asymmetry and unpredictability of existence.

Published in 1968, *The Back Country* collects poems from across the first decade and a half of his career, including "A Berry Feast," which he read at Six Gallery in 1955. The collection resonated with readers, even though, unlike much of Ferlinghetti's work of the late 1960s, it does not address the cultural tumult and political turmoil of those pivotal years. Although the collection ranges beyond Snyder's personal experience, it is, for the most part, very pointedly grounded in that experience. It is divided into four sections. The first section, "Far West," again draws on Snyder's experiences on logging crews and in other manual jobs, as well as his more leisurely sojourns into the wilderness. He is variously an observer of nature, a communer with nature, and a companion to others who are sharing the experience of being out in the wilderness. Although few of the poems deal primarily with Native American topics, the indigenous attitude toward the natural landscape, in terms of both the physical resources and the spiritual meaning and symbolism that it provides, is integral to understanding many of the poems. The second section, "The Far East," provides a complementary aggregate of Snyder's experiences in East Asia, ranging from the sort of largely sensory impressions that a casual visitor might have to the more coincidental observations of someone more interested in the mundane moment than in the broad sensation, to the spiritual recognitions of the Euro-American immersing himself in the cultures and rituals of an adopted Buddhist faith. The longest poem in this section, "Six Years," is sort of a poetic journal in which the daily entries are compressed into twelve monthly sections. Thus, structurally, the poem acknowledges both the chronological passage of time and the idea that all of time merges together in a manner than transcends the artificial, human distinctions between past, present, and future experience. The third section, "Kal," largely focuses on Snyder's relationships with women, exploring issues related to sexuality, intimacy, love, and, more broadly, fertility and the archetypal elements and spiritual purpose of existence. This section is linked to the two previous sections metaphorically (for instance, the female body is in several poems described as having the contours of a landscape) and symbolically (with the synthesis of the symbols associated with sexual and spiritual fulfilment—though Snyder never links them as explicitly as Ferlinghetti does in "Kyrie Eleison Kerista or the Situation in the West, Followed by a Holy Proposal"). The fourth section, "Back," includes some poems that might fit in the three earlier sections. But this section seems largely focused on the question of how we derive meaning from the endless and generally inexplicable swirl of experience. The poems address this theme on many levels—from contemplations on the natural cycles of a garden and reflections on people who become familiar to us even as the basic truths of their lives remain remote, to considerations of the often bewildering combination of events and personalities that shape political decisions and world events. This section closes with translations of a substantial group of poems by Miyazawa Kenji.

The poems in *Regarding Wave*, which was initially published in 1969 and then re-released a year later in a somewhat enlarged edition, were for the most part written after the birth of Snyder's son and his return from East Asia to the United States. As is the case with all of Snyder's poems, these poems are rooted in the poet's sense of deep connection to the natural world. But, although most of Snyder's poems also have a starting point in the poet's personal experience, the poems in this collection are strikingly different from his previous work because instead of moving from personal experience to the ways in which and levels on which that experience resonates with what he knows about the broader world, these poems move from the more intimate details of his very personal experience to an exploration of the ways in which that experience is incrementally but profoundly reshaping his view of himself and the world beyond his immediate family and home. Paradoxically, in the aftermath of the convulsive events of the late 1960s, this shift from public concerns to a much more narrowly personal focus was not anomalous. Moreover, in retrospect, this collection has come to seem to represent a necessary, restorative pause in Snyder's developing vision of himself as a more public activist. Certainly, the publication in the mid-1970s of poems such as "Smokey the Bear Sutra" demonstrate that Snyder's voice as an environmental activist had taken on an edgier confidence. And, of course, the publication of the collection *Turtle Island* in 1974 would mark Snyder's emergence not just as a notable Beat poet or an important environmental poet but, more broadly, as one of the major American poets of his generation.

## KEN KESEY (1935–2001)

Ken Kesey is regarded as a major novelist of the Counterculture, despite the fact that his output during the 1960s consisted of just two novels—*One Flew over the Cuckoo's Nest* (1962) and *Sometimes a Great Notion* (1964)—both of which were published in the first half of the 1960s before the Counterculture suddenly emerged as a major counterpoint to mainstream American cultural values. Indeed, until the great success of the film adaptation of *One Flew over the Cuckoo's Nest* in 1975, Kesey may have been known most widely for Tom Wolfe's portrait of him and the Merry Pranksters, the group of Counterculture figures who gathered around him and toured the United States in a repurposed and psychedelically redecorated school bus that they named "Further." Wolfe's *The Electric Kool-Aid Acid Test* became not just a major work of the New Journalism but an enduring account of the psychedelic period and the freewheeling experimentation with hallucinogenic drugs that marked the period.

Kesey's two novels contrast in almost every way imaginable—except in the essence of their critiques of American contemporary culture. *One Flew over the Cuckoo's Nest* is set largely in the very regimented and claustrophobic environment of a ward in a mental hospital. In contrast, *Sometimes a Great Notion* is set in an Oregon wilderness in which logging is still the primary industry. *One Flew over the Cuckoo's Nest* is narrated by Chief Bromden, a half–Native American patient in the mental hospital. Although Chief Bromden is ultimately the one character who transcends a system that treats the mentally ill as "mental *cases*" and equates treatment consistently with control, Chief Bromden is himself mentally ill and subject to hallucinations. So, as a narrator he is not entirely reliable, though he is clearly the only character from whom a truthful version of the story might be expected. The central paradox of his narration is that he passes himself off as deaf and dumb to avoid having to speak about the issues that led to his being institutionalized. In contrast, *Sometimes a Great Notion* includes an omniscient third-person narrator and first-person narration by most of the major characters, and it shifts often very abruptly among those narrators with, at best, very subtle markers of the shifts. Even more complexly, the novel shifts in the same abrupt way between chronologically separated events and in some instance from one location to another. In essence, the Stamper family is a collective narrator, much as the Bundrens are in William Faulkner's *As I Lay Dying*. But, in the Faulkner novel, each chapter title indicates the narrator, and Kesey's novel is about three times as long as *As I Lay Dying* and more comparable in its length to *Light in August*.

In *One Flew over the Cuckoo's Nest*, the event that sets everything in motion is Randle McMurphy's decision to behave in an erratic way so that he avoids being sentenced to a prison work farm and is committed instead to the mental hospital. Instead of just quietly serving out his time, however, McMurphy becomes increasingly annoyed at the regimented daily routine of the institution and, more specifically, the authoritarian temperament, barely concealed behind a clinical detachment, that is exhibited by the head nurse, Nurse Ratched. McMurphy begins to make it his mission to disrupt the institutional routine and to give his fellow patients a sense of the liberating possibilities in rebellion. But McMurphy does not take into account that the other patients do have serious psychological issues that prevent them from functioning outside of the hospital, and the pointlessness of his rebellion is emphasized by its most notable result—his being subjected to electroshock treatments and then a lobotomy that reduces him to a near vegetative state. The novel ends with Chief Bromden smothering McMurphy, liberating him from a system that he can no longer escape, and throwing a water fountain through a window through which he himself then escapes.

In *Sometimes a Great Notion*, the Stampers are independent loggers at a time when the industry has become almost completely corporatized. Not surprisingly, the Stampers are barely surviving economically, but when the unionized loggers in corporate employ decide to strike in a desperate attempt to preserve their jobs and wages in the face of increasing automation, the Stampers seize on the strike as an opportunity to save their family business—or at least to forestall its inevitable failure and all of the personal and family choices that its failure will involve. As in Faulkner's novel, the challenge that the family patriarch is determined to meet inevitably comes at a cost, fracturing the family in some fundamental and irrevocable ways. Many readers of the novel have balked at the apparent equivalence that Kesey makes between the Stampers' self-reliance and its suggestion of fundamental American values and their willingness to be strike breakers, or "scabs." But Kesey demonstrates that in a corporatized society that has little room for such values as self-reliance, they are not only anachronistic but inevitably compromising and somewhat willfully delusional. Paradoxically, the strikers are not going to be able to forestall automation and the resulting lost wages and jobs any more than the Stampers are going to be able to forestall the failure of their family business and their tenuous economic independence. The ultimate senselessness in the standoff between the Stampers and the strikers has a parallel in the long-standing conflicts between Hank Stamper and his estranged half-brother Lee. In the end, when Hank and Lee decide to make a futile effort to deliver downriver the rafts of timber that they have cut, they are not just reconciling with each other but are also reconciling themselves individually to the end of the family story that has provided a context for their personal conflicts. Like Chief Bromden, they are going to disappear into the anonymity of the American landscape, just as the shrinking peninsula on which their family home has been built is about to disappear into the Wakonda River. As in *One Flew over the Cuckoo's Nest*, there may be a certain dignity in resisting a culture that has been designed to render meaningless most expressions of individuality, but there is not any victory for Chief Bromden or the Stampers in any of the usual, conventional senses of a satisfying ending. Instead, there is a deep sense of pathos leavening perhaps with the consolation that despite the futility of resistance, some people nonetheless have the impulse to resist.

It is impossible at this point to separate the response to *One Flew over the Cuckoo's Nest* as a novel from the response to its film adaptation. But *Time* magazine did include it in its list of the best one hundred novels published between 1923 and 2005. And although neither novel made it onto Modern Library's list of the best one hundred novels of the twentieth century, as selected by literary critics, on the competing list selected by readers, *One Flew over the Cuckoo's Nest* was ranked ninetieth and *Sometimes a Great Notion* several spots behind it, at ninety-three. For a while, *Sometimes a Great Notion* had something of a resurgence in critical interest because of Kesey's postmodern narrative experimentation, but as the postmodernists on the immediate postwar decades have lost some critical ground with the ascendancy of novelists such as Don DeLillo, Jonathan Franzen, Johnathan Lethem, and Richard Powers, who have combined some experimentation with a renewed interest in more conventional storytelling, Kesey's novel seems to have become more of a minor or footnote work in the critical deliberations over the postmodern canon.

## CHARLES BUKOWSKI (1920–1994)

If Ken Kesey and the Merry Pranksters became the Counterculture equivalent of celebrities, Charles Bukowski seems to have been determined to remain an "underground" writer throughout a long career that began two decades ahead of the heyday of the Counterculture and extended to his death some three decades later. Despite a lifestyle that Bukowski himself described as irredeemably dissolute, he was extraordinarily prolific, producing some sixty books that, despite his penchant for producing work that challenged classification, included novels and collections of short fiction, poetry, essays, and other nonfiction.

In the 1940s and 1950s, Bukowski's work was sporadically published, mainly in little magazines. Ironically, his first published work of short fiction, "Aftermath of a Lengthy Rejection Slip," published in *Story* when he was twenty-three, would be followed by countless rejection slips. For almost the entire decade of the 1960s, Bukowski worked as a letter sorter with the U.S. Post Office in Los Angeles, one of his very few periods of "regular" employment. The experience would provide the material for his first novel, *Post Office*, published in 1971. But, during the 1960s, Bukowski finally started to get his work published by small presses—initially in broadsides and chapbooks, but eventually in books. His poetry collections of the 1960s include *Flower, Fist, and Bestial Wail* (1960), *It Catches My Heart in Its Hands* (1963), *Crucifix in a Deathhand* (1965), *At Terror Street and Agony Way* (1968), *Poems Written before Jumping Out of an 8 Story Window* (1968), *A Bukowski Sampler* (1969), and *The Days Run Away Like Wild Horses over the Hills* (1969). He also began to publish short stories, and his collections published in the 1960s include *Confessions of a Man Insane Enough to Live with Beasts* (1965), *All the Assholes in the World and Mine* (1966), and *Notes of a Dirty Old Man* (1969). The title of the last of those collections came from a column that he wrote for the Los Angeles underground newspaper *Open City*. The column was so popular that when *Open City* folded, the *Los Angeles Free Press*, as well as the underground New Orleans newspaper the *NOLA Express*, both arranged with Bukowski to continue publishing it. Between this exposure and his regular readings throughout the Los Angeles metro area, Bukowski became a fixture in the city's Counterculture.

In 1970, Bukowski turned fifty years old; so his age alone made him an unlikely cult figure in a period that placed so much emphasis on youthful idealism and animated rebellion. Although Bukowski's work focuses sympathetically on those, like himself, who survive on the grim margins of American material prosperity, Bukowski was also a cultural throwback whose more paradoxical personal traits were very pronounced in his public persona. Often openly misogynistic, he was involved in a series of relationships on which he seemed to depend emotionally and yet undermined with countless casual affairs with other women. His sympathy for the down and out was not so much a paean to the unlikely triumphs of underdogs as an acknowledgment of persistence in the absence of escape. Indeed, Bukowski sometimes seems to welcome degradation because it provides a justification for his rejection of respectability and for his scorn for and even rage at everything that it represents and everyone who embraces it. Bukowski himself has identified various modernists as the major influences on his work. But if one wants to locate his work stylistically and thematically, one can do worse than seeing it as a synthesis of the following: Steinbeck's humanizing of those reduced to hard choices by hard times; Nelson Algren's almost lyrical sense of the eccentric rhythms of life, and in particular night life, on the underside of American society; Henry Miller's benedictions to the undeniable and insistent attraction of the tawdry; and Hubert Selby Jr.'s recognition that no matter how low a person has sunk into degradation, there is always someplace even lower to which one can still sink. In Bukowski's work, hyperrealism and surrealism, as well as horror and farce, often converge and become indistinguishable.

In the mid-1960s, Bukowski's work was showcased by Jon and Louise Webb, who published the literary magazine *The Outsider*. They also founded the small press Loujon Press and, under that imprint, published the first two full-length collections of his work, *It Catches My Heart in Its Hands* (1963) and *Crucifix in a Deathhand* (1965). At the end of the 1960s, Bukowski found in John Martin of Black Sparrow Press a publisher committed to not just publishing but to actively and effectively promoting his work. So, somewhat paradoxically, Bukowski's work remained outside of the literary mainstream and yet reached an ever broader audience of readers very likely to be receptive to his singular voice. If it is now almost impossible to separate the response to Kesey's novel *One Flew over the Cuckoo's Nest* from the response to its very successful film adaptation, it is also almost impossible to distinguish Bukowski's contributions to the Counterculture during the 1960s from his career-long association with the Counterculture, for he retained his "underground" appeal even as he achieved a level of popularity and a level of critical attention and recognition that many, more mainstream writers never achieve. Indeed, almost a quarter-century after his death, Bukowski's reputation has, if anything, become more fixed.

## FURTHER READING

Alsen, Eberhard. *J. D. Salinger and the Nazis*. Madison: University of Wisconsin Press, 2018.
Altman, Dennis. *Gore Vidal's America*. Cambridge, MA: Polity, 2005.
Arlen, Michael. "Notes on the New Journalism." *The Atlantic*, May 1972.
Barber, John F., ed. *Richard Brautigan: Essays on the Writings and Life*. Jefferson, NC: McFarland, 2007.
Bloom, Clive. *Bestsellers: Popular Fiction since 1900*. New York: Palgrave Macmillan, 2002.
Bloom, Harold, ed. *James Baldwin*. Philadelphia: Chelsea House, 2006.
Bloom, Harold, ed. *J. D. Salinger's "The Catcher in the Rye."* New York: Chelsea House, 2007.
Bloom, Harold, ed. *John Updike*. New York: Chelsea House, 1987.
Bloom, Harold, ed. *Ken Kesey's "One Flew over the Cuckoo's Nest."* New York: Bloom's Literary Criticism, 2008.
Bloom, Harold, ed. *Kurt Vonnegut*. Philadelphia: Chelsea House, 2000.
Bloom, Harold, ed. *Norman Mailer*. Philadelphia: Chelsea House, 2003.
Bloom, Harold, ed. *Philip Roth*. New York: Chelsea House, 2003.
Bloom, Harold, ed. *Thomas Pynchon*. New York: Chelsea House, 2003.
Bonn, Thomas L. *Under Cover: An Illustrated History of American Mass-Market Paperbacks*. New York: Penguin, 1982.
Boyer, Jay. *Richard Brautigan*. Western Writers Series. Boise, ID: Boise State University Press, 1987.
Braxton, Joanne M. *Black Women Writing Autobiography: A Tradition within a Tradition*. Philadelphia: Temple University Press, 1989.
Brier, Evan. *A Novel Marketplace: Mass Culture, the Book Trade, and Postwar American Fiction*. Philadelphia: University of Pennsylvania Press, 2010.
Brim, Matt. *James Baldwin and the Queer Imagination*. Ann Arbor: University of Michigan Press, 2014.
Bryfonski, Dedria, ed. *Mental Illness in Ken Kesey's "One Flew over the Cuckoo's Nest."* Detroit: Greenhaven, 2010.
Burns, Glen. *Great Poets Howl: A Study of Allen Ginsberg's Poetry, 1943–1955*. New York: Peter Lang, 1983.
Calonne, David, ed. *Conversations with Gary Snyder*. Jackson: University Press of Mississippi, 2017.
Calonne, David Stephen. *Charles Bukowski: Sunlight Here I Am—Interviews and Encounters, 1963–1993*. Northville, MI: Sun Dog Press, 2003.
Campbell, Jeff H. *Updike's Novels: Thorns Spell a Word*. Wichita Falls, TX: Midwestern State University Press, 1987.
Capote, Truman. *"In Cold Blood": A True Account of a Multiple Murder and Its Consequences*. New York: Random House, 1966.
Chambers, Judith. *Thomas Pynchon*. New York: Twayne, 1992.

Chandarlapaty, Raj. *The Beat Generation and Counterculture: Paul Bowles, William S. Burroughs, Jack Kerouac.* New York: Peter Lang, 2009.
Cherkovski, Neeli. *Ferlinghetti: A Biography.* Garden City, NY: Doubleday, 1979.
Cochran, David. *America Noir: Underground Writers and Filmmakers of the Postwar Era.* Washington, DC: Smithsonian Institution Press, 2000.
Connolly, Andy. *Philip Roth and the American Liberal Tradition.* Lanham, MD: Lexington, 2017.
Dalsgaard, Inger H., Luc Herman, and Brian McHale, eds. *The Cambridge Companion to Thomas Pynchon.* New York: Cambridge University Press, 2012.
Detweiler, Robert. *John Updike.* Boston: Twayne, 1984.
Dickstein, Morris, ed. *James Baldwin.* Pasadena, CA: Salem, 2011.
Donner-Grau, Florinda. *Being-in-Dreaming.* New York: HarperCollins, 1992.
Dyer, Richard. *The Culture of Queers.* New York: Routledge, 2002.
Elam, Michelle, ed. *The Cambridge Companion to James Baldwin.* New York: Cambridge University Press, 2015.
Fahy, Thomas Richard. *Understanding Truman Capote.* Columbia: University of South Carolina Press, 2014.
Feiffer, Jules. *The Great Comic Book Heroes.* New York: Dial Press, 1965.
Fletcher, Joel L. *Ken and Thelma: The Story of "A Confederacy of Dunces."* Gretna, LA: Pelican, 2005.
Foster, Edward Halsey. *Richard Brautigan.* Twayne's United States Authors Series. Boston: Twayne, 1983.
Foster, Edward Halsey. *Understanding the Beats.* Columbia: University of South Carolina Press, 1992.
Freer, Joanna. *Thomas Pynchon and the American Counterculture.* New York: Cambridge University Press, 2014.
French, Warren G. *J. D. Salinger, Revisited.* Boston: Twayne, 1988.
Glenday, Michael K. *Norman Mailer.* New York: St. Martin's, 1995.
Gonnerman, Mark. *A Sense of the Whole: Reading Gary Snyder's "Mountains and Rivers without End."* Berkeley, CA: Counterpoint, 2015.
Greenspan, Emily. "Work Begins at 35." *New York Times,* July 6, 1980, Sec. 6, 21.
Gunn, Drewey Wayne, and Jaime Harker, eds. *1960s Gay Pulp Fiction: The Misplaced Heritage.* Amherst: University of Massachusetts Press, 2013.
Hajdu, David. *Positively 4th Street: The Lives and Ties of Joan Baez, Bob Dylan, Mimi Baez Farina, and Richard Farina.* New York: Farrar, Straus and Giroux, 2001.
Harris, Oliver. *William Burroughs and the Secret of Fascination.* Carbondale: Southern Illinois University Press, 2006.
Hayes, Patrick. *Philip Roth: Fiction and Power.* Oxford: Oxford University Press, 2014.
Hollowell, John. *Fact and Fiction: The New Journalism and the Nonfiction Novel.* Chapel Hill: University of North Carolina Press, 1977.
Horn, Maurice, and Pierre Couperie. *A History of the Comic Strip.* New York: Crown, 1968.
Hulse, Ed. *The Blood n Thunder Guide to Pulp Fiction.* n.p.: Muraina, 2013.
Johnson, Kevin. *The Dark Page II: Books That Inspired American Film Noir (1950–1965).* New Castle, DE: Oak Knoll, 2009.
Johnson, Nora. "Housewives and Prom Queens Twenty-Five Years Later." *New York Times Book Review,* March 20, 1988, 1.
Kiernan, Robert F. *Gore Vidal.* New York: Ungar, 1982.
Kline, Michael. "Narrating the Grotesque: The Rhetoric of Humor in John Kennedy Toole's *A Confederacy of Dunces.*" *Southern Quarterly* 37, 3–4 (Spring/Summer 1999), 283–291.

Klinkowitz, Jerome. *Kurt Vonnegut's America*. Columbia: University of South Carolina Press, 2009.
Klinkowitz, Jerome. *The Vonnegut Effect*. Columbia: University of South Carolina Press, 2004.
Lundquist, James. *J. D. Salinger*. New York: Continuum, 1988.
Lupton, Mary Jane. *Maya Angelou: The Iconic Self*. Santa Barbara, CA: Greenwood, 2016.
MacLauchlin, Cory. *Butterfly in the Typewriter: The Tragic Life of John Kennedy Toole and the Remarkable Story of "A Confederacy of Dunces."* New York: Da Capo, 2012.
Mailer, Norman. *The Armies of the Night*. New York: New American Library, 1968.
Mailer, Norman. *Miami and the Siege of Chicago*. New York: Signet, 1968.
Malpas, Simon. *Thomas Pynchon*. Manchester, UK: Manchester University Press, 2013.
Marvin, Thomas F. *Kurt Vonnegut: A Critical Companion*. Westport, CT: Greenwood, 2002.
McBride, Dwight A., ed. *James Baldwin Now*. New York: New York University Press, 1999.
McCann, Sean. *Gumshoe America: Hard-Boiled Crime Fiction and the Rise and Fall of New Deal Liberalism*. Durham, NC: Duke University Press, 2000.
McKinley, Maggie. *Understanding Norman Mailer*. Columbia: University of South Carolina Press, 2017.
McMahon, Gary. *Kurt Vonnegut and the Centrifugal Force of Fate*. Jefferson, NC: McFarland, 2009.
Mentak, Said. *A (Mis)reading of Kurt Vonnegut*. New York: Nova Science, 2010.
Merrill, Robert. *Joseph Heller*. Boston: Twayne, 1987.
Merrill, Robert. *Norman Mailer Revisited*. New York: Twayne, 1992.
Merrill, Thomas F. *Allen Ginsberg*. Twayne's United States Authors Series. Boston: Twayne, 1988.
Mickle, Mildred, ed. *Maya Angelou*. Ipswich, MA: Salem, 2016.
Miles, Barry. *Charles Bukowski*. New York: Virgin Books, 2006.
Milsom, Rosemary. "The Books That Changed Me: Interview with Anne Fine." *Sydney Morning-Herald*, October 24, 2004, 79.
Morse, Donald E. *The Novels of Kurt Vonnegut: Imagining Being an American*. Westport, CT: Praeger, 2003.
Murphy, Patrick, D. *Understanding Gary Snyder*. Columbia: University of South Carolina Press, 1992.
Newman, Judie. *John Updike*. New York: St. Martin's, 1988.
Newman, Robert D. *Understanding Thomas Pynchon*. Columbia: University of South Carolina Press, 1986.
Olster, Stacey, ed. *The Cambridge Companion to John Updike*. Cambridge: Cambridge University Press, 2006.
Parini, Jay, ed. *Gore Vidal: Writer against the Grain*. New York: Columbia University Press, 1992.
Parrish, Timothy, ed. *The Cambridge Companion to Philip Roth*. New York: Cambridge University Press, 2007.
Pinsker, Sanford. *Understanding Joseph Heller*. Columbia: University of South Carolina Press, 2009.
Porter, M. Gilbert. *One Flew over the Cuckoo's Nest*. Boston: Twayne, 1988.
Potts, Stephen W. *From Here to Absurdity: The Moral Battlefields of Joseph Heller*. San Bernardino, CA: Borgo, 1995.
Pozorski, Aimee, ed. *Roth and Celebrity*. Lanham, MD: Lexington, 2012.
Rabinowitz, Barbara. "Tupperware and Terror: The Rise of 'Chick Noir.'" *Chronicle of Higher Education*, January 3, 2016.
Radford, Jean. *Norman Mailer: A Critical Study*. New York: Barnes & Noble, 1975.

Reed, Terry. *Truman Capote*. Boston: Twayne, 1981.
Rodgers, Bernard F. *Philip Roth*. Boston: Twayne, 1978.
Royal, Derek Parker. *Philip Roth: New Perspectives on an American Author*. Westport, CT: Praeger, 2005.
Ruderman, Judith. *Joseph Heller*. New York: Continuum, 1991.
Safer, Elaine B. *Mocking the Age: The Later Novels of Philip Roth*. Albany, NY: SUNY Press, 2006.
Sanchez, Victor. *The Teachings of Don Carlos: Practical Applications of the Works of Carlos Castaneda*. Rochester, VT: Bear & Company, 1995.
Schiff, James A. *John Updike Revisited*. New York: Twayne, 1998.
Schiff, James A. *Updike's Version: Rewriting "The Scarlet Letter."* Columbia: University of Missouri Press, 1992.
Schuler, Robert Jordan. *Journeys toward the Original Mind: The Long Poems of Gary Snyder*. New York: Peter Lang, 1994.
Seed, David. *The Fiction of Joseph Heller: Against the Grain*. New York: St. Martin's, 1989.
Server, Lee. *Encyclopedia of Pulp Fiction Writers*. New York: Checkmark, 2002.
Silesky, Barry. *Ferlinghetti: The Artist in His Time*. New York: Warner, 1990.
Simon, Richard Keller. "John Kennedy Toole and Walker Percy: Fiction and Repetition in *A Confederacy of Dunces*." *Texas Studies in Literature and Language* 36, 1 (Spring 1994), 99–116.
Skau, Michael. *Constantly Risking Absurdity: The Writings of Lawrence Ferlinghetti*. Troy, NY: Whitston, 1989.
Skirl, Jennie. *William S. Burroughs*. Twayne's United States Authors Series. Boston: Twayne, 1985.
Smith, Larry R. *Lawrence Ferlinghetti, Poet-at-Large*. Carbondale: Southern Illinois University Press, 1983.
Sounes, Howard. *Charles Bukowski: Locked in the Arms of a Crazy Life*. New York: Grove, 1998.
Southern, Terry. "Twirling at Ole Miss: Adventures in Dixie." *Esquire*, February 1963.
Steuding, Bob. *Gary Snyder*. Twayne's United States Authors Series. Boston: Twayne, 1976.
Sumner, Gregory D. *Unstuck in Time: A Journey through Kurt Vonnegut's Life and Novels*. New York: Seven Stories, 2011.
Sutherland, John. *Bestsellers: A Very Short Introduction*. New York: Oxford University Press, 2007.
Tanner, Stephen L. *Ken Kesey*. Twayne's United States Authors Series. Boston: Twayne, 1983.
Thomas, P. L. *Reading, Learning, Teaching Kurt Vonnegut*. New York: Peter Lang, 2006.
Thompson, Hunter. *Hell's Angels: The Strange and Terrible Saga of the Outlaw Motorcycle Gangs*. New York: Random House, 1967.
Thompson, Hunter. "The Motorcycle Gangs: A Portrait of an Outsider Underground." *The Nation*, May 17, 1965.
Tomedi, John. *Kurt Vonnegut*. Philadelphia: Chelsea House, 2004.
Tovey, Paige. *The Transatlantic Eco-Romanticism of Gary Snyder*. New York: Palgrave Macmillan, 2013.
Unrue, John C. *J. D. Salinger*. Detroit: Gale Group, 2002.
Wagner, Roy. *Coyote Anthropology*. Lincoln: University of Nebraska Press, 2010.
Wagner-Martin, Linda. *Maya Angelou: Adventurous Spirit*. New York: Bloomsbury Academic, 2016.
Wallace, Amy. *Sorcerer's Apprentice: My Life with Carlos Castaneda*. Berkeley, CA: North Atlantic Books, 2003.

Warner, Simon, ed. *Howl for Now: A Celebration of Allen Ginsberg's Epic Protest Poem*. Pontefract, UK: Route, 2005.

Weber, Ronald. *Hired Pens: Professional Writers in America's Golden Age of Print*. Athens: Ohio University Press, 1997.

Weizmann, Daniel, ed. *Drinking with Bukowski: Recollections of the Poet Laureate of Skid Row*. New York: Thunder's Mouth Press, 2000.

Wenke, John Paul. *J. D. Salinger: A Study of the Short Fiction*. Boston: Twayne, 1991.

Wenke, Joseph. *Mailer's America*. Hanover, NH: University Press of New England, 1987.

Whalen-Bridge, John, ed. *Norman Mailer's Later Fictions: Ancient Evenings through Castle in the Forest*. New York: Palgrave Macmillan, 2010.

Wolf, Felix. *The Art of Navigation: Travels with Carlos Castaneda and Beyond*. n.p.: Millichap Books, 2010.

Wolfe, Tom. *The Electric Kool-Aid Acid Test*. New York: Farrar, Straus and Giroux, 1968.

Wolfe, Tom. *The Kandy-Kolored Tangerine-Flake Streamline Baby*. New York: Farrar, Straus and Giroux, 1965.

Wolfe, Tom, and E. W. Johnson, eds. *The New Journalism*. New York: Harper & Row, 1973.

Yardley, Jonathan. *Misfit: The Strange Life of Frederick Exley*. New York: Random House, 1997.

# CHAPTER 5

# Sports

## BASEBALL

Up until the late 1950s, Major League Baseball did not extend much beyond the Mississippi River. The St. Louis teams were the only ones west of the river. The Cardinals had been in existence since the nineteenth century, and for about fifty years, the city also fielded an American League team, the Browns, who relocated to Baltimore in the early 1950s and became the Orioles. At about that same time, the Boston Braves relocated to Milwaukee, where they would play for a little more than a decade. Along with the Cardinals and the Cubs and the White Sox in Chicago, those were the westernmost Major League teams. Then, in 1958, the owners of the Brooklyn Dodgers and the New York Giants announced that they would be relocating two of the most storied teams in baseball history to the Pacific Coast cities of Los Angeles and San Francisco. There were multiple reasons why there was a sudden impetus for the leagues to expand beyond their historical bases in the Northeast and the Midwest. The postwar expansion of commercial air travel meant that teams could travel faster between cities than they had been able to do so by train. Dramatic population growth in the Sun Belt was made possible by the development of air conditioning, which caused the rapid expansion of retirement communities. And the growth of television ownership and viewership in the 1950s created a new revenue stream from the broadcasting of games.

Today, it has largely been forgotten that in 1959, a third league, to be called the Commonwealth League, was organized not to compete with the American and National Leagues but to partner with them as a third major league. Eventually, eight cities were proposed as sites for teams in the new league. Except for one, all were in cities in which there were then no Major League teams. The eighth team was proposed for New York, where William Shea, with the support of the city government, spearheaded the effort to replace the Dodgers and the Giants with another National League franchise. After first trying to lure existing teams to the city, Shea became a major force in organizing the Commonwealth League. But when Major League Baseball committed to expansion, with one of the first new teams being located in New York, the Commonwealth League lost much of its reason for being and one of its driving forces. The New York Mets would begin playing as a National League team in 1962, and the stadium in which they played would be named after Shea. Of the other seven cities proposed as sites for Commonwealth League teams, all but Buffalo would eventually get a Major League team: Minneapolis–St. Paul would get the Twins in 1961 (the relocated and renamed Washington Senators); Houston, the Colt 45s, eventually renamed the Astros, in 1962; Atlanta, the Braves (relocated from Milwaukee) in 1965; Dallas–Fort Worth, the Texas Rangers in 1972 (relocated and renamed Senators, reestablished in Washington in 1962, after the original franchise relocated to Minnesota); Toronto, the Blue Jays in 1977; and Denver, the Colorado Rockies in 1993.

Major League Baseball in the 1960s reflected the general cultural shift that occurred from the first half of the decade to the second half. From 1960 to 1964, the New York Yankees extended a three-decade dominance on Major League Baseball. Between 1936 and 1964, the Yankees appeared in 22 of the 29 World Series, winning 16 of them. In 1960, the Yankees won 97 games during the regular season, winning the American League by eight games over the Baltimore Orioles and posting a winning record against every other American League team. In the World Series, the Yankees dominated the Pittsburgh Pirates in the three games that the Yankees won, while Pittsburgh won the other four games by close margins—including the seventh game that was decided by a walk-off home run by Pirates second baseman Bill Mazeroski, a hit that put him in the Hall of Fame. In the 1961 season, the Yankees fielded one of the greatest teams in Major League history, winning 109 games and winning the American League pennant again by eight games, this time over the Detroit Tigers. The team hit a total of 240 home runs, with Mickey Mantle and Roger Maris both chasing Babe Ruth's record of 60 home runs in a season. Nicknamed the "M&M Boys," Mantle and Maris combined for 115 home runs and 270 runs batted in. Maris finished with 61 home runs and Mantle with 54. But three other Yankees also hit more than 20 home runs: first baseman Bill Skowron hit 28; left fielder Yogi Berra, 22, and catcher Elston Howard, 21. To no one's surprise, the Yankees beat the Cincinnati Reds in the World Series, four games to one. In 1962, the Yankees won 96 games in the regular season, winning the American League by five games over the Minnesota Twins. Mantle was the American League's Most Valuable Player, but he and Maris combined for just 63 home runs and 189 runs batted in. The Yankees won the World Series, four games to three, over the San Francisco Giants. In 1963, the Yankees won 104 games during the regular season, winning the American League pennant by ten and a half games over the Chicago White Sox. Nonetheless, Mantle and Maris played only 155 games combined, accounting for just 38 home runs and 88 runs batted in, combined. The Yankees were swept in the World Series by the Los Angeles Dodgers, four games to none. The Dodgers starting pitchers Sandy Koufax, Don Drysdale, and Johnny Podres, along with reliever Ron Perranoski, allowed only four runs over

The "M&M Boys," Roger Maris and Mickey Mantle, chased Babe Ruth's home-run record as teammates on the 1960 New York Yankees. Maris broke the record on the last day of the season. (Underwood Archives/Getty Images)

the four games. It was the first time that the Yankees were swept in a World Series. In 1964, the Yankees won 99 games during the regular season, but won the American League pennant by just a single game over the Chicago White Sox. Mantle and Maris bounced back from the previous year, combining for 61 home runs and 182 runs batted in. But the Yankees lost the World Series to the St. Louis Cardinals, four games to three. The Cardinals were led by pitcher Bob Gibson. Notably, Mickey Mantle hit three home runs in the series, giving him a total of 18 home runs in World Series and breaking the record he held with Babe Ruth with 15 each.

As improbable as it might have seemed at the end of the 1964 season, the Yankees would not appear in another World Series for another twelve years. In fact, for the rest of the 1960s, they would be one of the worst teams in the Major Leagues. In 1965, they had their first losing season in forty years, finishing eight games under .500 and in sixth place in the ten-team league. In 1966, they would finish 19 games under .500 and in last place; in 1967, 18 games under .500 and in ninth place; in 1968, four games over .500 and in fifth place; and in 1969, one game under .500 and in fifth place in the newly formed six-team Eastern Division of the American League. Over that five-year span, the Yankees finished 25, 26.5, 20, 20, and 28.65 games out of first place. The team's one bright spot was that pitcher Stan Bahnsen won the Rookie of the Year Award in 1968, but his rookie season turned out to be one of the best in his career, and the Yankees traded him three years later.

If it can be said of the Yankees of the 1960s that seldom has a major sports franchise gone so quickly from historic dominance to haplessness, then it can be said of the New York Mets of the 1960s that seldom has a franchise gone so dramatically from being the epitome of haplessness to World Champions. In 1962, the Mets set a Major League record by losing 120 games. Only four teams in Major League history had won fewer games than the 40 that the Mets managed to win. They finished 60.5 games out of first place. Since the major reason for the team's existence had been the relocation of the Dodgers and the Giants from New York to the Pacific Coast, it is not surprising that the Mets would use the expansion draft to select players with some history with the Dodgers and the Giants. The former Dodgers included starting pitcher Roger Craig, catcher Joe Pignatano, and infielder Gil Hodges, while the former Giants included relief pitcher Ray Daviault and catcher Hobie Landrith. Until Shea Stadium was opened in 1964, the Mets played their home games in the Polo Ground, where the giants had played for decades, and to appeal further to New York fans, the Mets hired Casey Stengel, who had been forced into retirement by the Yankees after the 1960 season, at age seventy. Although Stengel had led the Yankees to ten American League pennants over twelve years and seven World Series wins, his four years with the Mets, in combination with two earlier managerial stints with the Brooklyn Dodgers and Boston Braves, were so opposite his success with the Yankees that he would end his long managerial career with just a .508 winning percentage. The 1962 Mets were so extraordinarily inept that players such as catcher Choo-Choo Coleman and first baseman Marv Thronberry, nicknamed "Marvelous Marv," became beloved for their lack of production. Stengel once drily gave Coleman the backhanded compliment of saying that his foot speed was apparent in how quickly he was able to scramble after passed balls. Of the players on the 1962 roster, only pitcher Al Jackson and rookie first baseman Ed Kranepool would remain with the team through the end of the decade. In contrast to Kranepool, who would become a mainstay on the Mets roster, Jackson was traded to the St. Louis Cardinals in 1966 and, despite a respectable earned run average, extended his string to five consecutive seasons with 15 or more losses (the Major League record is six such seasons). Still, Jackson held the Mets team record for wins, with 43, until Tom Seaver broke it in 1969. In that year, Jackson was traded back to the Mets in the spring, but then traded away in June because he was ineffective as a relief pitcher.

From 1963 to 1968, the Mets finished no higher than ninth out of the ten teams in the National League. In 1963 and 1964, they did marginally improve their record, though one could hardly say that there was much reason for hope in their improvement. In 1963, they won 51 games and finished in tenth place, 48 games out of first place. In 1964, they won 53 games and again finished in last place, 40 games out of first place. In 1964, a Mets fan is supposed to have called the *New York Daily News* to ask about the final score of a game between the Mets and the Chicago Cubs. When told that the Mets had scored 19 runs, the fan reportedly paused and then asked, "Did they win?" Although the story is very likely apocryphal, it has become part of the lore of the team and the sport. In 1965, the Mets slipped back to 50 wins, finishing in last place, 47 games out of first place. In 1966, however, they won 66 games and finished in ninth place, "just" 28.5 games out of first place. It was the first season in which they did not finish in last place, as well as the first season in which they did not lose 100 games. But, in 1967, they won only 61 games, finishing again in last place, 40.5 games out of first place. So, in 1968, when they had 71 wins, good for another ninth-place finish, "just" 24 games out of first place, it seemed as if the team had dramatically improved.

In 1969, the Mets, in effect, reversed the whole previous history, winning 100 games and the National League's new Eastern Division by eight games over the Chicago Cubs. On August 14, they had been trailing the Cubs by ten games, but they won 38 of their last 49 games to complete the 18-game turnaround in the standings. What was most impressive is that the team finished with almost identical home and away records of 52–30 and 48–32. The team had acquired and developed a core group of young pitchers. Tom Seaver won the Cy Young Award after compiling a regular-season record of 25–7, with a 2.21 earned run average and 208 strikeouts. The other starters included: Jerry Koosman, who finished with a 17–9 record and a 2.28 earned run average in his third season with the Mets; Jim McAndrew, who finished 6–7 with a 3.47 earned run average in his second season with the team; rookie Gary Gentry who finished 13–12 with a 3.38 earned run average; and Nolan Ryan, who finished 6–3 with a 3.43 earned run average while being used as a spot starter and reliever in his second full season with the Mets. In addition, journeyman starter Don Cardwell had a record of 8–10, with a 3.01 earned run average, and Ron Taylor and Tug McGraw anchored an excellent bullpen.

Even given that pitching dominated hitting in the late 1960s, the Mets lineup was anything but intimidating. Leftfielder Cleon Jones hit for a .340 average, but only three other hitters who played regularly had averages above .240. Likewise, centerfielder Tommy Agee hit 26 home runs and drove in 76 runs, but only four others hit between 10 and 15 home runs, and only one other player had more than 50 runs batted in. In addition to Jones and Agee, the everyday players included Jerry Grote at catcher, Ken Boswell at second base, and Bud Harrelson at shortstop. Ed Kranepool and Donn Clendenon platooned at first base, rookie Wayne Garret and Ed Charles, the oldest player on the roster, platooned at third base, and Ron Swoboda and Art Shamsky platooned in right field. None of these players made it past a first ballot in the Hall of Fame voting. In fact, most of them had careers marked by inconsistency, if not underachievement. Yet, during this season, they all provided very timely hits and some spectacular fielding plays that, in combination with the team's pitching, not only produced a completely unexpected regular season but a sweep of the Atlanta Braves in the first National League Championship Series and a five-game World Series win over the heavily favored Baltimore Orioles. Indeed, the Mets win over the Orioles was every bit as shocking as the New York Jets victory over the heavily favored Baltimore Colts in the Super Bowl played ten months earlier, in January 1969. The "Loveable Losers" of most of the 1960s certainly earned their new nicknames, the "Miracle Mets" and "the Amazing Mets."

In addition to the players already mentioned in this essay, the 1960s featured great hitters such as Hank Aaron of the Milwaukee/Atlanta Braves, Willie Mays and Willie McCovey of the San Francisco Giants, Frank Robinson of the Cincinnati Reds and the Baltimore Orioles, Pete Rose of the Reds, Roberto Clemente of the Pittsburgh Pirates, Harmon Killebrew of the Minnesota Twins, Carl Yastrzemski of the Boston Red Sox, Al Kaline and Norm Cash of the Detroit Tigers, Ernie Banks, Billy Williams, and Ron Santo of the Chicago Cubs, and great pitchers such as Whitey Ford of the Yankees, Juan Marichal of the Giants, Jim Bunning of the Philadelphia Phillies, and San McDowell of the Cleveland Indians.

The expansion of the Major Leagues discussed at the beginning of this essay had a major impact on the Minor Leagues. Long ignored, the Minor Leagues lost some of their strongest franchises when Major League teams located in the same cities, and the expansion also created the need for Minor League teams at every level (AAA, AA, A, and developmental) for the new franchises. In addition, the integration of the Major Leagues required the integration of the Minor Leagues because it spelled the end of the Negro Leagues that initially had served as feeders of talent. Likewise, the takeover of Cuba by the authoritarian government of Fidel Castro and the subsequent American embargo of the island eliminated what had been the Major Leagues' major source of foreign players and led to the recruitment of talent from other Latin American nations and eventually east Asian, or the nations of the Pacific rim. So, during the 1960s, the Minor Leagues became a much more organized system, with the Major League teams ensuring that most Minor League teams would be financially stable. Moreover, an amateur draft was instituted so that the richer teams with superior scouting resources could less easily monopolize talent; and eventually, in the mid-1970s, the MLB Scouting Bureau would be established, again to foster greater competitiveness.

Equally momentous, in the 1960s, both the players and the umpires formed unions. The players' union would, in the 1970s, secure the right to free agency, dramatically changing not only the nature of the game but the financial prospects of the players, especially those who were most talented but also those players who happened to meet a need for a specific team or more than one team. Initially, fans would bemoan the fact that few of the star players with which they most identified would remain with their teams throughout their careers, as they had generally done for the preceding half-century. But free agency would also mean that teams could become more competitive almost overnight. Although there is still an obvious imbalance in the financial resources of "big market" and "small market" teams, the game has also become much more specialized, and it is much more difficult for any team to have any sort of extended dominance such as that of the Yankees in the two decades from the end of the Second World War through the mid-1960s.

## FOOTBALL

The 1958 championship game of the National Football League (NFL) between the New York Giants and the Baltimore Colts ended in sudden-death overtime and almost immediately became known as "the "Game of the Century." It made the NFL into a television ratings driver, and the competition to purchase the broadcast rights drove up league revenues. At the same time, however, it created an incentive for the creation of a competing league. Established in 1960, the American Football League (AFL) competed with the NFL in only four markets: New York, Dallas, Los Angeles, and the San Francisco metro area. The franchises in Dallas and Los Angeles soon relocated to Kansas City and San Diego. The franchises in New York and the San Francisco Bay area struggled to find a fan base, but with changes in ownership in the mid-1960s, both franchises began to flourish. The other six franchises were located in northeastern and midwestern cities that did not have NFL franchises—Boston, Buffalo, and Cincinnati—and in cities outside of the Northeast and Midwest that had not to that point attracted major sports franchises—Miami, Houston, and Denver. Miami was an expansion team in 1966, and Cincinnati, in 1969, just a year ahead of the eventual merger between the NFL and the AFL. The AFL staked out territory in the Sun Belt states, where the NFL and, in fact, most professional leagues were looking to expand as the development of air conditioning began dramatically to increase the populations and expand the economies of those states, especially in the major metro areas.

Just as television contracts were making NFL teams more financially lucrative, an initial contract with ABC and then a much richer contract with NBC first legitimized the AFL and then made it a legitimate competitor with the NFL. In the middle of the decade, the AFL began successfully to compete with the NFL in signing college football stars and then to sign veteran NFL players by beating the contract offers made by their NFL teams. The competition between the two leagues was undermining the financial stability provided by the increased television revenues, and so the champions of the two leagues competed for three years in an interleague championship game that soon became known as the Super Bowl, before the leagues finally merged in 1970.

The first two Super Bowls seemed to demonstrate, however, that the NFL was still the superior league, even if the AFL was narrowing the gap in coaching and talent between the two leagues. That said, the Green Bay Packers were clearly the most dominant NFL team in the 1960s. Of the ten league championship games, Green Bay appeared in six, winning five—against the New York Giants in 1961 and 1962, the Cleveland Brown in 1965, and the Dallas Cowboys in 1968 and 1969—and with the only loss coming at the very beginning of the decade, in 1960 to the Philadelphia Eagles. The Packers were led by the legendary coach Vince Lombardi and Hall of Fame quarterback Bart Starr. Their style of play epitomized the hard-nosed football for which the NFL had become known, with an emphasis on establishing a running game on offense and a dominating presence on defense. This style of play contrasted with the offensive style that characterized the AFL, which placed more emphasis on the passing game and, in general, on speed. That style was, in fact, gradually being adopted by some NFL teams, especially the most recent expansion teams such as the Dallas Cowboys and Minnesota Vikings. In the so-called Ice Bowl, the 1967 NFL championship game between the Cowboys and the Packers that was played in Green Bay, the speed and flash of the Cowboys was ground down in the subzero temperatures, and the Packers' final drive, which ended with Bart Starr driving into the end zone beyond the block of guard Jerry Kramer, very memorably epitomized the temporary triumph of the Packers' very disciplined style of play.

Other notable NFL teams of the 1960s included the New York Giants, who in the six years between 1958 and 1963 made it to the championship game in every year but 1960 but lost all five times. The Cleveland Browns, led first by fullback Jim Brown and then by halfback Leroy Kelly, made it to the championship game four times—in 1964, 1965, 1968, and 1969—but won just once in 1964, defeating the Baltimore Colts. The Colts returned the favor, beating the Browns in 1968. The Chicago Bears made their only appearance in the title game in 1963, defeating the Giants. This championship was notable because it was legendary owner-coach George Halas's eighth and final title win, because the team had the rare distinction of leading the league in every major category—fewest rushing yards, fewest passing yards, fewest total yards, and fewest points allowed—and because the Bears would not appear in another championship game for twenty-two years, when another overwhelming defense led them to a Super Bowl win. The coach in the 1985 season was Mike Ditka, who had played tight end on the 1963 squad and had been one of the few offensive stars on that team.

In the AFL, the Houston Oilers appeared in the four championship games, winning the first two in 1960 and 1961, behind halfback Billy Cannon, and losing in 1962 and 1967. The Los Angeles and then San Diego Chargers appeared in five championship games, losing in 1960, 1961, 1964, and 1965, and winning just once in 1963, when they defeated the Boston Patriots in their only appearance in an AFL championship game. Ironically, neither the Oilers (now the Tennessee Titans nor the Chargers have ever won a Super Bowl, though each has made one appearance in the game, whereas the New England Patriots have appeared in eleven Super Bowls, winning six. Likewise, the Buffalo Bills, led by quarterback Jack Kemp, appeared in three straight AFL championship games, winning in 1964 and 1965, and losing in 1966, whereas the Denver Broncos were the only one of the eight original AFL franchises never to appear in an AFL championship game. Yet, between 1990 and 1993, the Bills would appear in four straight Super Bowls without winning any of them, while since the NFL-AFL merger, the Denver Broncos have appeared in eight Super Bowls, winning three of them (though they did go 0–4 before they won two straight). Toward the end of the decade, the AFL's two most initially dysfunctional franchises, the Oakland Raiders and the New York Jets would, along with the Kansas City Chiefs, perhaps the league's most consistent franchise, would dominate the league. The Raiders would appear in three straight championship games from 1967 through 1969, winning in 1967; the Jets would win the championship in 1969; and the Chiefs, who won the championship in 1962 when they were still located in Dallas, won again in 1966 and 1969.

In the first two Super Bowls, Green Bay won decisively 35–10 over the Kansas City Chiefs and 33–14 over the Oakland Raiders. In 1969, the Baltimore Colts had finished the regular season with a 13–1 record, and even though star quarterback Johnny Unitas had had an injury-riddled season, they entered the Super Bowl as prohibitive 18-point favorites over the New York Jets, who were

New York Jets quarterback "Broadway Joe" Namath became a legend during Super Bowl III by leading his team to an upset win over the Baltimore Colts. (Bettmann/Getty Images)

led by their young star quarterback "Broadway Joe" Namath, who brashly predicted that the Jets would win the game. The contrast between the quarterbacks was reversed with the head coaches: the veteran Jets coach, Weeb Ewbank, had been fired as the Colts head coach in the middle of the decade before taking the job with the Jets, and his replacement with the Colts was one of the youngest head coaches in NFL history, Don Shula. In one of the biggest upsets in professional football history, the Jets would prove Namath right, winning 16–7. Then, as if to prove that the AFL's goal of achieving parity with the NFL was being realized, in the fourth and final Super Bowl before the merger of the leagues, the Kansas City Chiefs, led by quarterback Len Dawson, decisively defeated the Minnesota Vikings, 23–7.

The NFL's All-Decade Team for the 1960s includes the following players on offense: quarterbacks—Sonny Jurgensen, Bart Starr, and Johnny Unitas; halfbacks—John David Crow, Paul Hornung, Leroy Kelly, and Gale Sayers; fullbacks—Jim Brown and Jim Taylor; split ends—Del Shofner and Charley Taylor; flankers—Gary Collins and Boyd Dowler; tight end—John Mackey; tackles—Bob Brown, Forest Gregg, and Ralph Neely; guards—Gene Hickerson, Jarry Kramer, and Howard Mudd; and center—Jim Ringo. The all-defensive team includes: ends—Doug Atkins, Willie Davis, and David "Deacon" Jones;

tackles—Alex Karras, Bob Lilly, and Merlin Olsen; linebackers—Dick Butkus, Larry Morris, Ray Nitschke, Tommy Nobis, and Dave Robinson; cornerbacks—Herb Adderley, Lem Barney, and Bobby Body; and safeties—Eddie Meador, Larry Wilson, and Willie Wood. The special teams players are kicker Jim Bakken and punter Don Chandler. Of the forty players on the NFL's All-Decade Team for the 1960s, twenty-seven have been inducted into the Pro Football Hall of Fame.

The AFL's All-Time Team (it existed only from 1960 to 1969) includes the following players on offense: quarterbacks—Joe Namath and Len Dawson; running backs (halfbacks and fullback)—Clem Daniels, Cookie Gilchrist, Abner Haynes, Paul Lowe; wide receivers (split ends and flankers)—Lance Alworth, Charlie Hennigan, Don Maynard, and Art Powell; tight ends—Fred Arbanas and Dave Kocourek; tackles—Steve Barber, Winston Hill, Ron Mix, and Jim Tyrer; guards—Ed Budde, Bill Shaw, Walt Sweeney, and Bob Talamini; and centers—Jim Otto and Jon Morris. The all-defensive team includes: ends—Rich Jackson, Jerry Mays, Ron McDole, and Gary Philbin; tackles—Houston Antwine, Buck Buchanan, Tom Keating, and Tom Sestak; linebackers—Bobby Bell, Nick Buoniconti, Dan Connors, Larry Grantham, Mike Stratton, and George Webster; cornerbacks—Willie Brown, Butch Byrd, Miller Farr, and Dave Grayson; and safeties—Goose Gonsoulin, Kenny Graham, Johnny Robinson, and George Saimes. The special teams players are: kickers—George Blanda and Jim Turner; punters—Bob Scarpeto and Jerrel Wilson. Of the forty-eight players on the AFL's All-Time Team, only thirteen have been inducted into the Pro Football Hall of Fame.

College football in the 1960s was not quite the industry that it has become today. The big games and the much smaller number of bowl games were televised, but networks were not yet contracting with the leagues for the television rights to their games. The rankings of the teams were much less formalized than they are now, and although there were consensus national champions, there were sometimes two teams identified as consensus champions, and there were often three or four teams identified as national champions by the eight different groups that provided rankings throughout the decade. Still, it is not an oversimplification to say that college football in the 1960s was dominated by the teams fielded by five schools with highly regarded, if not legendary, coaches: the University of Alabama coached by Paul "Bear" Bryant; Notre Dame University coached by Ara Parseghian; the Ohio State University coached by Woody Hayes; the University of Southern California coached by John McKay; and the University of Texas coached by Darrell Royal. Alabama won the consensus national championship or shared the consensus national championship in 1961 and 1965; Notre Dame, in 1964 and 1966; Ohio State in 1961 and 1968; USC, in 1962 and 1967; and Texas, in 1963 and 1969. The only other team with comparable success was Michigan State, which shared the consensus national championship in 1965 and 1966, but its coach, Duffy Daugherty never achieved quite the stature of the other coaches. Daugherty is deservedly in the College Football Hall of Fame, but the career winning percentages of the other coaches range from Parseghian's .739 to Bryant's .780, while Daugherty's was .623.

Some individual college football teams deserve mention for social or technical reasons. In a 1963 game between Maryland and North Carolina State, Darryl Hill, an offensive split end playing for Maryland became the first African American to play for one of the three major conferences in the Deep South—the Atlantic Coast Conference (ACC), the Southeastern Conference (SEC), and the Southwest Conference (SWC). In a 1967 game between Kentucky and Mississippi, Nathaniel Northington, a running back playing for Kentucky, became the first African American to play in an SEC game. In 1969, the largely white football team of the University of Tampa played the African American team of Florida A&M University, a historically black university. It was the first game that could be described as truly interracial.

On the technical side, the 1962 Rose Bowl between UCLA and the University of Minnesota was the first college football game to be broadcast in color. In the 1963 Army-Navy game, instant replay was used for the first time in any sports broadcast. In 1968, the game between the University of Alabama and Miami University (in Florida) became the first college football game to be broadcast in prime time. But, in the same way that the NFL championship game between the Baltimore Colts and the New York Giants turned professional football into a television staple, the 1967 game between UCLA and USC attracted a viewing audience that ensured that college football would get more exposure. The game not only determined the champion of one of the predecessors of the PAC-12 Conference, the Athletic Association of Western Universities, but ultimately the national championship. It also featured the two leading contenders for the Heisman Trophy: Gary Beban, the quarterback for UCLA, and O. J. Simpson, the running back for USC. Beban won the Heisman, but USC won the very close game, 21–20, and went on to win the national championship.

## BASKETBALL

Just as the New York Yankees dominated Major League Baseball in an unprecedented and subsequently unmatched way from the end of the Second World War to the middle of the 1960s, the Boston Celtics dominated professional basketball from the late 1950s through the end of the 1960s. In 1956, the Celtics drafted Bill Russell, who had led the University of San Francisco to consecutive NCAA championships in 1955 and 1956 and the U.S. Olympic basketball team to a gold medal in 1956. Russell would set a record for North American professional team sports by winning eleven NBA championships with the Celtics. Despite somewhat modest offensive skills and numbers, Russell was such a dominant defensive player and such a consummate team player that he won the NBA's Most Valuable Player award five times and was selected as an all-star in twelve of his thirteen seasons in the NBA. Over those thirteen seasons, the players around Russell changed, but the Celtics' team-oriented style of play remained consistently dominant. In the 1960s, the Celtics starting lineup included, in addition to Russell at center, point guard Bob Cousy, shooting guard Bill Sharman, small forward Frank Ramsey, and power forward Tommy Heinsohn. By the mid-1960s, Cousy, Ramsey, and Heinsohn had been replaced in the starting lineup by players such as K. C. Jones, Sam Jones, and Thomas "Satch" Sanders. In 1962, first-round draft pick John Havlicek, who had played college basketball at Ohio State, established himself as a all-star despite initially coming off the bench as the "sixth man." Later in the 1960s, small forward Bailey Howell and power forward Don Nelson became starters. All of these Celtics players except for Sanders and Nelson have been inducted, as players, into the Naismith Memorial Basketball Hall of Fame, and Nelson was inducted as a coach.

In 1957, the NBA's eighth season, the Celtics went to the finals for the first time, beating the St. Louis Hawks four games to three. The next year, the Celtics and Hawks were again in the finals, but the Hawks beat the Celtics four games to two. The Hawks featured such players as Bob Pettit, Cliff Hagan, and Clyde Lovellette. From 1959 to 1966, the Celtics then won eight straight NBA titles. In 1960 and 1961, they again defeated the Hawks, four games to three and four games to one. But in five of the other finals in that eight-year stretch, the Celtics' opponent was the Lakers, who were still located in Minneapolis in 1960 but in 1962, 1963, 1965, and 1966 were in Los Angeles. The Lakers were led by Jerry West and Elgin Baylor, and at the end of the decade, they added Wilt Chamberlain to the team. Nonetheless, they lost again to the Celtics in 1968 and 1969, despite having leads in both series. Although Chamberlain was the most dominant player that the league had seen to that point and remains one of the most dominant players in the league's history, his San Francisco Warriors had lost to the Celtics four games to one in 1964. But in 1966–1967, after Chamberlain had been traded to the Philadelphia 76ers, the team set a league record by winning 68 games in the regular season. (The record would stand for only five seasons, however, when the Lakers, with Chamberlain, would win 72 games and their first NBA title since relocating to Los Angeles.) In addition to Chamberlain, the 1966–1967 76ers included Hal Greer, Chet Walker, and Billy Cunningham. They defeated the Celtics four games to one in the Eastern Conference finals and then Chamberlain's former team, the San Francisco Warriors, in the finals, four games to two. During Russell's last three seasons with the Celtics, he was a player-coach, replacing longtime coach Red Auerbach who remained the team's general manager. Russell was the first

Center Wilt Chamberlain made basketball history throughout the 1960s. Some of his records still stand. (Bettmann/Getty Images)

African American to coach a professional team in a major sport, and his leadership was also very evident in his very public involvement in the Civil Rights Movement. Ironically, despite Boston's reputation as a very racially divided city, a reputation reinforced by the sometimes fierce opposition to using busing to integrate the public schools, in 1964 the Celtics became the first NBA team to start a game with an entirely African American team on the floor.

Although Bill Russell won far more championships, Wilt Chamberlain's dominance as an individual player cannot be overstated. Chamberlain still holds the following individual single-game NBA records: most points in a game—100, scored against the Knicks in 1962, a game in which he also set the records for most field goals attempted, most field goals made, and most free throws made in a game (the last is surprising because Chamberlain gained notoriety for his troubles at the free-throw line, which led him to shooting them underhanded late in his career); most rebounds in a game—55, in a game against the Celtics in 1960. In 1961–1962, Chamberlain set the following records for a single season: most minutes played per game—48.53; most total minutes—3,882; highest points per game average—50.32; most points—4,039; most 50-point games—45; most 40-point games—63; most consecutive 50-plus-point games—7; most consecutive 40-plus-point games—14; most consecutive 30-plus-point games—65; most consecutive 20-plus-point games—126 (1961–1963); most field goals made—1,597; most field goals attempted—3,159; most field goals missed—1,562; most free throws attempted—1,363; most rebounds per game—27.2; and most rebounds—2,149. In 1967–1968, he also set the record for most consecutive triple-doubles in a season with 9. Chamberlain also holds the following career records: most minutes per game—45.8; most consecutive seasons leading the league in points—7 (shared with Michael Jordan); most 60-plus-point games—32; most 50-plus-point games—118; most 40-plus-point games—271; most consecutive seasons leading the league in field goals attempted and made—7 for both; most consecutive field goals made—35 (in 1967); most consecutive seasons leading the league in free throws attempted—9; most rebounds—23,924; highest average rebounds per game—22.9; and most seasons leading the league in rebounds—11.

Beyond the players for the Celtics, Hawks, Lakers, and 76ers who have already been mentioned, the lists of the greatest players of the 1960s would include: Oscar Robertson, who played for the Cincinnati Royals and Milwaukee Bucks, with whom he won an NBA title; Jerry Lucas, who played for the Cincinnati Royals, San Francisco Warriors, and New York Knicks, with whom he won an NBA title; Richie Guerin, who played for the New York Knicks and for the St. Louis and Atlanta Hawks; Jack Twyman, who played for the Cincinnati Royals; Lenny Wilkins, who played for the St. Louis and Atlanta Hawks and the Seattle Supersonics, Cleveland Cavaliers, and Portland Trailblazers; Walt Bellamy, who played for the Chicago Packers, the franchise that became the Baltimore Bullets, the New York Knicks, the Detroit Pistons, the Atlanta Hawks, and the New Orleans Jazz; and Willis Reed, who played for his entire career for the New York Knicks.

The NCAA Basketball Tournament has been held annually at the end of each season since 1939. A year earlier, the National Invitational Tournament (NIT) had been established, and through the mid-1950s, the NIT was the more prestigious of the two postseason tournaments. Notably, teams from conferences in racially segregated parts of the nation usually chose to play in the NIT to avoid hosting regional games on their campuses that would involve racially integrated teams. Although the NCAA Tournament became more prestigious by the 1960s, it was not televised at all until 1969, and then only partially. During the 1960s, the number of invited teams fluctuated between 22 and 25. The expansion, in stages, of the tournament field to 64 and more teams went hand in hand with the rapid increase in the popularity of the tournament and in the television revenues generated being by the tournament for the television networks and participating teams and conferences. All of these developments have combined to make the NIT a sort of consolation prize for the teams that do not make the NCAA Tournament.

From 1960 through 1963, the NCAA Tournament was dominated by Ohio State and the University of Cincinnati. Ohio State teams were led by All-Americans Jerry Lucas and John Havlicek, and the University of Cincinnati was led by Oscar Robertson, though from 1960 to 1964, seven other players on the teams were named to the All-American teams. In 1960, Ohio State won its only national title, defeating the University of California. In 1961 and 1962, Cincinnati defeated Ohio State in the finals to win the national title. And in 1963, Cincinnati finished second to Loyola University of Chicago.

Over the eleven years from 1964 to 1975, UCLA would win the title in ten of the twelve years. UCLA's unprecedented and unmatched dominance of college basketball overlapped and is comparable to the Boston Celtics period of dominance in the NBA. During this period, UCLA had four undefeated seasons and set a record with 88 consecutive wins. The streak was ended when the University of Houston team that featured Elvin Hayes defeated UCLA 71–69. It was the first televised regular-season college basketball game and became known as the "Game of the Century." Coached by John Wooden, who earned the sobriquet "The Wizard of Westwood," UCLA featured in succession two of the greatest centers in the history of college basketball, Lew Alcindor, who changed his name to Kareem Abdul-Jabbar, and Bill Walton. But the teams also featured many other All-Americans, including Walt Hazard, Gail Goodrich, Keith Erickson, Lucius Allen, Mike Warren, Sidney Wicks, Curtis Rowe, Mike Bibby, Keith Wilkes, Richard Washington, David Meyers, and Marques Johnson.

In 1966, the only year in this twelve-year period in which UCLA did not make the Final Four, the NCAA Tournament was won by Texas Western University, now known as the University of Texas at El Paso, a team that featured an all–African American starting lineup and that defeated an all-white University of Kentucky team coached by the legendary Adolph Rupp.

Beyond the players already mentioned, All-Americans from the 1960s included such players as Darrel Imhoff (California, 1960), Jerry West (West Virginia, 1960), Tom Stith (St. Boneventure, 1960, 1961), Terry Dischinger, 1962, 1963), Bill Bradley (Princeton, 1964, 1965), Rick Barry (Miami [FL], 1965), Cazzie Russell (Michigan, 1965, 1966), Dave Bing (Syracuse, 1966), Jimmy Walker (Providence, 1966, 1967), Wes Unseld (Louisville, 1967, 1968), Pete Maravich (LSU,

1968, 1969, 1970), Spencer Haywood (Detroit, 1969), Calvin Murphy (Niagara, 1969, 1970), and Rick Mount (Purdue, 1969, 1970).

## THE WINTER AND SUMMER OLYMPICS

The 1960 Winter Olympics were held in Squaw Valley, California. The organizers spent $80 million developing the site, but despite the cost, they did not build a bobsled run, and for the only time in the history of the Winter Olympics, bobsledding competitions were not included. Thirty nations sent athletes to compete, and of the 665 athletes, 521, or about 78 percent, were men. The United States was represented by 79 athletes, the most of any nation, and about 12 percent of the total competing. (The United Team from Germany, with 74, and the Soviet Union, with 62, had the second and third highest numbers of athletes competing.) In total, there were 27 events and 81 available medals. The United States finished with the second highest total medals, with 10, but trailed the Soviet Union's 21 by a significant margin. The United States won the third highest number of gold medals—trailing the Soviet Union, with 7, and the United Team of Germany, with 4, and tied with Norway and Sweden, with 3. The gold medal winners from the United States were David Jenkins in men's figure skating, Carol Heiss in women's figure skating, and the ice hockey team. Penny Pitou was the only American athlete to win multiple medals, winning two silver medals in Alpine skiing events. CBS paid $50,000 for the rights to broadcast the games and provided selective coverage of the events.

The 1960 Summer Olympics were held in Rome. In contrast to the Winter Games, CBS agreed to pay almost $400,000 to broadcast the games. Because there were still no satellites to transmit the coverage, it was recorded on videotape and flown to New York to be broadcast. Eighty-three nations sent athletes to compete, and of the 5,338 athletes, 4,727, or almost 89 percent, were men. The United States was represented by 292 athletes, or about 5.5 percent of the total. It was the second highest total for a nation, trailing the United Team of Germany with 293 athletes and ahead of the Soviet Union with 283 athletes. The United States finished with 71 total medals, or just over 20 percent of the total awarded, trailing the Soviet Union with 103 medals and ahead of the United Team of Germany with 42 medals. The United States finished with 34 gold medals, trailing the Soviet Union with 43 gold medals and ahead of Italy with 13 gold medals. Four stories involving athletes stood out. First, Wilma Rudolph, an African American sprinter who had been afflicted with polio when she was a child, won three gold medals and was proclaimed by commentators as "the fastest woman in the world." Rafer Johnson won the decathlon, posting a record number of points but just narrowly beating C. K. Yang who was representing Taiwan but who had trained with and become friends with Johnson at UCLA. Cassius Clay (later Muhammad Ali) won the gold medal in boxing as a light-heavyweight. And the U.S. basketball team, led by immediate NBA all-stars Oscar Robertson, Jerry West, Jerry Lucas, and Walt Bellamy won the fifth straight gold medal by the U.S. teams.

The 1964 Winter Olympics were held in Innsbruck, Austria. Thirty-six nations sent athletes to compete in the games, and of the 1,091 athletes, 892, or almost

82 percent, were men. The United States was represented by 89 athletes, or just over 8 percent of the total. It was the second highest total for any nation, trailing the United Team of Germany with 96 and ahead of Austria with 83. Yet, the United States finished sixth in the total medal count, tied France and Sweden with just 7 medals, or just over 7 percent of the 97 total medals awarded, and far behind the Soviet Union's 25 total medals. Only one U.S. athlete won a gold medal—Terry McDermott in speed skating. Although the United States had dominated figure skating over the previous decade, the bronze medals won by Scott Allen in the men's singles competition and by Vivian Joseph and Ronald Joseph, who were siblings, in the pairs competition were a pleasant surprise. The entire U.S. figure skating team had perished in a plane crash in Belgium in 1961, on their way to the world championships. Allen was only 15 years old when he won the bronze medal. The Josephs' bronze medals were actually awarded after the fact. They had finished fourth at the Olympics but several years later, the German team, which had won the silver medal, was disqualified because they had signed a pro contract before the Olympics. The original bronze medalists, the Canadian team, were given silver medals, and the Josephs, bronze medals. Then, two decades later, the International Olympic Committee (IOC) reversed itself, and the silver medals were restored to the German pair, though the Canadians and the Josephs were also allowed to keep their medals.

The 1964 Summer Olympics were held in Tokyo. They were the first Olympics to be held in Asia and to be televised from a satellite link and partly in color. A total of 5,151 athletes representing 93 nations competed. Although multiple new events for women were added, 4,473, or almost 87 percent of those athletes, were male. The United States had the highest number of athletes competing, with 346, or almost 7 percent of the total; the United Team of Germany had the second highest number, with 337. Following these Olympics, the West and East Germans would field separate teams. The U.S. athletes would win the most gold medals, with 36; the Soviets would win the second highest number of gold medals, with 30. But the total medal count for U.S. athletes would be 90, six behind the Soviets final total of 96. Three American athletes attracted considerable attention. Joe Frazier won the gold medal for boxing in the heavyweight division. Within a decade, he and Muhammad Ali would be squaring off in a series of three of the most watched, most celebrated, and most brutal heavyweight bouts in boxing history. Bob Hayes won a gold medal as a sprinter. Nicknamed "Bullet Bob," he had the distinction of holding the world records at four distances—60 yards, 100 yards, 200 yards, and 100 meters—all at the same time. After the Olympics, he was drafted as a split end by the Dallas Cowboys as they attempted to imitate the more offensive-oriented style of the AFL teams that placed a greater emphasis on passing and speed. Hayes and Jim Thorpe are the only Olympic gold medalists in the Pro Football Hall of Fame, and Hayes is the only person to have won both an Olympic gold medal and a Super Bowl ring. Less celebrated was Billy Mills, a distance runner who unexpectedly won the 10,000-meter race, becoming the first and still the only American runner to do so. Lastly, American swimmer, Don Schollander, won four gold medals in swimming. Although swimming was a sport in which Americans usually excelled, Schollander was the first swimmer to have that sort of individual success. Unfortunately for Schollander, his achievement would be dramatically eclipsed by Mark Spitz in 1972; in fact, Spitz would win more medals than Schollander when they both competed with the U.S. team at the 1968 Olympics.

The 1968 Winter Olympics were held in Grenoble, France. For the first time, ABC secured the broadcast rights to the games for the Western Hemisphere and covered them from start to finish for the American viewing audience. Likewise, for the first time, the site organizers provided accommodations specifically for broadcasters, including a central site that provided all sorts of technical support that itself included computer support for the first time. The emphasis on marketing these Olympic games was so pronounced that for the first time a mascot specific to these games was created. The games attracted 1,158 athletes from 37 nations; 947, or almost 82 percent, of those athletes were men. The United States was represented by 95 athletes, or over 8 percent of the total, with West Germany having the second largest contingent, with 87. The United States finished with 7 of the 92 medals that were awarded, or about 7.5 percent of the total. In the total medal count, the U.S. finished tied with West Germany for the seventh highest total. The only gold medal won by a U.S. athlete was won by Peggy Fleming in figure skating. The U.S. television coverage made Fleming and French downhill skier Jean-Claude Killy, who won three gold medals, into the stars of these Olympic games.

The 1968 Summer Olympics were held in Mexico City. It was the first time that the Olympics were held in a Latin American or, for that matter, Spanish-speaking country. Because of the concerns about the hot weather during the summer months, these Summer Olympics, like those in Tokyo, were actually held in October. Because they coincided with the Mexican Student Movement, which broadly paralleled the political activism among American college students at the time, these Olympic games have been remembered for the political statements made through them. In total, 5,516 athletes representing 112 countries participated, with 4,735, or almost 86 percent, of those athletes being men. So, despite the addition of some women's sports, progress toward gender balance in the athletes participating was almost nonexistent over the 1960s. The United States again fielded the largest number of athletes, with 357, or about 6.5 percent of the total. The Soviet Union had the second highest number, with 312. The United States dominated these games, winning 107 of the 364 total medals that were awarded, or over 29 percent. More impressively, U.S. athletes won 45 of the 133 gold medals, or almost 34 percent of the total. The Soviet Union finished second in both categories, with 91 total medals and 29 gold medals. Given the total number of gold medals won by American athletes, it is not surprising that a number of their performances stood out. Swimmers Debbie Meyer and Charlie Hickcox each won three gold medals. Three athletes in track-and-field events other than running also made headlines. Al Oerter won his fourth straight gold medal in the discus throw, becoming the first track-and-field athlete and only the second athlete in Olympic history to achieve that recognition. Bob Beamon so surpassed the previous world's record in the long jump that his new record would stand for 23 years. And in the high jump, Dick Fosbury won the gold, proving that his unconventional technique, which purists referred to somewhat disdainfully as the "Fosbury flop," was in fact revolutionary. George Foreman dominated the heavyweight boxing division, as he would after turning professional, and while receiving his gold medal, he waved a small U.S. flag. This was seized upon as a contrast to what became the most signature moment of this Olympics. Tommie Jones and Juan Carlos won the gold and bronze medals in the 200-meter race, and at the medals ceremony, they wore black socks without shoes and, wearing black gloves, raised their fist during the playing of the national anthem. The reaction to this symbolic demonstration in support of Black Power cannot be overestimated. The IOC banned Smith and Carlos from participation in any future Olympic games, and Peter Norman, the Australian runner who had won the silver medal and had worn a badge in support of civil rights, was effectively banned from the 1972 Olympics.

## FURTHER READING

Allen, Neil. *Olympic Diary: Tokyo, 1964*. London: N. Kaye, 1965.
Bass, Amy. *Not the Triumph but the Struggle: The 1968 Olympics and the Making of the Black Athlete*. Minneapolis: University of Minnesota Press, 2004.
Brasher, Christopher, ed. *The Road to Rome*. London: W. Kimber, 1960.
Bryant, Howard. *Legends: The Best Players, Games, and Teams in Basketball*. New York: Philomel, 2017.
Carlos, John, with Dave Zirin. *The John Carlos Story: The Sports Moment That Changed the World*. Chicago: Haymarket, 2011.
Castañeda, Luis M. *Spectacular Mexico: Design, Propaganda, and the 1968 Olympics*. Minneapolis: University of Minnesota Press, 2014.
Coenen, Craig R. *From Sandlots to the Super Bowl: The National Football League, 1920–1967*. Knoxville: University of Tennessee Press, 2005.
Daniels, George G. *The XIX Olympiad: Mexico City, 1968, Sapporo, 1972*. Los Angeles: World Sport Research and Publications, 1996.
Flaherty, George F. *Hotel Mexico: Dwelling on the '68 Movement*. Oakland: University of California Press, 2016.
Fleder, Rob, ed. *The College Football Book*. New York: Sports Illustrated Books, 2008.
Florio, John, and Ouisie Shapiro: *One Nation under Baseball: How the 1960s Collided with the National Pastime*. Lincoln: University of Nebraska Press, 2017.
Frommer, Harvey. *When It Was Just a Game: Remembering the First Super Bowl*. Lanham, MD: Taylor Trade, 2015.
Fury, Shawn. *Rise and Fire: The Origins, Science, and Evolution of the Jump Shot—and How It Transformed Basketball Forever*. New York: Flatiron, 2016.
Gerlach, Larry R., ed. *The Winter Olympics: From Chamonix to Salt Lake City*. Salt Lake City: University of Utah Press, 2004.
Gmelch, George. *Playing with Tigers: A Minor League Chronicle of the Sixties*. Lincoln: University of Nebraska Press, 2016.
Gruver, Ed. *The American Football League: A Year-by-Year History, 1960–1969*. Jefferson, NC: McFarland, 1997.
Hartmann, Douglas. *Race, Culture and the Revolt of the Black Athlete: The 1968 Olympic Protests and Their Aftermath*. Chicago: University of Chicago Press, 2003.
Heisler, Mark. *Giants: The 25 Greatest Centers of All Time*. Chicago: Triumph, 2003.

Hensler, Paul. *The American League in Transition, 1965–1975: How Competition Thrived When the Yankees Didn't.* Jefferson, NC: McFarland, 2013.

Hensler, Paul. *The New Boys of Summer: Baseball's Radical Transformation in the Late Sixties.* Lanham, MD: Rowman & Littlefield, 2017.

Hoffer, Richard. *Something in the Air: American Passion and Defiance in the 1968 Mexico City Olympics.* New York: Free, 2009.

Kirchberg, Connie. *Hoop Lore: A History of the National Basketball Association.* Jefferson, NC: McFarland, 2007.

Maraniss, David. *Rome 1960: The Olympics That Changed the World.* New York: Simon & Schuster, 2008.

Miller, Jeff. *Going Long: The Wild 10-Year Saga of the Renegade American Football League in the Words of Those Who Lived It.* Chicago: Contemporary, 2003.

Oriard, Michael. *Bowled Over: Big-Time College Football from the Sixties to the BCS Era.* Chapel Hill: University of North Carolina Press, 2009.

Peterson, Robert. *Cages to Jump Shots: Pro Basketball's Early Years.* New York: Oxford University Press, 1990.

Ross, Charles Kenyatta. *Mavericks, Money, and Men: The AFL, Black Players, and the Evolution of Modern Football.* Philadelphia: Temple University Press, 2016.

Ryczek, William J. *Baseball on the Brink: The Crisis of 1968.* Jefferson, NC: McFarland, 2017.

Smith, Tommie, with David Steele. *Silent Gesture: Autobiography of Tommie Smith.* Philadelphia: Temple University Press, 2007.

Stark, Douglas. *Breaking Barriers: A History of Integration in Professional Basketball.* Lanham, MD: Rowman & Littlefield, 2019.

Stewart, Wayne. *Remembering the Greatest Coaches and Games of the NFL Glory Years: An Inside Look at the Golden Age of Football.* Lanham, MD: Rowman & Littlefield, 2018.

Surdam, David G. *The Rise of the National Basketball Association.* Urbana: University of Illinois Press, 2012.

Thomas, Ron. *They Cleared the Lane: The NBA's Black Pioneers.* Lincoln: University of Nebraska Press, 2002.

Walker, J. Samuel. *ACC Basketball: The Story of the Rivalries, Traditions, and Scandals of the First Two Decades of the Atlantic Coast Conference.* Chapel Hill: University of North Carolina Press, 2011.

Whalen, Thomas J. *Dynasty's End: Bill Russell and the 1968–69 World Champion Boston Celtics.* Boston: Northeastern University Press, 2004.

Wiggins, David K., and Patrick B. Miller, eds. *The Unlevel Playing Feld: A Documentary History of the African American Experience in Sport.* Urbana: University of Illinois Press, 2003.

Witherspoon, Kevin B. *Before the Eyes of the World: Mexico and the 1968 Olympic Games.* DeKalb, IL: Northern Illinois University Press, 2008.

Zimniuch, Frank. *Baseball's New Frontier: A History of Expansion, 1961–1998.* Lincoln: University of Nebraska Press, 2013.

# CHAPTER 6

# Art

**POP ART**

Perhaps the most defining movement in visual art during the 1960s was what quickly became known as pop art. Although it seemed a radical reconception of what art is and should be, pop art was in many ways a natural progression from the artistic movements that preceded it.

Over the modern era, artists had moved away from the medieval emphasis on religious subjects to a much broader range conception of appropriate subject matter that included landscapes, architecture, still-life paintings of arranged objects, historically significant figures and events, and portraits of aristocratic patrons. As the merchant class and then the gradually expanding middle class became patrons of artists and buyers of art—or visitors to museums—the subject matter expanded further to include scenes of everyday life and then, in response to increasing political democratization, industrial subjects and working-class life and even the squalor of underclass life. When realism had seemingly gone as far as it could be taken, artists began to experiment with ways of forcing viewers to look at the subjects of their paintings in fresh and even radically new ways. Through movements such as impressionism, expressionism, cubism, and surrealism, viewers were also forced to recognize the difference between reality and art: that is, if realism sought to represent the real world as accurately and as vividly as possible, the modernists sought to compel viewers to reconsider the ways in which they view the real world and to reshape their expectations of art and the function of art. In the middle decades of the twentieth century, abstract art completely eliminated "reality" as the subject of art, and abstract expressionism eliminated even recognizable shapes and forms from works of art.

Pop art went to the opposite extreme from abstract expressionism, reproducing and repurposing images from the material culture of postwar America.

The two main sources were, first, American advertising and commercial packaging and, second, American visual media including but not limited to film, television, magazines, and comic books. There were also typographical experiments and experiments of collages of text and images. Pop art did not look like much of the art that preceded it, but, of course, its imagery was extremely familiar. Three basic issues attracted the most discussion. First, was pop art was simply plagiarizing commercial art and other artifacts, or was it repurposing it in some significant way? Second, if it were a meaningful repurposing of familiar imagery, at what point would the repurposed imagery amount to an original work of art? And, lastly, if it were judged an original work, at what point would it deserve to be considered a serious work of art?

Clearly, pop art is fairly easy to identify and even to define, but its relation to the art movements that preceded and have followed, as well as the degree to which it deserves to be taken as seriously as those other movements, has remained a matter of some contention. Works of pop art continue to sell for amazingly high prices at auction, but there is still some argument over whether the sale prices reflect their actual, enduring value as art or are more a reflection of their current, perceived value as historical artifacts. Certainly, an argument can be made that the changes in American popular culture that began in the 1950s and were associated with the postwar economic boom came to fuller fruition in the 1960s and radically changed the "reality" in which people were living. Although advertising had become a self-contained industry in the early decades of the twentieth century, it became a major industry with the postwar boom in new consumer products. As grocery chains and other retail chains began aggressively competing, food and product packaging became less utilitarian and more a very important marketing device. In combination with the rapid development of the new medium of television and the revival of high-gloss magazines, both of which became major venues for advertising, the culture of celebrity become a more pervasive influence than it had been even during the so-called Golden Age of the Hollywood film studios. Celebrity typically attracted endorsement offers, which for performers and athletes increasingly became almost as important as a source of income, if not a more important source of income, as their salaries. These commercial and cultural phenomena came together at the grocery checkout, where racks of tabloid newspapers and magazines were positioned to spur last-minute impulse buying.

To some degree, pop art was justified by the sudden ubiquity of the materials that it repurposed. One could justifiably ask how relevant the art of the period would have been if it did not draw on those materials—or, to put it even more pointedly, how relevant would it have been if it ignored those materials. In an increasingly urbanized society in which communication and entertainment were increasingly electronic, human experience seemed to be becoming less direct and more vicarious, less active and more passive—concerns that would become much more pressing with the development and pervasive adoption of digital technologies. Moreover, the much intensified media saturation of American culture justified the claim that art that presented such commonplace details of our reality was forcing us in a serious way to recognize that those details were largely surfaces without much substance, or, perhaps more precisely, with implications that were seldom being considered. Because much commercial art relies on relatively simple and very defined lines and shapes and on relatively few and very bold colors, pop art forced viewers to confront, at least at an intuitive level, how they were being affected by branding and packaging. When the art involved the juxtaposition of images or collage, the effect was even more dramatic and ironic, but even when the focus was on a single image, the effect could be ironic simply because the commercial imagery was effectively breaking down the conventional distinctions between representational and abstract art. That the same advancements in printing technologies and techniques that facilitated developments in packaging could be employed in creating pop art meant that there was a very visceral, as well as conceptual, bridging of the traditional divisions between commercial art and "serious" art.

It needs to be emphasized that highly regarded artists had been blurring the distinctions between commercial and "serious" art for more than a century—for instance, the figures in Toulouse Lautrec's paintings and his posters advertising dance hall shows. Likewise, the Dadaists and some of their successors not only incorporated commercial imagery into some of their works, but they explored how photography and other developments exploited by commercial artists might change the conception of what a painting or other work of art is or might be.

That said, like many artistic and other movements associated with the 1960s, pop art, as a movement, had its beginnings in the 1950s, and like a number of other elements of 1960s popular culture, including popular music and fashion, it first came to wide notice in Great Britain. But, ironically, the British artists who became known as the Independent Group were responding to the pervasiveness of American products and popular culture in postwar Europe, where it would take several decades to recover from just the most visible devastation caused by the Second World War. Most notably, Eduardo Paolozzi and Richard Hamilton created collages that were amusing and satiric, placing images and objects into conventional settings in which they were startlingly out of place. For instance, in Paolozzi's "I Was a Rich Man's Plaything," the top two-thirds of the painting is a cover of a tabloid newspaper or "men's magazine" called *Intimate Confessions*. Below it are images of an American bomber with the propagandistic slogan "Keep 'em Flying" and the then iconic bottle of Coca-Cola alongside the company's logo. In one of Hamilton's collages called "Just What Is It That Makes Today's Homes So Different, So Appealing?," the background setting is a living room in a nicely furnished middle-class home, but it is crowded with images that might very well have been found in a magazine on the coffee table or end tables but are laughably out of place as life-sized presences. The man and woman of the house are nude—the man, a bodybuilder posing to accentuate his physique, and the woman, with one hand in her hair and the other holding a breast, posing as if for a pornographic photo spread. The incongruity is emphasized by their being presented in black-and-white when everything else in the room is in color. The living room is crowded with other images, including a canned ham standing on end in the center of the coffee table and a Ford emblem on a lampshade, suggesting how commercialization is crowding out other aspects of contemporary life. British pop art tended to be more unmistakably satiric and ironic than American pop art, which sometimes seemed so inexpressive that commentators wondered whether it was, in fact, satiric or ironic, or whether it was, instead, indifferent or even celebratory.

## ANDY WARHOL (1928–1987)

Andy Warhol is the artist most associated with the pop art movement. Indeed, while he was alive, he was frequently referred to as the "Pope of Pop." After graduating from the Carnegie Institute of Technology (later Carnegie Mellon University) in the late 1940s, he had relocated from his hometown of Pittsburgh to New York City, and he had fairly quickly found success as a commercial artist. By the late 1950s, he was exhibiting some of his commercial artwork at galleries and making the transition from being a commercial artist to being regarded as a "serious" artist. For his main subjects, Warhol focused on brand-name commercial products, celebrities, and sensational news stories. He was particularly interested in finding new ways to manipulate the relatively new technology of silk-screen printmaking. Early on, he mixed some of the paint dripping associated with abstract expressionism with the silk screening, but he ended up experimenting more with smudging the various layers of paint.

Although Warhol's celebrity persisted across the last three decades of his life, his period of greatest influence was the 1960s. He founded a studio known as the "Factory," which attracted all sorts of avant-garde visual and performing artists, who collaborated with Warhol on his diverse projects, inspired his art with the eccentric personas that they had adopted, or became celebrities in their own right because he brought those personas to wider public attention. In 1968, Valerie Solanas, a radical feminist whose *S.C.U.M. Manifesto*, advocating the elimination of men, had been published in 1967, shot Warhol and art critic Mario Amaya, who happened to be with Warhol. Afterward, she explained the attempted murder by asserting that she had no other way of escaping Warhol's influence. She had been, however, only very loosely associated with the group at the Factory, and in presentencing psychological examinations, she was diagnosed as a paranoid schizophrenic. The shooting was very nearly fatal for Warhol, with surgeons having to massage his heart to keep it beating while he was on the operating table, and he would be affected physically and psychologically by the trauma for the rest of his life. In the 1970s, he would retreat from the spotlight, but he remained much in demand for commissioned art projects, and in the last decade of his life, he began to be seen again at clubs in the company of other celebrities. He would die in 1987 of cardiac arrest following gall bladder surgery.

Warhol became controversial, first, because his works seemed to demand being taken seriously as art even as they represented a rejection of everything then associated with serious art. Even though no one could quite reproduce what Warhol was doing, in large part because much of the impact of the work was in his doing it before it occurred to anyone else to do it, art critics and broader cultural commentators began to focus on the flatness of his

Artist Andy Warhol became the center of the New York art scene in the 1960s and collected around him followers who would influence film and popular music as well as art. (Mario De Biasi/Mondadori via Getty Images)

works—on the lack of humor, irony, or any other indication of an attitude toward his subjects. Warhol himself remarked that he was fascinated by plastic and, in particular, the notion that plastic was all surface. Second, as Warhol enlisted assistants in creating his paintings and prints, critics wondered how much of the work was actually his own and how seriously the work should be taken as art if it was being created in a manner that suggested the mass production of the goods that it was often representing. Third, as the cast of artists and other "personalities" associated with the Factory expanded, Warhol began to experiment with all sorts of other genres beyond painting and printmaking: drawings; sculptures; photography; documentary and feature films, including the first widely distributed pornographic films; experimental plays; multimedia projects that, with the advent of personal computers, eventually began to include digital elements; audio recordings of his conversations in person and on the telephone; and "time capsules" of the detritus of his daily life. He also became an author, publishing both experimental fiction and more conventional nonfiction, and a record producer for experimental rock and new wave groups. Although his work in all of these forms attracted attention and was seen as innovative and in some instances cutting-edge, commentators began to see more than a little self-indulgence and even dilettantism in his seemingly continuous chasing after some new form within which he could experiment. Lastly, when Warhol increasingly took on commissioned projects, it seemed to some commentators as if he were reversing the course that made him famous as a "serious' artist—producing ostensibly "serious" art in the manner that one produces commercial art, turning "art" into a commodity indistinguishable in many fundamental ways from the commodities that are the mainstays of commercial art.

Nonetheless, the Andy Warhol Museum in Pittsburgh is the largest museum in the world devoted to the work of a single artist, and Warhol's paintings remain very much in demand. The following are the works by Warhol that rank among the one hundred works of art with the highest selling prices in history: *Silver Car Crash (Double Disaster)* (created in 1963; sold in 2013), $105.4 million; *Eight Elvises* (created in 1963; sold in 2008), $100 million; *Triple Elvis* (created in 1963; sold in 2014), $81.9 million; *Turquoise Marilyn* (created in 1964; sold in 2007), $80 million; *Green Car Crash (Green Burning Car 1)* (created in 1963; sold in 2007), $71.7 million; *Four Marlons* (created in 1966; sold in 2014), $69.6 million; and *Men in Her Life* (created in 1962; sold in 2010), $63.4 million.

Warhol's most famous works are, of course, of Campbell's soup cans. The original series of thirty-two paintings were each 16 inches wide by 20 inches long. Produced over a number of months in 1962 and 1963, the series represents the thirty-two kinds of Campbell's soup available at the time. The entire series is currently part of the permanent collection at the Museum of Modern Art (MOMA) in New York City. Warhol continued to produce paintings of the soup cans throughout his career. Some of the paintings depicted damaged cans— cans on which the labels were torn or cans that had become dented or seriously deformed in transit—or cans with other objects, most famously a can opener. The largest Campbell's soup can painting is 6 feet wide by 8 feet 4 inches long. The most expensive Campbell's soup can painting is *Small Torn Campbell Soup Can (Pepper Pot)*, which was painted in 1962 and sold for $11,776,000 in 2006.

## ROY LICHTENSTEIN (1923–1997)

Roy Lichtenstein had a longer life and career than Andy Warhol, and like Warhol, he remained productive throughout his life. But he never sought or reached the level of celebrity that Warhol achieved, and although several of his paintings rank among the one hundred works of art with the highest selling price in history, his work has not become fixed in the popular culture in the same way that some of Warhol's paintings have become broadly, if not almost universally, recognizable as his work. Yet, both artists produced their most impactful and enduringly influential works over the first half of the 1960s, and both artists faced broadly similar criticism about the subject matter, style, and originality of their work.

Lichtenstein's most well-known and influential works were taken from comic book panels. In changing the scale and subtly but significantly altering the style of the images, Lichtenstein sought to emphasize how pulp art might be turned into "serious" art and thereby to raise questions about the efficacy of such categories and assumptions about the value of different kinds of art. Specifically,

Lichtenstein utilized more emphatic outlines, more vivid colors, and exaggerated Ben-Day dots to distinguish his paintings from the original comic book panels. Ben-Day dots were used in printing comic books: basically, dots of the four base colors were overlaid in the printing process to create other colors and shades of color. Lichtenstein made the dots more prominent so that they would be obvious enough for the viewer to notice them without being completely distracted from the subject of the painting by them. In effect, the painting broke down the distinctions between subject and technique.

Lichtenstein's most famous paintings include *Look Mickey* (1961), *Masterpiece* (1962), *Whaam!* (1963), *Drowning Girl* (1963), and *Oh, Jeff . . . I Love You, Too . . . But . . .* (1964). *Look Mickey* shows Mickey Mouse and Donald Duck fishing off a dock. Donald Duck thinks that he has hooked a fish, and a dialogue bubble shows him exclaiming, "Look, Mickey. I've hooked a big one!!" Seeing that Donald Duck has actually hooked the back of his own sailor's shirt, Mickey holds his hand over his mouth to keep from laughing out loud. *Masterpiece* focuses on a striking blonde with a dark-haired, handsome man, who are shown only from the shoulders up. The corner of a painting on an easel is visible on the left side of the painting, and the dialogue bubble shows her exclaiming, "Why, Brad Darling, this painting is a masterpiece! My, soon you'll have all of New York clamoring for your work!" This painting sold in 2017 for $165 million, the tenth highest price ever paid for a painting up to that time. In *Whaam!*, an American fighter plane has just shot at and hit an enemy plane, which is bursting into yellow and red flames. The exclamation is in a white starburst between the two planes. *Drowning Girl* shows a blue-haired woman struggling to stay afloat in rough water. The swirling water is white, a much lighter shade of blue than her hair, and black. And under her mascara-darkened eyebrows and eyelashes, thick white tears have collected just below her closed eyes. A thought bubble shows her resolving, "I don't care. I'd rather sink—than call Brad for help!" *Oh, Jeff . . . I Love You, Too . . . But . . .* shows a close-up of a blue-eyed, red-lipped blonde with a white phone just barely visible at her right ear. The painting is so zoomed in on her pained expression that the top of her forehead and her chin are not visible in the frame. A less well-known painting has sold for the second highest price ever paid for one of Lichtenstein's paintings. *Nurse* (1964) shows another blue-eyed blonde from the shoulder up. Her nurse's cap and white uniform make it clear that she is a nurse. She looks very concerned, but there is no dialogue bubble or thought bubble indicating the cause of her concern. In 1995, the painting sold for $1.7 million, but 20 years later, in 2015, it sold for $95,365,000.

## PSYCHEDELIC ART

In the 1960s, the pursuit of alternative lifestyles had a parallel in the interest in entering into altered states of mind. The underlying idea was that contemporary society had become defined by conformity, and individuals had become so thoroughly conditioned to deeply ingrained, accepted ways of thinking that they had lost a true sense of their selves. As a consequence, freeing oneself from such social and psychological constraints in order to explore one's subconscious and one's spiritual possibilities required some sort of external agent. Hallucinogenic drugs such as LSD were promoted as a means of opening one's consciousness to fantastic possibilities, and the physical effects of those drugs inspired psychedelic rock music, psychedelic fashion, and psychedelic art.

To a society that a decade earlier had been defined by the gray flannel suit, psychedelic fashion was a truly shocking rejection of norms. And, unlike pop art, which appropriated the mainstream material culture, psychedelic art was most deeply meaningful to those committed to the Counterculture, and it became commodified to satisfy mainstream curiosity about the Counterculture. Popular representations of psychedelic imagery, such as those used on the television variety show *Rowan and Martin's Laugh-In*, were essentially a more mediated version of the buses carrying middle-aged tourists through the Haight-Ashbury district of San Francisco during and after the "Summer of Love." Such representations typically reduced the Counterculture to trite memes. But no one commodified psychedelic art more profitably than Peter Max, who became an international celebrity by giving a Counterculture cast to print and television advertisements and to corporate and product branding.

Psychedelic art was meant to imitate or to heighten the effect of hallucinogenic drugs. To that end, the artists employed: wavy or swirling lines; prismatic or warped shapes; suggestions of concentrated, diffracted, or fragmented light; bright, kaleidoscopic, or unusual colors; surrealistic combinations of imagery or collages of fragmented images and texts; or distorted and stylized scripts. Some psychedelic art had a Gothic style suggesting the darker corners of the subconscious.

This genre is now largely remembered for such things as record album covers and concert posters, such as those done by Wes Wilson to advertise acts appearing at the Filmore in San Francisco. The more stylized psychedelic art borrowed heavily from art nouveau, such as the work of Victor Moscoso. British artist Brigid Kelly would garner international attention for paintings that created optical illusions, and that type of work was created by a number of artists on both sides of the Atlantic.

## OTHER MOVEMENTS IN THE VISUAL ARTS

### Minimalism

Conceived as a reaction against the intense subjectivism of abstract expressionism, minimalism was intended to stress "objectivity"—to direct the focus onto the object without mediation. Minimalist artists created geometric shapes, stripped of any context and suggestion of figurative meaning, and emphasized the arrangement and repetition of the shapes. Many minimalist paintings were monochromatic, and few had more than a very limited set of colors or shades of color. Sculptors typically used industrial materials, and functional elements of architecture and machinery were isolated so totally from their sources that any suggestion of their utilitarian function was largely, if not completely, eliminated. A list of the most significant minimalist artists would almost certainly include Frank Stella (1936–), Carl Andre (1935–), Donald Judd (1928–1994), Robert Morris (1931–2018), and Robert Ryman (1930–2019).

**Lyrical Abstraction**

Lyrical abstraction was a reaction against pop art and minimalism. In its techniques and effects, it was a sort of synthesis between minimalism and its predecessor abstract expressionism, while incorporating some of the technical innovations adopted by pop artists. Noteworthy American artists in this movement include Natvar Bhavsar (1934–), Stanley Boxer (1926–2000), Lamar Briggs (1935–2015), Dan Christensen (1942–2007), David Diao (1943–), Friedel Dzubas (1915–1994), Sam Francis (1923–1994), Dorothy Gillespie (1920–2012), Cleve Gray (1918–2004), Paul Jenkins (1923–2012), Ronnie Landfield (1947–), Pat Lipsky (1940–), Joan Mitchell (1925–1992), Robert Natkin (1930–2010), Jules Olitski (1922–2007), Larry Poons (1937–), Garry Rich (1943–2016), John Seery (1941–), Jeff Way (1942–), and Larry Zox (1937–2006).

**Conceptual Art**

Conceptual art was in many ways a logical development from minimalism. For these artists, the work of art itself was secondary to the fully realized idea of the work. In fact, some conceptual artists argued that the work of art did not even need to be produced—that a description of the artist's conception was itself art. In effect, by reducing art's conventional commodification, conceptual artists eliminated established galleries as the primary marketplaces for their works and created their own venues. One of the most well-known conceptual artists working in the United States in the mid-1960s was Joseph Kosuth (1945–). His work was heavily influenced by his interests in psychoanalysis and in the philosophy of language: in the relationship between the individual psyche and the external world—between memory and experience, between the subconscious, consciousness, and reflexive response to sensory stimuli—and in the relationship between language and the realities that it signifies. Kosuth's most well-known work is *One and Three Chairs* (1965), in which a chair is exhibited with both a photograph of the chair and a blown-up copy of the dictionary definition of the word "chair."

**Fluxus**

Fluxus is the term given to the efforts of diverse artists who combined different media in experimental ways, placing the emphasis on the act of creation, rather than on the completed work. The movement was inspired by the experimental musical compositions of John Cage, and it is itself credited as being the starting place from which conceptual art, performance art, video art, and intermedia all developed. Notable American artists associated with the Fluxus movement include George Brecht (1924–2008), Henry Flynt (1940–), Al Hansen (1927–1995), Dick Higgins (1938–1998), Alison Knowles (1933–), George Maciunas (1931–1978), Yoko Ono (1933–), Nam June Paik (1932–2006), and Ben

Patterson (1934–1982). Of course, given the nature of the art, not as much of the work produced by these artists survives in museums, but most of the artists involved would likely not measure the importance of their work in that way.

### Video Art

Video art is different from cinema in that it does not have the identifiable settings, storyline(s), and characters that conventionally define feature films. The distinctions do, however, become more ambiguous when the point of comparison is experimental films that attempt to subvert the conventions and conventional elements of feature films. In its earliest stages in the 1960s, video art consisted of gallery installations or performance art that incorporated television sets and/or projected images along with live or recorded sounds. Over subsequent decades, as video tapes, DVD, and Internet technologies developed, video art began to be distributed over and even designed specifically for those media. Notable American video artists of the period included Vito Acconci (1940–2017), John Baldessari (1931–), Peter Campus (1937–), Doris Totten Chase (1923–2008), Frank Gillette (1941–), Dan Graham (1942), Joan Jonas (1936–), Bruce Nauman (1941–), Nam June Paik (1932–2006), Martha Rosler (1943–), and William Wegman (1943).

### Performance Art

In the same ways that video art is distinguishable from cinema, performance art is distinguishable from theater. In fact, some performance artists and commentators on the form have described it as the antithesis of theater. The elements that define performance art are very straightforward: it requires a performer, an audience, and some sort of nondramatic performance that includes the fine arts. Beyond that, the options and opportunities are literally open-ended: the performance can be live, recorded, or remotely transmitted; it can be scripted, outlined, or entirely improvised; it can include any level of audience participation or none at all; the performance can be extended or very brief, segmented, or continuous; the performance can include a great deal of movement or almost none at all. The key thing is to lead the audience to focus on the art in a fresh, if not provocative, way. Major performance artists of the period include Allen Kaprow (1927–2006), Yoko Ono (1933), and Carolee Schneemann (1939).

### Happenings

Happenings were a type of performance art in which the core aim was to engage the audience actively as an element of the resulting work of art. Therefore, although there was a great deal of allowance for improvisation, there was generally at least a tentative plan for how the audience might become part of the art. Artists known for creating happenings included Robert Delford Brown (1930–2009), Jim Dine (1935–), Red Grooms (1937–), Claes Oldenburg (1929–), Robert Rauschenberg (1925–2008), Lucas Samaras (1936–), Carolee Schneemann (1939–), and Robert Whitman (1935–).

### Process Art

Process art went beyond audience engagement to placing the entire emphasis on the conceptual processes and inventive impulses involved in the creation of art. The process was conceived of as something between a therapy session, a sacramental rite, and an animistic ritual. To take the interest away from the work of art as a durable artifact, process artists often used natural materials that were already showing degradation and decay or would be very shortly subject to it—in some cases, making use of even dead animals. In this way, art was reconceived not as a representation of nature but a part of the natural world, which was accepted as the ultimate work of art. The most notable American process artists of the period were Lynda Benglis (1941–), Eva Hesse (1936–1970), Gary Kuehn (1939–), Barry Le Va (1941–), Bruce Nauman (1941–), Robert Morris (1931–2019), Richard Serra (1939–), Keith Sonnier (1941–), and Richard Van Buren (1937–).

### Junk or Trash Art

Junk or trash art can be viewed as a descendant of found art and a parallel to process art. Found art involves the staging or modification of a commonplace object or combination of objects in a manner that reconceptualizes the object or objects as art, and it had been popularized by Dadaist artists in the first several decades of the twentieth century. Junk or trash art was largely a product of the 1960s—a response to the rapidly expanding material culture, the increasing commercial emphasis on packaging, and the growing concern about the disposal of refuse and its environmental impact. Major American junk or trash artists of the period include John Chamberlain (1927–), Bruce Conner (1933–2008), Arman (Armand Fernandez) (1928–2005), Ed Kienholz (1927–1994), David Smith (1906–1965), and Richard Stankiewicz (1923–1983).

### Earth or Land Art

Generally executed in somewhat remote areas, earth or land art was a reaction against the increasing commercialization of art. It could be exhibited only in photographs of the sites where it had been created, and although some of the sites have become major curiosities and thus commercially important, earth or land artists relied on grants from patrons rather than on sales to collectors. Earth or land art thereby undercut the paradigm by which the value of works of art was increasingly being measured by the prices they brought at auction. In general, earth or land artists seek to use natural materials to create works that are consistent with the natural contours of the land and that suggest its psychological and spiritual impact on a human observer. The artists have taken as their models the more organically conceived structures created by ancient and indigenous peoples, whether those structures were monumental or mundane. These artists are also obviously linked to contemporary movements such as minimalism and conceptual art. Major American earth or land artists of the period include Walter De Maria (1935–2013), Hans Haacke (1936–), Michael

Heizer (1944), Neil Jenney (1945–), Robert Morris (1931–2019), Dennis Oppenheim (1938–2011), and Robert Smithson (1938–1973).

### Graffiti

Although graffiti's association with "serious" art has become more pronounced over the last three to four decades with the rise of hip-hop culture, it had its roots in the 1960s. For graffiti artists, the development of aerosol paints was as important as the development of silk-screen printmaking technologies was for pop artists such as Andy Warhol. In its style, graffiti also has a great deal in common with pop art that borrowed from comics and with psychedelic art. In the deindustrialized urban wastelands of America's inner cities, graffiti became a form of land art, with the artists using the contours of dilapidated and abandoned structures to shape their work. Likewise, installation art is often seen as a development from earth or land art, and in an artist such as Banksy, installation art and graffiti art seem to have come together.

## JASPER JOHNS (1930–)

Jaspar Johns is typically identified as a major figure in the pop art movement, but he has generally not appropriated the imagery of commercial art and celebrity photography in the same ways that Andy Warhol and other pop artists have done so. He has focused, instead, on rendering symbols such as letters, numbers, and flags that are so universally recognized that they go almost unnoticed as subjects. By the late 1950s and the 1960s, for instance, the American flag had become such a universally recognized symbol that the many meanings attached to it were, in effect, canceling themselves out, making it no more resonant as a symbol than the cross at the top of the steeple of every Christian church in the United States. Johns himself explained that he was attempting to separate the painter from the painting, noting that the work of abstract expressionists such as Jackson Pollock and Willem de Kooning had such signature styles that the painters had, in effect, become the subjects of their paintings in which they were so thoroughly avoiding representations of any identifiable subjects. The use of letters, numbers, and universal symbols as subjects gave the viewer something to focus on as the subject and thereby forced them to focus on the painting itself, rather than on its creator or creation. In this way, the artist's every artistic choice became a point of focus.

Like Warhol and Lichtenstein, Johns continues to be most known for the work that he produced in the late 1950s and 1960s. His paintings have repeatedly set records for the highest prices paid for the work of a living artist, with his painting *Flag* (1958) selling for $110 million in 2010. Another of Johns's most well-known works is *Numbers* (1964), a 9-foot by 7-foot commissioned installation that hangs over the entrance to the David H. Koch Theater at Lincoln Center for the Performing Arts in New York City. Other notable works by Johns from the 1960s include *Painted Bronze* (1960), *Painting with Two Balls* (1960), *0 through 9* (1960), *Coat Hangar* (1960), *Painting Bitten by a Man* (1961), *Target* (1961), *Fool's House*

(1962), *Study for Skin* (1962), *Device* (1963), *Periscope (Hart Crane)* (1963), *The Critic Sees* (1964), *Figure Five* (1964), *Watchman* (1964), and *Voice* (1967).

## DIANE ARBUS (1923–1971)

After a decade working with her husband as a commercial and fashion photographer, Diane Arbus separated from him, and in the late 1950s, she began to support herself, albeit somewhat inconsistently, with feature assignments for major magazines and with private commissions. At the same time, she focused increasingly on refining the techniques that allowed her to take compelling portraits of people who, for the most part, either posed for her on the spot or were captured by her in the middle of their daily lives. Some of the people whom she photographed were very ordinary working-class and middle-class Americans—the mostly faceless people who fill the streets of New York and any other major city. Arbus photographed them in the places where they lived and worked—doing their jobs, running errands, enjoying a brief break, or socializing with coworkers, friends, or relatives. She managed to produce portraits of many of them as individuals, momentarily and vividly isolated from the crowded backdrop of the streets. But she also photographed couples, mothers with their children, and the elderly, somehow suggesting the subtle dynamics of personal relationships and small groups. Beyond making the ordinary seem extraordinary simply because of the clarity and honesty with which she focused on it and captured it, she also made many of the people who existed

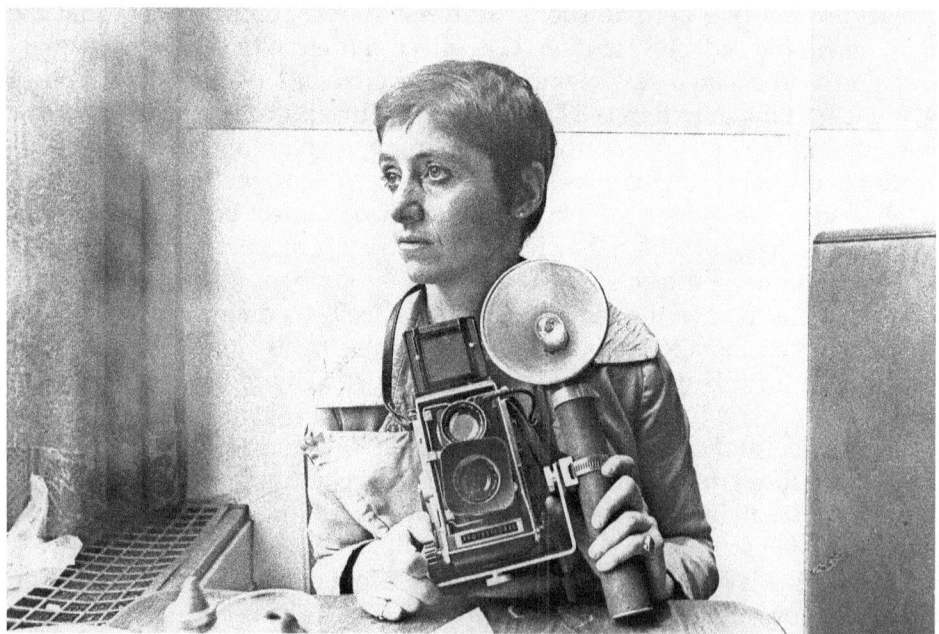

Diane Arbus brought a new sensibility to photography, bringing the marginalized to center stage. (Roz Kelly/Michael Ochs Archives/Getty Images)

on the margins of mainstream American life seem every bit as much a part of the social fabric as the "normal" folks. She photographed people who often were dismissed as lowlifes or freaks—the physically and mentally impaired, prostitutes, strippers, and transvestites, sideshow acts, hustlers and scroungers, transients and derelicts, individuals with unusual physical features and eccentric styles of dress, the whole spectrum of idiosyncratic and fantastic characters— and because she photographed them as directly as she photographed "normal" folks, she permitted them a measure of human dignity that was quite extraordinary, for their time and her time, and for any time.

In the second half of the 1950s, Arbus began to compile portfolios of her work, received several grants, and achieved considerable notice with a showing of her work at the Museum of Modern Art (MOMA), along with that of Lee Friedlander and Garry Winogrand. That show titled *New Documents* attracted more than a quarter of a million visitors to MOMA. Still, it was only after Arbus committed suicide in 1971 that her genius was truly appreciated. A retrospective showing of her work at MOMA in 1972 was turned into a national traveling exhibition that over the next three years attracted more than 7 million people to museums that hosted it. A book of the photographs in the show that was published to commemorate the show became so enduringly popular that it has never been out of print. Critics and historians have identified it as one of the most important books of photography ever published. Another selection of Arbus's work became an international traveling exhibition that extended from 1973 to 1979. It is difficult to overestimate the impact of Arbus's work on subsequent photographers and, more broadly, on the perception of and potential of photography as one of the fine arts. At the same time, many of the more remarkable aspects of Arbus's work have been imitated so frequently and widely that they now are commonplace and might seem to diminish the appreciation of her significance. But, as any number of commentators have pointed out, even today her photographs have a compelling singularity that remains largely elusive to even the most talented photographers who have been inspired by her work.

## VISUAL ARTS AND THE CIVIL RIGHTS MOVEMENT

Although the Black Arts Movement took shape in the second half of the 1960s and describes a determined exploration and celebration of African American identity through writing and the performing arts, it is loosely connected to a substantial body of work in the visual arts that accompanied the Civil Rights Movement. That movement inspired artists working in a number of genres— painting, sculpture, conceptual art, and photography. The most highly regarded paintings associated with the movement include: *Soldiers and Students* (1962), by Jacob Lawrence (1917–2000); *Birmingham* (1965), by Jack Whitten (1939–2018); *The Confederacy: Alabama* (1965), by Robert Indiana (1928–2018); *Three Witnesses* (1966), by Emma Amos (1938–); *Witness* (1968), by Benny Andrews (1930–2006); *Wives of Shango* (1969), by Jeff Donaldson (1932–2004); *City Limits* (1969), by Philp Guston (1913–1980); and *Lawdy Mama* (1969), by Barkley L. Hendricks (1945–2017). Noted sculptures and conceptual artworks include: *It Takes Two to Integrate*

(1961), by Edward Keinholz (1927–1994); *Homage to My Young Black Sisters* (1968), by Elizabeth Catlett (1915–2012); and *The Door* (1969), by David Hammons (1943–).

The most well known of the photographers capturing the Civil Rights Movement was Gordon Parks (1912–2006). On assignments for *Life* magazine, he covered Malcolm X and the March on Washington in 1963. Another contributor to *Life* was Dan Budnik (1933–), who compiled a lengthy photo essay of the Selma to Montgomery march. The photographs taken by James "Spider" Martin (1939–2003) of the violence during that march on what became known as "Bloody Sunday" created a national sensation. Employed by the Southern Christian Leadership Conference, Bob Fitch (1930–2006) photographed the March against Fear in Mississippi. In 1964, Matt Herron (1931–) organized the Southern Documentary Project to create a photographic record of Freedom Summer, and Herbert Eugene Randall Jr. (1936–) intensively documented Freedom Summer efforts in Hattiesburg, Mississippi. Art Shay (1922–2018) covered the race riots in Chicago in 1966 and in Detroit in 1967. And in 1969, Moneta Sleet Jr. (1926–1996) won the Pulitzer Prize for Feature Photography for his photos of Coretta Scott King at her husband's funeral. Sleet was the first African American to win a Pulitzer Prize for journalism.

## ARCHITECTURE

Major skyscrapers constructed in U.S. cities in the 1960s include: One Chase Manhattan Plaza, the MetLife Building, the Marine Midland Bank Building, and One New York Plaza; the Prudential Tower in Boston; the Phoenix Life Insurance Building in Hartford; the Casino Tower and the Skylon Tower in Niagara Falls; the Marina City Towers, the Richard J. Daley Center, the Lake Point Tower, the Bank One Plaza, and the John Hancock Center in Chicago; the Founders Tower in Oklahoma City; the Exxon Building in Houston; the Tower of the Americas in San Antonio; the Bank of America Center in San Francisco; and the Lovejoy Plaza in Portland, Oregon. But the project that received the most attention was started in the mid-1960s and was not completed until the next decade—the World Trade Center Towers in New York.

Other architectural landmarks constructed during the decade include: the Philharmonic Hall at the Lincoln Center for the Performing Arts, the Whitney Museum of Modern Art, the TWA Terminal at J.F.K. Airport, and the Verrazzano Narrows Bridge in New York; the Smithsonian's Museum of History and Technology and its Hirshhorn Museum and Sculpture Garden in Washington, DC; the Jefferson National Expansion memorial and the Gateway Arch in St. Louis; the Los Angeles County Museum of Art; and the Space Needle in Seattle. In 1964, however, an infrastructure project hailed as "one of the Seven Engineering Wonders of the Modern World" was opened—the 23-mile-long Chesapeake Bay Bridge–Tunnel, which connects the Delmarva Peninsula with Virginia.

Other notable projects undertaken over the course of the decade include major sports stadiums, arenas, and civic centers in a number of American cities; shopping malls designed by notable architects; and the construction of the campuses of newly established universities in just about every state.

The Pennsylvania Station in New York was perhaps the most notable architectural landmark to be demolished during the 1960s. But the number of such landmarks to be sacrificed to new construction projects would be dramatically reduced by the National Historic Preservation Act. Passed in 1966, the act established new standards for the protection, maintenance, and, where necessary, the rehabilitation of historically significant structures.

Some of the most influential, architecture-related books of the 1960s were Jane Jacobs's *The Death and Life of Great American Cities* (1961), Lewis Mumford's *The City in History* (1961), and Robert Venturi's *Complexity and Contradiction in Modern Architecture* (1966).

## FURTHER READING

Alkalimat, Abdul, Romi Crawford, and Rebecca Zorach, eds. *The Wall of Respect: Public Art and Black Liberation in 1960s Chicago*. Evanston, IL: Northwestern University Press, 2017.

Alloway, Lawrence. *Roy Lichtenstein*. New York: Abbeville, 1983.

Alloway, Lawrence, et al. *Modern Dreams: The Rise and Fall and Rise of Pop*. Cambridge, MA: MIT Press, 1988.

Baas, Jacquelynn, ed. *Fluxus and the Essential Questions of Life*. Chicago: University of Chicago Press, 2011.

Bernstein, Roberta. *Jasper Johns' Paintings and Sculptures, 1954–1974: "The Changing Focus of the Eye."* Ann Arbor, MI: UMI Research Press, 1985.

Bigham, Julia. *Pop Art Book*. London: Black Dog, 2007.

Bockris, Victor. *Life and Death of Andy Warhol*. New York: Da Capo, 2003.

Bosworth, Patricia. *Diane Arbus: A Biography*. New York: Knopf, 1984.

Carbone, Teresa A., and Kellie Jones. *Witness: Art and Civil Rights in the Sixties*. New York: Monacelli, 2014.

Cateforis, David, ed. *Decade of Transformation: American Art of the 1960s*. Lawrence, KS: Spencer Museum of Art, 1999.

Crow, Thomas E. *The Rise of the Sixties: American and European Art in the Era of Dissent*. New Haven, CT: Yale University Press, 1996.

Doris, Sara. *Pop Art and the Contest over American Culture*. New York: Cambridge University Press, 2007.

Elderfeld, John, ed. *American Art of the 1960s*. New York: Museum of Modern Art/Abrams, 1991.

Francis, Mark, ed. *Pop*. New York: Phaidon, 2005.

Francis, Richard. *Jasper Johns*. New York: Abbeville, 1984.

Goldstein, Ann, ed. *A Minimal Future? Art as Object 1958–1968*. Cambridge, MA: MIT Press, 2004.

Greenberg, Jan, and Sandra Jordan. *Andy Warhol: Prince of Pop*. New York: Delacorte, 2004.

Grunenberg, Christoph, and Jonathan Harris, eds. *Summer of Love: Psychedelic Art, Social Crisis, and Counterculture in the 1960s*. Liverpool, UK: Liverpool University Press, 2005.

Hathaway, Norman, and Dan Nadel, eds. *Electrical Banana: Masters of Psychedelic Art*. Bologna, Italy: Damiani, 2011.

Hendrickson, Janis. *Roy Lichtenstein*. Cologne, West Germany: Benedikt Taschen, 1988.

Herscher, Andrew. "American Urbicide." *Journal of Architectural Education* 60 (September 2006), 18–20.

Houston, Joe. *Optic Nerve: Perceptual Art of the 1960s*. London: Merrell, 2007.

Johnson, Ken. *Are You Experienced? How Psychedelic Consciousness Transformed Modern Art.* New York: Prestel, 2011.
Koch, Stephen. *Stargazer: Andy Warhol's World and His Films.* New York: Praeger, 1973.
Koestenbaum, Wayne. *Andy Warhol.* New York: Viking, 2001.
LeFalle-Collins, Lizzetta, and Cecil Fergerson. *19 Sixties: A Cultural Awakening Re-Evaluated, 1965–1975.* Los Angeles: California Afro-American Museum Foundation, 1989.
Lubow, Arthur. *Diane Arbus: Portrait of a Photographer.* New York: Ecco, 2016.
McCarthy, David. *Pop Art.* New York: Cambridge University Press, 2000.
Mercer, Kobena, ed. *Pop Art and Vernacular Cultures.* Cambridge, MA: MIT Press, 2007.
Owen, Ted, and Denise Dickson. *High Art: A History of the Psychedelic Poster.* London: Sanctuary, 1999.
Papadakis, Andreas C., ed. *Pop Art.* New York: St. Martin's, 1992.
Rosenthal, Nan, and Rith E. Fine. *The Drawings of Jasper Johns.* New York: Thames & Hudson, 1990.
Scherman, Tony, and David Dalton. *Pop: The Genius of Andy Warhol.* New York: HarperCollins, 2009.
Shanes, Eric. *The Pop Art Tradition: Responding to Mass-Culture.* New York: Parkstone, 2006.
Shanes, Eric. *Warhol.* New York: Abrams, 1989.
Sooke, Alastair. *Pop Art: A Colourful History.* London: Penguin, 2016.
Steinberg, Leo. *Jasper Johns.* New York: G. Wittenborn, 1963.
Stern, Robert A. M., Thomas Mellins, and David Fishman. *New York 1960: Architecture and Urbanism between the Second World War and the Bicentennial.* New York: Monacelli, 1995.
Stouffer, Hannah, and Eric Betz, eds. *Juxtapoz Psychedelic.* Berkeley, CA: Gingko, 2013.
Sussman, Elisabeth, and Doon Arbus. *Diane Arbus: A Chronology, 1923–1971.* New York: Aperture, 2011.
Van Wyk, Gary. *Pop Art: 50 Works of Art You Should Know.* New York: Prestel, 2013.
Whiting, Cécile. *Pop L.A.: Art and the City in the 1960s.* Berkeley, CA: University of California Press, 2006.
Willis, Deborah. *Reflections in Black: A History of Black Photographers, 1840 to the Present.* New York: Norton, 2000.
Yau, John. *A Thing among Things: The Art of Jasper Johns.* New York: Distributed Art, 2008.

# CHAPTER 7

# Fashion

## BIKINI

The bikini was created in France in 1946. Louis Reard, the French designer who created the original swimsuit, was considering names for it when just days before the show in which it was to be introduced, the United States performed the first test of a nuclear weapon at the remote Bikini Atoll in the South Pacific. Reard exploited the tremendous media attention to that event and even claimed that he thought that the bikini would have an equally explosive impact within the popular culture. The bikini was very controversial—in fact, so controversial that it did not become popular in the United States until the early 1960s. In the context of the conservative mainstream mores of the 1950s, it was not just considered daring to wear such a swimsuit, but also considered very immodest if not immoral. The first *Miss World* contest, held in 1951, was initially promoted as the Festival Bikini Contest at the Festival of Britain, and it was publicly condemned by Pope Pius XII.

But the pope's opinion of the bikini proved to have less enduring influence than a film starring a young French actress named Bridgette Bardot. She created a sensation when promotional stills from the film *Manina, la filles sans voiles* (or *Manina, the Girl Unveiled*) were distributed at the Cannes Film Festival. In fact, some historians have attributed the increased stature of the film festival and the rise in the popularity of the beach town of Saint-Tropez to Bardot's impact on the popular culture. The film, released in the United States as *Manina, the Girl in the Bikini*, undercut the ban on showing women's navels on film, though it would hang on a while longer on television (most famously in the sitcom *I Dream of Jeannie*). In 1962, Ursula Andress wore a white bikini in the James Bond film *Dr. No*, which was made in Great Britain, and instantly became a star on both sides of the Atlantic. But Andress's star power was nothing compared to that instantly achieved by Raquel Welch four years later, when she appeared in an animal-pelt bikini in the 1966 film *One Million Years B.C.* One

Ursula Andress and her bikini set 1960s style in the 1962 film *Dr. No*. (United Artist/Getty Images)

can argue that *Dr. No* was of interest to audiences because it was part of the James Bond franchise, but no one went to see *One Million Years B.C.* for any reason other than to see Raquel Welch in that bikini. The poster for the film became an iconic image of the popular culture of the decade, and even Americans who had not been born when the film was released can identify Welch by name from the poster.

Ironically, by the time that Welch appeared in *One Million Years B.C.*, the bikini had become a part of mainstream American culture. In 1962, the year in which Andress appeared in *Dr. No*, *Playboy* featured a model wearing a bikini on its front cover, and two years later, in 1964, Babette March appeared in a bikini on the cover of the debut issue of *Sports Illustrated*'s "swimsuit issue." But, the moral uproar over the bikini may have been undermined more than anything else by an infectiously silly pop song, Brian Hyland's 1960 hit "Itsy Bitsy Teenie Weenie Yellow Polka Dot Bikini." Yet, paradoxically, Annette Funicello, who starred with Frankie Avalon in a very popular series of teen-romance beach movies, was initially not permitted to appear in a bikini or even a two-piece bathing suit that exposed her navel. Almost every other actress in the films was wearing a bikini, but it was not until relatively late in the seven-film series that Funicello wore one. It has been argued that Funicello's finally appearing in a bikini made it socially acceptable for "good girls" to wear a bikini, but it can also be argued that Funicello's wearing a bikini was an indication that it had become suddenly anachronistic for her not to be wearing a bikini. Ironically, the arguments over the morality of the bikini primarily among those with conservative religious beliefs would be echoed in arguments among feminists, some of whom saw the freedom to wear a bikini as symbolic of liberation, and others of whom were concerned that the popularity of the bikini was further encouraging the objectification of women.

## MINISKIRTS, MINIDRESSES, AND MICROMINIS

The miniskirt, like the bikini, is considered an iconic garment of the 1960s. Like the bikini, the miniskirt had existed previous to the decade, but it had largely been restricted to costumes worn by skaters and dancers. It did not become a fashion fad until the mid to late 1960s, and like most fads, particularly in fashion, its origins have become a source of some dispute. Part of the problem is that hemlines began to rise gradually from the just-above-the-knee length most common at the beginning of the decade; so it is difficult to agree on when shorter skirts became definable as miniskirts. In addition, several designers in different locations were responding to the trend toward higher hemlines at about the same time. Nonetheless, British designer Mary Quant is generally credited with doing the most to popularize the miniskirt—to provoke intensive media attention to it as a new fashion choice.

The broadening popularity of the miniskirt also incited increasing controversy. Indeed, it provoked much more controversy than the bikini because the miniskirt was worn in more places than at pools and beaches. Some thought that it ought to be banned completely for being so immodest as to be offensive, but others thought that although it might be appropriate for casual wear, it was not appropriate in workplaces, houses of worship, and in other locations and situations where it either would be seen as constituting an unwanted distraction or might be regarded as demonstrating a lack of appropriate respect. Since a large part of the appeal of the miniskirt was its suggestion of rebellion and freedom from tired social constraints, the backlash against its popularity only increased its popularity and even led to ever more extremely short hemlines—or the development of the micromini, which barely covered any of the wearer's legs. Moreover, as the critics of the miniskirt began to argue that wearing a miniskirt was an invitation to sexual assault—and thereby partly, if not largely, shifting the blame from the attacker to the victim—the debate among feminists over wearing miniskirts became even more complex than that over wearing bikinis and allowing pornography to be more readily available. For, in this instance, the issue went beyond the tension between freer self-expression and reinforcing the objectification of women to tacitly endorsing the assumption that anything that a woman is wearing can be presenting as a justification for, or a mitigating circumstance in, a sexual assault upon her.

## BELL-BOTTOMS

Bell-bottom pants had become standard dress for those serving in the U.S. Navy. In the 1960s, the Beats helped to popularize wearing pea coats, denim work shirts, bell-bottoms, and other military surplus clothing available at Army-Navy surplus stores, and despite the increasing antiwar sentiment from the mid-1960s onward, the surplus clothing remained popular because it was inexpensive and durable—and perhaps, at least to some extent, because it represented an appropriation of the uniforms associated with militarism. By the mid-1960s, bell-bottoms became popular enough for them to be produced for direct retail sale not only by the major makers of blue jeans but by other producers of men's and women's apparel. As the decade drew to a close, the bell shape became more and more pronounced, the colors on the pants became bolder and more unusual, and the fabric was sometimes printed with striking and even extravagant geometric or psychedelic patterns. The wide bells would go out of fashion, but the basic style has remained popular.

## MOD CLOTHING AND PSYCHEDELIC PRINTS

In the late 1950s in Great Britain, the Mod and Rocker subcultures emerged among young people from working-class backgrounds as competing "alternatives" to what they saw as the drabness of their surroundings, the drudgery of their daily lives, and the socioeconomic constraints on their prospects. While the Rockers were influenced mainly by the leather-jacketed American motorcycle clubs and by the rockabilly sound and style of emerging American performers such as Elvis Presley and Jerry Lee Lewis, the Mods were very much influenced by French and Italian films and by the new hair and clothing styles sported by the young actors and actresses in those films. In terms of American musical influences, the Mods were influenced more by the increasing, mainstream popularity of rhythm and blues (R&B) music performed primarily by African American singers and musicians and by their discovery of the blues sources of that R&B music. And in contrast with the Rockers' interest in motorcycles, the Mods favored the motor scooters that were more popular in Italy and France. As a number of commentators have pointed out, the contrasting choices in transportation aligned with the fashion choices of each group, with the shape of the scooters making it easier for the more fashion-conscious Mods to keep their clothing clean.

Ironically, Mod fashion came to the United States with the so-called British Invasion in popular music that introduced white American audiences to the African American performers and genres of music that were already having a dramatic impact on American popular music. On the other hand, the Mod style was disconnected from most of its roots in the British subculture and from the tension with the Rocker subculture. As a result, in the United States, the signature elements of the Mod style—very tailored suits and low boots for young men and miniskirts or minidresses with high boots for young women—gradually morphed with the even more flamboyant psychedelic style that became more broadly associated with hippies and the Counterculture. Paisley became popular. The colors of men's clothing became more flamboyant, and women's clothing featured bold geometric prints and images and patterns borrowed from pop art, op art, and minimalism. The most enduringly popular item of psychedelic clothing was the tie-dyed T-shirt. White T-shirts were bound with rubber bands or cords before they were dipped into die, and the process could be repeated with multiple colors. Since almost anyone could do it and since there was generally no desire for a cleanly defined pattern, creating tie-dyed T-shirts became, at least for a while, do-it-yourself projects or exercises in self-expression. Eventually, because of the breakdown in styles, fabrics, and colors associated with male and female dress, much clothing became more gender-neutral, and the term "unisex" entered common usage.

## JACKIE KENNEDY (1929–1994)

If John Kennedy's youthfulness provided a very marked contrast with his predecessors, the contrast between Jackie Kennedy and the previous first ladies—Eleanor Roosevelt, Bess Truman, and Mamie Eisenhower—was even more strikingly dramatic. Whatever fine qualities those previous first ladies had and whatever contributions they made to American public life, they were all older and more matronly—and Jackie Kennedy, who was twelve years younger than her husband, who was then the youngest person ever elected to the presidency, was anything but matronly. During her husband's presidential campaign, Jackie had attracted notice for her personal charm and her sense of style. She generally wore clothing by French designers, and after her husband's election, there was some discussion that it would be politically advantageous for her to begin wearing clothes by American designers. But after working with several American designers who essentially copied French designs, she finally settled on the designer Oleg Cassini. Although he had been born in Paris and got his start as a designer in Italy, Cassini was the son of a Russian aristocrat who had fled the Russian Revolution and an Italian noblewoman. After spending the early years of their exile in various parts of Western Europe, the family eventually settled for a while in Italy, where the children began to use their mother's maiden name, Cassini. In his youth, Cassini became enamored with American sports and with tales of the American West and, in particular, with the culture of Native Americans. It is therefore not surprising that after establishing himself as a designer, he sought work as a designer for the Hollywood film studios. His clothing became known for its understated elegance and suggestion of youthful vitality. In short, if Oleg Cassini was not exactly the American-born designer that Jackie Kennedy's advisers thought was advisable, he was American enough to not be a liability—and had an exotic background that gave the first lady's stylishness an international cache.

What became known as the "Jackie Look" consisted of sleeveless, A-line dresses and gowns and tailored suits. The suits had waist-length jackets with narrow, notched lapels and three-quarter length sleeves and straight skirts that fell to the middle of the knee. The shoes were generally low-heeled pumps, and beyond formal occasions for which gowns were required, she often wore long gloves that matched the color of her suit or dress. But the most often-remembered element of the "look" was her popularizing of the matching pillbox hat. That signature element of the "look" was very wryly acknowledged in Bob Dylan's song "Leopard-Skin Pillbox Hat," which includes the lyric—"Well, you must tell me, baby how your/Head feels under somethin' like that/Under your brand new leopard-skin pill-box hat." The "look" was so popular that retailers rushed to provide affordable knockoffs of Cassini's designs. But, for all of its elegant simplicity, the "look" did not come cheaply for the first lady herself. At a time when the president's annual salary was $100,000, she reportedly spent about one and a half times that amount annually on her clothing. No matter, the pink outfit that she wore on the day on which her husband was assassinated, and that she refused to change out of even though it was splattered with his blood and brains, became one of the most iconic artifacts of U.S. history. Moreover, not only is the exhibition of her clothing one of the most popular attractions at the John F. Kennedy Library and Museum, but in 2001, seven years after her death, the Metropolitan Museum of Art featured the very popular exhibition "Jacqueline Kennedy: The White House Years." The enduring appreciation of her style is reflected in the fact that, in 2012, she was included in *Time* magazine's list of one hundred all-time fashion icons and, in 2016, in *Forbes* magazine's list of ten fashion icons—with both recognitions of her influence coming more than a half-century after she was named to the Best Dressed List International Hall of Fame in 1965.

## TWIGGY (1949–)

Born Lesley Hornby, the British model who became known as Twiggy became an international sensation in the second half of the 1960s. She came from a working-class family and grew up in a town northwest of London; so, her sudden fame was as transformative for her as it was for the popular culture. The name "Twiggy" was an extension of her childhood nickname "Twig," and it aptly described her very slender and minimally curvy figure. Twiggy herself admired the model Jean Shrimpton and had grown her hair long in an effort to imitate Shrimpton's appearance. But when a hair stylist experimentally cut Twiggy's hair very short, she was very quickly "discovered." In the space of just a single year, 1967, she went from appearing in *Vogue* for the first time to being featured in more than a dozen photo spreads in the various international editions of the magazine, being featured on the covers of dozens, if not hundreds, of other magazines, and being the subject of countless articles in newspapers and magazines that sought to explain the "Twiggy phenomenon" and offered commentary on what it meant for fashion, the popular culture, and the well-being of young women. In 1967, even the venerable *New Yorker* published multiple articles on Twiggy, devoting more space to her than to any other celebrity except perhaps The Beatles.

Indeed, from 1967 to 1970, when she stopped modeling, the attention to Twiggy approached Beatlemania. When she first came to the United States, a large crowd of screaming fans and media greeted her as she got off the plane—something that had become commonplace for British musical acts but was unheard of for a fashion model.

Twiggy (Lesley Hornby) became the ideal "waif," rocketing to fame as a model in 1967. (Hulton Archive/Getty Images)

She continued to attract such large crowds and such intensive media attention that she became recognized, in retrospect, as the first supermodel. But few subsequent supermodels have had quite the same cultural impact. Not only did Twiggy endorse her own lines of clothing and cosmetics, but she also endorsed a wide range of other products that exploited her popularity with preadolescent girls, such as school supplies, lunchboxes, and toys. She became the "face" of the "mod" generation as it was being commodified for mainstream consumption. Her androgynous appearance was perfectly suited for the clothing that she modeled, which was blurring traditional gender boundaries in clothing styles. But there was not only an immediate backlash from those who were uncomfortable with the sudden challenging of conventional gender distinctions and gender roles, but there was also a growing concern from across a broader spectrum of viewpoints that Twiggy's thinness was setting an unrealistic and unhealthy standard for girls and young women. Although Twiggy herself consistently asserted that she was naturally very thin and that she did not have to endure extreme diets in order to stay thin, her fame did clearly create a standard for subsequent models that was damaging to many of them, never mind the millions of girls and young women who judged themselves or felt that they were being judged ultimately by that standard. In any case, over subsequent decades, Twiggy found success as an actress, a singer, and an author, proving that she was more than just a fad and creating a paradigm for future supermodels to follow after they quit modeling.

## FURTHER READING

Cassini, Oleg. *A Thousand Days of Magic: Dressing Jacqueline Kennedy for the White House.* New York: Rizzoli, 2015.

Heiman, Jim. *60s Fashion: Vintage Fashion and Beauty Ads.* Koln, Germany: Taschen, 2007.

Mulvaney, Jay, and Dominick Dunne, foreword. *Jackie: The Clothes of Camelot.* New York: St. Martin's Press, 2001.

Paulicelli, Eugenia, Drake Stutesman, and Louise Wallenberg. *Film, Fashion, and the 1960s.* Bloomington: Indiana University Press, 2017.

Rielly, Edward J. *The 1960s.* Westport, CT: Greenwood, 2003.

Twiggy. *Twiggy: An Autobiography.* London: Hart-David, MacGibbon, 1975.

Walford, Jonathan. *Sixties Fashion: From Less Is More to Youthquake.* New York: Thames & Hudson, 2013.

Wills, David. *Switched On: Women Who Revolutionized Style in the 60's.* New York: Weldon Owen, 2017.

# CHAPTER 8

# Media and Advertising

## ADVERTISING IN THE MEDIA

In the 1960s, advertising moved to new heights and depths. It lost power over television but gained greater than ever influence over consumers. It reflected American culture and it changed it. Without ever meaning to, but knowing full well, it changed the American landscape.

At the end of the decade, even the movies were holding it up for ridicule (while also relying on it). *Putney Swope*, Robert Downey Sr.'s 1969 satire of it, placed advertising at the center of American racism, greed, sexism, and corruption. And the business was all that—and more.

As television grew stronger, both technologically (the addition of color, the development of larger and better sets) and in coverage (almost the whole country could pull in the three networks, or at least two of them with the third, ABC, coming up fast), advertising had to grow from its 1950s line drawings (kept simple due to poor reception and primitive sets) and staid product displays and announcers. Even its jingles had to get better: 1950s Choo-Choo Charlie, in his cartoons for Good & Plenty candy, could not compete in the 1960s, no matter how catchy the tune might have been.

There were other momentous changes caused by television's continued development. Early on, individual advertisers had been able to sponsor entire shows, much as they had done in the heyday of radio. Now, reacting to the new possibilities being opened up by color transmission and improvements such as microwave transmission and the expansion of coverage into almost every home, television studios were finding they could no longer produce shows on the cheap if they wanted to compete. The costs of production also reflected new studio techniques, higher costs for talent, and the desire for better sets and for "on location" shooting. All of this together, by the early 1960s, made single sponsorship prohibitively expensive leading to a "spot buy" system in which networks (with some spots reserved for local-station sales) sold individual time units within or adjacent to specific shows. In this system, product placement within shows began to go down so as not to compete with spot sales, and talent was no longer used, again within the shows, for product endorsement.

The upshot of this was that advertisers began to find they had less control over the content of shows in which their commercials ran. Though they could still pull ads from shows they found objectionable, they no longer were able to insist on approval of scripts or to oversee production. This sort of oversight now fell exclusively on the studios and the networks, leading to problems like those CBS experienced with *The Smothers Brothers Comedy Hour* (eventually leading to its cancellation) and to the power to push content barriers exhibited by the most popular show at the end of the decade, *Rowan & Martin's Laugh-In*, where the power of Nielsen ratings inoculated the show against advertiser interference.

All of these changes together gave advertising agencies a great deal more flexibility during the 1960s and even more freedom to experiment with types of ads that might not have been found acceptable earlier. Alka Seltzer's 1964 (with a 1966 color version) "No Matter What Shape (Your Stomach Is In)," for example, talked not at all about the product but showed a fast montage of stomachs to a catchy tune that was soon released as a single under the name of a concocted band and that charted. In 1969, Alka Seltzer made fun of the filming process for commercials in its "Spicy Meatball" ad, one of the first "meta" commercials, commenting on creation of the medium while selling a product. At the same time, political admakers were also beginning to be more daring, producing spots like the 1964 "Daisy" ad showing a little girl counting and pulling petals off a daisy that shifts into a countdown for the launch of a nuclear bomb.

The early years of the decade were especially filled with what we would now call "sexist" advertising. Slogans like "The most important quality in coffee is how much it will please your man," "Women are desperate for home appliances and will cry to get them," "Blow in her face and she'll follow you anywhere," and "Keep her where she belongs" were so common as to be unnoticed. Only in the later part of the decade, with the rise of feminism, would national attention start to be drawn to the negative depiction of women in these ads.

Advertising characters that continued in use for decades after the 1960s began to appear, created with more depth than the line drawings of previous years. Notable among these is Ronald McDonald, whose genesis is not clear but who was a major figure in McDonald's ads from the mid-1960s. The giggly Pillsbury Doughboy first appeared in 1965, a year after Lucky the Leprechaun for Lucky Charms cereal. Though there had been mascots for a long time, these set a new bar for detailed creation that has inspired ad agencies ever since.

With close to half of the American population under twenty-five by the middle of the decade, it is no surprise that advertising in the 1960s was increasingly aimed at the young and was a major factor in the 1960s fascination with youth culture.

The greatest advertising battle in the 1960s was over cigarettes. As the decade started, the Federal Trade Commission (FTC) began to limit, through negotiation with tobacco-product manufacturers, even implied claims that "low tar and nicotine" in cigarettes had a health benefit—unless such claims could be substantiated (they could not be). This led to a return to advertising based on claims of flavor and taste instead of hints about possible health benefits. The paradox here was that, by curtailing advertising on dubious and implied claims that some cigarettes were safer than others (claims the industry would deny it was making for, in its public stance, all cigarettes were safe), the FTC encouraged emphasis on the worst cigarettes, from a public-health standpoint.

Even in the face of tremendous advertising for cigarettes as a positive aspect of life, outside of the tobacco industry itself, both medical and public opinion was forming into a single opinion, that tobacco is indeed dangerous, and that it is a prime cause of lung disease. This did not stop young people from being seduced by the glamorous image advertisers created, but it did lead to the 1964 surgeon general's report, which concluded that cigarette smoking is a major cause of chronic bronchitis, that there is a relation between smoking and pulmonary emphysema, and that it is a cause of chronic bronchopulmonary disease, among other things. Soon, warnings were required on packages of tobacco products and, by the end of the decade, on print advertisements as well, and movement had begun toward disallowing tobacco advertising from all electronic media.

As advertisers began to see the impact of television advertising compared to any other medium, buys in print, in particular, began to decline. This had an especial impact on the oversized magazines such as the *Saturday Evening Post*, *Life* and *Look*. The *Post*, which a generation earlier was the single more ubiquitous magazine in the country, did not survive the decade, ceasing publication in 1969. *Life* and *Look* would soon follow. *Life*, ironically, had its heyday in the 1960s as purveyor of high-quality news photography at a level beyond its achievements of earlier decades. It was particularly important in bringing into American homes images of the Vietnam War with a clarity and impact that could not be achieved by the television images of the time.

## FOOD AND ADVERTISING

The 1960s were a decade of very visible changes. In some arenas, those changes seemed almost to bifurcate the decade, but in terms of food, the trends were fairly consistent: foods became more pre-prepared and prepackaged, and Americans' diets became more varied, especially due to an increasing interest in international cuisines.

Tang, a powdered drink mix, was first sold in 1959. But the sales were disappointing until John Glenn used the mix during a space flight in 1962. After that, Tang was marketed as "the breakfast drink of astronauts," and sales increased dramatically.

In 1960, the processes for making instant mashed potatoes and instant sweet potatoes from flakes were developed. In that same year, frozen bagels were first sold. In 1969, Pringles potato chips were introduced. The uniform size and shape of the chips that allowed them to be sold in a tubular can, instead of in a bag, was made possible by their being made from dehydrated and mashed potatoes.

In 1966, Nabisco introduced Snack Mate, a cheese spread dispensed from what is commonly described as an aerosol can but what is actually a synthesis of a squeeze tube and an aerosol can in which the aerosol does not mix with the ingredients but instead pushes against a piston that forces the processed cheese toward and out of the nozzle. Snack Mate was marketed as a more convenient alternative to Kraft's Cheeze Whiz, which had been available for more than a decade but only as a conventional spread available in a small tub. Oddly, Cheese Whiz would be "improved" by reducing the amount of cheese that it actually contained until Kraft finally forced to admit that it contains no cheese but only "cheese cultures."

In addition to an increase in the popularity of backyard barbeques and cocktail dinners, the following international themes for dinner parties became popular in the United States in the 1960s: Swedish smorgasbords, quick Oriental dinners, Pacific Island feasts, casual curry buffets, Mexican fiestas, Italian suppers, American-style skillet chicken suppers, and buffet-style suppers featuring casseroles.

As Americans became more interested in international foods, some foods were introduced that today would hardly seem exotic. For instance, in 1960, Granny Smith apples were first imported from New Zealand and available in American supermarkets. The advertising for Spice Islands seasoning declared that it "puts the seasoning secrets of the world in your hands."

In 1966, in a move that many saw as a very dramatic change in practice, the Roman Catholic bishops in the United States removed the prohibition against eating meat on Fridays outside of Lent, dealing a blow to the producers of frozen fish sticks and fish cakes. And in that same year, in an even more forward-looking event in the popular culture, during the first episode of the now landmark television series *Star Trek*, the crew of the starship *Enterprise* ate chemically synthesized food.

In 1968, General Mills introduced the fourth Betty Crocker. The completely fictional character had been created in the 1920s, but a "portrait" had not been created until 1936. It was then updated in 1955, 1965, 1969, 1972, 1980, 1986, and 1996. In each of the renderings, the character was a woman in her thirties with medium to dark brown hair, who was wearing a white blouse under a dark red jacket (except in 1965 when the blouse was also red). The rate of change in the representations of this character reflect the rate of change in the place of women in American society. The first portrait remained unchanged for just under two decades, but in the slightly more than two decades from the mid-1960s to the mid-1990s, there were six different updates. Interestingly, none of the images were based on real women, though actresses were employed to portray the character first on radio and then on TV. Most famously, Adelaide Hawley Cumming played Betty Crocker on various television shows and in countless personal appearances from 1949 to 1964, when she was told that the character needed updating—specifically, to be less matronly and to look a little less like a housewife. In a 1945 poll, Betty Crocker was ranked as the second most popular woman in America, trailing only Eleanor Roosevelt. That level of popularity—and perhaps confusion of the fictional character with a real person—carried into the early 1960s before the character started to seem completely anachronistic, especially to many younger women.

Foods advertisements in the 1960s emphasized taste and convenience: "Outflavors any single juice"—V-8; "The complete protein breakfast that's quick as instant coffee"—Kellogg's Special K; "How does Mrs. Burke stay as slim as her teenage daughter?"—Grape Nuts cereal; "They always eat better when you remember the soup," "Only Campbell's Tomato Soup does so much—so deliciously," and "Good things begin to happen ... when the lady of the house has soup for lunch"; "Either make it yourself or make it with Knorr"—Knorr soup mixes; "Happiest meat for sandwiches"—Spam; "Burgers really swing with real mayonnaise ... Hellmann's"; "'Backyard Banquets' always include Van Camp's Pork and Beans"; "Trust Swanson for specially selected cuts of lean beef in natural gravy"; "Dinner's all here with the sauce all ready"—Chef Boyardee Complete Spaghetti Dinner; "Don't just have a Meat Loaf Dinner. Have iPolpettoni Saporiti instead"—Chef Boyardee Spaghetti Sauce; "A meal in a minute with the Chef's touch in it"—Chef Boyardee Pizza with Cheese; "Hurried? You get a whole wonderful meal quick in Dinty Moore Beef Stew!"; "Be the Farmer's Daughter tonight"—Banquet Fried Chicken Frozen Dinner; "We know 498 desserts you can make with Whip'n'Chill. None takes more than 12 minutes"; "It's so easy to add color and flavor"—McCormick; "Now Jello has the just-picked flavor of fruit"; "Quicker cooking pudding that gives you a perfect creamy set every time"—Royal Pudding and Pie Filling; "Betty Crocker dips into the candy jar and comes up with two new Nugget Frosting Mixes"; and "Butterscotch Yule Log—Almost as easy as falling off a you-know-what."

3 customers for Campbell's coming up

Though Campbell's soup labels were made iconic by Andy Warhol, the company's advertisements were ubiquitous anyway during the 1960s. (Apic/Getty Images)

In the 1960s even more than in previous decades, advertising and corporate branding led to the creation of characters created to personalize the consumer's association with certain food products. In 1961, Pillsbury introduced the "Poppin' Fresh" Pillsbury Dough Boy. In 1964, Campbell's Soup Company, under its Franco-American brand, introduced SpaghettiOs, small circular pieces of pasta packaged in a can with tomato sauce. To parents, SpaghettiOs were marketed as a neater alternative to spaghetti for small children. To the children, they were marketed with the jingle, "Uh-oh! SpaghettiOs!" Kraft Singles (single slices of cheese) were advertised as being "tops with the lunch box crowd." Just about every breakfast cereal especially marketed to children had a character associated with it, but few were as popular or as enduring as Tony the Tiger who pitched Kellogg's Sugar Frosted Flakes by saying "Put a tiger in your tank" or "Put a tiger on your team, or by shouting, "They're great!" Green Giant tried to make its canned vegetables more palatable to children by creating the Jolly Green Giant to advertise them. The company even marketed a 4-foot-tall Jolly Green Giant rag doll for $3.50. Candies and snacks were an easier sell, but there was still competition. Rolo candies were advertised with a kid in a cowboy outfit overlaid with the text, "The Necco Kid packs his saddlebags with Necco."

### Food Packaging

In the 1960s, as supermarket chains expanded and gradually replaced independent grocers, food packaging was made more uniform and sturdy to facilitate its handling and shelving. Because products had to stand out on the supermarket shelves, branding became more important, and food packaging also became, in effect, its own form of advertising.

Some of the food packaging was intended to appeal directly to children. In 1960, Big Top began selling its peanut butter in a mug, with a picture of Hopalong Cassidy on the side. Cassidy was a star of the serial Westerns once shown in theaters on Saturday afternoons and now being shown on television on Saturday mornings. In 1968, Smucker introduced Gooper Grape, a swirled combination of grape jelly and peanut butter packaged in a clear plastic jar.

In 1960, food was packaged for the first time in aluminum cans, and two years later, in 1962, the pull tab to remove the lids of the cans was introduced. In 1964, Royal Crown Cola introduced the 12-ounce beverage can; Coca-Cola would not follow suit for another three years. By 1969, more canned beer than bottled beer would be sold in the United States. In 1961, "boiling bags"—frozen foods packaged in plastic bags that could withstand boiling water—became available. In 1964, Shake-n-Bake provided breading in a bag into which slices of meat could be added. In that same year, milk was sold in plastic bottles for the first time.

In 1963, producers of dried fruits and vegetables began to irradiate their products to reduce the development of mold and insect damage. Initially hailed as another illustration of science-driven progress, the process would become controversial because of growing concerns over nuclear power and technologies and the association with that sort of radiation.

In 1960, single-serving ketchup packages were introduced, and within a short time most condiments were also available in this way. And in 1965, an engineer with the Swedish company Celloplast secured a patent for the first disposable plastic grocery bag—an innovation that seemed extremely practical at the time but which has since become a symbol of ecological carelessness.

### Fast Food

During the 1960s, fast-food franchises became a fixture on the American landscape, but it is important to note that the industry did not have anything approaching its current scope or concentration. Many of the current fast-food franchises were just getting established, first as individual restaurants and then as local or regional franchises. Moreover, before the national chains became entrenched, there were many more local and regional chains than there are today. Some of those chains became defunct for other reasons, but a very large percentage were forced out of business or absorbed by the national chains. The state of the fast-food industry in the 1960s was in almost every way the opposite of what it is today—when many of the surviving, successful chains have been bought up by conglomerates, when the consolidation of the industry is even more pronounced than it might seem.

The fast-food chains that were founded in the 1960s included the following. In 1960, the original Hardee's was opened in Greenville, North Carolina, by Wilbur Hardee. In 1960, Tom Monaghan and his brother bought a pizzeria in Ypsilanti, Michigan. Within three years, Monaghan traded a Volkswagen Beetle for his share of this business, opened two other pizzerias, and named the beginning of what would become a nationwide chain Domino's. In 1961, Glen Bell Jr. founded the Taco Bell chain in Downey, California. Bell had opened a Taco Tias restaurant in 1951, and he opened more Taco Tias, as well as El Taco, restaurants throughout the 1950s. In 1962, John Galardi, a former employee of Bell, with support from Bell, opened the first Der Wienerschnitzel hot dog restaurant next door to a Taco Bell. In 1964, Tim Horton, a former hockey player, and a partner opened the first Tim Horton's Café and Bake Shop in Hamilton, Ontario. As Tim Horton's restaurants, this chain of coffee and doughnut shops soon expanded its menu and its scope, becoming a chain with franchises throughout North America and then internationally. In 1965, Fred DeLuca and Peter Buck founded Pete's Super Submarines in Bridgeport, Connecticut. Within a year, they began to locally franchise the sandwich shops, and in 1968, as the chain spread beyond New England, they changed the name to Subway. In 1968 and 1969, the seafood chains Red Lobster and Long John Silver's were founded. The first Red Lobster was opened in Lakeland, Florida, by Bill Darden and Charley Woodsby. The first Long John Silver's was opened in Lexington, Kentucky, by Jim Patterson.

Kentucky Fried Chicken had been founded by Col. Harland Sanders in North Corbin, Kentucky, in 1930 and turned into a chain in 1952 when its first franchise was opened in Salt Lake City, Utah. By the mid-1960s, it had become one of the major fast-food chains in the United States. In 1964, when Sanders was seventy-four years old, he sold the chain to private investors for $2 million, while agreeing to remain the spokesperson for it. Seven years later, those investors sold the chain to Heublein in 1971 for $285 million. Interestingly Heublein's focus to that point had been almost entirely on alcoholic beverages, with the one exception being its purchase of Gray Poupon mustards in the mid 1930s. A decade after acquiring Kentucky Fried Chicken, Heublein would be acquired by R. J. Reynolds Tobacco Company, which would then merge with Nabisco, and the resulting corporation, RJR Nabisco, would then sell the fast-food chain, now known as KFC, to Pepsico. In 1969, Dave Thomas opened the first Wendy's in Columbus, Ohio, selling square hamburgers, the corners of which hung somewhat out the round hamburger buns.

In 1965, Subway contracted with a company called ICEE to provide machines that made slushy drinks in all of its stores. ICEE had been founded by Omar

Knedlik, the owner of a soda fountain who, in the late 1950s, had invented a machine that made frozen carbonated drinks. A malfunction of that machine had turned the frozen drinks to slush, and when those slushy drinks proved very popular with Klednik's customers, he was inspired to create the ICEE machines. 7-Eleven called the slushy drinks Slurpees, and they quickly became the convenience stores' signature product. At the opposite end of the spectrum, in 1969, the country music and television star Jimmy Dean founded the Jimmy Dean Sausage Company, marketing the processed meats as down-home food prepared the old-fashioned way. Dean's pitch was so appealing that he remained a spokesperson for the brand even after it was bought by Sara Lee.

Of course, McDonald's had gotten a head start on its competitors. In 1961, Ray Kroc purchased McDonald's from the McDonald's brothers who had started the regional chain in the 1940s in Southern California. Kroc, who had been a sales agent for the McDonalds', immediately trademarked the name McDonald's, and after a single golden arch had been replaced by a double golden arch that after several iterations became the M-shaped arch that is almost universally recognized today, Kroc trademarked the symbol in 1968. Seeing the national potential for the chain, Kroc relocated the headquarters to the Midwest. In 1961, the same year that Kroc purchased the company, Fred Turner, the corporate operations manager for McDonald's, opened the first iteration of Hamburger University in the basement of a restaurant in Elkins, Illinois, one of the first franchises in the Midwest. This oxymoronic innovation was the first step in institutionalizing the emphasis on uniform food preparation throughout the whole chain of McDonald's restaurants nationwide. In 1963, Kroc served the one billionth McDonald's hamburger on the *Art Linkletter Show*, which was a staple of daytime television from 1952 to 1970 (though the name of the show changed several times). In that same year, the clown Ronald MacDonald was introduced, demonstrating the company's intent to market very pointedly to children. The character was created by Willard Scott, who is now remembered more for his thirty-year run as the weatherman on the *Today Show*. After about three years of playing the character at public appearances, Scott was replaced as Ronald McDonald because he had gained weight and the company was already concerned about the association of fast food with obesity.

In 1962, Edwin Traisman, an actual scientist working for McDonald's, secured a patent on a process for creating frozen French fries. In 1968, another McDonald's scientist named Ken Strong perfected the process by adding steps that would preserve the flavor of the French fries before they were frozen. In 1968, the Big Mac, a sandwich developed by Jim Delligatti, the owner of a McDonald's in Pittsburgh, was introduced nationally by the company. It initially cost 49 cents.

## TOBACCO AND ADVERTISING

Smoke-filled rooms were the norm for most of the 1960s. Restaurants, airplanes, offices, college classrooms—it didn't matter where—people were smoking there. One did not expect a hotel lobby, or a hotel room, to smell of anything but tobacco. Anyone who complained was looked upon as a killjoy.

During most of the decade, about half of American adults smoked or used tobacco in some form. Cigarettes, cigars, pipes, chewing tobacco, and snuff: these were all popular, though it was cigarettes that were the tobacco form of choice for most people. There were still plenty of cigar smokers around, and pipes, though considered stodgy and professorial, remained commonplace; snuff had all but disappeared though chewing tobacco continued to be popular in some rural areas. Rolling one's own, though it had nearly disappeared thanks to the cheap and universal availability of commercially rolled cigarettes, would even make a comeback during the decade, in part because of increased popularity of marijuana—which required the same paper for the rolling of a joint. Brands like Zig-Zag and Top began to serve a double use.

Though spittoons were a relic of the past, ashtrays were everywhere and were incorporated into almost every popular decor for homes, restaurants, and even cars. Stores and restaurants offered free matchbooks by the cash registers "for our matchless friends." Lighters, including the nearly ubiquitous Zippo, were in most every pocket or purse, and large ones sat atop desks and on coffee tables. Boxes of cigarettes also sat on tables and desks, available as a courtesy to guests at home and in the office. From hotel lobbies to courtrooms and even to hospitals, a tobacco haze of a sort that cannot even be imagined today covered the United States.

Even though few people believed tobacco-company claims that tobacco was healthy, smokers protected their prerogative belligerently; people who didn't smoke had little voice. So, wherever they went, nonsmokers would be surrounded by tobacco smoke. They had little choice. After all, the tobacco companies were working hard to convince even more Americans to smoke even in the face of increasing evidence of danger, trying to show the nonsmokers as, at best, an unimportant and even unhappy minority. The power of their advertising seemed, in the early years of the decade, unstoppable. One 1960s television ad campaign featured a man on the back of a pickup truck holding up a sign saying, "Show us your LARK pack!" while a cameraman filmed the responses of smiling people who pulled out their packs of that new brand. Everyone smoked, this ad assumed, and the happiest enjoyed Larks. The cacophony of tobacco advertising made it impossible, at least as the decade started, for antismoking to get a foothold.

Or so it seemed.

But things were about to start to change, making the 1960s a watershed decade in terms of American attitudes toward tobacco.

Even in the 1950s, there had been signs of trouble for the tobacco industry. As early as 1954, in its "A Frank Statement to Cigarette Smokers" group ad, the tobacco industry had promised to establish a Tobacco Industry Research Committee that would impartially investigate the claims that were beginning to be made connecting cigarettes and lung cancer. This, of course, wasn't really true, but it did give the industry enough breathing room to ramp up its advertising and to start developing brands it could market as healthier. By the start of the 1960s, all of this was in full swing.

But the science could not be denied.

The 1964 "Smoking and Health: Report of the Advisory Committee to the Surgeon General of the Public Health Service," showing connections between lung and heart disease and tobacco, gave a huge boost to what had been, until then, a sluggish antismoking movement. It started a change in American society and in people's everyday environment the extent of which is hard to understand by anyone who did not experience those days of a constant indoor tobacco haze. Soon after the surgeon general's report, airline stewardesses started pushing to ban smoking on airplanes or, at least, to limit it by creating smoking sections. People began to push for no-smoking sections in restaurants, too. Though these stirrings had little impact in the 1960s, evidence of the damage tobacco does continued to grow and antitobacco sentiments began to build.

During the 1960s, though, the tobacco companies still had the upper hand. Cigarettes had been central to American culture for a generation and were a symbol of freedom and success. American troops were supplied with cigarettes during the Second World War when cigarettes, compact and easy to ship and distribute, became what sometimes seemed universal addiction among American soldiers. After the war, the tobacco companies were able to build on the fact that returning veterans smoked heavily, implying that only sissies and cowards didn't smoke, moving quickly over the next few years to the image of the smoker as the athlete and outdoorsman—and, eventually outdoorswoman. By the 1960s, they had added filters to the mix to expand their attraction and partially as a way of insulating themselves from claims of health danger, and had invented all sorts of variations on them including things like charcoal layers.

After the 1964 surgeon general's report, smoking did begin a slow decline among adults so the tobacco companies, ever attuned to avenues for increasing sales, began to turn their focus more to youth. Smoking had long been associated with rebellion but now even more so. New warning labels on cigarette packs, required after 1965, were largely ignored by young potential smokers who saw that as part of the thrill of the illicit.

By the end of the 1960s, smoking wasn't seen as a sign of thralldom to that economic powerhouse, the tobacco industry, but a sign of individualism and independence, a paradox in that this had been developed through a commercial enterprise and the advertising that promoted it. The victory of the sellers of tobacco seemed all but complete, even though its opposition was gaining strength. The battle lines, then, for the coming decades were clear, though it was not yet certain which side would win.

## FURTHER READING

Brant, Allan M. *Cigarette Century: The Rise, Fall, and Deadly Persistence of the Product That Defined America*. New York: Basic Books, 2007.

Friedman, Laurie S., ed. *Fast Food*. Detroit: Greenhaven, 2010.

Fryar, Cheryl D., and R. Bethene Ervin. *Caloric Intake from Fast Food among Adults: United States, 2007–2010*. Hyattsville, MD: U.S. Department of Health and Human Services, Centers for Disease Control and Prevention, National Center for Health Statistics, 2013.

Haugen, David, and Susan Musser, eds. *The Food Industry in Eric Schlosser's Fast Food Nation*. Detroit: Greenhaven, 2013.

Ogilvy, David. *Confessions of an Advertising Man*. New York: Dell Books, 1963.

Pollay, Richard W. *How Cigarette Advertising Works: Rich Imagery and Poor Information*. Toronto: Ontario Tobacco Research Unit, 2002.

Schlosser, Eric. *Fast Food Nation: The Dark Side of the All-American Meal*. New York: Harper Perennial, 2005.

Thompson, Tamara, ed. *Fast Food*. Farmington Hills, MI: Greenhaven, 2015.

Ward, Christina. *American Advertising Cookbooks: How Corporations Taught Us to Love Spam, Bananas, and Jell-o*. Port Townsend, WA: Process Media, 2019.

# CHAPTER 9

# Controversies

## ASSASSINATIONS

It is not an exaggeration to assert that more than any other decade in U.S. history, the 1960s were marked by political assassinations. The decade seemed bracketed by the assassination of President John F. Kennedy in 1963 and the assassinations of the civil rights leader Martin Luther King Jr. and senator and presidential candidate Robert F. Kennedy in 1968. But, in addition to those iconic political figures, several other figures were also assassinated during the course of the decade, reinforcing the idea that the nation was experiencing unprecedented political, racial, socioeconomic, and cultural convulsions.

November 22, 1963, the day on which President John F. Kennedy (1917–1963) was assassinated during a political trip to Texas, has become one of the pivotal dates around which periods of American history and culture have been defined. Because of his grudging acceptance of the need for civil rights legislation, Kennedy felt that he needed to shore up his political support in the Deep South ahead of his reelection campaign in the following year. While his motorcade, including the convertible in which he preferred to ride, was passing through Dealey Plaza in Dallas, a series of shots rang out, killing Kennedy and seriously wounding Texas governor John Connally, who was sitting in the seat in front of Kennedy. Kennedy was struck initially in the throat, and then another bullet blew off the back of his head. Although the car sped off toward Dallas's Parkland Hospital, the president was clearly beyond saving.

Within hours, the suspected assassin, Lee Harvey Oswald, who worked in the Book Depository building from which the shots were fired, was arrested following the murder of Dallas police patrolman J. D. Tippitt, who had apparently attempted to stop and question Oswald. Even before Oswald was apprehended in a movie theater, the rifle believed to be the murder weapon was recovered on the floor where Oswald had worked. Moreover, it fairly quickly

President John F. Kennedy with his wife Jackie and Texas governor John Connally and his wife Idanell just moments before shots rang out in Dallas on November 22, 1963, ending Kennedy's life. (Library of Congress)

was widely reported that Oswald had defected to Russia and then returned to the United States with his Russian wife and that he had gotten some media attention as a proponent of "Fair Play for Cuba." Then, three days later, Oswald himself was murdered on live television as he was being transferred out of Dallas Police Headquarters, ostensibly for security reasons. Oswald's killer was Jack Ruby, the owner of a nightclub that featured exotic dancers and someone with long-standing ties to organized crime, albeit as a minor figure.

Given such revelations, it is not surprising that even by the time that Kennedy was being laid to rest in a solemn manner deliberately echoing the funeral ceremonies for Abraham Lincoln almost a century earlier, two competing views of the assassination had already been essentially defined. One view has been that all of the basic evidence points to Oswald as a lone assassin and almost all of the disputative evidence has been shown to be based on flawed assumptions. The competing view has been that the arguments for Oswald as a lone assassin are deliberately or coincidentally reflective of some sort of conspiracy to conceal the real perpetrators. It is not at all an exaggeration to say that every aspect of the case, from the ballistic evidence, the eye-witness testimony, and the videotapes of the assassination to comments made by even those most tangentially involved, sometimes decades after the event, has been endlessly reexamined and relitigated in the court of public opinion. Even though several thousand books, and counting, have now been written about the assassination, the debate shows no sign of losing steam. It has survived—and arguably has been stoked by—five major, government-commissioned investigations, from the Warren Commission established by Lyndon Johnson in the immediate aftermath of the assassination to the U.S. House Select Committee on Assassinations, which deliberated in the late 1970s. To date more than 200 distinct theories about who actually assassinated Kennedy or who was behind the assassination have been proposed. But the most commonly accepted of these theories involve foreign governments, the upper echelons of the U.S. government, rogue elements within the U.S. intelligence agencies, far-right extremist groups, and organized crime—or some combination of those groups acting on some shared interest.

The assassination had such a profound impact on the American psyche for a variety of reasons. Geopolitically, it occurred at the height of the Cold War—following the construction of the Berlin Wall, the failed Bay of Pigs Invasion of Cuba, and the Cuban Missile Crisis. In terms of domestic politics, the Kennedys were the most glamorous first couple in U.S. history. His sometimes debilitating health problems were concealed behind publicity shots of touch football games and sailing in the waters near the Kennedy compound in Hyannis Port. Jackie quickly but demurely became a style icon, and her young children and several miscarriages, one of which had occurred just months before the trip to Dallas, made her an empathetic figure. The images of the children at the president's funeral—in particular, footage of John Jr., who was just a toddler, saluting his father's casket—had a very profound effect. It just did not seem possible that an ineffectual loner with ambiguous allegiances and grudges could have been the sole cause of so much grief.

In combination with the simmering political and cultural backlash against the anticommunist witch hunts of the late 1940s and the 1950s and the growing discontent with corporate culture and materialism, the conspiracy theories surrounding the Kennedy assassination increased the distrust of government—in particular, the distrust of the unelected agencies associated with the military-industrial state—and were a major contributing factor in the skepticism about the official pronouncements about the escalating U.S. involvement in the Vietnam War. Even more directly, in April 1968, when Dr. Martin Luther King Jr. (1929–1968) was assassinated on the porch of the Lorraine Motel in Memphis, there was immediate skepticism about whether James Earl Ray had perpetrated the crime himself. And just two months later, when Sirhan Sirhan assassinated Robert F. Kennedy (1925–1968) in a hallway outside the kitchen of the Ambassador Hotel in Los Angeles, where Kennedy's campaign supporters were celebrating his victory in the California primary, there were inevitable theories about second or alternative assassins. Even granting that it was crowded and somewhat chaotic as Kennedy passed through that hallway, he was shot at point-blank range and Sirhan was immediately wrestled to the ground. So the persistence of theories not just about a conspiracy to kill R.F.K., but about the real assassin's escaping as Sirhan was apprehended demonstrates just how entrenched the notion of governmental and extra-governmental conspiracies had become in the American psyche.

The assassination of John F. Kennedy has often been described as marking the end of American innocence. But, very arguably, the assassinations of Martin Luther King Jr. and Robert F. Kennedy can be described as marking the end of the sort of progressive liberalism that extended from Roosevelt's New Deal and Johnson's Great Society, when the divisions caused by the Vietnam War enabled a conservative-led backlash against Johnson's domestic policies. Following King's assassination, the riots that had already been reducing many major American cities flared up with renewed intensity, and the more militant alternatives to the nonviolent resistance promoted by King gained ground and, arguably, undermined some of the gains made by the Civil Rights Movement. Likewise, following Robert F. Kennedy's assassination, the "old guard" of liberalism, from Hubert Humphrey to Walter Mondale, lost its ability to animate voters. As the Counterculture produced a cultural progressivism that has been challenged but not reversed over the intervening half-century, its political complement has largely remained dormant—a minority force within even the Democratic Party.

In addition to the assassination of Martin Luther King Jr., there were other race-related killings that have typically been described as assassinations. In June 1963, Medgar Evers (1925–1963), a prominent civil rights activist in Mississippi, was assassinated by Byron De La Beckwith, a member of the White Citizens Council, a Klan-related supremacist group. Evers was shot from behind as he walked from his car toward the front door of his home. Due to national outrage, Beckwith was tried twice in the 1960s for the killing, but he was not convicted until a third trial in 1994. One of the many dark ironies in this crime was that because of his prominence and the graveness of his wound, Evers became the first African American to be treated at a white-designated Mississippi hospital.

In February 1965, Malcom X (previously known as Malcolm Little and at the time of his death known as el-Hajj Malik el-Shabazz) was assassinated by three members of the Nation of Islam. As he recounted in his extremely influential *Autobiography of Malcolm X*, he lost his father at age five and his mother was hospitalized for mental illness when he was thirteen. After spending the rest of his adolescence in foster care, he was convicted of larceny and sentenced to prison. In prison, he became a convert to the Nation of Islam. After his release from prison, he developed into one of the group's most prominent advocates, asserting the superiority of the black race and arguing for segregation and against integration. In effect, he positioned the Nation of Islam in opposition to the Civil Rights Movement, rejecting even Martin Luther King Jr.'s emphasis on nonviolent resistance. Ultimately, however, Malcolm X became increasingly disillusioned with the Nation of Islam and, more specifically, with its leader, Elijah Muhammed. After returning from Saudi Arabia, where he completed the Hajj, he started his own mosque and organization, emphasizing racial equality rather than racial superiority, Pan-Africanism rather than racial segregation, and the right of blacks to defend themselves rather than aggressive racial violence. Ironically, he was assassinated in order to silence his opposition to the Nation of Islam, but his assassination focused more intense attention on his differences with the group.

In August 1967, George Lincoln Rockwell (1918–1967), the founder of the American Nazi Party, was murdered by a former member whom Rockwell had expelled from the group. While Rockwell certainly represented the opposite end of the spectrum from a civil rights activist such as Medgar Evers, his relationship with the Nation of Islam was considerably more complex. Although Rockwell believed fervently in white supremacy, he praised the Nation of Islam for its advocacy of segregation and did so with little if any sense of irony. Like much of the messaging from the Nation of Islam, Rockwell's ideology was pointedly virulently anti-Semitic, and from the Nation of Islam, he adopted the successful, if pernicious, linkage between religious zeal and racial purity—though in his case it became a linkage between Christian fundamentalism and white supremacy, rather than between Islam and black power. Rockwell's ideology of hatred was based on an unmitigated and often incoherent disdain for Jews and communists, whom he often treated as one and the same group of enemies and whom he denounced for advocating racial mixing that was intended to undermine white superiority. Yet, if Rockwell had a gift for promoting his ideology of hate, that gift was primarily for appropriating the tactics of his ostensible enemies. For instance, when the Freedom Riders went by bus into the Deep South to promote black voting rights and an end to Jim Crow segregation, Rockwell transformed a VW van that he drove to rallies into an immediately identifiable "Hate Bus." Similarly, when folk music became a popular vehicle for advancing progressive ideals, Rockwell started promoting "hatenannies," with recordings sold under the label Hatenanny Records. Rockwell's stature as, at most, a footnote figure in U.S. history is illustrated by his being mentioned in the Bob Dylan song "Talkin' John Birch Paranoid Blues": Rockwell is mentioned by name and then his views are deftly caricatured in the line "I know for a fact that he hates Commies, 'cause he picketed the movie *Exodus*." Likewise, he became a minor character in the television miniseries *Roots*, and Marlon Brando won an Emmy Award for the role. In the end, it is difficult to say whether Rockwell deserves credit for originating the sort of hate groups that have continued to find followers in the post–civil rights era, or he simply exploited some decline in the appeal of the Klan and other more prominent hate groups and turned the promotion of hate into something indistinguishable from a sort of relentless self-promotion.

The last killing worth mentioning in this context was clearly a politically motivated murder, though not the sort of killing usually classified as an assassination. In December 1969, Fred Hampton (1948–1969) and Mark Clark (1947–1969), two leaders of the Illinois chapter of the Black Panther Party, were killed in a joint police raid on Hampton's apartment. The raid involved units of the Chicago Police Department, the Cook County prosecutor's office, and the F.B.I. Hampton had become a target of law enforcement because he had had considerable success in organizing alliances between the Black Panther Party and several large black street gangs, as well as gangs representing several other ethnic groups. The raid had been preceded by several shootouts between police and members of the Black Panthers, and the ostensible purpose of the raid was to seize a weapons cache in Hampton's apartment. In all, fourteen police officers participated in the 4 a.m. raid. Between ninety and one hundred rounds were fired, and it was later determined that all but one round had been fired by the police. That round had been fired from Mark Clark's gun; he was the only one of the seven people in the apartment at the time of the raid, and it was later determined that the round may have been squeezed off by involuntary reflex when he was shot to death. The five others in the apartment besides Hampton and Clark were seriously wounded—most, like Hampton, having been shot where they had been sleeping. Despite all of these dubious facts, the five who survived were charged with multiple felonies, and a quick judicial review found that the shootings were justified. But the outrage over the case never quite dissipated, and after a series of inquests and trials, in 1982 the three police agencies involved in the raid and killings settled a civil rights suit brought by nine of Hampton's and Clark's survivors for $1.85 million, then a record amount for such a settlement. By 2004, the views of the case had changed so dramatically that the city of Chicago designated December 4, the day of the raid, as "Fred Hampton Day in Chicago."

All of these assassinations taken together, but especially the assassination of President Kennedy, not only led to the publication of the thousands of books and perhaps tens of thousands of articles written over the next fifty-plus years, but they also inspired a number of novels and films. Some of these novels and films have very directly treated the actual events of the 1960s, but others have focused on more historically remote assassinations or on entirely fictional events. Some of these treatments have been memorable, but most have not. Many in the latter category have simply been forgettable, but a few have been execrable.

The first film to treat the assassination of President Kennedy directly was *The Trial of Lee Harvey Oswald* (1964). Released just months after the assassination, the film features Charles Mazyrack as Lee Harvey Oswald, George R. Russell as Oswald's defense attorney, Arthur Nations as the prosecutor, and George Edgley as the presiding judge. So, it was not a cast that featured any "stars." But it was a creditable, if workmanlike, effort. The prosecution argued, in essence, that Oswald was driven to the crime by his communist beliefs, while the defense argued that he was suffering from paranoid schizophrenia. Since no official reports had yet been released on the case, the filmmakers hedged their bet by having the audience serve as the jury—with all arguments presented to the viewers on the other side of the screen just as if they were sitting in the jury box.

The only other film about the assassination of President Kennedy that was made in the 1960s was Andy Warhol's *Since* (1966). Whatever merit this film may have as an experimental work, it does not illuminate much about the assassination—even if one accepts the premise that it is not so much treating the event itself as it is exploring the way in which the media turned the historical moment into a media event. Not just the dialogue but the action was entirely improvised, and the released film was advertised as "unfinished." Any average viewer would find it incoherent. Even the roles were arbitrarily assigned, with Mary Woronov playing John F. Kennedy, Ondine playing Lyndon Johnson, Ingrid Superstar playing both Jackie Kennedy and Lady Bird Johnson, and Gerard Malanga and Ronnie Coutrone alternating between playing Lee Harvey Oswald and Jack Ruby.

The film of the 1960s most associated with the assassination of President Kennedy was not about the assassination. Based on a novel by Richard Condon,

# Controversies

*The Manchurian Candidate* stars Laurence Harvey and Frank Sinatra playing two soldiers in a platoon captured by the communists during the Korean War. All of the captured soldiers are subjected to brainwashing, with the soldier played by Harvey, Sergeant Raymond Shaw, mindlessly murdering two of the other soldiers at the command of his captors, who wish to confirm their ability to direct him. Yet, when the rest of the platoon is released to make their way back to the American lines, all of the survivors praise Shaw for saving their lives, and the platoon's commanding officer, Captain Bennett Marco, played by Sinatra, even recommends him for a Congressional Medal of Honor. Then when they return to the states, Marco, who is haunted by muddled dreams of Shaw's killing of the two soldiers, begins to work for military intelligence and gradually to unravel what happened when they were captured. Meanwhile, Shaw rejoins his prominent family. His mother, played memorably by Angela Lansbury, is a completely Machiavellian character. Now remarried to a demagogic politician modeled in many ways on Joe McCarthy, she is maneuvering him toward a run for the presidency. The film climaxes with Shaw's getting a phone call that triggers his mental programming and directs him to assassinate his own stepfather, with Sinatra following closely behind in a desperate attempt to prevent the crime that he knows that Shaw is about to commit.

This film is noteworthy in its own right: it was nominated for several Academy Awards, as well as other prestigious awards, and its critical standing has further increased over time. It has been added to the United States National Film Registry, and it has been included on the American Film Institute's list of the greatest one hundred films in the first one hundred years of commercial filmmaking, as well as a number of other lists of noteworthy films. But the film is also noteworthy because it became a sort of cultural corollary to the conspiracy theories that were proliferating about the assassination of President Kennedy. Although it does not treat the assassination, the film does link an assassination to Cold War politics and sinister plots by hostile governments at a time when it was absolutely unclear who may have been responsible for the assassination. It became accepted as fact that, following the assassination, Frank Sinatra, due to his friendship with the Kennedys, had bought out the rights to the film and had permanently removed it from circulation. This reasoning ignores, of course, that Sinatra had already become estranged from the Kennedys, and, in actuality, the film had simply completed its initial theatrical run shortly before the assassination had occurred, and in the months following the assassination it was shown in theaters that showed rereleased films and in drive-in theaters. Moreover, it was broadcast on CBS in prime time in September 1965, and not long after Sinatra did acquire the rights to the film in 1972, it was shown on NBC. As a sort of footnote to this apocrypha about the film adaptation, all of the attention to the film led to the discovery that Condon had clearly plagiarized parts of the novel from Robert Graves's *I, Claudius*. Although C. J. Silverio has been credited with making the initial discovery of the plagiarism, Jonathan Lethem brought it to more mainstream attention in his essay "The Ecstasy of Influence," in which he considers the thin lines between literary influence, creative borrowing, and plagiarism. A more cinematic footnote to this discussion is that although Sinatra plays the protagonist in *The Manchurian Candidate,* almost a decade earlier, in 1954, he had played John Baron, an assassin-for-hire who is targeting the U.S. president as his train stops in a small California town named Suddenly, which gives the film its name. In that film, John Baron is likely much closer to Oswald in his personality and motives than the exotically programmed Shaw is in *The Manchurian Candidate;* indeed, if one accepts that Oswald was not the lone gunman, it is very likely that the additional assassin(s) might have been "doing the job" for purely mercenary motives.

Another assassination-related film of the decade that is notable is Z. Based on the novel by Vassilis Vassilikos and directed by Costa-Gravas, this thriller was the first film to be nominated for the Academy Awards for both the Best Picture and the Best Foreign Language Film. It was also very successful commercially, both in the United States and internationally. It concerns another very public assassination that occurred in 1963—the assassination of Grigoris Lambrakis, a prodemocracy Greek politician who was assassinated while Greece was being ruled by a military dictatorship.

In subsequent decades, the Kennedy assassination has become the subject of several works by notable novelists: Don DeLillo's *Libra* (1988), James Ellroy's *American Tabloid* (1995), Stephen King's speculative novel *11-22-63* (2011), and Norman Mailer's biography, *Oswald's Tale: An American Mystery* (1995), which has many of the characteristics of Mailer's earlier nonfiction novel, *The Executioner's Song* (1979). But, in the 1960s, the fictional treatments of the Kennedy assassination and assassinations more broadly were more in the popular genres—in fact, largely in novels published only in paperback. Nick Carter is almost certainly the literary character with the longest active life as an ongoing character. From the start, the Nick Carter stories were written by unidentified authors and largely written in the first person, as if the character were the author. This device allowed the character not only to have a credibly extended shelf life but also to evolve. In the mid-1880s, Nick Carter was introduced in a series of dime novels as a detective modeled on the Pinkerton agents. For more than three decades, that version of the character was featured in several book series and a magazine carrying his name. Then for about a decade and a half, the character became just one in a stable of characters featured by its publishers in pulp novels and pulp magazines. As the hard-boiled detective genre emerged in the late 1920s and 1930s, Nick Carter was transformed into a tough gumshoe. Then, as the appeal of that genre began to wane in the early 1960s and the espionage genre, especially the James Bond novels and films, became extremely popular, Nick Carter was again transformed into an intelligence operative. This version of the character was featured in the series of paperback novels called *Nick Carter—Killmaster,* which ran for more than three decades into the mid-1990s and included about 260 novels. In the decade after the assassination of President Kennedy, the titles in this series reflect the unflagging interest in stories treating assassinations: in *Run, Spy, Run* (1964), Carter thwarts a plot to kill President Kennedy in September 1963; in *Temple of Fear* (1968), he prevents the assassination of Japanese emperor Hirohito; in *Assault on England* (1972), he is partially successful in foiling a plot to assassinate those holding all of the major positions in the British Cabinet; and in *Agent Counter-Agent* (1973),

Carter thwarts a plot to assassinate both the vice president of the United States and the president of Venezuela.

## RACIAL UNREST

In the 1910s and 1920s, African Americans from the rural Deep South began to move in large numbers to the industrial cities of the Northeast and Midwest. Known as the Great Migration, it was accelerated by the Great Mississippi Flood of 1927 and then stalled by the Great Depression. It had a parallel in the migration of poor whites from Appalachia to the same industrial cities, and it resumed during the Second World War when the conscription of large numbers of men into the military services created a labor shortage in factories that were not just suddenly running at full capacity but were even expanding to meet the demand for the ever-increasing production of military equipment and supplies.

Although the industrial cities of the Northeast and the Midwest did not have the sorts of statutes that institutionalized segregation as the Jim Crows laws codified it in the Deep South, racial segregation was, with few exceptions, very rigidly enforced. In fact, the Great Migration very much intensified attention to issues of race relations, and the rise of the Ku Klux Klan in the Midwest in the late 1910s and 1920s was directly related to the increasing numbers of African Americans participating in the Great Migration.

The racial segregation and the rising racial tensions in the affected cities were related to four focal issues that eventually led to public unrest. First, in almost all cities, African Americans were restricted by homeowner compacts and other legal devices to residing in certain very well-defined and rather confined neighborhoods. Worse, because the boundaries of these neighborhoods remained fixed even as the African American population dramatically increased, there was inevitable overcrowding. Moreover, because the migrants from the Deep South had typically been sharecroppers or tenant farmers or had been employed in other low-paying jobs, they lacked the financial resources to buy property and, instead, became renters. And since most of the rental properties were owned by white landlords who lived well outside the African American neighborhoods and because of increasing demand had little incentive to maintain the properties, the rents, the number of occupants per unit, and the deterioration of the properties all increased in tandem.

Second, the Great Migration occurred somewhat ahead of the successful unionization of major industries. Initially, most industrial plants were located in or near the inner city, and their labor forces lived within walking distance or a short trolley or bus ride of the plant. Finding employment within a plant often depended on family or social connections, relationships that African Americans were unable to build because of the segregation in housing and the extension of that segregation to social and civic organizations. So, African Americans were often excluded entirely from many heavy industries, and this exclusion was particularly prevalent among smaller companies that supplied parts or specialized machining to larger plants. Where African Americans were able to secure employment, they were typically relegated to the most physically demanding and low-paying jobs. Their inability to get the apprenticeships that would lead to skilled and higher-paying jobs was further exacerbated in some instances by their apathy, if not antipathy, toward labor unions. In some instances, most notably at Ford in Detroit, companies used clergy to recommend African Americans for employment. The clergy typically viewed labor unions as Marxist and antagonistic toward religion. And even where this sort of system did not promote suspicions of unions, the ever more entrenched segregation of the industrial workforce made the practices of the labor unions seem as much an obstacle to the employment and advancement of African American workers as company policies were. Even when the statewide and national leadership of labor unions began to recognize that the integration of the industrial workforce was not just a pragmatic necessity but a moral obligation, they had difficulty enforcing that change of mind-set at the local level.

Third, as tensions rose within the African American communities, the white city governments authorized the white police departments to maintain order and suppress any sort of dissent with whatever ruthless efficiency was deemed necessary. As a result, many African Americans began to view the authorities as fundamentally antagonistic to them—as the foremost enforcers of their oppression, rather than as their last line of defense against racism and the vigilantism that was its all-too-common manifestation. The authorities essentially lost touch with what was going on in African American neighborhoods and lost any opportunity to address simmering issues before they boiled over into civic crises.

Even as all three of these issues began to be addressed, several phenomena in the development of American metro areas served only to exacerbate, rather than to mitigate, the issues. First, somewhat ahead of the development of the interstate highway system, major cities began to build expressways to facilitate the movement between their suburbs and their downtowns. These expressways rather quickly had the unintended consequence of moving business and industrial plants outside of the inner city to locations along the expressways. The suburbs attracted residents from the middle and upper economic classes, and businesses followed their best customers. As automobiles and tractor-trailer trucks replaced buses, trolleys, and trains as the primary means of moving commuters and products, industrial plants moved out of the inner city because the land around the plants could not accommodate the automobiles of a workforce increasingly composed of suburban commuters, and the trucks carrying loads to and from the plants had difficulty navigating the increasingly congested streets. Moreover, industrial corporations discovered that moving their plants to locations outside of the city, and in other cities, made it more difficult for the labor unions to organize workers and facilitated automation.

So, just as the urban workforces began to become more integrated and African Americans began to move out into previously segregated neighborhoods, the property- and income-tax bases of the inner cities began to erode. Not only were African Americans gaining ground in cities that were in decline, but as they marshaled their political power within those cities, they were very often blamed for the decline. But, in the 1990s through the 2010s, the so-called white flight from the inner cities would be followed by an African American exodus from those same inner cities to the suburbs. The movement away from the inner cities was ultimately very clearly more economic than racial, but to some degree, that has always been the case. But, in contrast with complex economic developments, racial tensions have always been easier to reduce to compelling images and headlines, regardless of the news medium.

The "white flight" from the inner cities began in most cases in the 1950s and extended into the 1960s and the 1970s. But because African American frustrations boiled over in the "race riots" of the mid and late 1960s, it has become a commonplace assumption that the riots caused the "white flight" and were a cause, rather than at least in part a consequence, of the deterioration of the inner cities.

In the 1960s, the first major race riot in a major U.S. city occurred in Harlem in late July 1964. A fifteen-year-old African American boy was shot three times by an off-duty white policeman, who claimed that the boy had lunged at him with a knife after he had interceded in an escalating confrontation between the boy and two of his friends and a white building superintendent. The rioting lasted for six days and eventually spread to the Bedford-Stuyvesant neighborhood in Brooklyn, another predominantly African American community in New York City. Like most subsequent disturbances, this one was marked by lulls in which groups within the community in effect competed to tamp down and to inflame emotions. At the same time, the police response was so often out of sync with what was happening within the affected community that it generally did more to intensify rather than to quell the tensions. What was perhaps most unusual about these specific riots was that they often involved the police being targeted with objects thrown from the rooftops, rather than being confronted on the ground, in the streets. In the end, one person was killed, some 500 were injured, 465 were arrested, and there was $.5 million to $1 million in property damage. Although the riots were a major shock to the city government and the psyche of the city's residents, they were, in retrospect, largely a harbinger of worse unrest to come.

In the following year, on the other side of the continent, a confrontation with police similarly triggered large-scale rioting centered in Watts, the largely African American section of Los Angeles. An African American young man who was on parole for a robbery conviction was stopped for a traffic violation. An argument between him and the police quickly escalated as onlookers gathered. As the disturbance began to spread, the anger in the community was intensified by a rumor that a pregnant woman had been abused by the police. The rioting would last for six days, until some 4,000 National Guardsmen were mobilized to restore order. In the end, 34 people were killed, 1,032 were injured, 3,438 were arrested, and there was more than $40 million in property damage. California governor Pat Brown empowered former CIA director John A. McCone to head an investigation into the riots. The McCone Commission eventually issued a report that not only accurately identified the socioeconomic and political issues that had created tremendous sense of underlying resentment in Watts but also made perceptive recommendations on how those issues might be addressed and at least gradually mitigated. Unfortunately, few of those recommendations were put in place in any sort of substantive way, and a little more than a quarter of a century later, the same issues would fuel the riots that

Police and National Guard soldiers work to quell rioting in the Watts neighborhood of Los Angeles on August 14, 1965, during one of the first and worst urban upsets of the decade. (Bettmann/Getty Images)

convulsed South Central Los Angeles following the verdict in the trial of the police who brutally beat Rodney King after he attempted to flee from police because he feared that his being stopped for speeding would result in a DUI charge, which would violate the conditions of his parole.

In June 1966, Chicago was convulsed by three days of rioting. At their core, the so-called Division Street riots were a response to the same sort of root causes that led to the other riots throughout the 1960s. But there were several distinctive elements to these riots. Most notably, they involved Puerto Ricans, not African Americans. The Puerto Rican population of Chicago had increased from several hundred in 1950 to more than thirty thousand in 1960. But at the same time as the population was increasing, gentrification and racial segregation combined to reduce dramatically the housing available to these generally poorer, working-class transplants to the city. Moreover, although most of them were Roman Catholics, the Chicago diocese both failed to provide them with their own parish and largely ignored the fact that they were racially excluded from most of the parishes nearest to the neighborhoods in which they were concentrated. Recognizing the cultural tensions that were compounding the socioeconomic issues with which this ethnic community was grappling, the city of Chicago designated the first week in June as Puerto Rican Heritage Week and cosponsored a festival celebrating Puerto Rican culture. Unfortunately, the celebration turned into a confrontation when police attempted to arrest a young man and ended up shooting him in the leg. The riots, which extended over three days, were much smaller in scale than those in Watts, and they were quelled after more than 500 police were brought into the affected neighborhoods. In the end, no one was killed, but 16 were injured, 49 were arrested, and more than 50 buildings were damaged.

As destructive as the Watts riots were and for as long as they have lingered in the cultural memory of not just the Los Angeles region but of the nation, they were eclipsed by the events of the summer of 1967, which is remembered as the "Long Hot Summer." Racial rioting occurred in 159 cities across America, from Buffalo to Portland, Oregon, and from Minneapolis to Houston. The worst of these riots occurred in Newark and Detroit.

The "white flight" from Newark over the decade and a half preceding the riots had made the city the first major city in the United States in which the majority of the population was African American. Nonetheless, the major city offices were held by whites, and most of the police force was white. The underlying unrest caused by the segregation in housing and employment that was common in most U.S. cities was being exacerbated in Newark by the decision to raze a large African American neighborhood to build a new University of Medicine and Dentistry. As in most of the riots of the period, the immediate cause was the police mistreatment of an African American during a traffic stop. In this instance, an African American taxi driver was pursued after he went around a double-parked patrol car and then was beaten by two white officers after he stopped. Rumors spread that the police officers had been seen dragging away his lifeless body, and events rapidly escalated. Ultimately, almost 8,000 police and National Guardsmen were deployed to restore order. In the end, after six days of rioting, 26 people were dead, 727 were injured, 1,465 were arrested, and the property damage was estimated at more than $10 million.

Even worse than the Newark riots were those in Detroit. As was the case in the cultural memory of the Newark riots, those in Detroit have typically been remembered as a cause of the "white flight" from the city and of its rapid decline from being regarded as one of the most prosperous and dynamic cities of America's industrial age. But as in Newark, the riots in Detroit were at least as much an effect of and a response to the "white flight" and its economic impact as they were a cause of it. The population of Detroit peaked in 1950, and the out-migration to the suburbs was as pronounced in the 1950s and the 1960s as it was in the 1970s in the aftermath of the riots. Without at all minimizing the deep racial issues that have contributed to Detroit's problems, the out-migration has been at least as driven by economics as it has been defined by race. In the 1990s and the 2000s, the out-migration escalated as many, more affluent African Americans joined the movement out to the suburbs and beyond.

In the African American communities of Detroit, the 1967 riots are often remembered as the "Rebellion"—a rejection of the common characterizations of the events as almost entirely involving a convulsive outbreak of lawlessness spilling out of the African American sections of the city. As was the case in the 1943 riots in Detroit, such characterizations ignore the fact that the violence involved large numbers of whites, often organized in gangs, with African Americans often defending their own properties from damage rather than willfully destroying the property of others. The fact that African Americans were disproportionately represented in the numbers of those killed, injured, and arrested is a testament to the racial segregation of the city's police force as much as it is a reflection of who was most responsible for the mayhem.

The riots in Detroit began with a police raid on an unlicensed bar (known as a "blind pig") operating after-hours in an African American neighborhood. Most of the more than eighty people in the bar were celebrating the return of two soldiers from a tour of duty in the Vietnam War. The police who conducted the raid were surprised at the size of the group inside, and after deciding to take everyone into custody, they had to wait for a sufficient number of police vans to arrive. Meanwhile, despite the very late hour, a crowd gathered outside the bar, and when the police attempted to load the vans, the situation became chaotic. Although the police vans managed to get away from the scene, rioting began, and because the police response was very slow, it quickly escalated and spread. As areas beyond the African American neighborhoods began to be affected, Governor Romney called out the National Guard, but when those troops proved ill-equipped to handle the situation, President Johnson sent in units of the 101st Airborne Division. By all measures, these riots were the worst in U.S. history since the 1863 draft riots in New York City and until the Rodney King riots in South Central Los Angeles in 1992. In the end, 43 people were killed, 1,189 people were injured, 7,231 were arrested, and there was more than $40 million in property damage. More than 400 structures had to be demolished, and more than 2,500 stores and businesses were damaged and/or looted.

If the unrest of the summer of 1967 seemed both unprecedented and unlikely to be repeated, 1968 quickly proved those assumptions wrong. On April 4, Dr. Martin Luther King Jr. was assassinated in Memphis, and over the next week, 125 American cities were convulsed by rioting, with the riots in at least three dozen of those cities being characterized as major disturbances. The worst of the rioting took place in Chicago, Baltimore, and Washington, DC. Because the federal government adopted and promoted a policy of containing, rather than aggressively suppressing, the unrest, the property damage sustained in these riots was generally higher than in the riots of the previous summer, but the level of violence was lower. As was the case in the Detroit riots of the previous summer, in African American communities and commentary, these disturbances have often been referred to as the "Easter Uprising" in an effort to emphasize not just the immediate precipitating event of Dr. King's assassination but also the endemic, broader causes, instead of the effects.

In Chicago, the riots lasted for two days, and because the police efforts to suppress the unrest were particularly aggressive, there were more casualties than elsewhere. In the end, 11 people were killed, several hundred were injured, including 90 police officers and 48 people wounded by police gunfire, 2,150 were arrested, and there was about $10 million in property damage. More than 200 buildings were destroyed or damaged severely enough that they had to be demolished, and the damage was especially concentrated and conspicuous along a 2-mile stretch of West Madison Street. Ironically, in some African American neighborhoods, gang members, who had had personal contact with Dr. King, managed to maintain order much more effectively than the police.

Indeed, when the same aggressive tactics used to suppress these riots were used later in the summer against protesters who had gathered during the Democratic National Convention, the tactics escalated the unrest and were a public-relations disaster for Mayor Richard Daley's administration.

In response to the escalating rioting in Baltimore, Maryland governor Spiro Agnew first mobilized the state police and then the state National Guard, and when both of those forces seemed inadequate, he requested that federal troops be deployed. The rioting in Baltimore would be notable because it was one of the few instances in which the white "counter-rioting" was so pronounced that the media coverage could not avoid addressing it. In the end, 6 people were killed, about 70 people were injured, 5,800 were arrested, and property damage totaled more than $12 million. More than 1,000 businesses reported physical damage due to the disturbances. Notably, although more than 1,200 fires were reported, only five of those arrested were arrested for arson. Today, one of the main reasons that the riots are remembered outside of Maryland is that Spiro Agnew's decisive response to the riots and his strong declarations about his commitment to law and order brought him to the attention of Richard Nixon, who was making the restoration of law and order a major talking point in his campaign for the Republican nomination for president and, a few months later, asked Agnew to be his running mate in the 1968 presidential election.

The worst of the 1968 riots occurred in Washington, DC. These riots were notable for several reasons. First, African American political radicalism, in the person of Stokely Carmichael, played a focal role in framing the immediate response to the assassination of Dr. King, which involved the demand that the white businesses close in order to mark the assassination, and in framing the subsequent violence as the only available response to the tragic rejection of Dr. King's dream of non-violent change. Second, in contrast to the confrontational tactics employed in Chicago, the chief of police in Washington, DC, attempted to control and then suppress the disturbances using tear gas and the weight of numbers. Nonetheless, in the end, the riots in Washington, DC, would leave 13 people dead, 1,097 injured, and about 7,600 arrested. The property damage would total $25 million, or more than twice the damage reported for Baltimore and more than two and a half times the damage reported for Chicago. Third, because the rioting occurred near the Capitol district, the national media made very visible not only the effects of the rioting but also the military response to it. In addition to the mass mobilization of police, almost 14,000 federal troops were deployed to protect federal buildings. The imagery seemed both literally and symbolically to suggest that American institutions were under siege and that American society was unraveling in a very violent way. Indeed, the damage in Washington, DC, was so extensive that it would take several decades for the physical scars to fade, and, thus, the nation's capital would remain a reminder of the socioeconomic causes and consequences of the nation's unresolved issues of race. Likewise, because the riots occurred so close to the center of government and therefore had a very visceral effect on federal lawmakers, they led to the rapid passage to the Civil Rights Act of 1968 and the Fair Housing Act. That legislation was passed even before the report of the Kerner Commission, established by President Johnson, issued its report on the socioeconomic conditions that were the underlying causes of racial inequality and unrest, a report that included very astute recommendations on how those conditions might best be addressed. But the enduring physical scars of the rioting on the capital's cityscape served to emphasize the difficulty in addressing entrenched racial inequality, even through landmark legislation and very well-intentioned and thorough investigations.

## VIETNAM WAR

The history of Vietnam as an identifiable entity is both long and complex. Likewise, although the history of the U.S. military involvement in Vietnam represents a relatively brief episode in that long and complex history, it was also one of the most protracted and complex in U.S. military and political history. Moreover, it convulsed and reshaped American society and culture in ways that few events have done—outside of the four major wars (the Revolutionary War, the Civil War, the First World War, and the Second World War) and the Great Depression.

Although the U.S. military involvement in Vietnam began in the immediate aftermath of the Second World War and the onset of the Cold War shortly thereafter, it never made much of an impression on the public consciousness because it was just one of a number of proxy wars in the Cold War and because the U.S. initially used the French forces who were attempting to reassert control over the colony known as French Indochina (the current nations of Vietnam, Laos, and Cambodia) as surrogates in its effort to check the spread of communism in Asia. The United States supported the French by providing almost all of their military commitment, additional financial support, and ancillary assets such as intelligence and disinformation services. The intelligence support is memorably depicted in *The Quiet American*, an important work by the British novelist Graham Greene (1955). That novel was adapted into the first film to treat the U.S. involvement in Vietnam, directed by Joseph L. Mankiewicz and starring Audie Murphy, Michael Redgrave, and Giorgia Moll. Murphy had been the most decorated U.S. soldier of the Second World War; Redgrave was a highly respected British actor; and Moll was an Italian film actress, whose active career lasted less than a decade and a half, from the mid-1950s to the late 1960s. Ironically, her career basically spanned direct U.S. involvement in Vietnam, but her role in this film, one of her most notable outside of Italian films, is now most remembered as an example of "whitewashing," or the casting of Caucasians in Asian roles. The film itself was made on the heels of the McCarthy hearings and communist hysteria of the early 1950s, and it emphasizes the function of the intelligence services in combating the spread of communism. Not coincidentally it was released a year after the defeat of the French in the Battle of Dien Bien Phu that effectively ended French colonial rule in Indochina. More recently, the novel was adapted to a film directed by Philip Noyce and starring Michael Caine, Brendan Fraser, and Do Thi Hai Yen (2002). This later adaptation is truer to the themes of Greene's novels, emphasizing the moral compromises that defined U.S. engagement in Vietnam from the very beginning and on all levels.

Beyond those moral compromises, there was also a persistent lack of understanding of the complexity of the political issues in Vietnam, a lack of understanding that undermined strategies based on framing the conflict simply as a Cold War confrontation between communism and capitalism, never mind one between authoritarian government and democracy. Although a Vietnamese kingdom had secured its independence from China in the tenth century, that kingdom had been centered in what became North Vietnam. There was another kingdom in what are now the central provinces of Vietnam, and the southern provinces were dominated by the Khmer kingdom centered in Cambodia. Indeed, although the Vietnamese kingdom in the north fairly persistently expanded southward, from the fifteenth through the early nineteenth century, there were recurring wars as that kingdom's political unity and military power waxed and waned. Although more than 85 percent of the current population is ethnically defined as Vietnamese, there is more lingering ethnic and cultural diversity than those statistics reflect.

Moreover, when the division of North and South Vietnam became more entrenched in the aftermath of the French exodus, Ngo Dinh Diem rather rapidly seized control of the government of South Vietnam. In terms of representing an alternative to the communist government under Ho Chi Minh in North Vietnam, Diem's greatest strength was that he was an ardent nationalist. His major competing liability was, however, that he was also an ardent Roman Catholic. Most of the population of South Vietnam, particularly in the rural hinterlands, were Buddhists or practiced folk religions. In the cities where the political power was concentrated, the majority were Buddhists, with the Roman Catholics constituting a powerful minority, in large part because they were holdovers from the French colonial regime. Their understanding of the functions of government and military organization was a sizable advantage, but their association with European colonialism was a liability in terms of maintaining popular support. Diem squandered his advantages by putting family members and political cronies in key positions within his government and creating circumstances under which corruption became rampant. He also made a major strategic error in initiating a persecution of the Buddhist majority, creating a political environment in which military operations against the communist insurgents in South Vietnam—the Viet Cong—were compromised by his wanting to preserve his military forces to suppress attempted coups against his government.

In terms of American popular culture, the first images related to U.S. involvement in Vietnam to be ingrained into the American public consciousness were in televised news reports of Buddhist monks immolating themselves to protest the attacks on Buddhists by the Diem government. Although most viewers of the evening news broadcasts could still not locate Vietnam on a world map, the horrific images of the monks sitting cross-legged in the middle of a street while someone poured gasoline over them and their then igniting themselves made the conflicts in Vietnam stand out among the almost continuous stories of political and ethnic convulsions that were shaping the former European colonies as they secured their independence and they attempted to establish self-government. Diem would be executed in a CIA-backed coup shortly before President Kennedy was himself assassinated. The ironies in those closely spaced events would not become public knowledge for some time, and just as the elimination of Diem would not appreciably improve the fractures that persisted in the South Vietnamese government, it would not substantially alter the deepening U.S. involvement in a conflict that required more than military power and political will to win.

Over the course of Kennedy's tragically shortened presidency, the number of U.S. military advisers in Vietnam had increased from about 2,000 to 16,000. The strategies for making South Vietnam more secure were publicly described as the Strategic Hamlet Program. Modeled on the establishment of forts on the Western frontier in late-nineteenth-century America, this plan attempted to make agricultural villages secure by creating fortified strongholds to which the villagers would return at night and into which they could retreat if the village were attacked. Support for this strategy was undermined by the return to a landlord system of landholding aggressively pursued by the Diem government (and ironically paralleling an equally unpopular attempt to collectivize agriculture in North Vietnam). The Diem government also failed to commit fully to this effort because Diem feared that fragmenting his forces would undermine his hold on power. Moreover, because this strategy was essentially defensive and could not be put into effect across the whole countryside, it ceded most of the military initiative to the Viet Cong and allowed them to develop more secure bases of operation.

Near the end of this period, the U.S. military responded to these developments by introducing Special Forces into the conflict, with the specific mission to undermine the Viet Cong's insurgency by conducting clandestine search-and-destroy operations against them. *The Green Berets* (1968), starring John Wayne, would be the only major American film about the Vietnam War released during the 1960s. The film is almost laughably mediocre. It was filmed in the Carolinas, on a landscape that does not at all replicate that of Vietnam. John Wayne was already too old and paunchy to credibly play a combat officer. And although the film ostensibly addresses the moral ambiguities of U.S. involvement in the war, it does so with the patriotic heavy-handedness of Wayne's films about the Pacific theater of the Second World War, in which the Japanese are depicted as cartoonishly sinister and vicious figures. Nonetheless, if the film had been released four years earlier when the war had not yet become unpopular, it might have been better received. But, because it was released as the protests against the war were beginning to reach a crescendo, it was dismissed as amateurish propaganda and eroded Wayne's stature as an iconic American figure, making him seem not just anachronistic, but something of a stooge for those who were persisting in their support for a war that was being increasingly regarded as having no clear political or moral purpose and no well-defined or achievable military aim.

In 1965, the Johnson administration dramatically changed course on the conflict in Vietnam, though it was slow in acknowledging the shift. Instead of asserting that the United States was assisting the military forces of South Vietnam (ARVN) with training and tactical support, the American military took over the conduct of the war. The new strategy had three components: first, a rapid expansion in the numbers of U.S. and allied forces; second, coordinated campaigns in which overwhelming force would be brought against Viet Cong strongholds in order to cause maximum casualties and eliminate their capacity to undertake capacity to initiate offensive operations; and third, an intensification of the strategic bombing campaigns against North Vietnamese cities and infrastructure and against the supply routes through Laos known as the Ho Chi Minh Trail. In the nine months between March and December of 1965, American combat forces in South Vietnam increased from 3,500 to 200,000. These forces rapidly began to undertake campaigns against the Viet Cong that involved a complex coordination of airpower and concentrated artillery and armored forces in support of infantry that were often rapidly delivered and extricated from the battlefield by helicopters. The aim of the American military was to search out and destroy the Viet Cong in order to seriously degrade their capacity to control territory, rather than to seize and hold territory themselves. The body count of the enemy killed in each engagement became the measure of progress toward victory. And while tactical airpower was supporting these ground campaigns, high-altitude bombers began to drop what would ultimately add up to a higher tonnage of bombs than what was dropped on both Germany and Japan during the Second World War. Specifically, some calculations have suggested that more bombs were dropped on the supply routes and the bases of the communist insurgents in Laos than on any comparable landscape of targets before or since.

Despite the persistently optimistic assessments and public pronouncements of American military and political leaders, the new approach to the conduct of the war had some fundamental flaws. First, the continuing expansion of U.S. forces to two and then almost three times the 200,000 deployed at the end of 1965 meant an increasing reliance on the military draft. The troops deployed in 1964 and 1965 were largely experienced professionals, but from 1966 onward, an increasing percentage of the American forces had had more limited training, were deployed for one-year tours of duty before being discharged back into civilian life, and lacked the sort of unit cohesion that motivates combat veterans when the strategic and even the tactical goals begin to seem ambiguous, or even irrationally divorced from reality, and begin to undermine morale. The body bag became a symbol of the erosion of morale as much as the body count became the new measure of supposed progress that never culminated in victory. The Americans underestimated the capacity of the Viet Cong and the North Vietnamese to suffer severe casualties and then reconstitute their forces. Similarly, when the North Vietnamese managed to bring down some of the American strategic bombers, they became adept at producing film footage of the shattered wrecks of the planes and, when any of the crews survived, the detention of airmen, who, for all of their heroic perseverance, did not look at all as if they were representatives of the greatest military power on earth or impervious to the possibility of defeat. The attention in the U.S. media to the plight of the POWs provided an opening for the North Vietnamese to shift attention to the human toll of the strategic bombing, which inevitably caused civilian casualties and displaced whole communities of survivors. This resurrected the moral issues raised after the Second World War about the saturation

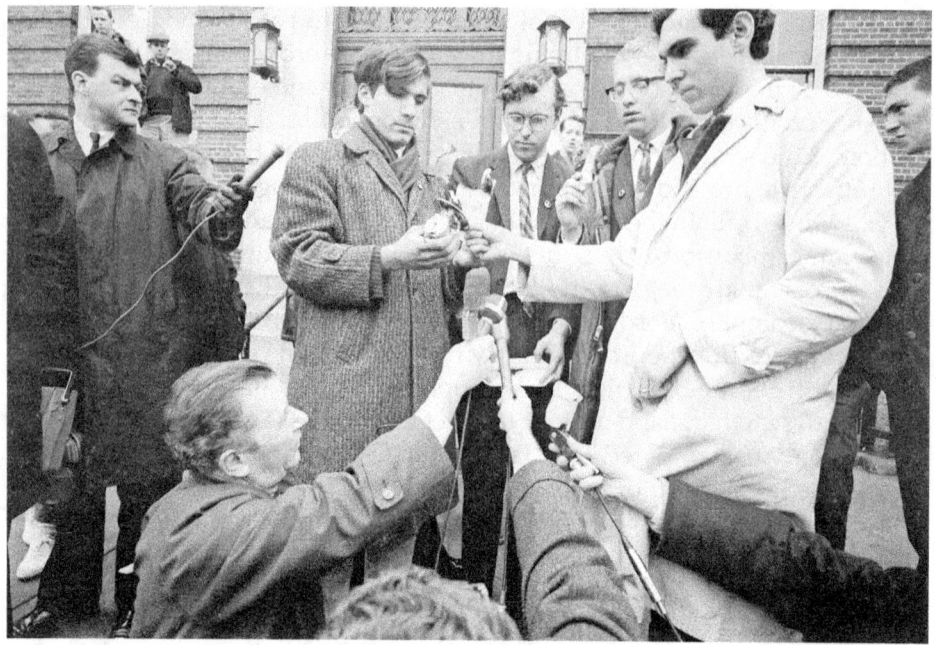

Anger at the Selective Service System (the draft) boiled over in the mid-1960s as the Vietnam War escalated. Here, young men are burning their draft cards in an act of defiance. (Bettmann/Getty Images)

bombing of German and Japanese cities, especially those such as Dresden with great historical significance and very little military significance. The bombing campaign became the first focal point in the accusations that the U.S. military was committing war crimes in its prosecution of the war. And those accusations would turn the protests against the war into the first truly international protest movement. In fact, the first organized protests against U.S. involvement in the war occurred not in the United States but in the United Kingdom and Australia in May 1963, well ahead of the initiation of the strategic bombing campaign.

The protests against the war in the United States itself began in a very limited way in September and October of 1964, with protests outside the United Nations headquarters in New York City that focused on the persecution of Buddhists by the Diem government and the U.S. support of that government, and outside the Waldorf Astoria Hotel, where Diem's sister-in-law, Madame Ngo Dinh Nhu (commonly referred to as Madame Nhu and the first lady of South Vietnam) was speaking. In April 1964, the *National Guardian* published the first call for draft resistance, and in May, the first public burning of draft cards as a symbol of resistance to the war and the draft occurred when a dozen men publicly burned their draft cards in New York City. Also in May, hundreds of students marched in loosely coordinated protests in such cities as New York, Boston, San Francisco, Seattle, and Madison, Wisconsin—with New York and San Francisco becoming the focal points of such protests going forward. In December, the first organized protests attracted a larger number of students—more than 1,000 in New York and San Francisco—with protests also occurring in such cities such as Boston, Philadelphia, Washington, DC, Minneapolis, Miami, Cleveland, Minneapolis, Austin, and Sacramento.

In 1965, notable antiwar protests occurred in every month but January and September. In 1962 Jerry Rubin had drafted the Port Huron Statement, which would become the manifesto for Students for a Democratic Society (SDS). In March 1964, at the University of Michigan, the SDS organized the first teach-in against the war and the draft, and the event was so popular that the concept rapidly spread to other campuses across the nation. In April, the SDS organized the largest protest to date against the war; held in Washington, DC, it attracted 15,000–20,000 marchers. In the fall of 1964, Mario Savio had organized the Free Speech Movement at the University of California at Berkeley, asserting the right of students to engage in political organizing and political protests on the campus. In 1965, at Berkeley, Jerry Rubin and Peter Smale organized the Vietnam Day Committee, and a protest in October attracted 35,000 protesters. The success of the protest represented a rebound from the truncation of a march from Oakland to Berkeley when the protesters dispersed somewhat chaotically in the face of massed police. The protests were not at all confined to the coastal cities. For instance, in April, college students in Oklahoma managed to mail out and otherwise distribute hundreds of thousands of pamphlets with photos of infants who had become horrific "collateral damage" in U.S. military operations. In mid-October, the first coordinated international protests, called Days of International Protest, took place in cities worldwide, with the largest protests occurring in such European cities as London, Brussels, Copenhagen, Stockholm, and Rome. In March 1966, groups including the SDS, SANE, Women Strike for Peace, and the Committee for Nonviolent Action joined together to form the National Coordinating Committee to End the War in Vietnam. That group coordinated with international groups to organize a follow-up to the previous year's Days of International Protest. In addition to mass protests in cities outside the United States such as Ottawa, London, Lyon, Oslo, Stockholm, and Tokyo, large protests occurred in Boston, Philadelphia, Washington, DC, Detroit, Chicago, Oklahoma City, and San Francisco.

In 1965, hardly a week would go by without a news report about some public burning of draft cards. The image became so associated with the Antiwar Movement that it was featured on the cover of the August issue of *Life* magazine. It was inevitable that the government would react, and in October, David J. Miller became the first person charged and convicted under an amendment to the forty-year-old selective service act that now prohibited the mutilation of draft cards. In March 1967, David Paul O'Brien and three others were arrested for burning their draft cards on the steps of a courthouse in Boston. O'Brien would appeal his conviction all the way to the U.S. Supreme Court. But in a ruling in the following year, the court was persuaded by the government's arguments that, in this case, the individual right to freedom of expression was outweighed by the need to protect the national interest. More grimly, as the Buddhist monks had done to protest the Diem government's persecution of Buddhists, Americans began to self-immolate to protest the war. The first to do so, in March 1965, was Alice Hertz, an eighty-two-year-old woman in Detroit. In November, Norman Morrison, a Quaker from Baltimore and a thirty-two-year-old father of three, immolated himself just outside the Pentagon, under the windows of Defense Secretary Robert McNamara's offices.

In 1967, the Civil Rights Movement and the Antiwar Movement became more formally interconnected when Dr. Martin Luther King Jr. spoke at Riverside Church in New York City in early April: "Somehow this madness must cease. We must stop now. I speak as a child of God and brother to the suffering poor of Vietnam. I speak for those whose land is being laid waste, whose homes are being destroyed, whose culture is being subverted. I speak for the poor of America who are paying the double price of smashed hopes at home and death and corruption in Vietnam. I speak as a citizen of the world, for the world as it stands aghast at the path we have taken. I speak as an American to the leaders of my own nation. The great initiative in this war is ours. The initiative to stop it must be ours." In the spring of the previous year, the group Clergy and Laymen against the War had been formed, and clergy began to take a more prominent role in the opposition to the war. In November 1966, Rev. James L. Bevel became the leader of the Mobilization Committee to End the War in Vietnam (MOBE), which coordinated several nationwide protests in the spring of 1967. On October 16, MOBE-coordinated protests were staged in thirty major U.S. cities, and a week later, MOBE organized the March on the Pentagon: 100,000 protesters gathered on the National Mall, and some 35,000 to 50,000 gathered at the Pentagon. The events at the Pentagon were chronicled in Norman Mailer's award-winning "nonfiction novel" *The Armies of the Night*.

In October 1967, Philip Berrigan, a Josephite priest and veteran of the Second World War and three fellow protesters, who together became known as the Baltimore Four, entered a draft board office in Baltimore, poured blood over the records kept in the office, and then remained at the site until they were arrested. Berrigan would become one of the most well-known protesters against the war. At the opposite end of the spectrum, Dr. Benjamin Spock, the pediatrician who had become a household name by writing *Baby and Child Care* (1946), the "bible" of child-rearing for baby boom parents, was arrested in December 1967 while participating in demonstration against the draft in New York City. If Lyndon Johnson thought that Walter Cronkite's public questioning of the war marked a turning point in terms of public support for the war effort, for most Americans Dr. Spock's arrest during a protest against the draft marked a turning point in their unquestioning confidence in the government's justifications of the human and material costs of the war.

Although individual members of the active military and veterans of the Vietnam War had joined protests in previous years, in 1967 the veterans against the war became more formally organized and more prominent both in the media coverage of the war protests and in the public consciousness of the ways in which the war was fracturing American society. In June 1967, the formation of the Vietnam Veterans against the War was announced, and later that month, *The Bond* appeared, the first underground newspaper published by servicemen in Vietnam.

In the second half of 1967, General William Westmoreland, the commander of the U.S. forces in South Vietnam, began measuring the success of U.S. military operations by the "body counts" of enemy combatants killed in search-and-destroy campaigns that had been conducted over the previous two years across much of South Vietnam. This messaging about the war ultimately led him to declare that the enemy forces had been so degraded that their ability to conduct any large-scale operations had been seriously compromised. What Westmoreland messaging failed to convey was that most U.S. military operations were reactive, not proactive—that the Viet Cong were largely determining when and where they would fight. Likewise, the search-and-destroy operations had created a very large internal refugee population within South Vietnam, much of which naturally migrated into the larger cities, exacerbating the effects of a burgeoning underground and illicit economy and of endemic institutional corruption associated with the expansion of the U.S. war effort. The U.S. war effort was, in effect, opening much of the rural countryside to the insurgents while making it easier for insurgents to establish themselves in the major cities.

Not long after Westmoreland proclaimed that the Viet Cong's offensive capabilities had been dramatically degraded, they, along with North Vietnamese troops, launched their largest offensive operation of the war on January 30, 1968. Known as the Tet Offensive, this was a coordinated attack against more than one hundred cities and towns across South Vietnam, including five of the six autonomous cities, thirty-six of the forty-two provincial capitals, and the capital city of Saigon. The offensive involved more than 80,000 Viet Cong and North Vietnamese troops, and for the most part, both the U.S. and South Vietnamese forces were caught completely off guard. One of the key aims of the offensive, provoking a popular uprising across South Vietnam, never materialized in any significant way. Furthermore, within a week or two, most of the attacks on South Vietnamese cities were decisively suppressed, with heavy losses being inflicted on the Viet Cong and North Vietnamese forces. Nonetheless, the attacks on key buildings in Saigon received very heavy television and other media coverage worldwide, and it took almost five weeks of heavy fighting for U.S. forces to recapture strongholds in the provincial capital of Hue, including the historically, architecturally, and culturally significant Citadel that was finally reduced to rubble as a last resort. The Viet Cong and North Vietnamese would launch three successive offensives, following the Tet Offensive with somewhat smaller scale offensives in May and August of 1968. Their losses in these offensives have been estimated at about double the total forces involved in the Tet Offensive, with more than 45,000 killed and more than 110,000 wounded. So, the Tet Offensive was, in fact, a decisive military defeat for the Viet Cong and the North Vietnamese. But, politically, it marked a dramatic turning point in the war because it so undermined the U.S. public's confidence in the possibility of victory that even many ardent political supporters of the military began very earnestly to consider exit strategies.

About a week before the initiation of the Tet Offensive, several North Vietnamese divisions attacked the U.S. combat base at Khe Sahn in northwestern

South Vietnam. The base was in a rather isolated area, and after the North Vietnamese seized control of the surrounding hills and isolated the base, comparisons to the isolation and decisive defeat of the French forces at Dien Bien Phu seemed ominously apposite. The American forces, however, had the benefit of massive reserves of airpower. During the three to four months during which the combat around the base was most intense, the U.S. Air Force not only dropped more than 100,000 tons of bombs on the North Vietnamese positions but supplied the base with more than 150,000 artillery rounds that were fired on those positions as well. In the end, the siege was lifted by the arrival of a sizable relief force. But what appeared to be a decisive victory in one of the few sustained fixed-site battles of the war was undercut by the decision to abandon the base in the early summer of 1968. Indeed, shortly after the base was dismantled and the remnants destroyed and the last U.S. troops abandoned the area in early July 1968, it became very clear that North Vietnamese troops had taken control of the area. So what was initially portrayed as a decisive, if costly, victory by U.S. forces very quickly became a singular illustration of the ultimate futility of the U.S. military strategy in the Vietnam War.

From 1965 through 1970, the period of escalated U.S. involvement in the Vietnam War, the numbers of those who enlisted and were drafted into the military remained relatively even. But the rationale for enlisting changed dramatically. In the earlier years of the conflict a fairly high percentage of those who enlisted chose to serve in infantry units, but by the end of the decade, when enlistment was increasingly seen as a way to avoid the service in infantry units that was the fate of most draftees, only between 2 and 3 percent of enlistees chose to serve in infantry units. Moreover, the number of college students who selected ROTC decreased by two-thirds (and that number would continue to plummet through the mid-1970s). As a result, a war that was largely being fought on the ground by soldiers with just one-year tours of duty was being fought increasingly by soldiers who had much less faith in the war effort, had much less unit cohesion, and were aware that they were, in effect, serving instead of not only those peers who had secured deferments by attending college but also by enlisting into support units rather than combat units. Over the second half of the 1960s, the number of desertions occurring within the United States increased fourfold, and the increasing popularity of the Counterculture meant that drug use among the military, in particular among combat units in Vietnam where hard drugs, in particular heroin, were readily available, increased dramatically.

The dramatic erosion of morale among U.S. forces was demonstrated in various ways. The military engagements with the Viet Cong continued to be much more reactive than proactive, and so what were already euphemistically described as "search-and-destroy" missions became openly referred to as "search-and-evade" missions. Units were often very slow to respond to the orders of their officers and thereby rendered their orders ineffectual. Increasingly, units openly disregarded the orders of their officers that were likely to place them in clearly perilous or even dubious situations, and in some extreme instances in which officers seemed recklessly aggressive or bent on disciplinary retaliation, they were killed by their own men, a phenomenon that became known as "fragging." At the opposite extreme, war crimes against Vietnamese civilians became more commonplace. It is notable that from 1965 through 1967, only one major war crime was committed by U.S. troops in Vietnam, the massacre by U.S. Marines of 145 Vietnamese at Thuy Bo over two days at the end of January and beginning of February 1965. (As a point of contrast, over those same three years, South Korean forces were blamed for three massacres in which more than 1,600 Vietnamese were killed.) But in March 1968, the most notorious war crimes of the conflict were committed by U.S. Army units at the village of My Lai, where on one day more than 500 Vietnamese were massacred. This war crime, in combination with the concerns about the civilian casualties resulting from the heavy U.S. bombing of North Vietnamese cities, reinforced the argument that the U.S. military involvement in Vietnam was an immoral enterprise, and it led to a very unfortunate stereotyping of the soldiers who served there as "baby killers." Indeed, the entire military-industrial complex was implicated in the stigmatization of the war effort as an immoral enterprise. In late fall 1967, students at the University of Wisconsin in Madison had staged the first Dow Day protest, at which it was asserted that Dow Chemical was guilty of war crimes because it was supplying the U.S. military with the napalm that was being used indiscriminately across Vietnam. This linkage between war crimes and crimes against the environment would be given a more pointed moral turn when the use of defoliants such as Agent Orange was later linked directly to high incidences of cancers among not only civilians who survived the war and returned to their homes in the affected areas of the Vietnamese countryside but also among U.S. veterans of the war.

The increasingly widespread disenchantment with the war in Vietnam, even among those who were not directly opposing it, spelled the end of Lyndon Johnson's presidency. After the New Hampshire primary, Johnson announced that he would not be seeking another term. The antiwar sentiment on the Democratic side initially gathered behind the candidacy of Senator Eugene McCarthy of Minnesota, whose strong second-place finish in the New Hampshire primary led to Johnson's decision to bow out. But then Robert F. Kennedy entered the race, and the combination of his family legacy and his charisma allowed him to eclipse McCarthy as the main challenger to Vice President Hubert H. Humphrey. It is important to remember that in 1968, there were Democratic presidential primaries in only thirteen states. Most delegates to the Democratic National Convention were chosen in state caucuses largely controlled by party leaders, and Humphrey, who did not actively compete in the primaries, was set to enter the convention with a plurality, though not a majority of the delegates. Robert Kennedy's victory in the California primary had given him much momentum heading into the convention, but his assassination during the celebration of that victory essentially gave Humphrey the nomination. Although Johnson was seeking to negotiate a peaceful end to the Vietnam conflict, and although his efforts were secretly being undermined by the Republican candidate Richard M. Nixon, Humphrey was saddled with the perception that he would continue the war while Nixon was publicly committing to bringing the war to an honorable conclusion. Still, as the campaign wore on through the fall of 1968, Humphrey steadily gained ground on Nixon, and the narrowness of the margin of the popular vote—about 500,000 votes—suggested to many that if the campaign had extended for several more weeks, Humphrey might have significantly narrowed, if not overcome, Nixon's 301 to 191 advantage in the Electoral College vote.

But, in 1968, George Wallace ran the most effective third-party campaign in modern American history, winning forty-six electoral votes and almost 10 million popular votes, and one can argue that Wallace's candidacy hurt Nixon as much as, if not more than, it hurt Humphrey. Granted, Wallace did siphon off blue-collar votes in the industrial states of the Northeast and the Midwest that might have gone largely to Humphrey, but Wallace also carried states in the Deep South that had already shifted to the Republican side in 1964, in response to Johnson's championing of civil rights and Goldwater's reassertion of states' rights. Since Nixon carried all of the southern states except Texas, it is very likely that he would have carried the states that Wallace carried if Wallace had not run.

Moreover, on its surface, the so-called Southern strategy meant that an increasingly conservative Republican Party balanced its losses in the multiracial, urbanized northern states by flipping the Deep South—by appealing to Southern whites who felt indignant at the abrupt end to a century of institutionalized racial segregation in their states, even if many of them were not quite willing to openly describe racial integration as an abomination. But, in much of the Northeast and the Midwest, racial segregation had been every bit as real as it had been in the Deep South, even if it had not been as formally institutionalized, and as African Americans gained increasing political and economic power in the cities, the so-called white flight to the suburbs created a cohort of white voters responsive to much of the same appeals that were effective with white voters in the Deep South.

Indeed, Nixon did not even have to emphasize "states' rights" in the same way that Goldwater had done in 1964. In 1968, in the wake of the major race riots that had convulsed almost every major city in the United States over the previous half-decade, Nixon proclaimed himself the "law and order" candidate, which allowed him to peel off blue-collar, increasingly suburban, and traditionally Democratic voters who felt alienated from the emerging, new Democratic coalition of nonwhite and aggressively progressive voters who were responsive to new values associated with the Counterculture. Moreover, Humphrey's problems with those white, more traditional Democratic voters were compounded by his being, at best, the default candidate for the new Democratic coalition that had coalesced first around Eugene McCarthy and then more enthusiastically around Robert F. Kennedy. Even more specifically, as Martin Luther King Jr. had done—though to an entirely different political purpose—Nixon linked the Civil Rights and Antiwar Movements in the public consciousness as phenomena that were fundamentally eroding faith in American social and cultural norms, American institutions, and American values.

To Humphrey's great disadvantage, the linkage that Nixon was asserting was seemingly illustrated in the streets of Chicago during the Democratic National Convention. Indeed, because the city's government had long been dominated by the Democratic political machine headed by Mayor Richard Daley, the very heavy-handed deployment of police forces to suppress antiwar demonstrations seemed to illustrate not only the broader degeneration of the political process and the threat of endemic civil disorder but also the profound fracturing of the Democratic Party itself. In much the same way that the daily coverage of the Vietnam War on the evening news broadcasts, over "color" television sets, had brought the war literally home to Americans with an immediacy and a graphicness that the black-and-white newsreels documenting past wars had not done, so, too, the much fuller coverage of the "chaos" in the streets of Chicago made many Americans just as uneasy about what was happening in their own country as they were about what was occurring in Vietnam. Even though the police outnumbered the demonstrators and the police tactics were, in retrospect, unnecessarily extremely aggressive, public opinion polls showed that most Americans were willing to give the police the benefit of the doubt. If the U.S. military itself was exhibiting many signs of war fatigue, the country as a whole was exhibiting a similar fatigue over the controversies created by the war. That eight of the organizers of the protests in Chicago would be charged with both inciting rioting and conspiring criminally to create civil disorder reinforced the notion that the Counterculture Movement and the Antiwar Movement were not just sinister phenomena but were being organized by sinister anti-American forces. That such a notion was seriously held by a minority of Americans did not mean that it was not in wide circulation and affecting opinions. That the defendants, by then known as the Chicago Seven (because Black Panther leader Bobby Seale was tried separately) were convicted only of the lesser charge of inciting a riot and not of conspiracy, and that even the convictions on inciting a riot would be overturned on appeal, did not matter in the immediate moment when so much hung in the balance politically.

As Nixon was being inaugurated, polling showed that about half of the nation expressed some confidence that his administration would find a way to conduct the war more effectively than the Johnson administration had conducted it, and a third still believed in the possibility of a decisive American victory in the war. The Antiwar Movement was still a minority movement, with only about 30 percent of those polled describing themselves as being against the war. By mid-October, however, millions of Americans in countless cities across the nation interrupted their daily lives to participate in the first national Moratorium to End the War in Vietnam. The scope of these demonstrations made it very clear that a political and cultural tipping point had finally been reached on the war. The moratorium was followed a month later by huge demonstrations in Washington, DC, and San Francisco, with the demonstration in the nation's capital attracting an estimated half a million protesters.

## THE SUMMER OF LOVE AND THE WOODSTOCK MUSIC FESTIVAL

The mainstreaming of the Counterculture can be said to have begun in the so-called Summer of Love. In the summer of 1967, several hundreds of thousands of young people from across the United States migrated toward those sections of major American cities that had become known as centers of the

Counterculture. More than 100,000 traveled to San Francisco alone, where for more than a decade the North Shore neighborhood had been a center of the Beatnik scene and a gathering place for the peripatetic poets, novelists, essayists, and spiritual seekers known collectively as the Beats. During the spring break weeks of 1967, thousands of college students had come to the Haight-Ashbury District of the city to take in the "scene," and local government officials had become so alarmed by the growing Countercultural appeal of the district that they inadvertently promoted it by issuing formal warnings that larger numbers of young visitors would not be welcomed. Then, in the late spring, Scott MacKenzie recorded "San Francisco (Be Sure to Wear Flowers in Your Hair)," a song written by his friend John Phillips of The Mamas and the Papas in order to promote the Monterrey Pop Festival. The great popularity of this song not only inspired young people from across the entire country to decide to travel to San Francisco, but also led the media to begin referring to those young people as "flower children."

In contrast with the city government, community leaders in the Haight-Ashbury District actively planned for the influx of young people—creating a Free Clinic and a Free Store, finding housing to accommodate the visitors, and organizing activities and events to engage them and thereby promote the values that local groups such as The Diggers espoused and hoped might become more widely adopted. Most young people were, of course, more interested in temporarily indulging in rebellion than in radically transforming their lives—that is, most were more interested in letting their hair grow long, in dressing like "hippies," in engaging in casual sexual relations, and in experimenting with mind-altering drugs than they were interested in "dropping out" permanently, in rejecting the material comforts and material ambitions that defined so much of late-twentieth-century American life, in committing to living "off the grid" in communal groups in which everything was shared, and in exploring their spiritual possibilities within a greatly simplified lifestyle in which all of the conventional limits to self-exploration might be more easily transcended. In retrospect, it seems a very naïve assumption that a summer spent in this way could have any sort of truly transformative impact. But the fact that a considerable number of young people did genuinely try to "drop out" and, even when that failed, made the ideals that inspired that effort a central part of their subsequent lives is a great testimony to the profound appeal of the Counterculture as an alternative to the mainstream American culture in the 1960s.

Indeed, by the end of the "Summer of Love," the permanent residents of the Haight-Ashbury District recognized that it had been permanently damaged by the "Summer of Love." No amount of planning could have been done to avoid the problems created by 100,000 young people crowding into a place to which they had no permanent connection in order to experiment, without any conventional constraints, in behaviors that would otherwise have been regarded as illicit, if not actually illegal. The district attracted all sorts of predatory types who exploited the interest in experimenting with psychedelic drugs by providing more highly addictive drugs such as heroin. The crime rates within the district began to soar as the general living conditions deteriorated. By the autumn, the permanent residents of the district were advising visitors to stay away—to find or to create in their own neighborhoods or cities what so many had been seeking in Haight-Ashbury. The irony was that many of the permanent residents of the district ultimately had to look elsewhere as well.

The most lasting cultural impact of the "Summer of Love" may have been in the "psychedelic" music that was a large part of its appeal. Much of this music was featured at the Monterey Pop Festival held in mid-June, at which such groups as The Grateful Dead, Jefferson Airplane, Quicksilver Messenger Service, The Jimi Hendrix Experience, The Byrds, and Big Brother and the Holding Company with Janis Joplin performed. In addition to Scott MacKenzie's signature song, the following songs are among those that have become closely associated with the "Summer of Love": Strawberry Alarm Clock's "Incense and Peppermints," The Turtles' "Happy Together," The Young Rascals' "Groovin'," The Mamas and the Papas' "Creeque Alley," The Young Rascals' "How Can I Be Sure," Buffalo Springfield's "For What It's Worth," The Doors' "Light My Fire," Jefferson Airplane's "Somebody to Love" and "White Rabbit," Jimi Hendrix's "Purple Haze," and The Animals' "San Francisco Nights."

If the "Summer of Love" is in many ways now remembered more for the music associated with it than as a truly transformative cultural experience, the opposite might be said for the Woodstock Music Festival. This observation is not meant to suggest that the musical performances were not memorable. Over four days in August 1969, a crowd of between 400,000 and 500,000 people gathered on a dairy farm in the Catskill Mountain region of upstate New York and listened to a somewhat improvised schedule of musical performances that included some of the most prominent groups and solo artists of the period. On Friday night, the last two performers, Arlo Guthrie and Joan Baez, who both performed after midnight, are the most likely to now be remembered. Baez closed that first night with a fourteen-song set that ended with a rendition of "We Shall Overcome." On Saturday, the first full day of performances, Santana was the most notable act to perform earlier in the day, but the last six acts were all headliners: The Grateful Dead, Creedence Clearwater Revival, Janis Joplin, Sly and the Family Stone, The Who, and Jefferson Airplane. On Sunday, every act was a headliner at the time, though The Band, Crosby, Stills, Nash, and Young, and Jimi Hendrix are probably the most likely to be remembered today, a half-century later. Joe Cocker opened the final day at 2:00 in the afternoon, and he was followed by Country Joe and the Fish. Since Country Joe MacDonald had performed on Friday as a solo act, he owns the distinction of being the only act who performed on two separate days of the festival. Between 9:00 and 11:00 on Monday morning, Hendrix closed the festival, with a sixteen-song set, performing "Hey, Joe" as an encore.

The Woodstock Music Festival was originally conceived of as a for-profit event, and close to 200,000 tickets were sold in advance. But even as those tickets were being sold, the festival organizers were having difficulty securing a site and were repeatedly assuring those who worried about the scale of the event that "only" about 50,000 people were expected to attend. In the end, of course, eight to ten times that number attended, and to no one's surprise, the available sanitary facilities, food services, and medical care were not close to being adequate for a crowd of that size. Worse, as several heavy downpours turned much of the site to mud, the general lack of shelter made the physical conditions fairly miserable for most of those in the crowd. Adding to the sense of potential disaster, the roads leading to and from the site were grossly inadequate for handling the volume of traffic, and there were serious concerns about not only how those experiencing medical emergencies might be evacuated from the site but also how the performers might be transported safely and efficiently to and from it.

But, in the end, the Woodstock Music Festival became an emblematic demonstration of the power of peace and love. Over the four days of the festivals, no felony crimes were reported. Only two deaths occurred—one involving a diabetic and one in an accident involving a tractor's being accidentally driven over a sleeping festival goer. Given the amount of conspicuous drug use, the lack of any fatal drug overdoses is astonishing and a testament to the skills and dedication of those who volunteered to provide first aid. The festival itself would have been important culturally simply because of its scope and its very improvised success, but the record album and the film that the organizers produced not only allowed them to make a profit but also ensured that the event would become one of the most iconic cultural events of the entire decade of the 1960s.

## MANSON FAMILY

Born in 1934 to an absent father and a neglectful mother, Charles Manson spent much of his childhood and adolescence living with relatives, in homes for neglected children, or in juvenile detention facilities. When he reached adulthood, he continued to add to an ever-lengthening criminal history. It is not an exaggeration to say that if he was not already incarcerated, he was being sought by law enforcement for his involvement in crimes ranging from check forgery and larceny to promotion of prostitution. By the time he was paroled for the final time in 1967, Manson estimated that he had spent half of his thirty-two years confined in juvenile detention facilities or in prisons.

Manson drifted to San Francisco just as the Hippie Movement was beginning to dominate the street life of that city. He soon gathered around him a fairly large group of young women who were attracted to the idea of a transient life free from conventional social and material expectations but nonetheless were seeking some sort of spiritual focus. These women and a few young men became known collectively as the Manson Family. Manson was a very unlikely cult leader, but his followers were as ardently attached to him as outsiders would be bewildered by his hold over them. Eventually, Manson and his followers found a home base at the Spahn Ranch, a former movie set just outside of Los Angeles.

Largely self-educated, Manson constructed and charismatically communicated a vision of the world that was a weird synthesis of random elements of Christian theology, scientology, the arcane rites of obscure sects, countercultural theories, and popular culture. One of the most notorious elements of Manson's world view was his interpretation of The Beatles' song "Helter Skelter" as a forewarning of a coming apocalyptic race war. When his attempts to

Controversies

promote himself as a songwriter and singer were frustrated, he convinced his followers that they needed to commit crimes that would be so shocking that they would exacerbate the already seething racial tensions and provoke the race war that would ultimately lead to his own emergence as a public figure singularly equipped to restore some sort of spiritual order.

On August 9 and 10, members of the Manson Family committed multiple murders at two different sites. On the night of August 9, they killed five people at the home being rented by the film director Roman Polanski and his wife, the actress Sharon Tate. Polanski was away, but Tate, who was eight months pregnant, and their friends Abigail Folger, Wojciek Frykowski, and Jay Sebring, along with Stephen Parent, who had been visiting the property's caretaker, were savagely murdered, shot, and slashed with knives, with the word "pig" left smeared on the door with the victim's blood. On the night of August 10, they killed supermarket executive Leno LaBianca and his wife Rosemary, stabbing them dozens of times with a bayonet and with knives and forks taken from the LaBiancas' kitchen. The crime was linked to the Tate murders when the killers left multiple messages on the walls, written with the victims' blood. They also carved the word "war" into Leno LaBianca's abdomen. Manson was not present for the Tate murders, and although he and Watson apparently tied up the LaBiancas before his followers murdered them, he was not actually in the house when they were murdered. The Tate murders may not have been entirely random; Manson may have been targeting a former occupant of the home who he believed had not delivered on a promised recording contract. But the LaBianca murders were entirely random.

The celebrity of the victims on the first night and the savagery of the murders, along with the seeming randomness of the murders and the escalated savagery of the murders on the second night made these crimes resonate profoundly in the affluent suburbs of Los Angeles and to become a major news story nationally and even internationally. When Manson and those who committed the murders were finally arrested, the investigation and the trial received more media attention than any crime story between the Lindbergh kidnapping in the 1930s and the O. J. Simpson murder trial in the 1990s.

In the second half of the 1960s, the Counterculture had merged into the daily, mainstream culture of America, and the effects had been convulsive. The benign expression of "flower power" had reached its apogee in the Woodstock Music Festival, but the peacefulness of that massive, spontaneous gathering stood in contrast with the violence of the race riots that were convulsing American cities and the antiwar protests that were disrupting university campuses and the cities in which they were located. To middle-aged, middle-class Americans who had grown up during the Great Depression, had entered adulthood during the Second World War, and had finally found prosperity and stability during two decades following that war, America seemed to be coming apart at the seams. The Manson murders seemed to represent the underside of the Counterculture, the inexplicable evil that could result from the complete abandonment of conventional cultural mores.

In the 1970s, revelations that the Manson Family had been responsible for less publicized murders both before and after the Tate and LaBianca murders, along with the arrest of Manson Family member, Squeaky Fromme, and the attempted assassination of President Gerald Ford, reinforced the associations of Manson's name with malevolence. In televised interviews conducted over the next several decades of his lengthening incarceration, Manson cultivated a persona that suggested his continuing capacity to project menace beyond the prison walls. Although he has lost his sway over most of his accomplices in the Tate and LaBianca murders—although most of them have eventually expressed great remorse for their participation in the murders and even bewilderment over their soulless acceptance of Manson's influence—Manson himself has remained defiantly uncontrite, his disdain for the society that has locked him away as enduring as the swastika that he carved into his forehead after his conviction for masterminding the Tate and LaBianca murders.

## MISS AMERICA PAGEANT PROTESTS, "BRA BURNING," AND THE MAINSTREAMING OF RADICAL FEMINISM

Certainly, the Women's Movement had gained considerable support and some notable media attention throughout the 1960s, but the movement was largely eclipsed by the much more visible Civil Rights and Antiwar Movements. Indeed, a group of feminists who called themselves New York Radical Women formed in the late 1960s precisely because they felt that the major social movements of the time were too dominated by men and giving too little attention to how the political and cultural issues of the period were inextricably related to women's issues. Most of the founding members of the group were in their twenties, and they began not only to speak publicly on the major issues of the day but to collect those speeches into pamphlets that were widely read and shared and very influential. As was the case with many activist groups of the period, New York Radical Women lasted only several years before its solidarity was undermined by ideological differences and its members joined other groups that more matched their evolving political views. But, despite the relatively brief period in which the group was active, it came to national attention in a manner that ensured that the Women's Movement would no longer be relegated to the background of the political and cultural tumult of the period.

In early September 1968, the New York Radical Women organized a protest at the Miss America Pageant in Atlantic City. Several hundred women showed up to demonstrate against the pageant, but a group of civil rights advocates were coincidentally protesting the event as well, and so the combined demonstrations attracted even more media attention than either one would have attracted by itself. Most of the protesting occurred on the Boardwalk outside of the hall in which the pageant was being held. But several protesters managed to get inside, to hold up a banner with the words "Women's Liberation" printed across it, and to chant the phrase a number of times before security escorted them out of the hall. The national television audience was not shown the protest and was, in fact, hardly made aware of it, but major newspapers across the country featured the wire story, including a photo of the women holding the banner, very prominently, and, literally overnight, "Women's Liberation" was transformed into a new cultural catchphrase.

Outside, the other demonstrators had gathered around a trash can with the words "Freedom Trash Can" printed down the side. Into the trash can, they tossed all sorts of items associated with the objectification and repression of women—from hair curlers and makeup to cooking utensils and mop heads. But what got the attention of the media were the girdles and bras tossed dramatically into the can. Ironically—as it turned out—the women had planned to burn the items in the trash can, but when they had applied for the permit for the demonstration, they had been told that fires were strictly prohibited on the wooden Boardwalk. But a reporter linked the feminist protest to the antiwar protests in which draft cards were often dramatically burned and referred to "bra burning," almost instantly creating yet another cultural catchphrase. Readers got the impression that the protesters had removed their bras on the spot and then had set them on fire when, in actuality, nothing quite that dramatic had actually occurred.

Somewhat lost in the focus on the "bra burning" were two send-ups of the Miss America Pageant. In addition to the trash can, the New York Radical Women had brought a sheep to the Boardwalk and crowned it, and to reinforce their description of the pageant as a meat market, one of the pamphlets that they distributed to passersby included a photo of a swimsuit contestant with her body parts marked in much the same way that butchers' posters of cows and pigs are marked to show the various cuts of meat. Less jaundiced about the concept of the pageant itself, the civil rights protesters were loosely linked to the organizers of the first Miss Black America Pageant, held in a hotel a short distance down the Boardwalk from the hall in which the Miss America Pageant was being held.

Like many of the protest movements of the 1960s, the Women's Movement provoked a backlash. For one thing, the Miss America Pageant remained very popular, and it would take a half-century before the organizers would make any sort of meaningful effort to reconceptualize it in the context of the #MeToo Movement. It turned out that, as a metaphor, "bra burning" had some confused associations. Some men and women viewed it as an extremist rejection of sexuality, while others viewed it either as being an implicitly sexually suggestive act or even as being a deliberately sexually provocative act. Although the effort to reduce feminism to "bra burning" rather quickly became a hollow trope, it nonetheless resonated with many men and women long after the actual act had become as passè as the peace-sign hand gesture.

## ORGANIZED CRIME

In the 1960s, organized crime emerged from the underside of American life and became not just an acknowledged phenomenon but a prominent part of American popular culture. The decade was bracketed by the Valachi hearings in 1963 and the publication of *The Valachi Papers* and *The Godfather* in 1967 and 1969. Although law enforcement was very ambivalent, at best, about the publication of the book, *The Valachi Papers*, by Peter Maas, reported the revelations made in a series of Senate hearings by Joseph Valachi, a mob enforcer who became the first mobster to violate very publicly the code of *omerta*, or secrecy.

*The Godfather*, written by Mario Puzo, was a novel, a work of fiction, but it drew heavily—very cleverly and credibly—on the revelations about the "Five Families" that dominated organized crime in New York City, as well as on the tabloid stories about Frank Sinatra's links to organized-crime figures and revelations about the mob's operation of Las Vegas casinos. Both best-selling books were adapted to films that were released in 1972. (It is arguable whether the tremendous critical and commercial success of the film adaptation of *The Godfather* had a positive or negative impact commercially on the film adaptation of *The Valachi Papers*, which was critically judged to be inferior.)

What we now define as organized crime developed in the 1920s during Prohibition. Although there had been criminal gangs in American cities going back to the 1850s when nativist and Irish gangs formed and competed in cities such as New York and Boston, the great sums of money to be made from the illicit importation or production and distribution of alcoholic beverages during Prohibition not only raised the stakes for the competing gangs but necessitated large increases in their membership and expansions of the rackets and the territories that they each controlled. Escalating violence between the gangs and the consolidation of the surviving gangs were inevitable.

By the early 1930s in New York City, a group of young and predominantly Sicilian American mobsters eliminated, in succession, Giuseppe "Joe the boss" Masseria and Salvatore Maranzano, who were competing to be the "boss of bosses." As an alternative, the younger mobsters formed a New York leadership group known as the Commission, which also included the heads of the Buffalo crime "family" and the Chicago "Outfit." On a national level, a more loosely organized but parallel group developed that became known as the Syndicate.

The five New York "crime families" were originally headed by Charles "Lucky" Luciano, Giuseppe "Joe" Profaci, Vincent "the Executioner" Mangano, Tomasso "Tommy" Gagliano, and Joseph Bonanno. Below the "bosses," the structure of the crime families included underbosses, "capos" who ran "crews," and "made Men" and "associates" who made up the "crews" and rose in the ranks by their ability to "earn" and their capacities for ruthless but selective violence. The Sicilian American crime "families" often had close working relationships with Jewish, Irish, and Polish American gangs—most notably the Jewish American gang headed by Meyer Lansky and Benjamin "Bugsy" Siegel in New York and the Jewish American "Purple Gang" in Detroit. But, across the United States, the Sicilian American "crime families" included many mobsters of other ethnicities as "associates."

In the Prohibition period, mobsters such as Al Capone received as much media attention as gangsters such as John Dillinger, Charles Arthur "Pretty Boy" Floyd, Lester Joseph Gillis a.k.a. "Baby Face Nelson," and Clyde Barrow and Bonnie Parker, typically referred to simply as "Bonnie and Clyde." These gangsters were primarily engaged in armed robberies, and their primary targets were banks. It is easy to see why the general public would, however, not have made much distinction between them and mobsters such as Al Capone since both groups made the most headlines when they were engaged in shoot-outs, which typically featured cars traveling at high speeds and submachine guns that produced a "hail" of bullets. It is less clear why J. Edgar Hoover, who made headlines bringing the gangsters to justice, chose largely to ignore the mobsters. It may have been that the gangsters were easier targets. In contrast, the organized- crime "families" ran much more complex operations; the "bosses" would be more difficult to "bring to justice"; and the agents working for Hoover's now widely acclaimed Federal Bureau of Investigation might have been more likely to be corrupted in investigating the organized crime, tainting the agency's carefully cultivated public image.

In the late 1940s, there was renewed attention to mob activity in cities throughout the country. In response, Tennessee senator Estes Kefauver, heading a Special Committee to Investigate Crime in Interstate Commerce, held public hearings in fourteen large cities. More than 600 witnesses would testify under oath, including many mobsters, but despite all of the attention that the hearings received, the so-called Kefauver Committee was never able to achieve its main goal of substantiating that organized crime did, in fact, have a national organization. Many of the hearings were televised, and most of the mobsters called to testify at the hearings refused to testify under their Fifth Amendment right to avoid self-incrimination. Frank Costello, then the "boss" of Luciano's "family," was an exception. He attempted to answer the questions selectively and ended up looking foolish. In the most memorable moment from all of the hearings, when Costello was asked what he had ever done for his country, he croaked the response, "Paid my taxes."

Although the Kefauver Committee ended up making twenty-two reasonable and well-received recommendations on how federal law enforcement should deal with organized crime, the hearings faded into the background, and nothing changed substantially for much of the 1950s. In November 1957, however, more than one hundred mobsters from around the country gathered at the home of mobster Joseph Barbara in Apalachin, New York. The meeting was supposed to resolve some long-standing issues among the New York "families," including conflicts arising from their competing interests in other parts of the United States and in other countries, in particular, Cuba. The meeting was also supposed to confirm Vito Genovese's position as the de facto head of the New York Commission and the national Syndicate. But when local police became suspicious about the gathering and called in state police as reinforcements, the meeting quickly degenerated into a fiasco. In the end about fifty of the more than one hundred mobsters in attendance were arrested—in many instances, ignominiously after they had tried to flee through the surrounding woods—and charged with engaging in a criminal conspiracy. Although most who were charged were convicted, those convictions were overturned on appeal. The main damage done by the event was in the intensified public demand for more attention to organized crime and in the loss of prestige of Vito Genovese.

The Kefauver hearings and the Apalachin conference brought organized crime unwanted public attention, confirming its existence, but neither event succeeded in exposing much of the workings of organized crime. The Valachi hearings, however, exposed the structure and operations of the Commission and the national Syndicate, the structure and interests of individual crime "families," the identities of the past and current leaders of those families, and the culture of being a "made man," from the rituals of induction to the penalties for committing various offenses against the code governing the behavior of everyone in the organization, from top to bottom. Beginning in October 1963, Valachi testified before the Senator John McClellan's Committee on Organized Crime, a subcommittee of the Senate Committee on Government Operations. Like many of the hearings of the Kefauver Committee, these hearings were nationally televised. Valachi was a relatively low-level member of the Genovese crime family, never rising above the level of an enforcer, but his longevity, his having been a "made man" since the formation of the Commission and the Syndicate meant that he had accumulated a great deal of inside information of the organization for which he worked, even if he had received some of that information second- or thirdhand.

One of the odd ramifications of the Valachi hearings was that New York's "Five Families" became permanently named for their bosses at the time of the hearings: Joseph Bonanno was the one holdover from the original bosses; the "family" originally headed by Charles "Lucky" Luciano became named for Vito Genovese; that originally headed by Giuseppe "Joe" Profaci became named for Joseph "Joe" Colombo; that originally headed by Vincent "the Executioner" Mangano became named for Carlo Gambino; and that originally headed by Tomasso "Tommy" Gagliano became named for Tommy "Three-Finger Brown" Lucchese.

Ironically, however, the leadership of these families was about to become even more tumultuous than it was in the 1950s, when Frank Costello was forced into retirement as head of the Luciano/Genovese "family" by an attempted assassination and Albert Anastasia was eliminated as the head of the Mangano/Gambino "family" when he was infamously gunned down in a barber's chair while getting a shave. In 1963, Joseph Bonanno failed in a scheme to take control of the Commission by assassinating Carlo Gambino and Tommy Lucchese. As a result, one of his allies, Joseph Magliocci, who had briefly headed the Profaci "family" was forced into retirement and replaced by Joe Colombo, who had exposed the plot to the other bosses. Bonanno himself was either kidnapped by his rivals or went into hiding, and the control of his family was given to several Commission-selected underbosses but contested by Bonanno's son, Salvatore "Bill" Bonanno. The conflict between these two groups became known as the "Bananas Wars." The conflict climaxed in 1968 with an extraordinarily inept attempted hit on Bill Bonanno, which involved hundreds of shots being fired without a single person being hit. In that same year, Joe Bonanno suffered a heart attack and retired with his son to Arizona, where they had long maintained second homes. Ironically, both Bonannos would publish memoirs of their time in organized crime. Joe Bonanno's *A Man of Honor* was published in 1983, and Bill Bonanno's *Bound by Honor: A Mafioso's Story* was published in 1999. Things had so changed in the decades since the Valachi hearings that these memoirs were no longer potentially fatal breaches of *omerta*.

Vito Genovese spent most of the decade in prison, and his "family" was overseen by two of his underbosses who continued their power-sharing arrangement after he died in 1969. In 1967, Tommy Lucchese died of a brain tumor, and the leadership of his "family" was somewhat tenuous until his leading underboss, Anthony "Tony Ducks" Corallo, was released from prison in 1970. Near the end of the decade, as federal pressure on organized crime intensified, Joe Colombo began developing the idea that the attention to the Mafia or La Cosa Nostra should be publicly countered as a negative stereotyping of all Italian Americans. In 1970, he would announce the formation of the Italian American Civil Rights League, organize a massive rally attended by an estimated 50,000 New Yorkers, and then, when the other bosses decided that the strategy was backfiring disastrously, be assassinated at a second, smaller rally.

While the other four New York "families" were dealing with these issues in their leadership, Carlo Gambino was consolidating his power and expanding the interests of his "family." By the time that he died in 1976, from natural causes and without ever having served time in prison, the Gambino "family' was the largest and wealthiest organized crime organization in the United States—though the "family" would go through its own convulsions with the assassination of Gambino's successor, Paul Castellano, and the much documented rise and fall of John Gotti.

Published at the end of a decade in which organized crime had received an unprecedented amount of media attention and public exposure, *The Godfather* was Mario Puzo's very deliberate effort to write a best seller and rescue his flagging career as a novelist. The novel exploits all of the insider information revealed in the Valachi hearings, and in creating a sixth New York "family" in the Corleones, Puzo provoked all sorts of speculation about who was the closest real-life model for Vito Corleone and who the other fictional bosses most resembled. Notably, Puzo's novel was much grittier in its depiction of the Corleones than the film adaptation on which Puzo would collaborate with Francis Ford Coppola. In both the novel and the film, Vito Corleone's sons are involved in the "family business," which, as Bill Bonanno's failed attempt to succeed his father illustrated, was extremely unusual in actual organized crime "families." But, in the film, there is much more emphasis on the aspects of the Corleones' family life that are (or at least were) typical of mainstream American life. Thus, the juxtaposition of the family with the "family" creates a broader thematic tension between legitimate and illicit business enterprises, as well as between conventional American values and the "code" by which members of organized crime "families" ostensibly conduct their business and personal lives. The novel was a best seller for two successive years, remaining a fixture on the list for sixty-seven consecutive weeks and selling more than 9 million copies over just those two years—or well before the film adaptation created a renewed interest in the novel. For a time, it was the best-selling novel of all time, but the novel has been so eclipsed by critical acclaim for the film that it is fair to say that the film has kept the novel in print.

## ALBERT DESALVO (1931–1973)

In the last three decades of the twentieth century, the United States would become obsessed with serial killers, real and fictional. Ted Bundy, John Wayne Gacy, and Jeffrey Dahmer would become immediately recognizable names, and films such as *Silence of the Lambs*, *Seven*, and *American Psycho* would achieve great commercial success and provoke considerable critical debate. From our current vantage point, it is easy to forget that serial killers were an anomaly in the 1960s.

Granted, Ted Bundy actually began killing in the early 1960s, and at about the same time, one of the most prolific serial killers in U.S. history, a drifter named Henry Lee Lucas also is thought to have committed the first of the 200-plus murders attributed to him. But a national database that facilitated the tracking of transient serial killers would not be established until the 1970s, and in 1974, David Meirhofer, a serial killer who preyed on children in rural Montana, would become the first serial killer whose apprehension was facilitated by the new science of criminal profiling. Meirhofer, like Ed Gein, the Wisconsin killer and grave robber, was a stable serial killer, or one whose crimes were committed in a fairly localized area. It is also worth noting that Gein inspired Alfred Hitchcock's *Psycho* (1960), which is now recognized as a landmark film and as one of the first notable serial killer films, even though the genre would not be defined for several more decades.

Another serial killer whose crimes were concentrated in a single area was the so-called Cincinnati Strangler, who raped and murdered seven elderly women in that city in 1965 and 1966. A cab driver named Posteal Laskey Jr. was convicted of one of the murders and commonly believed to have committed the others as well—largely because they abruptly stopped after his apprehension. But, with one other major exception, even localized serial killings would be uncommon—or at least go largely unrecognized—in the 1960s.

The Cincinnati Strangler case never provoked the intense and extended national media attention that the Boston Strangler case would provoke. Nor would the Cincinnati Strangler become as much a figure in the popular culture as the Boston Strangler. Nonetheless, there are some striking parallels between the cases. Most notably, in both instances, the killings abruptly stopped with the apprehension of the suspect, and the killer was never subsequently convicted of all of the killings, or even several of the killings. In the case of the Boston Strangler, Albert DeSalvo was never actually convicted of any murders. Beyond these similarities, the main difference between the two cases would be that it has been widely accepted that Laskey committed the murders in Cincinnati, but for decades, a broad range of arguments have been presented that DeSalvo was not in fact the Boston Strangler—and that many of the murders may not have been related in any way beyond their having occurred coincidentally within the same time period.

Between 1962 and 1964, thirteen women between the ages of nineteen and eighty-five were murdered in their apartments. The age range of the victims, along with significant differences in the ways in which they were murdered, made it unclear whether or not the murders were linked. In this same time period, police were also investigating a series of crimes dubbed variously as the "Green Man" and the "Measuring Man" rapes. Albert DeSalvo, whose criminal record dated back to his early adolescence but had included mostly petty crimes, was arrested for the rapes. While he was awaiting trial on those charges, he also confessed to being the Boston Strangler. Although there was no physical evidence linking DeSalvo to the murders, he knew some details about the crime that only the murderer would seemingly have known. He was convicted of the rapes and widely assumed to have committed the murders, but he was never tried on the murders.

Almost immediately, there were many skeptics, and some of them would devote considerable time and energy to developing alternative theories to the Boston Strangler case. Beyond the things that variations in the murders attributed to the strangler, some skeptics argued that it was unlikely that DeSalvo would have chosen only to rape some victims while also murdering others whom he had also raped. Furthermore, although DeSalvo seemed to have an intimate knowledge of the crimes, he also got some basic details wrong. This inconsistency led some to speculate that the murders had been committed by his cellmate, George Nassar, to whom DeSalvo had supposedly confessed but who may actually have shared details about the crimes that he had committed with DeSalvo. The skeptics included family members of Mary Sullivan, one of the strangler's last victims, whose nephew wrote a book in which he presented a very detailed argument that someone other than DeSalvo had murdered her. But, in the early 2000s, an analysis of some of the DNA evidence still in the crime files established very convincingly that DeSalvo had, in fact, raped and murdered Mary Sullivan.

It will likely never be established as definitively that DeSalvo committed all of the other murders attributed to the Boston Strangler. But his name will remain inextricably linked to the crimes. A half-century after the crimes, it seems especially paradoxical, if not ironic, that the skeptics about DeSalvo's guilt have often explained away his confession by pointing to his very obvious enjoyment of the notoriety. Likewise, DeSalvo's attorney, F. Lee Bailey, was a notorious grandstander whose efforts on behalf of his client sometimes seemed puzzling, if not dubious.

## RICHARD SPECK (1941–1991)

On the night of July 13–14, an itinerant laborer named Richard Speck broke into a townhouse that was the residence of eight student nurses working at the South Chicago Community Hospital. After tying each of them up, he spent the night tormenting, torturing, sexually abusing, and killing them, one after another. A ninth young woman who had been visiting the victims escaped Speck's notice, hid beneath a bed, and was subsequently able to provide a very accurate description of him. Once the police sketch was distributed to the newspapers and other media, Speck attempted suicide, and the physician in the emergency room to which he was taken almost immediately recognized him as the suspect in the multiple murders for whom the authorities were searching.

The scope and the brutality of the murders ensured that the case would receive national attention. It was profoundly shocking that in the midst of a crowded city, this one innocuous-looking man would not only randomly target a houseful of victims, but also be able to subdue them and then to brutalize them over a number of hours, without anyone outside the home being aware of the horrible crimes in progress inside of it. That Speck had no personal connection to his victims—that the crime seemed completely without motive—reinforced the disturbing awareness that just about anyone could be vulnerable to such violence. Speck's crimes seemed to compound the national unease following the assassination of President Kennedy. In the midst of increasing material affluence for most Americans, there were very unsettling reminders that the period of peace and prosperity was not being shared by everyone and was much more fragile than most of those who were enjoying it preferred to think.

As it turned out, of course, Speck paradoxically looked like an unlikely monster and yet had a background that made him a predictable candidate for committing monstrous acts. His father died when Speck was still very young, and his mother made a very poor choice in her second husband. Speck's stepfather, who was a heavy drinker and had a long record of petty crimes, was abusive to him. Combined with Speck's poor eyesight and his unwillingness to wear eyeglasses, his tumultuous home life ensured that he would have tremendous difficulties in school. When he dropped out of high school at age sixteen, Speck was several grades behind and had already started drinking heavily. Over the next eight years, Speck would have difficulty holding jobs, and he would have several relationships with young women that, very predictably, would be tumultuous and end badly. He began to accumulate a record of petty crimes and brief incarcerations that was similar to his stepfather's, and he began to exhibit an increasing capacity for violence. In the months immediately preceding his murders of the nurses, he likely committed at least two other murders about which he was questioned by police.

Although Speck's crimes were too horrific to be entirely forgotten, they were followed by such convulsive events—political assassinations, race riots, and the escalation of both the military involvement in Vietnam and the antiwar protests—that they receded in the public memory. In contrast to the lingering questions about Albert DeSalvo's guilt for the Boston Strangler murders, there was never any ambiguity about Speck's guilt. So, when he died in 1991, his death might have been simply a sort of historical footnote to events that occurred a quarter of a century earlier. But following Speck's death, videotapes were released showing Speck, in prison, doing drugs and engaging in explicit sex acts with other inmates. As if to give this scandalous revelation an even more lurid twist, Speck revealed that he was apparently taking female hormones that had been smuggled to him in prison and was developing secondary female sex characteristics.

## CHARLES WHITMAN (1941–1966)

At about 11:30 in the morning on August 1, 1966, Charles Whitman climbed to the deck of the tower at the top of the main building at the University of Texas at Austin and began shooting people walking across the campus in just about every direction from the tower. The rampage continued for just over an hour and a half, and in the end, Whitman had killed seventeen people and wounded thirty-one others. He himself was shot dead by two policemen who heroically made it to the tower through Whitman's fusillade and then up to the deck of the tower, where they surprised him. At the time, Whitman's rampage was the worst mass shooting in U.S. history. Indeed, even in our own period in which school shootings have become all too commonplace, Whitman's rampage still ranks as the third worst school shooting in U.S. history, with the toll in dead and wounded exceeded only by the massacres at Virginia Tech in 2007 and at Sandy Hook Elementary School in 2012. And Whitman's rampage still ranks as the eighth deadliest mass shooting at any sort of site in U.S. history. So, it is extremely difficult for us to understand the impact of this event on the American psyche.

Whitman had many of what have subsequently been defined as the hallmark characteristics of mass shooters. He grew up in a household in which his father abused both Whitman's mother and Whitman and his siblings. He was very intelligent and succeeded at a number of things that he tried as a child and adolescent, but he never really achieved any sustained success as an adult. After a beating by his father just after he had graduated from high school, he enlisted in the Marine Corps, excelling at marksmanship. He seemed ambitious, but after he received a military scholarship to study engineering at the University of Texas as a prelude to being considered for officers' training school, he was such an indifferent student that he lost his scholarship. Returning to active duty with the Marines as a noncommissioned officer, he let his gambling habit ruin any chance that he had at a career in the Marines. Returning to the University of Texas, he resumed his studies while working at a series of part-time jobs. During his initial enrollment at the university, he had married a schoolteacher whom he claimed to love deeply but whom he also admitted he had physically abused. He rescued his mother from his abusive father and brought her from Florida to Austin to live near him and his wife. Then less than two months later, in the middle of the night before he went on his rampage, Whitman killed both his mother and his wife by stabbing them through the heart while they were sleeping. In his suicide note, he reiterated his deep love for them and claimed that he had killed them to spare them any anguish in the aftermath of what he was about to do.

During the criminal investigation and then the formal government inquiry that followed the shooting, it was revealed that Whitman had been suffering from severe headaches, and in his suicide note, he himself had suggested that authorities conduct an autopsy and examine his brain. It turned out that he had a small but necrotic tumor in his brain, but experts could not agree on the degree to which it might have been a contributing cause of his actions. He had also been seeking some psychological counseling, and it turned out that with both the psychologist and with some acquaintances, he had been fairly open about his sudden feelings of uncontrollable rage. In at least several instances, he had even commented off-handedly about how someone could climb into the tower and cause a great deal of harm.

## FURTHER READING

Albanese, Jay S. *Organized Crime in America*. Cincinnati: Anderson, 1989.
Anderson, David L. *The Columbia Guide to the Vietnam War*. New York: Columbia University Press, 2002.

Altman, Jack, and Marvin Ziporyn. *Born to Raise Hell: The Untold Story of Richard Speck.* New York: Grove, 1967.
Ayton, Mel. *The Forgotten Terrorist: Sirhan Sirhan and the Assassination of Robert F. Kennedy.* Washington, DC: Potomac, 2007.
Babic, Annessa Ann. *America's Changing Icons: Constructing Patriotic Women from World War I to the Present.* Lanham, MD: Rowman & Littlefield, 2018.
Benson, Michael. *The Encyclopedia of the J.F.K. Assassination.* New York: Facts on File, 2002.
Berlatsky, Noah, ed. *The Assassination of Martin Luther King, Jr.* Detroit: Greenhaven, 2011.
Bingham, Clara. *Witness to the Revolution: Radicals, Resisters, Vets, Hippies, and the Year America Lost Its Mind and Found Its Soul.* New York: Random House, 2016.
Boyle, Brenda M., and Jeehyun Lim, eds. *Looking Back on the Vietnam War: Twenty-First Century Perspectives.* New Brunswick, NJ: Rutgers University Press, 2016.
Breo, Dennis L., and William J. Martin. *The Crime of the Century: Richard Speck and the Murder of Eight Student Nurses.* New York: Bantam, 1993.
Bugliosi, Vincent. *Reclaiming History: The Assassination of President John F. Kennedy.* New York: Norton, 2007.
Bugliosi, Vincent, with Curt Gentry. *Helter Skelter: The True Story of the Manson Murders.* New York: Norton, 1974.
Burns, Rebecca. *Burial for a King: Martin Luther King, Jr.'s Funeral and the Week That Transformed Atlanta and Rocked America.* New York: Scribner, 2011.
Campbell, W. Joseph. *Getting It Wrong: Debunking the Greatest Myths in American Journalism.* Oakland: University of California Press, 2017.
Chambers, G. Paul. *Head Shot: The Science behind the J.F.K. Assassination.* Amherst, NY: Prometheus, 2010.
Clarke, Thurston. *The Last Campaign: Robert F. Kennedy and 82 Days That Inspired America.* New York: Henry Holt, 2008.
Collins, Terry. *The Assassination of Martin Luther King, Jr., April 4, 1968.* Chicago: Heinemann Library, 2014.
Cooper, Ian. *The Manson Family on Film and Television.* Jefferson, NC: McFarland, 2018.
D'Alessandro, Jill, and Colleen Terry. *Summer of Love: Art, Fashion, and Rock and Roll.* San Francisco: Fine Arts Museums of San Francisco/Oakland: University of California Press, 2017.
De Stefano, George. *An Offer We Can't Refuse: The Mafia in the Mind of America.* New York: Faber and Faber, 2006.
Elegant, Robert S. *How to Lose a War: The Press and Viet Nam.* Washington, DC: Ethics and Public Policy Center, 1982.
Esper, George. *The Eyewitness History of the Vietnam War, 1961–1975.* New York: Ballantine, 1983.
Faith, Karlene. *The Long Prison Journey of Leslie Van Houten: Life beyond the Cult.* Boston: Northeastern University Press, 2001.
Fornatale, Pete. *Back to the Garden: The Story of Woodstock.* New York: Touchstone, 2009.
Gale, Dennis E. *Understanding Urban Unrest: From Reverend King to Rodney King.* Thousand Oaks, CA: Sage, 1998.
Gatten, Jeffrey N. *Woodstock Scholarship: An Interdisciplinary Annotated Bibliography.* Cambridge, UK: Open Book, 2016.
Gelb, Leslie H. *The Irony of Vietnam: The System Worked.* Washington, DC: Brookings Institution, 2016.
Gerdes, Louise I., ed. *Woodstock.* Detroit: Greenhaven, 2012.
Guinn, Jeff. *Manson: The Life and Times of Charles Manson.* New York: Simon & Schuster, 2013.

Hastings, Max. *Vietnam: An Epic Tragedy, 1945–1975*. New York: Harper, 2018.
Hellmann, John. *The Kennedy Obsession: The American Myth of J.F.K.* New York: Columbia University Press, 1997.
Hendley, Nate. *American Gangsters, Then and Now: An Encyclopedia*. Santa Barbara, CA: ABC-CLIO, 2010.
Hillstrom, Kevin, and Laurie Collier Hillstrom. *Woodstock*. Detroit: Omnigraphics, 2013.
Hoblin, Paul. *The Boston Strangler*. Minneapolis: ABDO, 2012.
Hoerl, Kristen. *The Bad Sixties: Hollywood Memories of the Counterculture, Anti-War, and Black Power Movements*. Jackson: University of Mississippi Press, 2018.
Hrach, Thomas J. *The Riot Report and the News: How the Kerner Commission Changed Media Coverage of Black America*. Amherst: University of Massachusetts Press, 2016.
Issitt, Micah L. *Hippies: A Guide to an American Subculture*. Santa Barbara, CA: Greenwood, 2009.
Kaiser, David E. *The Road to Dallas: The Assassination of John F. Kennedy*. Cambridge, MA: Harvard University Press/Belknap, 2008.
Kelly, Robert J. *Encyclopedia of Organized Crime in the United States: From Capone's Chicago to the New Urban Underworld*. Westport, CT: Greenwood, 2000.
Klaber, William, and Philip H. Melanson. *Shadow Play: The Murder of Robert F. Kennedy, the Trial of Sirhan Sirhan, and the Failure of American Justice*. New York: St. Martin's, 1997.
Lake, Dianne, and Deborah Herman. *Member of the Family: My Story of Charles Manson, Life inside His Cult, and the Darkness That Ended the Sixties*. New York: Morrow, 2017.
Lavergne, Gary M. *A Sniper in the Tower: The Charles Whitman Murders*. Denton: University of North Texas Press, 1997.
Levy, Peter B. *The Great Uprising: Race Riots in Urban America during the 1960s*. New York: Cambridge University Press, 2018.
Maclear, Michael. *The 10,000 Day War: Vietnam, 1945–1975*. New York: St. Martin's, 1981.
Makower, Joel. *Woodstock: The Oral History*. Albany, NY: Excelsior Editions/SUNY Press, 2009.
Manson, Charles, with Nuel Emmons. *Manson in His Own Words*. New York: Grove, 1986.
Mara, Wil. *Civil Unrest in the 1960s: Riots and Their Aftermath*. New York: Marshall Cavendish Benchmark, 2010.
McKnight, Gerald. *Breach of Trust: How the Warren Commission Failed the Nation and Why*. Lawrence: University Press of Kansas, 2013.
McLaughlin, Malcom. *The Long, Hot Summer of 1967: Urban Rebellion in America*. New York: Palgrave Macmillan, 2014.
Miller, Robert L., and Dennis Wainstock. *Indochina and Vietnam: The Thirty-Five-Year War, 1940–1975*. New York: Enigma, 2013.
Miller, Timothy. *The Hippies and American Values*. Knoxville: University of Tennessee Press, 2011.
Moldea, Dan E. *The Killing of Robert F. Kennedy: An Investigation of Motive, Means, and Opportunity*. New York: Norton, 1995.
Moretta, John A. *The Hippies: A 1960s History*. Jefferson, NC: McFarland, 2017.
Morrison, Denton E., and Carlin Paige Holden. *The Burning Bra: The American Breast Fetish and Women's Liberation*. East Lansing: Department of Sociology, Michigan State University, 1970.
Moss, George. *Vietnam, an American Ordeal*. Englewood Cliffs, NJ: Prentice Hall, 1990.
Neale, Jonathan. *A People's History of the Vietnam War*. New York: New Press, 2003.
Posner, Gerald L. *Case Closed: Lee Harvey Oswald and the Assassination of J.F.K.* New York: Doubleday, 1994.

Posner, Gerald L. *Killing the Dream: The Assassination of Martin Luther King, Jr.* New York: Random House, 1998.
Rahtz, Howard. *Race, Riots, and the Police.* Boulder, CO: Lynne Rienner, 2016.
Rogers, Alan. *The Boston Strangler.* Beverly, MA: Commonwealth Editions, 2006.
Rorabaugh, W. J. *American Hippies.* New York: Cambridge University Press, 2015.
Rosenbloom, Joseph. *Redemption: Martin Luther King, Jr.'s Last 31 Hours.* Boston: Beacon, 2018.
Sanders, Ed. *The Family: The Manson Group and Its Aftermath.* New York: New American Library, 1989.
Schulzinger, Robert D. *A Time for War: The United States and Vietnam, 1941–1975.* New York: Oxford University Press, 1998.
Sherman, Casey. *A Rose for Mary: The Hunt for the Real Boston Strangler.* Boston: Northeastern University Press, 2003.
Sifakis, Carl. *The Mafia Encyclopedia.* New York: Facts on File, 2005.
Smiley, Tavis. *Death of a King: The Real Story of Dr. Martin Luther King, Jr.'s Final Year.* New York: Little, Brown, 2014.
Sokol, Jason. *The Heavens Might Crack: The Death and Legacy of Martin Luther King, Jr.* New York: Basic, 2018.
Spector, Ronald H. *After Tet: The Bloodiest Year in Vietnam.* New York: Free Press, 1993.
Steel, Ronald. *In Love with Night: The American Romance with Robert Kennedy.* New York: Simon & Schuster, 2000.
Swanson, James L. *Chasing King's Killer: The Hunt for Martin Luther King, Jr.'s Assassin.* New York: Scholastic, 2018.
Swanson, James L. *End of Days: The Assassination of John F. Kennedy.* New York: Morrow, 2013.
Talese, Gay. *Honor Thy Father.* New York: Harper Perennial, 2009.
Udo, Tommy. *Charles Manson: Music, Mayhem, Murder.* London: Sanctuary, 2002.
Waldron, Lamar. *The Hidden History of the JFK Assassination: The Definitive Account of the Most Controversial Crime of the Twentieth Century.* Berkeley, CA: Counterpoint, 2013.
Ward, Geoffrey C. *Vietnam: An Intimate History.* Based on a Documentary Film by Ken Burns and Lynn Novick. New York: Knopf, 2017.
Wexler, Stuart. *The Awful Grace of God: Religious Terrorism, White Supremacy, and the Unsolved Murder of Martin Luther King, Jr.* Berkeley, CA: Counterpoint, 2012.

## CHAPTER 10

# Game-Changers

### THE CHICAGO SEVEN

The Chicago Seven—along with Bobby Seale, who was tried separately—were a group of activists put on trial in September 1969 for conspiracy to cross state lines to incite a riot at the 1968 Democratic National Convention. The defendants were Rennie Davis, David Dellinger, John Froines, Tom Hayden, Abbie Hoffman, Jerry Rubin, and Lee Weiner. All but Froines and Weiner were convicted of crossing state lines to incite a riot, convictions overturned on appeal.

The Chicago Seven were prominent personalities on the political left, particularly Dave Dellinger, Tom Hayden, Abbie Hoffman, and Jerry Rubin. An experienced leftist long before the advent of the 1960s, Dave Dellinger had been an activist even while in prison as a conscientious objector during the Second World War. He and others had successfully protested segregated dining halls. As a founding editor of *Liberation*, he developed contacts far beyond what other and younger 1960s radicals could muster. Though he was an advocate of the nonviolent tactic of Mahatma Gandhi, he still advocated for the protests at the 1968 Democratic National Convention.

Author of the 1962 "Port Huron Statement" that was the manifesto of the Students for a Democratic Society (SDS), Tom Hayden was influential in the organization through a number of changes in focus. Other members of the SDS didn't care for his late-1965 trip to North Vietnam, and Hayden began to focus his energies on the National Mobilization Committee to End the War in Vietnam (commonly referred to as "the Mobe") and was instrumental in organizing the protests at the 1968 Democratic National Convention in Chicago.

One of the favorite leftist activists with the media because of the stunts he pulled, Abbie Hoffman was best known for founding the Youth International Party (the "Yippies"), for a stunt at the New York Stock Exchange where he and others threw real and fake dollar bills from the gallery down onto the traders, and for telling the press and soldiers that he would levitate the Pentagon during the March on the Pentagon in October 1967.

An activist starting when he was a student at the University of California at Berkeley, Jerry Rubin became an early leader of antiwar protests against the U.S. actions in Vietnam. With Abbie Hoffman and others, he was a founder of the Youth International Party (the "Yippies") in 1967 and believed, like Hoffman, in publicity at almost any cost. Subpoenaed by the House Un-American Activities Committee, he showed up in a Revolutionary War–style uniform, telling the committee "nothing is more American than revolution."

The Chicago Seven trial was a mockery, made so both by the judge, who was openly disdainful of the defendants, and the defendants themselves, who used the trial to gain publicity for their antiwar agenda. It was a foregone conclusion, even at the time, that any convictions handed down would never stand.

## JOHN F. KENNEDY (1917–1963)

There are many ironies related to John F. Kennedy's place in history and, more specifically, his place within the history of the 1960s. The decade began with the 1960 presidential election, but his term in office, cut short by his assassination, lasted less than three years. His assassination cast a shadow over the rest of the decade and, arguably, much of the next decade, especially because its impact was compounded by the assassinations of both Martin Luther King Jr. and Robert F. Kennedy in 1968. So, although Kennedy's election to the presidency is often cited as setting the tone for the decade, with an emphasis on youthful optimism and transformative change, his assassination, which spawned more conspiracy theories than any event in history, radically reshaped many Americans—and especially many young Americans'—sense of what would be required to achieve transformative change.

By 1960, the first of the baby boomers were just in their midteens, but by the end of the decade, their generation would be providing much of the mass in most of the mass movements of the period. Most Americans were still not baby boomers, but the baby boomers were dominating just about every aspect of American life to a degree that no previous generation had ever done. The period was defined by "youth culture," and Kennedy was the youngest person ever elected to the presidency. (Theodore Roosevelt was the youngest to serve as president but he succeeded William McKinley after McKinley was assassinated and was not elected to the office in his own right until he was older than Kennedy was when he became president.) Indeed, Kennedy seemed the embodiment of youthfulness. He had served heroically during the Second World War, and he was the first person of the generation who had served in the ranks during that war to be elected to the presidency. He famously spoke of a "torch being passed to a new generation of Americans, and the physical contrast with his predecessor, Dwight D. Eisenhower, seemed as if it could not be more dramatic: Eisenhower was bald and had serious heart problems; Kennedy had a full head of hair, was tanned, and looked athletically trim. Of course, much of Kennedy's physical appeal was an illusion. For a young man, he had many serious health problems, the most significant of which were severe back problems, exacerbated by his wartime service, and Addison's disease. Ironically, the steroids administered to him to combat Addison's disease made his face look fuller and healthier than it had looked when he had run for the U.S. House and then the U.S. Senate, when he had appeared to be much more frail and even somewhat gaunt.

Kennedy's mystique depended, of course, on more than his good looks. He was part of a large, prominent, and generally appealing family. His family had been prominent in American business and politics for decades. Both of his grandfathers had been important political figures in Massachusetts politics. His father, Joseph P. Kennedy, had made millions as a stock trader and a film producer, and the celebrity that he had acquired in the process had contributed to his being named the first U.S. ambassador to Great Britain who was of Irish descent. The national attention to this appointment put the focus for the first time on the Kennedys' large brood of charming children. Kennedy's ambition was driven in part by his resentment toward the WASP establishment, but his ambassadorship became a political liability when he publicly promoted continued U.S. isolationism and even appeasement, instead of greater support for Great Britain, in response to mounting Nazi aggression. Interestingly, for his senior thesis at Harvard, John wrote an analysis of the failure of the appeasement strategy toward Nazi Germany, an analysis that, at his father's urging, he eventually turned into the book *Why England Slept* (1940). The book does not defend appeasement per se, but it does argue that it provided a necessary interim period in which Great Britain was able to arm itself sufficiently to withstand Nazi aggression. With America's entry into the conflict, both Joe Jr. and John enlisted in the military, and Joseph Jr., who had embraced his father's political ambitions for him, may have been driven to distinguish himself in combat. During a risky mission, he died when the bomber that he was piloting exploded. John, who had already distinguished himself after his PT boat had been rammed by a Japanese destroyer, became the willing agent of his father's ambitions.

In 1953, shortly after he was elected to the U.S. Senate, Kennedy married Jacqueline Bouvier, a young woman with a certain aristocratic poise, an air of sophistication, and great sense of style. Like her husband, she seemed to have an intuitive awareness of how the relatively new medium of television could be used to project accessibility while the White House actually controlled access to the first family. In many ways, Jackie became, in the minds of many Americans of the period, the epitome of what a first lady should be: it became a recurring trope of Kennedy's speaking engagements that he would claim to be almost overlooked in the midst of all of the attention that she was receiving, when, in fact, she was consistently his greatest political asset because she almost never did anything that did not reflect positively on him and that did not work to his political benefit. Moreover, it had been a long time since there were children in the White House, and when Kennedy was elected, Caroline was still a preschooler and John, known affectionately as "John-John," was born just weeks after the election. It was common knowledge that Jackie had had several miscarriages before Caroline was born, and the sympathy for her after the assassination was compounded by the public awareness that she had suffered another miscarriage earlier in that year.

In short, as the parents of the baby boomers were chasing the American Dream, the Kennedys seemed a dream family, but one humanized by an awareness that they were not immune to tragic turns of events—even before the assassination. Jackie sealed the perception of the Kennedy years as a special interlude in American history when, not long after the assassination, in an interview for *Life* magazine, she quoted the final lines of the very popular Broadway musical *Camelot*: "Don't let it be forgot,/that once there was a spot,/for one brief, shining moment/that was known as Camelot." And to ensure that no one could possibly miss the point of the analogy between their time in the White House and that highly romanticized treatment of the legends surrounding the Court of King Arthur, she added: "There'll be great presidents again ... but there will never be another Camelot." That such a conception of those years has survived myriad revelations about everything from the political calculations to the sexual infidelities of the president demonstrates that Jacqueline Kennedy understood more than most the profound and enduring power of myth-making, even in an increasingly media-saturated age—or perhaps all the more so in such an age.

In the context of such myth-making, it is perhaps not very surprising that, in public-opinion polling, Kennedy has remained one of the most remembered and most popular presidents. Yet, given the brevity of his presidency, it may be somewhat more surprising that he has continued to be judged to have been a very effective president in the fairly regular rankings of the presidents by professional historians in surveys sponsored by various media outlets and professional associations. In those rankings, Kennedy has consistently been included in the top quartile of presidents, with the latest aggregate of the rankings from 1982 to 2018 indicating that historians regard him as the tenth most effective president.

Certainly, one of Kennedy's greatest strengths was his ability to inspire Americans with expertly crafted oratory. At his inauguration, he famously called for a rededication to national service, asserting, "Ask not what your country can do for you. Ask what you can do for your country." It is not an exaggeration to say that those two brief sentences did as much as anything to make a success of the Peace Corps, in which American soft power was projected overseas through young volunteers committed to helping to meet the needs of individual, small communities in the postcolonial world. Likewise, in a speech delivered at the Rice University stadium in 1962, Kennedy proclaimed his goal of putting a man on the moon by the end of the decade in very memorable terms: "We choose to go to the moon in this decade and do the other things, not because they are easy, but because they are hard, because that goal will serve to organize and measure the best of our energies and skills, because that challenge is one that we are willing to accept, one we are unwilling to postpone, and one which we intend to win, and the others, too." Little wonder that as the network news divisions covered each rocket launch that marked progress toward this heady goal, millions of Americans stopped what they were doing and tuned in—with millions of American children being inspired in the most visceral way to study engineering and science. And, when Kennedy visited the divided city of Berlin during one of the most critical periods of the Cold War, he stirred the massive crowd by stating unequivocally, *"Ich bin ein Berliner,"* which translates as "I am a citizen of Berlin." And, in the same speech, he also observed: "Freedom has many difficulties, and democracy is not perfect. But we have never had to put a wall up to keep our people in, to prevent them from leaving us." The speech captured the pragmatic but idealistic tenor of much of the foreign policy aims that his administration pursued.

The focal foreign-policy crisis of his presidency was, of course, the Cuban Missile Crisis. After U.S. high-altitude surveillance planes had captured images of missile launch pads being constructed by the Soviet Union in Castro's Cuba, Kennedy decided to blockade the sea lanes to the island to prevent the missiles from being delivered. In a matter of days, the world came closer to nuclear Armageddon than at any time before or since. Ultimately, the Soviet Union avoided a confrontation and did not place missiles in Cuba, accepting the unpublicized American reciprocal offer to remove nuclear missiles from bases in Turkey. Kennedy's steadiness and quiet resolve during this unprecedented crisis won much-deserved admiration, especially since many of his advisers urged much more aggressive confrontational responses to the Soviet Union's attempt to create a nuclear base not just in the Western Hemisphere but in a suddenly hostile island nation just ninety miles off the southern coast of Florida. Some critics of Kennedy's foreign policy have insisted that his notable failures must also be taken fully into account—pointing, in particular, to the disastrous Bay of Pigs expedition in which anti–Castro Cuba exiles, with CIA backing, attempted to invade the island with the aim of ousting Castro's regime. But, one can also argue that Kennedy's subsequent skepticism about overly optimistic projections of military and intelligence experts very much informed his more deliberate choices during the Cuban Missile Crisis. Furthermore, just a year after the missile crisis, the Kennedy administration was able to negotiate the first Nuclear Test Ban Treaty with the Soviet Union (and Great Britain), eliminating all testing of nuclear weapons except for underground testing—that is, all atmospheric, above ground, and underwater testing of such weapons.

The two policy areas about which the tragic truncation of Kennedy's presidency has raised the most speculation are civil rights and U.S. military involvement in Vietnam. These two policy areas, one domestic and one foreign, would become the most divisive issues during the presidency of Lyndon Johnson. The Democratic support for civil rights would dramatically reshape the Democratic base, costing the party the solid base of support that it had had in the South since the Civil War. It would take decades for non-white voters to increase enough in both numbers and political engagement to offset the Republicans' advantages among white voters. Over several decades, the number of conservative Democrats and liberal Republicans would dramatically decline, making both parties more ideologically homogenous, and the long-standing regional divisions would increasingly become divisions between urban and rural voters. It would also take decades for the Republican Party to move so far to the right that suburban white voters would begin to vote Democratic in large enough numbers to make a decisive difference.

The growing opposition to the Vietnam War and Eugene McCarthy's emergence as an antiwar primary challenger in the 1968 presidential election would lead Johnson to the bitter political calculation that he could not be elected to a second term. In the longer term, the U.S. military would abandon the draft and move toward an all-volunteer force. This reconceptualization of military service was effective as long as the military was engaged in relatively brief and smaller-scale conflicts. But the post–9/11 wars in Afghanistan and Iraq have exposed the very real limitations of an all-volunteer force: the effects of repeated deployments into combat zones, with increased suicide rates among service members being only the most salient of those effects, and the disconnection between the general population and military families in terms of the impact and the personal costs of prolonged military conflicts. The efforts to create greater public awareness of this disconnection have led to a greater appreciation for the military but have not really addressed the limitations of relying on an all-volunteer force.

The impact of the Civil Rights Movement and the Vietnam War on Johnson's presidency has raised questions about whether Kennedy would have approached the issues in the same way. On civil rights, it is fairly clear that Kennedy was moving toward many of the same positions that Johnson would fully embrace. The Civil Rights Act of 1964 was introduced under Kennedy and was passed more easily because Johnson publicly framed its passage as a tribute to the assassinated president's memory and legacy. Ironically, much the same can be said for most of the domestic policy aims showcased in Kennedy's New Frontier proposals, few of which were passed during his own presidential term but almost all of which were passed, often in considerably expanded form, as part of Johnson's Great Society proposals. Nonetheless, even though Kennedy had visited Dallas in November 1963 to try to shore up his eroding political base in that state, the political implications for Kennedy might have been somewhat different for Kennedy than for Johnson—and for the Democratic Party—if the passage of the civil rights legislation had occurred during a second term of the Kennedy presidency. For, the fact that Johnson, a Southerner, stood so adamantly for the legislation was viewed by many whites in the South as a betrayal, and as effective as Johnson was as a political broker, he did not have the political charisma or some of the other political assets that Kennedy possessed.

Of course, even Johnson might have survived the political divisiveness of civil rights legislation if not for the dramatic escalation of the American military involvement in Vietnam and then the equally dramatic escalation in the public opposition to the war. Kennedy had, of course, significantly increased the number of U.S. "military advisers" in Vietnam, and although he seems to have authorized the coup against Diem, he seems also to have been genuinely shocked by Diem's assassination. Certainly, he recognized the conundrum that abandoning all of what had been French Indochina to communist governments was politically untenable but, at the same time, any war to prevent a communist takeover of South Vietnam, never mind of Laos and Cambodia, was very likely unwinnable. In January 1964, Kennedy was due to receive a thorough briefing on the political and military situation in Vietnam and the U.S. options for affecting that situation, and he was clearly intending to come to some sort of decision on that festering issue just ahead of the start of his reelection campaign. When Johnson succeeded him as the Democratic candidate in the 1964 election, the fact that his opponent Barry Goldwater was an ardent Cold Warrior meant that Johnson felt that looking weak on checking communism in Vietnam was a more immediate political liability than the possibility that the war was unwinnable. It was a poor political calculation that Kennedy, with a still fresh memory of the Bay of Pigs fiasco as a constant reminder of the risks on undue optimism, may not have made. And beyond his political charisma and his substantive accomplishments during his tragically truncated presidency, historians' persistently high opinion of Kennedy's presidency may be an acknowledgment of his considerable political skills beyond those most obvious to the voting public.

See Chapter 9 for information regarding the assassinations of John F. Kennedy, Martin Luther King Jr., Robert F. Kennedy, and several other figures.

## ROBERT F. KENNEDY (1925–1968)

During his lifetime, to the American public, Robert "Bobby" Kennedy could seem a mass of contradictions. That's because, as the 1960s progressed and American culture changed, Kennedy did, too. Not as simply a follower of cultural trends—at least, not completely—but because he grew and changed in response to new responsibilities and to the political events of the time, including such consequential events as the Bay of Pigs, the Cuban Missile Crisis, the Vietnam War, his brother John Kennedy's assassination, the Civil Rights Movement, the War on Poverty, and more. The public, though, doesn't much like it when the famous change, for a particular image of each is early settled on and movement away from it leads to confusion and dissatisfaction. So, Bobby came to be viewed with skepticism throughout most of the 1960s—right up until his own assassination when, of course, opinion about him changed completely.

Even so, there were always two sides to Bobby, the ruthless politician and the idealist leader. Often, they seemed at odds. After his brother Jack's election to the presidency in 1960, for example, journalist Murray Kempton asked Bobby if he was glad he had intervened with a Georgia judge to help get Martin Luther King Jr. released on bail (he had been arrested during a sit-in and bail had initially been refused and time on a prison work farm was threatened). "Sure I'm glad, but I would hope I'm not glad for the reason you think I'm glad" (Schlesinger 1978, 235). John Kennedy may have won the election because of the African American vote—the reason Kempton assumed Kennedy was glad. But Kennedy's feelings about his actions were more complicated, as his motivations had been at the time. He understood the political possibilities, but he acted also from a moral perspective.

This dichotomy and melding of the practical and the idealistic is central to any understanding of Bobby Kennedy as a public figure: he was a master of political manipulation and cutthroat gamesmanship, but his goal was never simply to win. He worked hard to dovetail the political and the moral but, at least not until the end of his life, he rarely publicized the moral, religious, and ethical aspects of his thinking. He had wanted King released as much because keeping him in jail was an outrage as he felt pressing for it would be advantageous politically (which it might not have been: advocating for King may have lost as many votes as it gained).

When he became active on the national political scene, working for his brother's presidential campaign, Bobby felt he needed to enunciate only one goal, Jack Kennedy's success. His role was not one of putting forth the ideas and goals of the candidate (he left that to Jack) but to making sure reaching them was possible. But the campaign did put Bobby squarely in the spotlight. As the decade passed, as Bobby assumed roles as attorney general, as senator from New York, and as a presidential candidate, he was never far from the public eye at any time during the decade—even beyond his assassination on the night of what might have proved the most important primary victory of the year. He was loved and loathed but never ignored by either the press or the American people.

Understanding that he needed to take control of his image during the pivotal 1968 Democratic primary season, Kennedy, well before he announced his own candidacy on March 16, 1968, began positioning himself as something more than an anti–Vietnam War candidate. That place, after all, had been staked out by Minnesota senator Eugene McCarthy, whose own candidacy began three-and-a-half months before Kennedy's. In fact, what Kennedy was now envisioning as a positive campaign had begun even earlier, in the wake of his brother's assassination and his own first run for office, for the Senate representing the state of New York, in 1964. The persona he presented to New York voters was of a self-deprecating almost gentle man, quite a change from his reputation as the pugnacious lawyer who had once worked for the right-wing demagogue Wisconsin senator Joseph McCarthy, who later took on Teamsters Union president Jimmy Hoffa by means that many saw as questionable, at best, and who had battled entrenched Federal Bureau of Investigation director J. Edgar Hoover while attorney general during his brother's administration.

The change might have been expected. Soon after Jack Kennedy's assassination, while speaking at the graduation ceremonies for the International Police Academy in Washington, DC, Bobby said:

> This may be the generation of rising expectations throughout the world. It may be the time when millions of people are released from the chains of ignorance, poverty, and disease which have bound them for centuries.
>
> But it is also the age of nails in the street and the plastic bomb; it is the age of arson, sabotage, kidnapping, and murder for political purposes; it is the age of hit-and-run terrorist activities coordinated on a global scale.
>
> And there is an inherent contradiction between these two conditions. (Adler, *A New Day*, 62)

That contradiction, between impetuous action and the rule of law, had long been apparent within Bobby himself. He was now learning that the idealism that had always been a part of him, but that was being brought to the fore through the personal reevaluations engendered by his brother's murder, could not be furthered by actions of anger, revenge, or immediate and unthinking response. Instead of increasing Bobby's anger at his enemies, the assassination had made him more thoughtful and restrained—and more positive in ways that the public had never seen from him. He had come to believe, as he said on October 22, 1966, during a speech at the University of California at Berkeley, that:

> Cruelty and wanton violence may temporarily relieve a feeling of frustration, a sense of impotence. But the damage of those who perpetuate it—these are the negation of reason and the antithesis of humanity, and they are the besetting sins of the twentieth century.
>
> Surely the world has seen enough, in the last forty years, of violence and hatred. Surely we have seen enough of the attempt to justify present injustice by past slights, or to punish the unjust by making the world more unjust. (Adler, *A New Day*, 74)

These are the words of a man who had been evaluating himself carefully in the wake of violence that had affected him personally and who had learned a lesson that he now wanted to share with the world.

Of course, Kennedy was in no way original in this line of thinking. Martin Luther King Jr. was already prominent in his quest to end violence, though particularly that between the races in America. Dr. Benjamin Spock, famous for his book of advice for parents, had become a national spokesperson against not only the Vietnam War but the culture of violence. Others were doing much the same. Bobby, certainly, was not a creator of the idealism of the 1960s, but he was just as certainly affected by it, made it personal, and rode it publicly. This new image for a man associated with deft and deadly political machinations created a lot of doubt about Kennedy, whose early reputation as a tough, no-holds-barred adversarial lawyer was hard to shake. A large percentage of the American public had always viewed Bobby much more cynically than they had Jack—and their opinions proved hard to change.

Not only had Bobby been the hard-charging leader of his brother's presidential campaign, but his later actions as attorney general and close adviser to the president did little to soften his image. He was actively involved in setting the grounds for the United States' ill-fated Bay of Pigs fiasco and its aftermath. He was also involved in creating responses and strategies during the Cuban Missile Crisis of October 1962 where toughness, and not compassion, was the byword—in public. Yet Kennedy was learning a pivotal lesson, that strength is not enough to resolve issues. As he wrote in *Thirteen Days*:

> The final lesson of the Cuban missile crisis is the importance of placing ourselves in the other country's shoes. During the crisis, President Kennedy spent more time trying to determine the effect of a particular course of action on [USSR leader Nikita] Khrushchev or the Russians than on any other phase of what he was doing. What guided all his deliberations was an effort not to disgrace Khrushchev, not to humiliate the Soviet Union, not to have them feel they would have to escalate their response because their national security or national interests so committed them. (Kennedy 1968, 95)

As his public pronouncements from 1964 on would show, Kennedy was soon applying this principle to almost all of his activities. Involvement at the top of the government of the United States had changed him in ways that were only ratified as he examined the world in the wake of his brother's death. He could, however, joke about his evolving views, many of which he began to express in earnest during his 1964 campaign for the Senate seat from New York. After he had won, in part as a result of his new, softer image, he quipped, knowing how cynically some viewed his change, "Now I can go back to being ruthless again" (Adler, *The Robert F. Kennedy Wit*, 114).

With his distinct Boston accent and upper-crust background, Bobby was easy to make fun of, and often was on television, radio, and even on record. Perhaps the most popular parody of Kennedy was William Minkin's version, in a Kennedy accent, of The Troggs' 1966 hit "Wild Thing." Recording as "Senator Bobby" with "The Hardly Worthit Players—Bill Menkin," Minkin saw his parody crack the top 20 on the *Billboard* chart in 1967. Minkin followed up in 1968 with "Senator Boddy" singing his version of the 1967 hit for Mitch Ryder and the Detroit Wheels "Sock It to Me, Baby." Kennedy was aware of this sort of satire concerning him but did not try to run away from it—just the opposite. Shortly before his assassination, Kennedy recorded a skit for the popular *Smothers Brothers Comedy Hour* with Tommy Smothers and Pat Paulson, who was involved in his own (fake) campaign for president. Though already scheduled to run, it was pulled after Kennedy's death.

Kennedy had long been known for an acerbic and often understated wit. Once, for example, during a campaign rally at the University of Pennsylvania in April 1968, he said, "I have a speech which it is my responsibility to give, and you have a responsibility to listen to it." After a pause, he continued, "And if you finish before I do, let me know" (Adler, *The Robert F. Kennedy Wit*, 38). Few in his audience likely caught the joke. Most of his jokes appeared almost as throwaway lines, and it sometimes took his listeners a great deal of time to get the punchlines.

On the other hand, there was always something about Bobby that seemed to portend tragedy. In his privately printed 1969 book *R.F.K. (1925–1968)* the poet Robert Lowell wrote "Doom was woven in your nerves, your shirt,/woven in the great clan." Hindsight gave a new appreciation for Bobby Kennedy to a nation, even to people like Lowell, who had not supported his presidential campaign. In death, Bobby became better loved than ever he was in life.

## GEORGE WALLACE (1919–1998)

At forty-one when the 1960s began, George Wallace was a Circuit Court judge and a politician who had lost the 1958 Democratic primary for Alabama governor. He was completely unknown outside of the state and would remain almost as much so even after being elected governor in 1962. That soon changed when he tried to stop two African Americans from enrolling in the University of Alabama. On June 11, 1963, he stood in front of Foster Auditorium, where registration was taking place on the Tuscaloosa campus until ordered to move aside by a National Guard general.

Though now at the forefront of resistance to desegregation and with a suddenly nationally known name, Wallace had not been nearly as ardent a segregationist in the 1950s as many other southern politicians. He had decided, after his 1958 loss, that the path toward political success in Alabama lay in overt appeal to racism. In 1962, he made resistance to civil rights a centerpiece of his campaign and managed to win a plurality in the Democratic primary and a majority in the subsequent runoff. With no Republican opponent, he won the November election by receiving almost every vote cast.

The incident, called by Wallace's supporters "the stand at the schoolhouse door," accomplished nothing for the proponents of segregation aside from providing them with a new leader. Wallace made sure he continued to be in the headlines over the following days through a series of telegraph exchanges with President John Kennedy. Though he was himself inciting resistance, he told Kennedy the president had "full responsibility . . . for preserving peace and order on the campus." In a subsequent telegram, Wallace wrote, "It is extremely unfortunate that you . . . do not have a better understanding of the situation which you have created." Wallace blamed the situation on the African Americans: "a continuous cause of the tension in Alabama is the presence of the three Negro students . . . and I suggest that you immediately secure their withdrawal." Wallace's continuing pugnacious attitude made him a hero to racist whites not only in the South but across much of the country.

Apologists for Wallace have long argued that his appeal was more populist than racist, but the fact that it was directed primarily at white voters (at least during the 1960s) belies that suggestion, though this is a distinction that is still used by politicians wishing to galvanize white voters without appearing outright racist. Wallace certainly held populist beliefs, some of them drawn from Louisiana's Huey Long, a governor and senator who was killed in the 1930s, but there's little doubt that he based his political career in the 1960s on championing segregation.

No doubt to capitalize on his newfound fame, Wallace decided to enter the 1964 Democratic primaries, challenging President Lyndon Johnson. He surprised the president's primary surrogates with strong showings in a number of places, including the northern states of Wisconsin and Indiana. However, when the Republicans nominated Barry Goldwater, support for Wallace quickly dried up. In fact, he folded his campaign on July 19, just three days after the end of the Republican National Convention. Seeing the enthusiasm for Goldwater, Wallace was shrewd enough to recognize that 1964 just was not his year.

At the time, Alabama was one of the few states where a governor could not run for reelection, so Wallace, in 1966, stepped aside for the candidacy of his wife Lurleen, who easily won the election. Less than halfway through her term, however, she would die of cancer—in May 1968 during Wallace's next run for the presidency.

Running on his own American Independent Party ticket in 1968, Wallace won five states (all from the former Confederacy) for forty-six electoral votes. In all, almost 10 million Americans voted for Wallace, 13.5 percent of the total votes cast. Though he would run for president, again as a Democrat, in 1972, Wallace's campaign then would be effectively ended by an assassination attempt that left him paralyzed from the waist down. Thus, 1968 represented the high-water mark of Wallace's national aspirations.

Wallace did not expect to win the election but knew he could succeed in enough states in the Deep South (following the Strom Thurmond pattern of 1948) to keep either the Republican or the Democrat from reaching an Electoral College majority, throwing the election to the House of Representatives. As it turned out, of course, Richard Nixon earned enough electoral votes on his own to assure his ascension to the presidency. Thus, Wallace's hope of being able to determine the presidency in return for concessions to his agenda (particularly opposition to desegregation) was shattered. However, he had shown Republicans that the once "solid south" of the Democratic Party was now up for grabs.

From a strong start, Wallace's support declined throughout the fall 1968 campaign, in part because of shrewd decisions by Richard Nixon undercutting his support by advocating positions similar to Wallace's but not quite as extreme and by union support for Humphrey that drew many members back to the Democratic fold.

In addition, Wallace made the mistake of choosing retired Air Force General Curtis LeMay, a right-wing hawk, as his running mate. LeMay believed that nuclear weapons should be a usable part of the American military arsenal. One of the tactics used against Barry Goldwater four years earlier was accusation that he might be too willing to use nuclear weapons, something most Americans distrusted. The early parts of the decade, especially right after the Cuban Missile Crisis when people were advised to create fallout shelters, learn to "duck and cover," and take other precautions against nuclear attack, had created a strong reaction against even the suggestion of use of nuclear weapons. Though Wallace, with his populist and racist stance, struck a chord with quite a few white Americans, LeMay's belligerent suggestions of the use of nuclear weapons—even in Vietnam—was a step too far.

## MARTIN LUTHER KING JR. (1929–1968) AND THE CIVIL RIGHTS MOVEMENT

For three-quarters of a century, racial segregation was institutionalized throughout almost all of the United States. In the Deep South and "border" states, the Jim Crow statutes made the segregation more formalized and blatant than it was in other parts of the country, but the resurgence of the Klan in the 1920s and its dramatic expansion into the Midwest, where it was for a time treated as if it were the equivalent of a fraternal organization, demonstrated that racism was not only prevalent but also widely accepted as a social, economic, political, and cultural norm.

In the mid-1950s, a series of events created momentum for the development of a broad-based movement to assert and to ensure equal rights for African Americans. In 1954, the U.S. Supreme Court issued a landmark decision in the case of *Brown v. Board of Education* (of Topeka, Kansas), which struck down the very dubious premise that racially segregated public schools were "separate but equal." In 1955, Emmett Till, an African American teenager falsely accused of talking suggestively to a white woman in a grocery store, was abducted and brutally murdered while visiting relatives in Mississippi. When his body was returned to Chicago, his mother decided to have an open casket so that everyone could see exactly what had been done to him, and a local hate crime became a national news story. In 1955, Rosa Parks was arrested for refusing to give up her seat in the "colored" section of a bus to a white passenger because the whites-only seats were full. Parks's act of civil disobedience inspired the Montgomery bus boycott, which lasted for over a year and led to a Supreme Court ruling that segregation on public transportation is unconstitutional. And in 1957, when nine African American students were accepted into the previously all-white Central High School in Little Rock, Arkansas, they were blocked from entering the school by crowds of protesters, who were encouraged by Governor Orval Faubus's deployment of the National Guard to prevent desegregation. Ultimately, President Eisenhower had to call out units of the 101st Airborne Division and to federalize the Arkansas National Guard to enforce the integration of the schools.

After his graduation from Crozer Theological Seminary and while he was completing his doctoral work in theology at Boston University, Martin Luther King Jr. accepted a position as pastor of the Dexter Avenue Baptist Church in Montgomery, Alabama, in 1954. A year later, following Rosa Parks's arrest for her defiance of the Jim Crow laws, King became one of the organizers of the Montgomery bus boycott, and this public activism brought him not just to regional attention but also to some national notice. In the late 1950s, he became one of the founding members of the Southern Christian Leadership Conference (SCLC). Unlike the NAACP, the SCLC initially did not initiate actions intended to advance civil rights but, instead, attempted to support efforts that had started organically in communities. The SCLC emphasized nonviolent resistance, but it was not a passive resistance; rather, the strategy was to provoke confrontations that would force the opponents of civil rights to overreact, exposing their viciousness to public scrutiny and turning public opinion toward support of civil rights. The SCLC was a loose association of African American religious congregations and church leaders, and it successfully linked the promotion and protection of Christian values to the promotion and protection of African American civil rights. Influenced by the very popular and influential crusades of the white evangelist Billy Graham, King not only adopted some of Graham's techniques, but he also forged linkages with Graham and other prominent white religious leaders.

The nonviolent strategies adopted by the SCLC were generally very effective, but they were challenged in the late 1950s and early 1960s by a spectrum of leaders critical of King's approach. These critics included: NAACP renegade Robert F. Williams who organized African American militias to provide armed self-defense against attacks by white supremacist groups such as the Ku Klux Klan; Malcom X who as a spokesperson for the Nation of Islam advocated segregation and militancy to preserve African American culture against the oppressive influence of white European culture; and Stokely Carmichael, who began his activism with the SCLC but developed into a militant advocate of racial separatism and Pan-Africanism, eventually associating himself with the Black Panther Party. That King's advocacy of nonviolent confrontation ultimately prevailed over these alternative beliefs and strategies is a testament to his personal qualities of leadership and his ability to inspire sympathy and support across a broadening spectrum of demographic and political groups.

In the late 1950s and the early 1960s, African American groups in a number of cities not only in the Deep South but also in the southern Plains states began to conduct sit-ins to force the integration of diners and other restaurants. The most famous of these sit-ins occurred in February 1960 at the lunch counter of the Woolworth's in Greensboro, North Carolina, by four students from the North Carolina Agricultural and Technical College, a historically black college. As the sit-ins became more widespread, the tactics became more refined, and the African Americans were often joined by representatives of allied white groups and white college students.

These same groups joined African American activists from the northern states in the "Freedom Rides" of 1960 and 1961. Traveling in buses, the "Freedom Riders" gathered supporters along the routes they traveled from one city to another across the South. The first "Freedom Ride" caravan set out from Washington, DC, and headed toward New Orleans. In a number of locations, white supremacists blocked the way, damaging the buses to the point where they could not be operated and seriously injuring many of the riders. Hundreds of "Freedom Riders" were arrested in Mississippi, and because they refused to pay the fines imposed on them, they were subjected to very harsh jail conditions and were often brutally tormented and beaten. Although it is widely remembered that the "Freedom Riders" succeeded, in spite of the violent opposition of segregationists, far fewer Americans will be able to identify that the purpose of the "Freedom Rides" was to end the segregation of interstate transportation, and few will understand in any vivid sense the terrible experiences endured by many of the "Freedom Riders" in support of the cause.

The "Freedom Rides" led to the development of the "Freedom Movement" across the South. At its core an effort to register African Americans to vote and to negate all of the mechanisms of Jim Crow that were designed to prevent them from voting, the "Freedom Movement" inevitably became an economic, as well as a political, cause, in part because African Americans had more immediate economic power than political power and in part because white supremacists often tried to retaliate economically against African Americans engaged in political activism—even to the extent of simply registering to vote. The "Freedom Movement" came to a climax in 1964, with the so-called Freedom Summer, during which thousands of activists from the northern states, including many idealistic college students, traveled to the South to assist in the voter registration efforts. The civil rights and voting rights legislation that President Kennedy had finally agreed to support had stalled in Congress in the aftermath of his assassination. "Freedom Summer" would make the passage of that legislation inevitable, though not in the way that its organizers anticipated. The calculated murders of three civil rights activists—James Chaney, Andrew Goodman, and Michael Schwerner—by KKK members, some of whom turned out to be members of local law enforcement, brought to a head the issues related to institutionalized segregation and the denial of full civil rights to peoples of color. At a pivotal political moment, the murders of Chaney, Goodman, and

Schwerner would be burned into the national conscience and the national memory. Their highly publicized murders provoked a degree of outrage that a century of lynchings and often brutal racial oppression had ironically failed to provoke.

This activism continued throughout the 1960s, as did the violence. Particularly noteworthy were the marches from Selma, Alabama, to the state capital of Montgomery, to protest the suppression of civil rights and voting rights of African Americans in Selma. On a Sunday in March 1965, thereafter remembered as "Bloody Sunday," police and white supremacists attacked marchers, killing several of them and seriously injuring many others. But the discontent led to the passage of much legislation meant to counter and reverse entrenched racism: most notably the Civil Rights Act of 1964, the Voting Rights Act of 1965, and the Civil Rights Act of 1968.

At key points during the history of the Civil Rights Movement in the 1960s, Dr. King produced statements that not only inspired his followers and attracted new followers but that defined the Civil Rights Movement as one of the most transformative political, socioeconomic, and cultural movements in U.S. history. These statements changed a fragmented effort to assert the rights of marginalized peoples into a defining test of the American character.

In 1963, King was arrested in Birmingham during an effort to desegregate the city's downtown business district. From his jail cell, he wrote "Letter from Birmingham Jail" in response to the criticisms of other African American clergymen who questioned the tactics and the timing of the protests. The letter includes this often quoted passage: "We know through painful experience that freedom is never voluntarily given by the oppressor; it must be demanded by the oppressed. Frankly, I have yet to engage in a direct action campaign that was 'well timed' in the view of those who have not suffered unduly from the disease of segregation. For years now I have heard the word 'Wait!' It rings in the ear of every Negro with piercing familiarity. This 'Wait' has almost always meant 'Never.' We must come to see, with one of our distinguished jurists, that 'justice too long delayed is justice denied.'"

In August 1963, Dr. King was the keynote speaker of the March on Washington. In front of the Lincoln Memorial, he delivered his "I Have a Dream Speech" to the crowd of 200,000–300,000 marchers gathered on the Capitol Mall. The speech, which has become almost as prominent in the canon of great American speeches as Lincoln's "Gettysburg Address," includes many moving passages but, perhaps none more moving than this passage: "I have a dream that my four little children will one day live in a nation where they will not be judged by the color of their skin but by the content of their character. I have a dream . . . I have a dream that one day in Alabama, with its vicious racists, with its governor having his lips dripping with the words of interposition and nullification, one day right there in Alabama little black boys and black girls will be able to join hands with little white boys and white girls as sisters and brothers." In another less often quoted but moving passage, King echoes his "Letter from Birmingham Jail": "We have also come to this hallowed spot to remind America of the fierce urgency of now. This is no time to engage in the luxury of cooling off or to take the tranquilizing drug of gradualism. Now is the time to make

One of the most iconic moments of the 1960s was Martin Luther King Jr.'s "I Have a Dream" speech during the March on Washington, August 28, 1963. (Bettmann/Getty Images)

real the promises of democracy. Now is the time to rise from the dark and desolate valley of segregation to the sunlit path of racial justice. Now is the time to lift our nation from the quicksands of racial injustice to the solid rock of brotherhood. Now is the time to make justice a reality for all of God's children."

And, in April 1968, on the evening before he was assassinated in Memphis, Dr. King gave his "I've Been to the Mountaintop" speech at the Mason Temple in Memphis, where he had come to support a strike of the city's sanitation workers. In the speech, he recalls in detail, the events in 1963 that had led to his being jailed in Birmingham, and the speech closes with this prescient response to the current threats to his life: "Well, I don't know what will happen now. We've got some difficult days ahead. But it really doesn't matter with me now, because I've been to the mountaintop. And I don't mind. Like anybody, I would like to live a long life. Longevity has its place. But I'm not concerned about that now. I just want to do God's will. And He's allowed me to go up to the mountain. And I've looked over. And I've seen the Promised Land. I may not get there with you. But I want you to know tonight, that we, as a people, will get to the promised land! And so I'm happy, tonight. I'm not worried about anything. I'm not fearing any man! Mine eyes have seen the glory of the coming of the Lord!"

Not surprisingly, given the origins and makeup of the Southern Christian Leadership Conference, the Civil Rights Movement's most pervasive representation in the popular culture was in music—in the songs sung by performers who were themselves activists and by more ordinary supporters, very often when they were facing down the intimidation of segregationists or law enforcement that had been directed to enforce Jim Crow statutes. That the Civil Rights Movement defined itself in both spiritual and political terms is reflected in the fact that the songs most associated with it were known as both "civil rights hymns" and "civil rights anthems." Indeed, a large percentage of the dozens of songs associated with the movement were originally spirituals, which were adapted to emphasize the cause of racial equality and to facilitate their being sung by large groups. The most enduringly significant of these songs were "We Shall Overcome" and "A Change Is Gonna Come," but other very popular songs included "Ain't Gonna Let Nobody Turn Me 'Round," "Certainly Lord," "Go Tell it on the Mountain," "Hold On," "Hymn to Freedom," "I Love Everybody," "If You Miss Me at the Back of the Bus," "I'm Gonna Sit at the Welcome Table," "I Woke Up This Mornin'," "Keep Your Eyes on the Prize," "Lift Every Voice and Sing," "Oh, Freedom," and "This Little Light of Mine." Two other songs, "If I Had a Hammer" and "We Shall Not Be Moved," were originally labor songs and were eventually adapted to multiple causes, demonstrating how in the popular culture and in popular perception, if not always in a more pragmatic way, the disparate economic, social, and political movements melded into a broad phenomenon that became known as the Counterculture.

Not surprisingly, the Civil Rights Movement has also become the topic of a fairly large number of documentary and feature films. Some of the documentary films appeared in the midst of the ongoing events in the 1960s: *Crisis: Behind a Presidential Commitment* (1963), *Nine from Little Rock* (1964), *The March* (1964), *Louisiana Diary* (1964), and *Cicero March* (1966). *King: A Filmed Record . . . Montgomery to Memphis* would be released in 1970, and other documentaries have continued to appear regularly over the half-century since Dr. King's assassination. In contrast, it would be almost two decades after his assassination before the first major feature film about the Civil Rights Movement would appear—*Mississippi Burning* (1988), which focuses on the FBI investigation of the murders of Chaney, Goodman, and Schwerner. Subsequent significant feature films have included *The Long Walk Home* (1990), *Malcolm X* (1992), *Ghosts of Mississippi* (1996), *Selma, Lord, Selma* (1999), *The Rosa Parks Story* (2002), *Freedom Song* (2006), *The Butler* (2013), *Selma* (2014), and *All the Way* (2016). The most important feature film of the 1960s to treat racial issues in the Deep South did not address the Civil Rights Movement directly. *In the Heat of the Night* (1967) stars Sidney Poitier as Virgil Tibbs, a Philadelphia police homicide detective who is visiting family in Mississippi and is coerced into helping a Mississippi sheriff, named Gillespie and played by Rod Steiger, to solve the murder of a northern businessman who was building a much-needed factory in the small town of Sparta. In a manner that still resonates very powerfully today, the film lays bare all of the ingrained racial assumptions that underlie prejudice. Indeed, that scenes such as the one in which Tibbs is slapped in the face by the biggest landowner in the area and slaps him back still have considerable shock value suggests the impact that the film had when it was released just over a half-century ago, when the Jim Crow South was officially being legislated into history but, in actuality, was still a very immediate and pervasive presence in many communities.

## JOHN WAYNE (1907–1979)

By the 1960s, John Wayne had become one of the most iconic figures in the history of American popular culture, a film star whose appeal far transcended his rather limited range as an actor and whose influence extended well beyond the entertainment industry and into both contemporary politics and broader discussions about the American national mythos and the American national character.

John Wayne's film career began in the late 1920s, when he appeared in twenty films as an extra or in small speaking roles. In fact, he often served in other capacities on these film sets. In his first billed acting role in *Words and Music*, a 1929 film that, with the advent of sound, was one of the first musicals, Wayne was identified as "Duke Morrison." He apparently sang in that film. In the 1930s, Wayne would actually star in several "singing cowboy" Westerns, but in each of those cases, the singing was dubbed.

Wayne's first starring role came in *The Big Trail* (1930), which was directed by Raoul Walsh. Because it was an expensive, projected blockbuster that bombed at the box office, it did not launch Wayne's career as he might reasonably have expected it to do. For most of the rest of the decade, Wayne was in demand but as a lead in B-Westerns and action-adventure serials. In 1931, he appeared in six films; in 1932, nine films; in 1933, twelve films; in 1934, nine films; in 1935, eight films; in 1936, seven films; in 1937, five films; in 1938, four films; and in 1939, six films. The range of the roles that he was offered was so limited that his roles in several films as union organizers and boxers are somewhat noteworthy. But his most unusual role during this period came in *The Deceiver* (1931), a crime drama in which Wayne plays the corpse of the main character, Reginald Thorpe. When the background to the murder is shown in extended flashback scenes, Thorpe is, however, played by Ian Keith.

Wayne's breakout role came in 1939 in the John Ford–directed Western *Stagecoach* in which Wayne plays the Ringo Kid, who has escaped from prison in order to avenge the murders of his father and brother; on a stagecoach ride from Arizona Territory to Lordsburg, New Mexico, he helps fight off attacks by Apaches and falls for a prostitute who also needs to find a more responsible and respectable life. Yet, despite the critical and commercial success of *Stagecoach*, it was the war films that Wayne made from the mid-1940s through the late 1950s that firmly established his stardom and his persona as an American hero. These films include *Flying Tigers* (1942), *The Fighting Seabees* (1944), *Back to Bataan* (1945), *They Were Expendable* (1945), *Sands of Iwo Jima* (1949), *Operation Pacific* (1951), *Flying Leathernecks* (1951), *The Sea Chase* (1955), and *The Wings of Eagles* (1957).

During late 1940s and the 1950s, Wayne also, of course, returned to the Western, teaming with major directors to make some of the most highly regarded films not just in the genre but of the immediate postwar decades. The first of these films, *Red River* (1948), and the next to last, *Rio Bravo* (1959), were directed by Howard Hawks. The others were directed by John Ford: *Fort Apache* (1948), *3 Godfathers* (1948), *She Wore a Yellow Ribbon* (1949), *Rio Grande* (1950), *The Searchers* (1956), and *The Horse Soldiers* (1959).

It was also during the postwar decade that Wayne demonstrated that his increasing stardom was not accompanied by any increasing range as an actor. Indeed, one especially ill-chosen project seems, in retrospect, to have showcased his limitations as an actor. In *The Conqueror* (1956), Wayne attempts to portray Genghis Khan in the years when he was coming to prominence and power, and the performance is so wooden and culturally disconnected that one almost has the sense that Wayne is deliberately parodying his film persona, which he was not. The film is included in almost every list of awful films, but it has also achieved a lasting notoriety because it was filmed in Utah at a site directly downwind of the above-ground nuclear test site in Nevada and approximately 40 percent of its cast were subsequently diagnosed with cancer. Unintentionally compounding the risks, Howard Hughes, who produced the film, even had tons of dirt shipped from the site in Utah to the Hollywood lot where the rest of the filming was done. Still, at least in the case of Wayne himself, it seems difficult to argue that his lung cancer was not just as likely to have been caused by his cigarette smoking, which peaked at six packs per day during the filming of *The Alamo*, about a half-decade before he had a lung removed. A strange detail in Hughes's own very strange personal saga is that *The Conqueror* was apparently one of the films that he watched repeatedly, in a continuous loop, in his very reclusive and disturbed final years. It is a reflection of just how iconic a figure Wayne became that this sort of story continues to be circulated and to resonate.

Wayne began the decade of the 1960s with the release of *The Alamo*, the first film that he not only starred in but produced and directed. The production would place such a strain on him that it would be the only film that he ever attempted to direct solo. The film had very high production values. A complete replica of the Alamo, built to three-quarters scale of the historical site, was constructed, and the film was nominated for Academy Awards in multiple technical categories. But, overall, it received a very mixed critical response, and although it drew large audiences, the high cost of its production meant that it was not very profitable. Moreover, the film was panned by historians for its many historical inaccuracies, and none of the stars, with the possible exception of then teen star Franky Avalon, would include it among their most noteworthy screen credits.

*The Man Who Shot Liberty Valance* (1962) would be Wayne's most notable Western of the decade. It is the last of his films to be shot in black-and-white and, with the exception of the sprawling saga *How the West Was Won* (1962), it is the last Western in which Wayne was directed by John Ford. In the film, Wayne plays a rancher who is good with a gun and secretly saves the lawyer who steals his girlfriend's heart. The lawyer, played by Jimmy Stewart, rides the notoriety from having supposedly gunned down Liberty Valance into a long political career and an equally long and satisfying marriage. In contrast, Wayne's character and what he represents pass from the scene much less dramatically but just as decisively as Liberty Valance exited.

Throughout most of the 1960s, Wayne would make Westerns that paired him with notable costars and that reworked the elements of the Westerns that he had made over the previous two decades. These films include *The Comancheros*

(1961), *McClintock!* (1963), *The Sons of Katie Elder* (1965), *The War Wagon* (1967), and *The Undefeated* (1969). One of Wayne's films of the 1960s, *El Dorado* (1966), is a fairly shameless remake of *Rio Bravo* (1959) redeemed only by the star power of Wayne and his costars. Despite the fact that the films were unapologetically formulaic, if not simply redundant, they were consistently popular—indeed, even more popular than the films of the late 1940s and the 1950s that they were echoing.

For twenty-five straight years, from 1949 to 1974, John Wayne was ranked in the top ten box office draws. Clint Eastwood ranks second in total years on the list, with twenty-one years, but no one has come close to Wayne's consistent popularity. That popularity is evident in his rankings throughout the 1960s: he ranked second on the list in 1963, 1965, and 1969; fourth on the list in 1961, 1962, 1964, and 1968; seventh in 1966; eighth in 1967; and tenth in 1960. Even though Wayne was not the top box office draw in any single year during the 1960s, IMDb lists Wayne as the top money-making star of the decade.

*True Grit* (1969) would end the decade that began with *The Alamo* on a decidedly higher note. Wayne would receive his only Academy Award for his portrayal of a one-eyed, drunken marshal named Rooster Cogburn. But the award clearly falls into the category of those that recognize the cumulative work of a long and remarkable career, rather than a singularly outstanding performance. Certainly, Wayne's starring role in *The Searchers* (1956)—his portrayal of Ethan Edwards, an ex-Confederate soldier and a real hard case who sets out on an unrelenting quest to find a niece kidnapped by Comanches—is now widely recognized as his most compelling performance. Moreover, some of his other performances in major Westerns released in the late 1940s and the 1950s can, arguably, be ranked above his performance in *True Grit*. Indeed, his performance in his final film, *The Shootist* (1976), in which he portrays John Bernard Brooks, an aging gunfighter who is dying of cancer and chooses to go out in a gunfight, is quieter but also much more nuanced than the larger-than-life, if rough-around-the-edges character that he plays in *True Grit*. But it is a testament to Wayne's iconic stature that the Motion Picture Academy felt that he deserved the Best Actor Oscar, rather than an Academy Honorary Award typically given to major stars who have not received a Best Actor or Best Actress Award.

Wayne's war films of the 1960s followed the opposite trajectory of his Western films. In 1962, he was one of the many major stars who participated in the making of *The Longest Day*, arguably the most notable film about the U.S. forces in the European theater of the Second World War up to that time and since, with the exception of *Saving Private Ryan*. Wayne has a larger role than most of the stars in the film, playing Lieutenant Colonel Benjamin Vandervoort, who led paratroopers in the airborne landings that preceded the assaults on the Normandy beaches on D-Day. Ironically, due to a leg injury suffered during the parachute drop, Wayne's character spends almost all of his time on screen being hauled around on a cart. That Wayne manages to make such a potentially ridiculous situation into a demonstration of hard determination and heroic perseverance is a testament to the force and solidity of his screen persona.

At the opposite end of the decade and at the opposite end of the spectrum in terms of Wayne's legacy is *The Green Berets* (1968). Like *The Alamo*, it was a project dominated by Wayne, although he delegated some of the directing to Ray Kellogg. When the film was conceived, the U.S. involvement was escalating, and the film was intended to frame the war, culturally and politically, in the same sort of lens through which Wayne had memorialized the heroic sacrifices made by Americans during the Second World War. But by the time the film was released, the nation was in the midst of an increasingly contentious presidential election, and the Tet Offensive had both undermined the official pronouncements about the aims and progress of the war and had given great impetus to the antiwar movement. For most younger viewers, *The Green Berets* was as anachronistic as it was jingoistic. Indeed, elements of the film seemed designed to emphasize how anachronistic it was: specifically, Wayne was too old and overweight for the role of someone leading a Green Beret company in combat; the film was made on locations in the American South that bore no resemblance to the tropical forests and rice farms of South Vietnam; and the film seemed a catalogue of character types commonplace in war films, down to the orphan adopted as a sort of mascot by the American troops, who is devastated by the combat death of his father figure. (In this last respect, *The Green Berets* borrows very heavily and very obviously from *55 Days at Peking*, which was released five years earlier.)

In the late 1960s, Wayne became a more overtly political figure, making controversial public statements not just on the war but on the genocide against Native Americans—justifying the conflicts by the need for land and decrying the "selfishness" of the Native Americans in attempting to keep it all for themselves—and on civil rights—asserting his acceptance of white supremacy and asserting that African Americans should demonstrate that they were "responsible" as a precondition for gaining full political rights. A former member of the John Birch Society, Wayne promoted himself as a lifelong crusader against communism, making no distinction between it and socialism and denouncing them as equally antithetical to American values. That Wayne expressed these opinions straightforwardly and unapologetically to some degree simply reinforced his entrenched public persona. But, the fact that Wayne's most objectionable views and remarks are now largely forgotten may simply be the result of timing. In the early 1970s, Wayne was diagnosed with stomach cancer and became a figure of widespread public sympathy as he contended with the disease—a sympathy that *The Shootist* entrenched in the public consciousness. Wayne's persistently large presence in the American cultural mythos probably derives from his public persona's not becoming inextricably linked to and even transformed by his reactionary cultural and political views, much as Charlton Heston's public persona would be.

## FRANK SINATRA (1915–1998)

In the mid-1940s, Frank Sinatra became the first teen heartthrob, first as featured singer with the big bands of Harry James and Tommy Dorsey and then as a solo artist. The teenaged girls of the period, known as bobby soxers, screamed, swooned, chased after him, and tore at his clothing—behaving in ways that prefigured Elvis's sexualized appeal and Beatlemania, though the memory of Sinatramania had faded enough over the intervening decade or two that it all seemed new again.

After the Second World War, Sinatra's appeal declined, in part because of rumors around the deferment that had allowed him to avoid military service during the war. He found himself singing in small venues in out of the way places, and for a time, he even had vocal issues. He reemerged in the public spotlight, with a critically acclaimed role in the film adaptation of *From Here to Eternity* (1953), James Jones's best-selling novel about Pearl Harbor in the days just ahead of the Japanese attack. He followed that performance with other notable roles in films that included *Guys and Dolls* (1955), *The Man with the Golden Arm* (1955), *Pal Joey* (1957), and the film adaptation of another James Jones's novel, *Some Came Running* (1958). That film was the first to feature the "Rat Pack," a group of Sinatra's friends who performed improvisationally at the Sands Hotel and Casino in Las Vegas. The group included Dean Martin, Sammy Davis Jr., Peter Lawford, Joey Bishop, and others. Along with Sinatra's "scandalous" affair and stormy marriage with Ava Gardner, the antics of the Rat Pack made Sinatra one of the most widely known celebrities of the era.

In the 1950s, Sinatra, who had lost his contract with Columbia Records at the start of the decade, signed on with Capitol Records and began a long and prolific collaboration with the conductor and arranger Nelson Riddle. From 1954 to 1962, Sinatra released sixteen critically acclaimed and commercially successful albums. Most were characterized by what Sinatra himself described as saloon ballads and torch songs. With albums such as *In the Wee Small Hours* (1955), *Songs for Swingin' Lovers* (1956), *Come Fly with Me* (1958), and *Frank Sinatra Sings for Only the Lonely* (1958), Sinatra not only resurrected his singing career but established himself as a mature artist with an enduring appeal.

So, at the start of the 1960s, Frank Sinatra was arguably the most popular and most acclaimed performer in the United States. In 1961, he left Capitol Records and founded his own recording label, Reprise Records. Although he gradually broadened his recordings to appeal to shifting musical tastes, the albums that he released in the 1960s remained true to his musical roots, critically appreciated, and commercially successful. From *Ring-a-Ding-Ding* (1961) to *Sinatra's Sinatra* (1963), to *September of My Years* (1965) and *A Man and His Music* (1965), to *That's Life* (1966), *Strangers in the Night* (1966), and *My Way* (1969), there was hardly a false note. Sinatra's recordings with Count Basie (1964), with Antonio Carlos Jobim (1967), and with Duke Ellington (1968) were regarded, and are still regarded, as landmark events.

As in the 1950s, Sinatra remained a fixture on network television throughout the 1960s. His son's kidnapping in 1963 and his relatively brief marriage to the much younger actress Mia Farrow (1966–1968) kept Sinatra's name in the news and in the tabloids. Likewise, Sinatra's very public support for the presidential candidacy of John F. Kennedy included his recording of the campaign's theme song, and his prominence as a performer and celebrity seemed to have gained him an insider's access to political power. But when Robert F. Kennedy became attorney general and began an aggressive campaign against organized crime, Sinatra's long association with various mobsters and his acquaintance with such mob leaders as Sam Giancana made him a political liability and led to his being ostracized from the Kennedys' circle, a slight that he never quite got over.

Ironically, one of Sinatra's best performances on film would be in *The Manchurian Candidate* (1962), which concerns the communist brainwashing of a young man from a prominent political candidate who is captured during the Korean conflict and becomes a preprogrammed assassin who targets a presidential candidate. Adapted from a Richard Condon novel, the film was initially released in the midst of the Cuban Missile Crisis, and for obvious political reasons, its release was limited. Then, after it had received favorable reviews and had been nominated for several major awards, its rerelease was ostensibly derailed by the assassination of President Kennedy. Or at least that was the story that got the most traction. Later film historians have noted that the film was being shown in some theaters in the weeks and months immediately following the assassination, and they have suggested that the film may simply have not found a wider or more persistent audience. Regardless of the actual facts, the film gradually became something of a cult classic, in part because of its association with the Kennedy assassination.

In the 1960s, Sinatra remained a successful film actor, starring in nineteen feature films. In 1960, the "Rat Pack" improvised its way through the film most closely associated with it, *Ocean's Eleven*, and in 1964, the group came together again for *Robin and the 7 Hoods*. Sinatra continued to find roles in war films, most notably *Von Ryan's Express* (1965). And in the last half of the decade, he gave several notable performances in detective films—as the private detective Tony Rome in both *Tony Rome* (1968) and *The Lady in Cement* (1968) and as police detective Joe Leland in the film adaptation of Roderick Thorp's novel *The Detective* (1968).

By the end of the 1960s, Sinatra had become a truly iconic figure not just in the United States but worldwide. Nonetheless, although his career was to have several more iterations in the 1970s and 1980s, the 1960s marked the end of his period of greatest productivity and achievement. Indeed, the end seemed even more abrupt at the time than it does now. In 1970, his concept album *Watertown* sold very modestly, and the film *Dirty Dingus Magee* was critically panned. Sinatra felt that popular tastes had simply changed too dramatically for him to remain relevant, and so he announced his retirement at a 1971 concert. The retirement did not last, but Sinatra would star in only one more film, the crime drama *The First Deadly Sin* (1980), and although he would release seven more albums of new material, those releases would stretch over more than two decades.

## ELVIS PRESLEY (1935–1977)

If Elvis Presley had disappeared from public attention or had passed away prematurely at the end of the 1950s, he would still be remembered as a major figure in the popular culture of that decade. His impact as popularizer of rock-and-roll music and as a major influence on the youth culture emerging in the postwar years would have ensured his continuing significance. His first four albums all reached number one on the Billboard charts. *Loving You* (1957) was certified as a Gold Record; *Elvis Presley* (1956) and *Elvis* (1956) were certified as

Platinum Records; and *Elvis' Christmas Album* (1957) was certified as a Multi-Platinum Record (3X). Moreover, although his fifth album, *Elvis' Golden Records* (1958), peaked at number three on the Billboard charts, it was certified as a Multi-Platinum Record (6X). Equally impressive were Elvis's singles sales: he had five number one hits in 1956, four in 1957, two in 1958, and another in 1959. (In the last two years of the decade, his output was limited by his much publicized military service.) In the 1950s, variety shows were one of the mainstays of television programming, and one can make the argument that Elvis's appearances, in quick succession in the middle of 1956, on some of the most popular variety shows of the decade—*The Milton Berle Show*, *The Steve Allen Show*, and *The Ed Sullivan Show*—brought rock and roll into the mainstream of American popular culture. Even as those appearances provoked a strong backlash, on the one hand, from those who condemned the music as vulgar and, on the other hand, from those who dismissed the music as noise, the ratings that Elvis's television appearances garnered made it inevitable that the music and its most popular performers would get a full hearing in the mass media.

In 1992, the U.S. postal service announced its intention to issue a postage stamp commemorating Elvis Presley's contributions to American popular culture, and it made the unprecedented decision to allow the public to choose between two Elvis stamps, almost immediately dubbed the "Young Elvis" and the "Old Elvis" options. Whatever significance this poll has in the history of our popular culture, it cemented the notion that Elvis's career had two distinct phases: in the first phase, he was a young and spontaneous revolutionary force, and in the second phase, he was a bloated, near-caricature of his younger self—an iconic figure reduced to a lounge act, a revolutionary figure who had sold out his talent to sustain a lifestyle characterized by excessive material consumption and by self-indulgence that often amounted to self-delusion. What this view of Elvis's career overlooks is most of the decade of the 1960s, during which Elvis's successes as a recording artist and a film star gave him a stature that most rock-and-roll stars have never reached and, very arguably, cumulatively gave him an iconic stature that has given his rise and fall much more complexity and resonance than most stories of meteoric success and self-destructive excess.

In the 1950s, Elvis did make four films: *Love Me Tender* (1956), *Loving You* (1957), *Jailhouse Rock* (1957), and *King Creole* (1958). It is important to note that the marketing of Elvis as a film star occurred in tandem with his becoming a major recording artist; it was not, as has often been suggested, a direction that his career took after his popularity as a recording artist—or, more precisely, his status as a ground-breaking recording artist—began to wane. It is easy to overlook the popularity and the impact of Elvis's films. None of the films was ever going to be nominated for an Academy Award, and Elvis himself was never given much room in his roles to develop beyond the level of an instinctive acting ability. Eventually, he seems to have given up on trying to earn legitimacy as an actor, and he started to very conspicuously ham it up on screen. Nonetheless, in its list of the highest-earning film stars of the 1960s, IMDb ranks Elvis number nine—behind John Wayne, Doris Day, Elizabeth Taylor, Cary Grant, Rock Hudson, Jack Lemmon, Paul Newman, and Julie Andrews, and ahead

Though Elvis no longer dominated the music charts in the 1960s, he was the single most influential figure of the decade's pop and rock genres. (Bettmann/Getty Images)

of Sean Connery, Sandra Dee, Lee Marvin, Steve McQueen, Sidney Poitier, and Jerry Lewis. From 1961 to 1966, Elvis was ranked in the top ten box office draws, ranking fifth in 1962, sixth in 1964 and 1965, seventh in 1963, and tenth in 1961 and 1966. In 1960, 1961, and 1963, he made two films in each year. In 1962, and 1964 through 1969, he made three films in each year. His continuing popularity as a major film star extended his appeal well beyond his original, largely teenaged audience, and it ensured that when he reemerged as a stage performer in the late 1960s, he had sustained a level of popularity and celebrity that made him much more than the typical retro-act. In sum, his film career ensured that he didn't lose his audience as it matured and that he actually attracted more fans beyond his base audience.

Many of the albums that Elvis released in the 1960s were the soundtracks from his films, though it is worth noting that not every film was accompanied by an album. These soundtracks are now often dismissed as schlocky forays into other musical styles, but the albums were as commercially successful as the films—arguably even more successful. Three of the fifteen soundtrack albums from the decade reached number one on the Billboard charts, and nine of the fifteen were top ten albums. Eleven of these albums were certified as Gold Records, two were certified as Platinum Records, and one, *Blue Hawaii*, was certified as a Multi-Platinum Record (3X). In that album, Elvis moves as far from his rockabilly roots as he does in any of the soundtrack albums.

It is undeniable, however, that by the late 1960s, both Elvis's musical career and his film career had stagnated at a moderate level of success that suggested that his career was in decline. So, in 1968, Elvis simultaneously returned to live performances for the first time since the early 1960s and made a major foray into television with the broadcast of an intimate performance in front of a small audience in Burbank, California. Commonly referred to as Elvis's *'68 Comeback Special*, the performance featured Elvis dressed in black leather. Although Elvis performed many of his hit songs, the performance had an undeniable freshness and force. The special was NBC's top-rated show of the year, arguably approaching the impact of Elvis's performances on the variety shows of the mid-1950s. The soundtrack of the television special became Elvis first top ten album in several years, and the special set the stage for the hit singles that he released the next year, "In the Ghetto" and "Suspicious Minds," which would be his last number one single, and the critically acclaimed album *From Elvis in Memphis*, which would be certified as a Gold Record.

The *'68 Comeback Special* would be followed by a series of live performances in much larger venues, most notably the Houston Astrodome. Elvis would also begin performing regularly in Las Vegas casinos, where the black leather outfit of the *'68 Comeback Special* segued into white sequined jumpsuits modeled on the outfits worn by the flamboyant stuntman Evel Knievel. Likewise, the return to his musical roots in the *'68 Comeback Special* would be followed by an increasing tendency to turn his own hits and songs that he chose to cover into big-production numbers in which certain lyrics were punched up for effect and every gesture seemed to become a practiced mannerism. Off stage, Elvis's personal behavior and relationships would become as much a staple of the tabloid newspapers and magazines as the press releases about him had become staples of the teen fan magazines of the 1950s. His very bizarre visit to Richard Nixon's White House would become, in retrospect, just one salient indication of his increasingly eccentric behavior. And, of course, following his premature but predictable death, the focus of the tabloid media would simply shift to propagating the endless rumors that his death was some sort of a ruse and that he had been sighted living a largely anonymous existence in every conceivable corner of the world. His former wife, Priscilla, his former fiancée, Linda Thompson, and his daughter, Lisa Marie, would also become the subjects of endless innuendo and speculation, a circumstance very much exacerbated by Lisa Marie's brief and dumbfounding marriage to Michael Jackson.

However successful Elvis's career as a performer was when he was alive, it has been superseded in many respects by his success since his death. When Elvis died, it was estimated that he had sold about 250 million records. It is now estimated that more than a billion of his records have sold worldwide. The catalogue of his recordings, which now includes live recordings and all sorts of other recordings recovered from his personal vaults, has expanded almost exponentially, with each landmark anniversary of his death seemingly becoming the occasion for some new multidisk repackaging of his hits or some genre-defined selection of his recordings. Because some of his early albums and singles preceded the formal designation of Gold and Platinum certifications of the sales of recordings, the bookkeeping on his catalog has been reviewed and brought up to date, with the result that more than 110 of his albums and singles have been certified as Gold or Platinum records—beyond those so designated at the time of his death.

The sales have been paralleled by the gradual but steady transformation of his home, Graceland, into not just a tourist attraction but a self-contained resort—invested with much of the grandeur of a national monument. Graceland has consistently attracted more than 500,000 visitors a year, and each year it contributes more than $150 million to the economy of the city of Memphis. Not only has the Presley estate fed the mania for all things Elvis by very systematically auctioning off all sorts of Elvis memorabilia, ranging from individual canceled checks to private jets, but it has also selectively and shrewdly marketed his name and likeness on a variety of products. Although it is true that all celebrities have public personas that conceal aspects of their actual personalities, this truism becomes especially applicable to iconic celebrities. And this truism is more applicable to Elvis than to any other iconic figure in the history of American popular culture. If the relatively simple country boy from Tupelo, Mississippi, became swallowed up and even lost within the celebrated performer created and carefully managed by his Colonel Tom Parker, then even that public persona has subsequently become swallowed up since his death in his transformation into a folk figure of very outsized proportions and necessarily caricatured attributes. He is a late twentieth century's version of Paul Bunyan, who sometimes indulged his whims by flying across the continent to procure and to consume gargantuan, grilled sandwiches filled with bacon, bananas, and peanut butter.

## THE BEATLES

Among the iconic entertainers covered in this section of the book, The Beatles are the only ones to achieve iconic status in the decade and to be associated almost entirely with the decade. The band lasted just a little more than a decade, forming in 1960 and disbanding in 1970. But the period of their actual influence is even shorter, from 1963 to 1970, and in that short period of time they not only transformed American and Western popular music and popular culture, but they did so by transforming themselves multiple times and in astonishingly rapid succession.

The Beatles were originally a bar band playing clubs in working-class Liverpool and for a time in Hamburg, Germany. From the beginning, the band played a considerable variety of genres of popular music. Beyond being influenced by American rock and roll and rhythm and blues, as well as British and American pop music, they played scuffle. Originally a form of what is now called American traditional or American roots music, scuffle was often played on simple and even homemade instruments, and it freely blended elements of folk, bluegrass, gospel, blues, and jazz. In the 1950s, this freewheeling style of music became something of a rage in the United Kingdom, especially among young musicians.

By 1962, the members of The Beatles had become fixed, with drummer Ringo Starr joining the three original members—Paul McCartney, John Lennon, and

George Harrison. McCartney and Lennon would collaborate in writing the majority of the band's songs, but Harrison would also become a very talented songwriter. Beyond the obvious complementary talents and cohesion of the group, their rise to international stardom was facilitated greatly by their manager Brian Epstein and their record producer George Martin. In 1963, the group had its first hit singles in the United Kingdom, where the nickname "The Fab Four" and the cultural term "Beatlemania" were coined. In 1964, they appeared on American television and performed live in the United States for the first time, becoming the leading edge of what would become known as the "British Invasion" of American popular music. Although their two appearances on *The Ed Sullivan Show* received somewhat mixed reviews, their first appearances attracted 73 million viewers, at the time the highest number of viewers for any television broadcast, and the second appearance attracted just a slightly smaller audience of 70 million viewers. In addition, their three concert dates were sell-outs, with the crowds including large numbers of clearly enraptured teenaged girls. The Beatles "mop top" haircuts were referred to condescendingly, if not dismissively or derisively, by many older commentators on the popular culture, but to young people, the hairstyles seemed fresh and even daring—even though in the matter of just a few years, the "look" of "early" Beatles would begin to seem cleanly groomed. The core paradox of The Beatles would remain their ability to seem, at once, irrepressibly upbeat, astonishingly experimental, unapologetically true to their own vision and values, and able to accommodate both the conventional and the radical without compromising either for the sake of the other.

Although The Beatles achieved tremendous success before they disbanded as a group in 1970 and had a tremendous impact on the popular culture of the 1960s, their enduring popularity and influence has been at least as remarkable. Their albums have remained available even as various compilation sets of their 217 recorded songs have been released. To date, the group has sold more than 800 million copies of their albums worldwide, making them the best-selling musical artists of all-time. More than 175 million copies of their albums have been sold in the United States alone. In total, they released seventeen studio albums in the United States. All seventeen of those albums went Platinum in the United States alone, with fourteen of the seventeen albums reaching number 1 on the Billboard charts. (The only three albums not to reach number 1 are *Introducing . . . The Beetles*, their first U.S. album, *Something New*, their fifth U.S. album, and *Yellow Submarine*—all of which reached number 2 on the Billboard charts.) *Abbey Road* went 12x Platinum; *Sgt. Pepper's Lonely Hearts Club Band*, 13x Platinum; and *The White Album*, an astonishing 19x Platinum. In total, The Beatles released sixty-three singles, twenty of which hit number 1 on the Billboard Hot 100 charts—a record that still stands.

The Beatles' first two albums included a mix of original songs and covers of other hit songs. On the first album released in the United States, *Introducing . . . The Beatles* (1963), which had been released in the United Kingdom as *Please, Please Me*, the most notable songs aside from the title song are "I Saw Her Standing There" and "Love Me Do." On the second album released in the United States, *The Beatles Second Album* (1963), which had been released in the United

Kingdom as *With the Beatles*, the most notable original song was "All My Loving." The first album to consist entirely of original songs would be *Hard Day's Night* (1964), which, in addition to the title song, includes "And I Love Her" and "Can't Buy Me Love." *Hard Day's Night* would be The Beatles' first feature film, and the album featured the soundtrack for the film on side 1 and other recordings on side 2. The same format would apply to *Help!* (1965), the album released with the group's second film, which was loosely conceived as a spoof of the James Bond espionage films. In addition to the title song, the album is notable for the songs "Ticket to Ride," "You've Got to Hide Your Love Away," and "You're Gonna Lose That Girl," all written by Lennon and McCartney, as well as "I Need You," written by George Harrison.

The Beatles' next album, *Rubber Soul* (1965) marked a considerable shift from their previous albums, all of which had featured fairly conventional pop songs focused on romantic relationships. Although *Rubber Soul* did include the romantic ballad "Michelle," it also included songs such as "Norwegian Wood," "Nowhere Man," and "In My Life," which anticipated the more psychedelic sound and vignette-like content that became a more striking characteristic of the later albums. The increasing experimentation in The Beatles' songwriting was even more strikingly apparent in *Revolver* (1966). Indeed, some critics have claimed that this album had a more transformative influence on the music of the period and more broadly on the developing notion of a Counterculture than either *Sgt. Pepper* or *The White Album* had. Some have even argued that *Revolver* stands as a more effectively integrated album than either of those more acclaimed albums. The album certainly shifts fluidly among a range of styles, from the more driving rock of "Taxman" and "Got to Get You into My Life" to the more fanciful rhythms of "Eleanor Rigby," "Good Day Sunshine," and "Yellow Submarine."

The Beatles' concerts had become stadium-sized events, and although they were both very popular and profitable, The Beatles became increasingly frustrated by the fact that they themselves could hardly hear the music they were playing and were tired of the inescapable media attention to and often frenzied intrusion by fans into just about every aspect of their lives on tour. By the end of 1966, they decided to stop touring and to focus on recording. Certainly, they had reached a level of international popularity that the touring was no longer necessary to drive record sales, and, in fact, their decision to stop touring ended up making the release of each new album into a media event as big as any concert that they had ever played.

With the release of *Sgt. Pepper's Lonely Hearts Club Band* (1967), The Beatles transcended pop stardom and achieved an iconic stature that has endured well beyond the period of their greatest relevancy. The album was an immediate sensation, spending fifteen weeks at number 1 on the Billboard chart and becoming the first rock album to win the Grammy award for Album of the Year. It has remained continuously available in its original format, and it has sold more than 30 million copies worldwide. Given the limiting four-track recording available at the time, the album was immediately lauded as an astonishing technical achievement because the band had painstakingly overlaid tracks to create an amazing density of musical elements and very unusual combinations of sounds. Moreover, the scope of the technical achievement was all the more amazing because, more often than not, the effects were very subtle and precise, rather than extravagantly showcased. In every respect, the parts of the album were made to serve the intention for the whole. The aim was to reconceptualize the album as more than a collection of singles—as, instead, a fully integrated work that itself had the structure of a well-constructed but in some ways delightfully unconventional song. The album became a touchstone work of psychedelic music, but it freely incorporates not only a broad range of rock styles, but also elements of source genres such as blues and jazz, of music hall tunes and circus music, of classical compositions, and of avant-garde experiments with atonality, as well as samplings of the very different tonal registers characteristic of North African and South Asian music. Even though "With a Little Help from My Friends" and "Lucy in the Sky with Diamonds" would be recorded as singles by other artists, and even though "A Day in the Life" stands out as a masterful piece of songwriting, it is telling that The Beatles chose not to release as singles any of the songs on this album.

If anything, the emphasis on psychedelia was even more pronounced on the next album, *Magical Mystery Tour* (1967). Conceptually, the album seems to have been modeled on Ken Kesey's Merry Pranksters who, three years earlier, had become Counterculture celebrities by taking a literal and LSD-fueled road trip in a psychedelically painted bus that they had named *Further*. Like *Hard Day's Night* and *Help!*, the album was part soundtrack and part a collection of previously released singles and new songs that had not found a place on other albums. Besides the title song, the album includes "Penny Lane" and "Strawberry Fields Forever," which had been released as the two sides of a hit single ahead of *Sgt. Pepper* and then left off that album. It also includes "The Fool on the Hill," "I Am the Walrus," "Hello, Goodbye," "Baby, You're a Rich Man," and "All You Need Is Love." Because so many of the songs on the album have been so memorable, some critics have argued that *Magical Mystery Tour* is not just a better album than *Sgt. Pepper* and *The White Album* but actually a more cohesive album. But the best evidence that that opinion remains a minority view is that on the fiftieth anniversaries of the albums' original releases, special anniversary editions of both *Sgt. Pepper* and *The White Album* were released, but not of *Magical Mystery Tour*.

Some of those who believe that *Sgt. Pepper* is overrated, especially in comparison to *The White Album* have argued that *Sgt. Pepper* may be historically and culturally more significant but *The White Album* is musically more transcendent. They have argued that, as a double studio album, *The White Album* has much more range and substance than *Sgt. Pepper* and risked creating more opportunities for missteps. Much has been written about how The Beatles exasperated each other and George Martin with the obsessive ways in which they reworked the smallest elements of each song until there seemed a very real danger that a sense of the integrity of the individual songs, never mind of the whole project, was being sacrificed. The group would never quite be the same after finishing this album, but that they had anything at all left to produce that was worthwhile may actually be a further testament to their collective talents.

For all of the obsessive tinkering, *The White Album* has a less polished and more spontaneous feel than *Sgt. Pepper*. It includes edgy rock songs with psychedelic elements, such as "Back in the U.S.S.R.," "Glass Onion," "Piggies," "Helter Skelter," "Revolution 1," and "Revolution 9." At the opposite extreme are songs that seem send-ups of silly pop songs, even while drawing on earlier folk and popular forms—songs such as "Ob-La-Di, Ob-La-Da," "The Continuing Story of Bungalow Bill," "Rocky Raccoon," and "Birthday." In between those two extremes are songs such as "Happiness Is a Warm Gun," "Why Don't We Do It in the Road," and "Everybody's Got Something to Hide Except Me and My Monkey," in which there is more underlying wit than pure silliness. Songs such as "Dear Prudence," "Blackbird," "Sexy Sadie," and "Savoy Truffle" are immediately recognizable as Beatles' songs and might have appeared on any album since *Revolver*. And "Why My Guitar Gently Weeps" has become a rock standard, a singularly great song that nonetheless fits seamlessly into a great album.

*Abbey Road* (1969) has the basically same mix of songs as those on *The White Album*, but one suspects that if it had not been preceded by *The White Album*, *Abbey Road* would have been perceived as more disjointed than even some critics have found it to be. For instance, it is hard to imagine three songs more different in style than the three most well-known songs on this album written by Harrison, Lennon, and McCartney: Harrison's "Something," Lennon's "Come Together," and McCartney's "She Came in through the Bathroom Window." Likewise, the shifts among the last four songs on side 1 from "Maxwell's Silver Hammer' to "Oh, Darling" and then from "Octopus' Garden" to "I Want You (She's So Heavy)" seem simply to be jarring rather than purposeful. It seems telling that side 2 seems more tonally coherent than side 1 is.

The Beatles' final album, *Let It Be* (1970), is remembered almost entirely for the title song, often described as Paul McCartney's response to Simon and Garfunkel's "A Bridge over Troubled Waters." It is indicative of the dissipation of the band's energy and commitment that two sides of the album end with versions of "Get Back," a single that was released in the year before the album's release. It is also indicative that in addition to "Let It Be," the most well-known song from this final album is "The Long and Winding Road." Although the breakup of the band has been much bemoaned, The Beatles had a much longer run, much more consistent success, and arguably much greater musical influence and more significant and enduring cultural impact than any other musical group of the period. And there were obvious signs that the creative tensions that accounted for their success were becoming festering conflicts that were undermining their collective creativity. That each one of The Beatles would find renewed inspiration, creative freedom, and commercial success as solo artists has often been viewed as a sort of extended epilogue to their decade together. But that seems as simplistic a view of their careers as blaming John Lennon's relationship with Yoko Ono for the breakup of The Beatles.

## MUHAMMAD ALI

Muhammad Ali was not only the greatest boxer and one of the greatest athletes of the twentieth century, but he was also one of the major figures in the popular culture of the century, not just in the United States but internationally. When he fought George Foreman in Zaire, Ali was embraced across the continent of Africa as much more than a celebrated athlete. He was embraced as an iconic figure who had come to represent the aspirations of people of color worldwide.

Ali was born in 1942 to a working-class family in Louisville, Kentucky, which until he was already an adult remained a racially segregated city. Although descended from slaves, at least one of whom became a heroic figure lauded by abolitionists, he was named for his father who had been named for a well-known segregationist politician named Cassius Clay. From a young age, he seems to have had a visceral resentment of any suggestion that his race made him in any way inherently inferior. When he was just twelve years old, Ali, who suffered from severe dyslexia, began boxing, and over the next half-dozen years, he would compile an amateur record of 100–5. He won six Gold Gloves titles in Kentucky and two National Gold Gloves titles. His career as an amateur climaxed at the 1960 Summer Olympics in Rome, where he won the gold medal boxing as a light heavyweight.

Following his Olympic success, Ali turned professional, as a heavyweight. Over the next three years, he compiled a record of 19–0, but although fifteen of the wins were by knockout, the quality of his opponents was questioned—especially by commentators who found his public persona to be very off-putting. Although Ali had a very unusual style for a heavyweight, combining very fast hands with being very quick on his feet, he became more widely known for running his mouth, freely touting his own skills and denigrating his opponents, very often in insulting personal terms. He later revealed that he had modeled his insufferably overconfident public persona after that of the professional wrestler known as Gorgeous George. In any case, his performances in some of his early fights did not seem to justify his overconfidence. He was knocked down twice, and in his eighteenth and nineteenth fights, he won an unimpressive decision over the number 2 contender Doug Jones and beat veteran British champion Henry Cooper after opening a bad cut over Cooper's eye, just a round after Cooper had knocked him flat and he had clearly been saved by the bell from being counted out.

So, as Ali entered his first bout against heavyweight champion Sonny Liston, he was a heavy underdog. Liston was a very menacing figure—a hard man from a hard background who had worked as a bouncer and an enforcer for people commonly believed to have underworld associations. His recurring run-ins with law enforcement reinforced the impression that he was a thug, albeit one with considerable boxing skills. He was a heavy puncher, and he had had certainly paid his dues as a fighter before winning the championship by knocking out Floyd Patterson in a title bout and then in a rematch. Indeed, even after his two unexpected defeats to Ali, Liston would continue to be ranked among the top heavyweights of all time. Ali won their first fight when Liston quit after six rounds, and he beat him in the second fight when he caught him with a short right a little more than two minutes into the first round. Because the result of the second fight was even more unexpected than that of the first, there was immediate speculation that Liston had thrown the fight, especially because it was not obvious to ringside observers that Ali had even hit him with a punch. And although analysis of the film of the fight showed that the "phantom punch"

After converting to Islam and changing his name from Cassius Clay to Muhammad Ali, the champion boxer was stripped of his heavyweight title for refusing to cooperate with the military draft. (Bettmann/Getty Images)

was a misrepresentation, many remained unconvinced that the punch had been capable of knocking out Liston.

After defeating Liston and winning the world championship, Ali had publicly been admitted to the Nation of Islam and had legally changed his name from Cassius Clay, his "slave name," to Muhammad Ali. The controversy that this decision created has been somewhat lost in that which surrounded his decision in 1966 to declare himself a conscientious objector and to refuse induction into the U.S. armed services. But his being a member of the Nation of Islam was enough to provoke several state boxing boards to revoke his license to fight and for some promoters to avoid his fights. Between November 1965 and March 1967, he would successfully defend his title eight times, with the second through fifth of those title defenses occurring either in Canada or Europe. If there had been any doubts about Ali's worthiness as a champion, those eight fights put them decisively to rest. The first of the title defenses came against Floyd Patterson, for whom Ali had tremendous respect. The fifteen-round fight ended with a TKO in the twelfth round, and many observers felt that Ali had been determined to avoid inflicting any serious damage on Patterson. In striking contrast, in the next to last of these fights, Ali seemed determined to extend the fifteen rounds against Ernie Terrell to their fullest length simply so that he could inflict as much punishment on Terrell as possible. Terrell had pointedly insisted on referring to Ali by his birth name, and it was obvious that Ali's usual prefight denigration of his opponent had taken on a real edge. Of the eight title defenses, Ali's win over Cleveland Williams in the sixth fight is generally considered to be one of his most thoroughly dominant performances against a legitimate opponent. Following as it did on Ali's demolition of Terrell, his last defense against Zora Foley has been as largely forgotten as Foley himself.

In 1967, Ali was convicted in a jury trial of draft evasion, but he was released on bail as his case went forward on appeal, until it was eventually appealed all the way to the Supreme Court. In June 1970, the court ruled 8–0 (with Thurgood Marshall recusing himself) in Ali's favor. What is little remembered is that the court did not actually comment on the merits of Ali's claim to conscientious-objector status. Instead, the court found that at no level had the prosecutors shown how Ali's claims not met the three standards for granting such status. At the time, some critics of Ali's stance did try to emphasize that he had, in effect, gotten off on a procedural technicality, rather than on the actual merits of his claim. But at that point, the Vietnam War had become so unpopular that Ali's position on the war had come to seem more mainstream than radical.

At the time, Ali's statements on the war seemed to put him in much the same public position as Jane Fonda—admired by a minority for taking a moral stand that put his personal fortunes at great risk but disdained by the majority of Americans who felt that the moral stand amounted to a very perverse sort of self-promotion and an ill-conceived betrayal of American values, if not outright treason. Ali is most remembered for this blunt statement of his views on the war: "I ain't got nothing against no Viet Cong; no Viet Cong never called me nigger." Such a provocative statement would completely overshadow any more thoughtful statements that he would make about why he believed that his conversion to Islam demanded that he embrace pacifism. Indeed, it was not just non-Muslims who wondered how a boxer, in particular a boxer who seemed to take inordinate pleasure in humiliating and, in some cases, in physically tormenting his opponents, could claim to be a pacifist. The Nation of Islam had itself been hesitant to accept Ali as a member not just because he was a boxer but especially because of his public persona as a boxer. To make the whole matter even more of a tangle of deeply contentious views, the murder of Malcom X, the linkages between members of the Nation of Islam and black radical groups, and the often virulent rhetoric of the group's leaders undermined the premise that violence was antithetical to the Islamic faith that the group was advocating.

When Ali resumed his career after a three-year interruption, there was a great deal of warranted skepticism about his prospects. As a boxer, he had, after all, lost what might have been the prime years of his career. And if large numbers of people had watched his earlier fights in anticipation of seeing him getting soundly beaten, even larger numbers now watched them for that reason. But, when he seemed to defy time and precedent and to come back as good as or even better than he had been before his career had been interrupted, he began to earn a grudging respect even from some of those who found his public persona most off-putting. Although it was natural for commentators to wonder what his career might have been like had it not been interrupted when it was, it has also become clear that Ali's iconic stature is directly attributable to his transcending the interruption of his career and achieving a level of success that actually eclipsed his earlier success. Some of that success resulted from his finally having opponents of equal caliber—opponents such as Joe Frazier, Ken Norton, and George Foreman who pushed him to his limits athletically in a way that Sonny Liston was expected to do but never did.

Although it would be foolish to think that Ali's athletic achievements were irrelevant to his broader stature as an activist, the perception of him as a cultural icon was very much rooted in the period in which his boxing career was interrupted. For young African Americans and, in particular, for young African American athletes, Ali's self-assertiveness, framed as it was as a rejection to institutionalized racism, was one of the few available models for how one might succeed within a racially disadvantaging economic system without muting or compromising one's racial identity. During the period in which his legal case was being appealed, Ali became a frequent and welcome speaker on college campuses and especially at historically black colleges and universities (HBCUs). He became as effective at public speaking as he was at prefight and postfight banter, and although the banter filtered into his public speaking and was a great part of his appeal, the speaking engagements gave him the opportunity to demonstrate that he was a very thoughtful person who understood conceptually as well as viscerally the issues of race that are always, in one way or another, close to the center of American political tensions, social and economic issues, and cultural debates.

## FURTHER READING

Adler, Bill, ed. *A New Day: Robert F. Kennedy*. New York: Signet, 1968.
Adler, Bill, ed. *The Robert F. Kennedy Wit*. New York: Berkley, 1968.
Ali, Muhammad, with Richard Durham. *The Greatest, My Own Story*. New York: Random House, 1975.
*All Together Now: The Beatles Reader*. New York: BPI Communications, 2001.
Berry, Joseph P. *John F. Kennedy and the Media: The First Television President*. Lanham, MD: University Press of America, 1987.
Bianculli, David. 2010. *Dangerously Funny: The Uncensored Story of the "Smothers Brothers Comedy Hour."* New York: Simon & Schuster.
Bingham, Howard L., and Max Wallace. *Muhammad Ali's Greatest Fight: Cassius Clay vs. the United States of America*. New York: M. Evans, 2000.
Bradlee, Benjamin C. *Conversations with Kennedy*. New York: Norton, 1975.
Brown, Peter Harry, and Pat H. Broeske. *Down at the End of Lonely Street: The Life and Death of Elvis Presley*. New York: Dutton, 1997.
Burner, David. *John F. Kennedy and a New Generation*. Boston: Little, Brown, 1988.
Burrow, Rufus, Jr. *God and Human Dignity: The Personalism, Theology, and Ethics of Martin Luther King, Jr.* Notre Dame, IN: University of Notre Dame Press, 2006.
Carter, Dan T. *The Politics of Rage: George Wallace, the Origins of the New Conservatism, and the Transformation of American Politics*. New York: Simon & Schuster, 1995.
Clarke, Donald. *All or Nothing at All: A Life of Frank Sinatra*. London: Macmillan, 1997.
Conklin, Thomas. *Muhammad Ali: The Fight for Respect*. Brookfield, CT: Millbrook, 1991.
Connolly, Ray. *Being Elvis: A Lonely Life*. New York: Liveright, 2017.
Dallek, Robert. *Camelot's Court: Inside the Kennedy White House*. New York: HarperCollins, 2013.
Davies, Hunter. *The Beatles*. New York: McGraw-Hill, 1978.

Davis, Ronald L. *Due: The Life and Image of John Wayne*. Norman, OK: University of Oklahoma Press, 1998.
Early, Gerald, ed. *The Muhammad Ali Reader*. Hopewell, NJ: Ecco, 2013.
Eig, Jonathan. *Ali: A Life*. Boston: Houghton Mifflin Harcourt, 2017.
Eliot, Marc. *American Titan: Searching for John Wayne*. New York: Dey St./Morrow, 2014.
Eyman, Scott. *John Wayne: The Life and Legend*. New York: Simon & Schuster, 2014.
Ezra, Michael. *Muhammad Ali: The Making of an Icon*. Philadelphia: Temple University Press, 2009.
Frady, Marshall. *Martin Luther King, Jr.: A Life*. New York: Penguin, 2006.
Freedland, Michael. *All the Way: A Biography of Frank Sinatra*. New York: St. Martin's, 1997.
Garrow, David J. *Bearing the Cross: Martin Luther King, Jr., and the Southern Christian Leadership Conference*. New York: Morrow, 1986.
Garrow, David J. *The FBI and Martin Luther King, Jr.: From "Solo" to Memphis*. New York: Norton, 1981.
Giuliano, Geoffrey. *The Beatles: A Celebration*. Toronto: Methuen, 1986.
Grove, Martin A. *Beatle Madness*. New York: Manor, 1978.
Hamill, Pete. *Why Sinatra Matters*. Boston: Little, Brown, 2003.
Hammontree, Patsy Guy. *Elvis Presley: A Bio-Bibliography*. Westport, CT: Greenwood, 1985.
Hansen, Drew D. *The Dream: Martin Luther King, Jr., and the Speech That Inspired a Nation*. New York: Ecco, 2003.
Harry, Bill. *Beatlemania, the History of the Beatles on Film: An Illustrated Filmography*. New York: Avon, 1984.
Hauser, Thomas. *Muhammad Ali: His Life and Times*. New York: Simon & Schuster, 1991.
Hauser, Thomas. *Muhammad Ali: A Tribute to the Greatest*. New York: Pegasus, 2016.
Hellmann, John. *The Kennedy Obsession: The American Myth of JFK*. New York: Columbia University Press, 1997.
Hoffer, Richard. *Bouts of Mania: Ali, Frazier, and Foreman and an America on the Ropes*. Boston: Da Capo, 2014.
Ingham, Chris. *The Rough Guide to Frank Sinatra*. London: Rough Guides, 2005.
Jackson, Troy. *Becoming King: Martin Luther King, Jr. and the Making of a National Leader*. Lexington: University Press of Kentucky, 2008.
Kaplan, James. *Frank: The Voice*. New York: Doubleday, 2010.
Kelley, Kitty. *His Way: The Unauthorized Biography of Frank Sinatra*. New York: Bantam, 1996.
Kennedy, Robert. 1968. *Thirteen Days: A Memoir of the Cuban Missile Crisis*. New York: Norton.
King, Martin Luther, Jr. *The Autobiography of Martin Luther King, Jr.* Ed. by Clayborne Carson. New York: Warner, 1998.
Kolkey, Jonathan Martin. *The New Right, 1960–1968: With Epilogue, 1969–1980*. Washington, DC: University Press of America, 1983.
Landesman, Fred. *The John Wayne Filmography*. Jefferson, NC: McFarland, 2004.
Lazo, Caroline Evensen. *Martin Luther King, Jr.* New York: Maxwell Macmillan, 1994.
Lehman, David. *Sinatra's Century: One Hundred Notes on the Man and His World*. New York: HarperCollins, 2015.
Lemert, Charles C. *Muhammad Ali: Trickster in the Culture of Irony*. Cambridge, UK: Polity, 2003.
Lesher, Stephan. *George Wallace: American Populist*. Boston: Da Capo Press, 1995.
Lowell, Robert. *R.F.K., 1925–1968*. Cambridge, MA: Laurence Scott, 1969.
Mailer, Norman. *The Fight*. Boston: Little, Brown, 1975.

Marcus, Greil. *Dead Elvis: A Chronicle of a Cultural Obsession*. New York: Doubleday, 1991.
Marqusee, Mike. *Redemption Song: Muhammad Ali and the Spirit of the Sixties*. New York: Verso, 2000.
Mason, Bobbie Ann. *Elvis Presley*. New York: Viking, 2003.
Matthews, Chris. *Bobby Kennedy: A Raging Spirit*. New York: Simon & Schuster, 2018.
Matthews, Christopher. *Jack Kennedy: Elusive Hero*. New York: Simon & Schuster, 2011.
McKeen, William. *The Beatles: A Bio-Bibliography*. New York: Greenwood, 1989.
McNally, Karen. *When Frankie Went to Hollywood: Frank Sinatra and American Male Identity*. Urbana: University of Illinois Press, 2008.
Miles, Barry. *The Beatles: A Diary: An Intimate Day by Day History*. London: Omnibus, 1998.
Mulligan, Kate Siobhan. *The Beatles: A Musical Biography*. Santa Barbara, CA: Greenwood, 2010.
Munn, Michael. *John Wayne: The Man behind the Myth*. New York: New American Library, 2004.
O'Grady, Terence J. *The Beatles: A Musical Evolution*. Boston: Twayne, 1983.
Pacheco, Ferdie. *Muhammad Ali: A View from the Corner*. New York: Carol, 1992.
Patterson, Lillie. *Martin Luther King, Jr., and the Freedom Movement*. New York: Facts on File, 1989.
Perret, Geoffrey. *Jack: A Life Like No Other*. New York: Random House, 2001.
Reddick, Lawrence Dunbar. *Crusader without Violence: A Biography of Martin Luther King, Jr*. New York: Harper, 1959.
Reeves, Richard. *President Kennedy: Profile of Power*. New York: Simon & Schuster, 1993.
Remnick, David. *King of the World: Muhammad Ali and the Rise of an American Hero*. New York: Vintage, 1998.
Riggin, Judith M. *John Wayne: A Bio-Bibliography*. New York: Greenwood, 1992.
Roberts, Randy, and James S. Olsen. *John Wayne: American*. Lincoln: University of Nebraska Press, 1995.
Rorabaugh, W. J. *Kennedy and the Promise of the Sixties*. New York: Cambridge University Press, 2002.
Scaduto, Anthony. *The Beatles*. New York: New American Library, 1968.
Schlesinger, Arthur. *Robert Kennedy and His Times*. New York: Ballentine Books, 1978.
Selverstone, Marc J. *A Companion to John F. Kennedy*. Malden, MA: Wiley Blackwell, 2014.
Simpson, Paul. *The Rough Guide to Elvis*. London: Rough Guides, 2002.
Stokes, Geoffrey. *The Beatles*. New York: Times Books, 1980.
Stravinsky, John. *Muhammad Ali*. New York: Park Lane, 1997.
White, Mark J. *Kennedy: A Cultural History of an American Icon*. New York: Bloomsbury, 2013.

# CHAPTER 11

# Legacy

The word "hippie" typically brings to mind very vivid images and provokes very strong associations, but it is in many ways a very amorphous term. It is neither a blanket term for activists of the period nor a definable subcategory of those activists. And so, not surprisingly, it is not as easy as one might expect to gauge the lasting impact of the hippies on American politics, American society, and American culture. In the hippies' political values, one can find the roots of the new progressive political forces that emerged in support of Barrack Obama's presidential candidacy and that, after the disappointment of the 2016 presidential campaign, emerged in a very galvanized way during the 2018 midterm elections. Certainly, many of the values espoused by the very diverse candidates who sought and won office in 2018 are very consistent with the values associated with the hippies in the late 1960s. But, then, the obvious question would be what had happened to those political forces over the forty years between 1968 and 2008, never mind the fifty years between 1968 and 2018.

The progressive wing of the Democratic Party did seize control of the party apparatus in 1972, alienating not just conservative Democrats but also important constituencies such as organized labor. The result was that George McGovern was defeated as decisively as any presidential candidate in U.S. history. That defeat was so decisive that even the resignation of Richard Nixon under threat of impeachment did not lead to any sustained resurgence of progressive Democrats. The two Democrats elected to the presidency between Johnson and Obama—Jimmy Carter and Bill Clinton—were both centrist Democrats from the Deep South. Indeed, over the same period, as the Republican Party moved farther to the political right, the long-standing progressive majorities in both the U.S. Senate and the U.S. House, as well as in many state legislatures, were eroded until Democrats either held just slim majorities that depended on centrists or became the minority party. Indeed, during this entire period, the word "liberal" became such a pejorative political term that liberal Democrats started referring to themselves as "progressives."

Over the whole of the last half-century, it has been easier to gauge the impact of the political values associated with the hippies by the opposition marshaled in opposition to those values than by any conspicuous evidence of their transcendence across a broad swathe of U.S. political life. Since Goldwater's candidacy in the 1964 presidential election, the Republican Party has made the end of the "welfare state" one of its primary objectives, but the centerpieces of GOP campaigns in most of the subsequent presidential elections have been divisive social issues that have allowed "traditional values" or "family values" to be defended in opposition to less prescriptive notions of social and sexual categories and less clear (and often black-and-white) conceptions of social, economic, and cultural issues. Those issues have included abortion rights, LGBTQ rights, racial profiling in policing, the criminalization of drug use, gun ownership, and immigration. The political right has become increasingly defined by what it opposes, and pronouncements about what it defends often fairly quickly devolve into catchphrases and truisms. The groups developed in opposition to progressive values have included evangelical conservatives or the Christian right, the Tea Party, various self-styled militia groups, and most recently Christian nationalists.

Moreover, it is arguable that the values promoted by the hippies have withstood the often intense opposition to them, have become increasingly mainstreamed culturally, and are finally emerging in the public sphere as viable policy proposals. Although many male hippies remained very sexist in their attitudes toward women even as they embraced the "sexual revolution," the idea that freer expressions of sexuality should not carry social stigmas did facilitate the broadening mainstream acceptance of both women's rights and LGBTQ rights. Indeed, the hippies' deliberate blurring of conventional gender distinctions in physical appearance and dress undoubtedly contributed to a greater willingness to take the issues related to transgender identity and rights more seriously in mainstream political discussions. The hippies' interest in Eastern and "alternative" religions not only has led to a greater tolerance for religious differences but also a broader societal acceptance of "otherness." Although the hippies' fascination with indigenous and folk cultures led to some degree of charlatanism that has been all too easy to satirize, it has also contributed to a more complex sense of American history and identity. The hippies' interest in living "off the grid" has very clearly contributed to a greater awareness of human impact on the natural environment, raising questions about the human costs—the medical, moral, and spiritual costs—of creating a society in which even food production has become increasingly industrialized. And, lastly, the hippies' attraction to communal living was, at least in some ways, a response to the deepening sense of being isolated in the midst of crowds that has resulted from increasing urbanization. Indeed, the rise of digital technologies, in particular the reliance on social media, has made the desire for real human connections all the more intense. And the fact that the last several years have seen the largest mass demonstrations since the 1960s suggests that large numbers of people are rediscovering the value of in-person social networks even if they are being much facilitated by digital social networks.

To give an additional turn to the idea that the impact of the hippies' values can be seen more clearly against the focused opposition to those values, it is also true that some of those values have actually been appropriated—or misappropriated—by groups typically considered to be at the opposite end of the political spectrum. For instance, the hippies' interest in living "off the grid" is now associated as frequently with far right survivalists as it is with those who are seeking a more ecologically balanced life. Likewise, the hippies' belief that individual choices related to sexuality should not be stigmatized and individual choices related to drug use should not be criminalized have become major tenets of contemporary libertarianism. The hippies' mistrust of government agencies and their seeming willingness to embrace conspiracy theories almost indiscriminately have become as typical of those on the far right as those on the far left. Indeed, one might argue that the hippies' general skepticism toward all institutions is reflected less in the groups at the political extremes and more in the increasing percentage of Americans who have become politically disengaged. In a parallel way, one might argue that the hippies' interest in Eastern and "alternative" religions as an alternative to deeply institutionalized "Western" religions has led not only to a greater tolerance of religious differences but also to a greater skepticism toward religion in general. This skepticism seems to be reflected in the fact that one out of four Americans now identify themselves as being nonreligious (rather than not being affiliated with a particular religion). Lastly, since so much of the hippies' cultural influence was through the music associated with them, it seems ironic that heavy-metal music, which is generally considered a direct offshoot of psychedelic music, is now used as a major recruiting tool for skinhead groups and other white nationalist groups.

Over the last forty years, the deepening partisanship that has characterized American politics has led to a reflexive acceptance of the depth of that partisan divide and the elimination of the political center, at least among candidates and lawmakers, if not among voters. But on a number of issues, the political extremes are actually united in their views, if not in their reasons for holding their views. It is as if a circle were the model, with the position of the far right and the far left on the circle being at once the farthest removed from each other and the closest to each other.

For instance, as the Russian interference in the 2016 presidential election has been investigated by the special counsel Robert Mueller, other divisions of the U.S. Department of Justice, and various congressional committees, a conspiracy theory has emerged suggesting that elements not only within the Department of Justice but also within the FBI, the CIA, and other even more shadowy agencies within the national security apparatus have been conspiring to produce evidence that will lead to President Trump's removal from office. On the far right, these participants in the "Deep State Coup" against Trump are political partisans, holdovers from the Obama administration and other Clinton sympathizers who have refused to accept the legitimacy of Trump's shocking defeat of Hillary Clinton in the 2016 presidential election. In this version of the conspiracy theory, the "Deep State" is attempting to subvert the democratic process by attributing to Trump, his family, his campaign team, and his administration the very sorts of unethical actions and outright criminal behavior that they themselves have engaged in in order to discredit his victory and suggest his illegitimacy. In the aftermath of the release of the redacted version of the Mueller report, President Trump has himself voiced this conspiracy theory, suggesting that the congressional committees that are demanding an unredacted version of the report, other related materials, and witness testimony are, in fact, part of this "Deep State" conspiracy to either impeach him or to prevent his reelection. Of course, this view ignores a great deal of evidence that Trump and his supporters have otherwise claimed cannot be criminal because it was done blatantly in full public view. On the far left, there is also a widespread acceptance of a "Deep State Coup" against President Trump. Among those conspiracy theorists, however, the explanation for the "Coup" is the long-standing hostility toward Russia and the reflexive attribution of all manner of nefarious motives and actions to the Russians on the flimsiest of bases. This acceptance of the "Coup" seems to be itself a reflexive response to the long history of red-baiting within the U.S. politics, the persecution of American communists and communist sympathizers by agencies of the U.S. government, and the Cold War demonization of the Soviet Union that was used to justify the unending expansion of the military-industrial complex to the detriment of individual rights. Of course, this view ignores the reality that Russia has not been a communist state for the last three decades—that the authoritarian elements of the communist regime have been retained but to serve the interests of oligarchs who engage in a sort of completely unregulated capitalism, with the only constraint being what Putin wishes to allow.

That the far right and the far Left should embrace this conspiracy theory, and others, seems to be an extended consequence of the conspiracy theories proliferated after the assassination of President Kennedy and that continue to be entertained and invented. Conspiracy theories had, of course, existed previous to the Kennedy assassination, and some of them even made it into wider public circulation, even if they never were given much credence—for example, the theory that President Roosevelt had received forewarnings of the Japanese attack on Pearl Harbor but had decided to suppress the warnings and allow the attack to occur so that he could justify U.S. entry into the Second World War. But the proliferation of conspiracy theories related to the Kennedy assassination effectively legitimized the notion that all conspiracy theories are not products of the febrile imaginations and ideological paranoia of those on the political lunatic fringe. Indeed, because of the proliferation of social-media platforms, it has become difficult to define what is on the lunatic fringe. For instance, the "Pizzagate" conspiracy theory that Hillary Clinton had been involved in a child sex ring operating out of a pizzeria has received a considerable amount of mainstream media coverage, albeit because some of those who advanced or embraced it have faced other political, legal, and professional issues. But the sad reality is that in the general scheme of things, "Pizzagate" is neither the most ridiculous nor the most scurrilous conspiracy theory receiving wide circulation on social media catering to the fringes of the far right and the far left.

The investigations into the Russian interference in the 2016 presidential election has put a great deal of pressure on the Trump administration, but it has brought even more scrutiny to some of the most important corporations in the digital-technology sector—Facebook most intensely, but also Twitter, YouTube, Google, and even Amazon. On one level, the issues are related to national security and the integrity of U.S. elections. But beyond those concerns, there are many issues related to digital media itself: the role of digital media in our political discourse; the need to regulate digital media in some way, if not in the same way as other media are; and the ways in which the business models of digital-media companies invite abuses of their platforms. At the heart of all of these issues is the fact that the commodity from which digital media-companies are primarily profiting is the personal data that they gather about their users. Beyond the privacy issues, and even beyond the issues related to the very precisely targeted political exploitation of personal attitudes, there is a disenchantment with the idea that our most successful corporations essentially now produce nothing of extrinsic value—that they have, instead, devised ways to facilitate and to monetize personal communications and social interactions. Each time that a platform is used, more data on the user is produced, and so the potential profits tied to the scope and specificity of that data would compound, increasing much more dramatically than the actual use of the platforms—and even exponentially increasing with a steady increase in users.

The skepticism about the business model of digital-media corporations has been compounded by a broader skepticism about the ways in which corporations produce profits and contribute to the national economy. One of the major causes of the 2008 financial crisis was the packaging of subprime mortgages as securities by the major banks. To casual observers, it might have seemed that the banks were simply spreading the risk inherent in extending mortgages to marginally qualified borrowers during an extended boom in home prices. But, by packaging the mortgages as highly profitable securities at a time when the risk seemed greatly mitigated by the boom in home prices, the banks were actually compounding the risk involved in making the initial loans. For the subprime mortgages further inflated housing demand and housing prices, and when the housing market finally became so overpriced that the pricing was no longer sustainable, the very high default rates on the subprime mortgages caused a collapse in home prices, rather than simply a stagnation or a decline in prices. Worse, every sector with holdings in housing-related securities saw their value drop precipitously; so the crisis in the housing sector had an immediate effect across other economic sectors, creating a major economic crisis.

Even the corporations that ostensibly exist to produce durable goods seem to have become less focused on production and on research and development and more focused on stock prices as a source of profit. For this reason, the large decrease in corporate tax rates in 2017 produced very little increase in employment or in wages. Almost all of the revenues that corporations saved due to the tax cuts was spent on stock buybacks. Because a stock buyback reduces the amount of stock available for purchase, it drives up the price of the stock, increasing the dividends of those who hold stock and the compensation of executives whose compensation is tied to stock prices and may even be paid partly in shares of stock. As with the packaging of subprime mortgages as securities, stock buybacks seem to be largely an exercise in moving money around in order to make money from the transactions. So, for the average American, the idea that General Motors would announce the closure of its Lordstown facility, one of its largest production facilities, even as it was being given massive tax breaks and reporting high profits illustrates the increasing disconnect between the truisms about the intrinsic value of major corporations and their relation to the communities in which their products are bought, never mind those in which their employees live—and their "downsized" former employees often still live.

The emphasis on corporate deregulation during the Reagan years and beyond was framed as a necessary response to the Counterculture's antipathy toward corporate culture, its deep skepticism about the intrinsic benefits of unfettered capitalism, and its rejection of the notion that the "Protestant work ethic" should be regarded as a core American value, especially if it is primarily being measured in profit-taking. The case for less fettered and more dynamic corporate growth had a broad appeal when the economic stagnation of the 1970s and early 1980s made it clear that the unprecedented postwar economic boom had run its course. It had a broad appeal when foreign competition in some major sectors, such as automobile and other durable goods manufacturing, allowed the effects of postindustrialization and increasing automation to be framed as the inability of American corporations to compete with cheap foreign labor. It had a broad appeal when labor unions, especially in the industrial sector, proved to be ineffectual in protecting employment, never mind in preserving wages and benefits.

But now, nearly four decades into one of the most probusiness periods in U.S. history, American workers are coming back to the Counterculture's skepticism about corporate culture. In a period in which workers are being told that they may need to change not just their places of employment or their jobs, but their fields several times over their working lives, there is little sense of employee loyalty to the corporations that now employ them. The days of implicit expectations of lifetime employment with a corporation are now so long gone that they are hardly remembered. In a period in which wealth inequality is higher than it has ever been—with the only available comparisons being the Gilded Age, which led to landmark Progressive reforms following a major economic depression in the mid-1890s, and the last years of the "Roaring Twenties," which led to the Great Depression and the wholesale reforms of the New Deal—there is less concern about the continued profitability of major corporations and more concern about personal financial solvency and the viability of any sort of financial planning. It is worth noting that although the 1950s and early 1960s were perceived as a period in which the corporate culture had a pervasive influence, that was also a period in which corporate tax rates were very high and executive compensation was very low in comparison to what they are today.

In a period in which large numbers of workers feel marginalized and undervalued, there is a resurgence of interest in collective bargaining. In the 1960s, labor unions were still strong enough that they were largely taken for granted. If anything, the Counterculture viewed labor unions as part of the corporate culture, rather than as oppositional to it. At present, it is noteworthy that although the most visible labor actions have been by teachers, by public-sector employees who have been especially vilified as ineffective and overvalued, those labor actions have had broad community support—even in "red" states considered least sympathetic to public employees and to organized labor. Indeed, in some of the states in which there have been mass actions, the teachers have had no right to unionize or their unions have had very restricted collective-bargaining rights. In the private sector, the greatest labor activism has been among low-wage service workers, and people have now forgotten that that is where the industrial unions first took hold, among low-paid, semiskilled workers on the first mass-production lines and in the mines. It is also noteworthy that there are many signs of discontent among workers in the digital technology sector, who feel that the profitability of the sector has, in large part, depended on their exploitation. In a sense, the questions asked by those in the Counterculture have remained the same, though the context in which they are being asked has changed dramatically. The central question is still how the individual finds real meaning within a mass culture. In the 1960s, the concern was that the individual would become a cog in the machine. Today, the concern is that the individual has become a very disposable corporate asset and is being turned into a corporate commodity.

That many of those involved in the teachers' strikes have been women and women of color should have come as no surprise to anyone. The 2016 presidential election activated this part of the electorate more than any other, and the record number of women and women of color elected to office in the 2018 elections, at the federal, state, and local levels, was facilitated by very well coordinated, grassroots voter registration, fund-raising, and get-out-the-vote efforts. All of these developments are very clearly linked to the efforts made and the gains achieved by the Women's Movement and Civil Rights Movement in the 1960s—as well as reflecting of some deep frustration that, over the last half-century, those gains have not translated into more equitable representation of women in political and corporate leadership positions, or even led to much more basic gains such as laws mandating equal pay for equal work and laws that continue to protect, rather than erode, a woman's right to choose to terminate a pregnancy. In comparison to the 1960s, the number of women who have completed college degrees, as well as the number who hold degrees in what have been male-dominated disciplines, has increased dramatically. But it is also true that a disproportionately high percentage of women carry a high level of student-loan debt. When combined with some continued gender bias in hiring, especially into high-paying positions, the burden of that debt is compounded. Like workers in general, women have been waiting for an often-promised broad improvement in their economic circumstances, and they are now losing patience with waiting. Likewise, the #MeToo Movement has been a dramatic demonstration of the dramatic increase in the power of women to demand changes in the public sphere, and the unwillingness to tolerate any sexual impropriety, never mind sexual harassment or sexual assault, is clearly connected to their demand for a greater voice in the workplace.

As impressive as the Women's Marches have been, they have not been the only mass demonstrations and protests that have both reflected and reshaped public opinion on important issues—and that have thereby provoked comparisons to the demonstrations that occurred throughout the second half of the 1960s. The demonstrations against the targeting and abuse of people of color by the police and the take-a-knee protests during the playing of the national anthem ahead of sporting events have provoked more controversy than the Women's Marches, but they have reflected the reality that when people of color cannot depend on equal treatment under the law, other lingering social, economic, and political issues related to race cannot be addressed in any sort of serious and meaningful way. At the same time as these protests against police brutality were occurring, there was a defiantly public resurgence in white nationalism. As troubling as it has been to see extremism given any measure of legitimacy, media attention to white nationalism had the effect of very quickly galvanizing mass opposition to it. In August 2017, "Unite the Right" marchers came to Charlottesville, Virginia, to protest the removal of a statue of Robert E. Lee. Counter-protesters gathered to stand against hate, and when one of the white nationalists drove his car into a street full of the counter-protesters, a woman named Heather Heyer was killed. That tragedy created a context in which footage of the white nationalists marching by torchlight while they shouted, "Jews will not replace us" was aired repeatedly. And it all had the effect of undercutting the criticisms of the African American protests against police brutality—of undercutting assertions that most charges of racism are self-serving, that they perpetuate a reflexive rationalization of criminality as an effect of socioeconomic and educational disadvantage, and that they are intended to take the focus and the onus off the suspicious or resistant behavior that provoked excessive use of force by police.

Colin Kaepernick was not the only African American athlete to take a knee, but he became a focal point for those who wished to criticize the protest as unpatriotic. It is not difficult to see Kaepernick as standing in a line that began in the 1960s with Muhammad Ali, John Carlos, and Tommie Smith. And although Kaepernick has not been signed by another professional football team since opting out of his contract with the San Francisco 49ers and becoming a free agent, he has successfully reached a settlement with the NFL on a suit alleging that team owners have colluded to deny him employment because of his activism. Moreover, when Nike selected him to be the face of its new advertising campaign in 2018, the campaign proved to be incredibly successful—in spite of, or perhaps because of, much criticism from the far right and even from President Trump. Furthermore, it is illuminating to compare Kaepernick's situation with that of John Carlos and Tommie Smith. After they gave the black power salute while receiving their medals at the 1968 Summer Olympics, they were expelled from the Olympic Village, and for more than a decade afterward, they were effectively ostracized. Their courage in making that protest was belatedly recognized in a formal way when they received the Arthur Ashe Award for Courage at the 2008 Espy Awards. In contrast with that long-delayed recognition, in 2017, Colin Kaepernick received the Muhammad Ali Legacy Award from *Sports Illustrated* and the Eason Monroe Courageous Advocate Award from the American Civil Liberties Union, and then in 2018, he received the Ambassador of Conscience Award from Amnesty International and the W. E. B. Du Bois

Award from Harvard University. Progress is often incremental, and it does not usually occur in a straight line. But it is sometimes measurable in ways that are significant at least in part because they are profoundly symbolic. When John Carlos and Smith were expelled from the Olympic Village, the president of the International Olympic Committee (IOC) expressed outrage at their politicization of the games. When it was revealed that he had expressed no objections whatsoever to the ubiquitous Nazi salutes at the 1936 Summer Olympics in Berlin, he answered that the Nazi salute was a national symbol to which no great stigma had been attached at the time of those games, whereas the black power salute made by Carlos and Smith was a subversive political gesture. It is indicative of some significant progress that fifty years later, such an indefensible rationalization would have absolutely ruined him.

Although student protests have certainly continued to occur in the decades following the Vietnam War, there have not been any student protests coordinated on a national scale on an issue of special importance to young people. All of that changed, for high school students, after the mass shooting in February 2018, at Marjory Stoneman Douglas High School in Parkland, Florida. Mass shootings have become all too common, and in the immediate aftermath of each shooting, there have been mass vigils at the site to commemorate those who lost their lives, and in some instances, vigils have been held in other locations around the country to show solidarity with the victims' families and to highlight the appalling lack of a national response to these recurring massacres. But, as President Obama said after the mass shooting at Sandy Hook Elementary School in Newtown, Connecticut, if that horrific massacre of very young children was not enough to cause legislators to buck the National Rifle Association (NRA) and pass some sort of gun-control measures, then appealing for government action on this issue was very close to an exercise in futility. Nonetheless, the surviving students at Marjory Stoneman Douglas High School were determined that they would demand change until they succeeded in effecting it. Students such as Emma Gonzalez, David Hogg, Alfonso Calderon, Sarah Chadwick, Jaclyn Corin, Ryan Dietsch, Cameron Kasky, and Alex Wind began by organizing local rallies at which they spoke out passionately about the moral and political unacceptability of doing nothing. The rallies received a great deal of media attention, statewide and nationally, and eventually students at other high schools started to organize complementary rallies and walkouts timed to commemorate the time of the mass shooting. The proliferation of the walkouts inspired the organization of a National March for Our Lives held in Washington, DC, in March 2018. The students created a political action committee called Never Again MSD and successfully pressured the Florida legislature to pass some gun-control measures—over the vocal objections of the NRA—and comparable measures began to be introduced and passed in other states. The students began to organize voter registration drives and to use their PAC to support candidates who were willing to vote for further gun-control measures. Although several of the students were featured on the cover of *Time* magazine, they also endured a great deal of very personalized and derisive criticism from conservative media and gun-rights advocates. But the criticism came across as so calculated and petty that it largely backfired. The students have succeeded in creating a national student movement that has achieved concrete progress on an issue that had seemed as intractable as any issue facing the nation.

In the 1960s, popular music was one of the major means by which social and political statements were made and new ideas were communicated. Although popular music is still used to address all sorts of current issues, it is not the same sort of organizing force as it was a half-century ago. But, at least to some extent, that role has been filled by social media, where memes and hashtags have much the same impact as a memorable refrain in a "protest song." In fact, although there have been all sorts of commentary on the antisocial side effects of social media, it is not surprising that the rise of social media has coincided with a level of social activism not seen since the 1960s. The Internet is, after all, basically a library of "underground" 'zines where just about any sensibility can find a way to express itself and find others who share that sensibility. The Internet has put many general news magazines out of business, but it has actually been a boon to specialized magazines. Several years ago, a media professor noted in an article in the *Chronicle of Higher Education* that three magazines devoted to keeping ferrets as pets were able to be profitable because the Internet allowed ferret owners to locate them with very little effort. The media that facilitates the sharing of such specialized interests can obviously be used to marshal activism on major issues of national interest.

## FURTHER READING

Aronowitz, Stanley. *The Death and Rebirth of American Radicalism*. New York: Routledge, 1996.
Bloom, Alexander. *Long Time Gone: Sixties America Then and Now*. New York: Oxford University Press, 2001.
Bothmer, Bernard von. *Framing the Sixties: The Use and Abuse of a Decade from Ronald Reagan to George W. Bush*. Amherst: University of Massachusetts Press, 2010.
Cantor, Paul A. *Gilligan Unbound: Popular Culture in the Age of Globalization*. Lanham, MD: Rowman & Littlefield, 2001.
Chappell, Marisa. *The War on Welfare: Family, Poverty, and Politics in Modern America*. Philadelphia: University of Pennsylvania Press, 2010.
Christie, Nancy, and Michael Gauvreau, eds. *The Sixties and Beyond: Dechristianization in North America and Western Europe, 1945–2000*. Toronto: University of Toronto Press, 2013.
Daniels, Robert Vincent. *The Fourth Revolution: Transformations in American Society from the Sixties to the Present*. New York: Routledge, 2006.
DeGroot, Gerald J., ed. *Student Protest: The Sixties and After*. New York: Longman, 1998.
Echols, Alice. *Shaky Ground: The '60s and Its Aftershocks*. New York: Columbia University Press, 2002.
Ehrenreich, Barbara. *Fear of Falling: The Inner Life of the Middle Class*. New York: Pantheon, 1989.
Fleming, Cynthia Griggs. *Yes We Did? From King's Dream to Obama's Promise*. Lexington: University Press of Kentucky, 2009.
Gitlin, Todd. *The Twilight of Common Dreams: Why America Is Wracked by Culture Wars*. New York: Metropolitan, 1995.

Jenkins, Philip. *Decade of Nightmares: The End of the Sixties and the Making of Eighties America*. New York: Oxford University Press, 2006.

Kauffman, Jonathan. *Hippie Food: How Back-to-the-Landers, Longhairs, and Revolutionaries Changed the Way We Eat*. New York: William Morrow, 2018.

Kimball, Roger. *The Long March: How the Cultural Revolution of the 1960s Changed America*. San Francisco: Encounter, 2000.

Magnet, Myron. *The Dream and the Nightmare: The Sixties' Legacy to the Underclass*. New York: William Morrow, 1993.

McMillan, John. *Smoking Typewriters: The Sixties Underground Press and the Rise of Alternative Media in America*. New York: Oxford University Press, 2011.

Roof, Wade Clark. *Spiritual Marketplace: Baby Boomers and the Remaking of American Religion*. Princeton, NJ: Princeton University Press, 1999.

Shafer, D. Michael, ed. *The Legacy: The Vietnam War in the American Imagination*. Boston: Beacon, 1990.

Steele, Shelby. *White Guilt: How Blacks and Whites Together Destroyed the Promise of the Civil Rights Era*. New York: HarperCollins, 2006.

Stone, Skip. *Hippies from A to Z: Their Sex, Drugs, Music, and Impact on Society from the Sixties to the Present*. Silver City, NM: Hip, 2000.

Tate, Greg, ed. *Everything but the Burden: What White People Are Taking from Black Culture*. New York: Broadway, 2003.

Thomson, Irene Taviss. *Culture Wars and Enduring American Dilemmas*. Ann Arbor: University of Michigan Press, 2010.

Turner, Fred. *From Counterculture to Cyberculture: Stewart Brand, the Whole Earth Network, and the Rise of Digital Utopianism*. Chicago: University of Chicago Press, 2006.

# Bibliography

Albert, Judith Clavir, and Stewart Edward Albert, eds. *The Sixties Papers: Documents of a Rebellious Decade*. New York: Praeger, 1984.
Ashby, LeRoy. *With Amusement for All: A History of American Popular Culture since 1830*. Lexington: University Press of Kentucky, 2006.
Baugess, James S., and Abbe Allen DeBolt, eds. *Encyclopedia of the Sixties: A Decade of Culture and Counterculture*. Santa Barbara, CA: Greenwood, 2012.
Bingham, Clara. *Witness to the Revolution: Radicals, Resisters, Vets, Hippies, and the Year America Lost Its Mind and Found Its Soul*. New York: Random House, 2016.
Bloch, Avital H., and Lauri Umansky, eds. *Impossible to Hold: Women and Culture in the 1960's*. New York: New York University Press, 2005.
Bloom, Alexander, and Wini Breines, ed. *"Takin' It to the Streets": A Sixties Reader*. New York: Oxford University Press, 2003.
Brackett, David. *The Pop, Rock, and Soul Reader: Histories and Debates*. New York: Oxford University Press, 2014.
Braunstein, Peter, and Michael William Doyle, eds. *Imagine Nation: The American Counterculture of the 1960s and '70s*. New York: Routledge, 2002.
Brick, Howard. *Age of Contradiction: American Thought and Culture in the 1960s*. Ithaca, NY: Cornell University Press, 2000.
Brode, Douglas. *Sex, Drugs, and Rock 'n' Roll: The Evolution of an American Youth Culture*. New York: Peter Lang, 2015.
Bromell, Nicholas Knowles. *Tomorrow Never Knows: Rock and Psychedelics in the 1960s*. Chicago: University of Chicago Press, 2000.
Chalmers, David Mark. *And the Crooked Places Made Straight: The Struggle for Social Change in the 1960s*. Baltimore: Johns Hopkins University Press, 1996.
DeLeon, David, ed. *Leaders from the 1960s: A Biographical Sourcebook of American Activism*. Westport, CT: Greenwood, 1994.
Dickstein, Morris. *Gates of Eden: American Culture in the Sixties*. New York: Basic, 1977.
Dubinsky, Karen, ed. *New World Coming: The Sixties and the Shaping of Global Consciousness*. Toronto: Between the Lines, 2009.

Farber, David. *The Age of Great Dreams: America in the 1960s*. New York: Hill & Wang, 1994.

Farber, David, ed. *The Sixties: From Memory to History*. Chapel Hill: University of North Carolina Press, 1994.

Farber, David, and Beth Bailey, eds. *The Columbia Guide to America in the 1960s*. New York: Columbia University Press, 2001.

Farber, David, and Jeff Roche, eds. *The Conservative Sixties*. New York: Peter Lang, 2003.

Fischer, Klaus P. *America in White, Black, and Gray: A History of the Stormy 1960s*. London: Continuum, 2007.

Frank, Thomas. *The Conquest of Cool: Business Culture, Counterculture, and the Rise of Hip Consumerism*. Chicago: University of Chicago Press, 1997.

Gaillard, Frye. *A Hard Rain: America in the 1960s, Our Decade of Hope, Possibility, and Innocence Lost*. Montgomery, AL: NewSouth, 2018.

Grogan, Jessica. *Encountering America: Humanistic Psychology, Sixties Culture, and the Shaping of the Modern Self*. New York: Harper Perennial, 2013.

Hall, James C. *Mercy, Mercy Me: African-American Culture and the American Sixties*. New York: Oxford University Press, 2001.

Hamilton, Neil A. *The ABC-CLIO Companion to the 1960s Counterculture in America*. Santa Barbara, CA: ABC-CLIO, 1997.

Hartman, Andrew. *A War for the Soul of America: A History of the Culture Wars*. Chicago: University of Chicago Press, 2015.

Heineman, Kenneth J. *Put Your Bodies upon the Wheels: Student Revolt in the 1960s*. Chicago: I. R. Dee, 2001.

Hill, Laban Carrick. *America Dreaming: How Youth Changed America in the Sixties*. New York: Little, Brown, 2007.

Isserman, Maurice. *America Divided: The Civil War of the 1960s*. New York: Oxford University Press, 2015.

Kaufman, David. *Jewhooing the Sixties: American Celebrity and Jewish Identity: Sandy Koufax, Lenny Bruce, Bob Dylan, and Barbra Streisand*. Waltham, MA: Brandeis University Press, 2012.

Kercher, Stephen E. *Revel with a Cause: Liberal Satire in Postwar America*. Chicago: University of Chicago Press, 2006.

Klein, Michael, ed. *An American Half-Century: Postwar Culture and Politics in the USA*. Boulder, CO: Pluto, 1994.

Kutschke, Beate, and Barley Norton, eds. *Music and Protest in 1968*. New York: Cambridge University Press, 2013.

Levine, Paul, and Harry Papasotiriou. *America since 1945: The American Moment*. New York: Palgrave Macmillan, 2005.

Levy, Peter B., ed. *America in the Sixties—Right, Left, and Center: A Documentary History*. Westport, CT: Greenwood, 1998.

Mackenzie, G. Calvin, and Robert Weisbrot. *The Liberal Hour: Washington and the Politics of Change in the 1960s*. New York: Penguin, 2008.

Martinez, Manuel Luis. *Countering the Counterculture: Rereading Postwar American Dissent from Jack Kerouac to Tomás Rivera*. Madison: University of Wisconsin Press, 2003.

Miller, Timothy. *The 60s Communes: Hippies and Beyond*. Syracuse, NY: Syracuse University Press, 1999.

Monhollon, Rusty, ed. *Baby Boom: People and Perspectives*. Santa Barbara, CA: ABC-CLIO, 2010.

Monteith, Sharon. *American Culture in the 1960s*. Edinburgh, UK: Edinburgh University Press, 2008.

Moretta, John. *The Hippies: A 1960s History*. Jefferson, NC: McFarland, 2017.

Morgan, Edward P. *The 60s Experience: Hard Lessons about Modern America*. Philadelphia: Temple University Press, 1991.

Morgan, Edward P. *What Really Happened to the 1960s: How Mass Media Culture Failed American Democracy*. Lawrence: University Press of Kansas, 2010.

Newhouse, Thomas. *The Beat Generation and the Popular Novel in the United States, 1945–1970*. Jefferson, NC: McFarland, 2000.

Patterson, James T. *The Eve of Destruction: How 1965 Transformed America*. New York: Basic, 2012.

Reed, Adolph, Jr. *Race, Politics, and Culture: Critical Essays on the Radicalism of the 1960's*. Westport, CT: Greenwood, 1986.

Rielly, Edward J. *The 1960s*. Westport, CT: Greenwood, 2003.

Schloss, Joseph Glenn, Larry Starr, and Christopher Waterman. *Rock: Music, Culture, and Business*. New York: Oxford University Press, 2012.

Spigel, Lynn, and Michael Curtin, eds. *The Revolution Wasn't Televised: Sixties Television and Social Conflict*. New York: Routledge, 1997.

Stark, Steven D. *Glued to the Set: The 60 Television Shows and Events That Made Us Who We Are Today*. New York: Delta, 1998.

Staub, Michael E., ed. *The Jewish 1960s: An American Sourcebook*. Waltham, MA: Brandeis University Press, 2004.

Stras, Laurie, ed. *She's So Fine: Reflections on Whiteness, Femininity, Adolescence and Class in 1960s Music*. Burlington, VT: Ashgate, 2010.

Waldschmidt-Nelson, Britta, Sharon Monteith, Clara Juncker, and Grzegorz Kosc. *The Transatlantic Sixties: Europe and the United States in the Counterculture Decade*. Bielefeld, Germany: Knowledge Unlatched, 2013.

Warner, Simon. *Text and Drugs and Rock 'n' Roll: The Beats and Rock Culture*. London: Bloomsbury, 2013.

Whitmer, Peter O., and Bruce Van Wyngarden. *Aquarius Revisited: Seven Who Created the Sixties Counterculture That Changed America: William Burroughs, Allen Ginsberg, Ken Kesey, Timothy Leary, Norman Mailer, Tom Robbins, Hunter S. Thompson*. New York: Macmillan, 1987.

Willis, Jim. *1960s Counterculture: Documents Decoded*. Santa Barbara, CA: ABC-CLIO, 2015.

# Index

*ABC's Wide World of Sports*, 55
Acid rock, 60–61
Action-adventure television series, 40–46
    detective series, 40–43
    espionage series, 44–45
    legal dramas, 43
    medical dramas, 46
    military series, 45–46
    self-aware thrillers, 43–44
Addams, Charles, 94
Advertising, 171, 194–203
African Americans, xxiv, xxvii, xix–xx, 55–56
    Black Arts Movement, xxvi–xxvii; links to Harlem Renaissance, xxvii
    "Bloody Sunday," 263
    *Brown v. Board of Education*, 260
    Civil Rights Movement, 260–264
    continuing impact of the Civil Rights Movement, 292–294
    documentary and feature films about the Civil Rights Movement, 264
    Freedom Movement, 262–263
    Freedom Riders, 262
    Great Migration, xxiv, 213
    lunch counter protests at Woolworth's in Greensboro, North Carolina, 262
    March on Washington, 263
    murders of Chaney, Goodman, and Schwerner, 262–263
    postwar racial segregation, xix–xx
    racial integration and sports broadcasts, 56
    racial unrest, 213–220
        Baltimore race riots in 1968, 219
        Chicago race riots in 1968, 218–219
        Detroit race riots in 1967, 217–218
        Division Street race riots in Chicago in 1967, 216–217
        Harlem race riots in 1964, 215
        "The Long, Hot Summer," 217–218
        Newark race riots in 1967, 217
        riots in response to the King assassination, 218–220
        underlying causes of racial unrest, 213–215
        Washington, DC, race riots in 1968, 219–220
        Watts race riots in 1965, 215–216
    songs associated with the Civil Rights Movement, 264
    Southern Christian Leadership Conference, 261–262
    visual arts and the Civil Rights Movement, 183–184
Ailey, Alvin, 65
Album covers (LP records), 83

Ali, Muhammad (Cassius Clay), 165, 279–283
   amateur boxing record, 280
   conscientious objector claim, 282
   emergence as an iconic figure, 282–283
   fights against Sonny Liston, 280–281
   name change and conversion to Islam, 281
   public persona, 280
   stripping of his title and eventual resumption of career, 282–283
   title defenses, 281–282
*American Bandstand*, 34–35, 77–78
Andress, Ursula, 22, 187
Andrews, Julie, 22
*The Andy Griffith Show*, 35
Angelou, Maya, 119–121
   genre issues of her seven autobiographical books, 120
   *I Know Why the Caged Bird Sings*, 121
Animated movies, 94–95
Ann-Margret, 22–23
Antinovelists, 105, 133
Apalachin conference, 239
Arbus, Diane, 182–183
Architecture, 184–185
Arledge, Roone, 55
Art, 170–186
   architecture, 184–185
   other movements in the visual arts, 177–181
      conceptual art, 178
      earth or land art, 180–181
      Fluxus, 178–179
      graffiti, 181
      happenings, 179
      junk or trash art, 180
      lyrical abstraction, 178
      minimalism, 177–178
      performance art, 179
      process art, 180
      video art, 179
   pop art, 170–173
   psychedelic art, 176–177
   visual arts and the Civil Rights Movement, 183–184
Assassinations, 205–213
   Evers, Medger, 208
   Hampton, Fred, and Mark Clark, 209–210
   Kennedy, John F., 205–207
      films related to the assassination released in the 1960s, 210–212
      novels related to the assassination published in the 1960s, 212–213
   Kennedy, Robert F., 207–208
   King, Martin Luther, Jr., 207–208
   Malcolm X, 208
   Rockwell, George Lincoln, 208–209
Auchincloss, Louis, 87
*The Avengers*, 45

Baby Boom, xviii–xix
Bakersfield sound, 64
Balanchine, George, 65
Baldwin, James, 118–119
   *Another Country*, 119
   *Blues for Mister Charlie*, 119
   *The Fire Next Time*, 118
   *Going to Meet the Man*, 119
   *Nobody Knows My Name*, 118
   *Tell Me How Long the Train's Been Gone*, 119
Baltimore race riots in 1968, 219
"Bananas Wars," 240
Bardot, Bridget, 23, 187
Baseball, 151–156
   great players of the 1960s, 156
   proposed Commonwealth League and MLB expansion, 151–152
   reorganization of the minor leagues, 156
   unionization of the players and umpires, 156
Basketball, 161–165
   National Basketball Association, 161–163
   NCAA and NIT tournaments, 163–164
   notable All-American basketball players of the 1960s, 164–165
   notable NBA players of the 1960s, 163
   rivalry between Bill Russell and Wilt Chamberlain, 162–163
   Texas Western University's all-black team's NCAA tournament victory over the University of Kentucky's all-white team, 164
The Beach Boys, 77
Beamon, Bob, 167

# Index

The Beatles, 275–279
   *Abbey Road*, 279
   Beatlemania, 276
   *Let It Be*, 279
   *Magical Mystery Tour*, 278
   record sales, 276
   *Revolver*, 277
   *Rubber Soul*, 277
   *Sgt. Pepper's Lonely Hearts Club Band*, 277–278
   *The White Album*, 278–279
Beats and beatniks, xviii
Beatty, Warren, 23
Bell-bottoms, 189
*Ben Casey*, 46
Bernstein, Leonard, 64
Berrigan, Philip, 226
Best sellers
   fiction, 87–90
   nonfiction, 90–92
Betty Crocker, 197–198
The bikini, 187–188
Biondi, Dick, 85
Black and White Ball, 97
Black Arts Movement, xxvi–xxvii, 183
   links to Harlem Renaissance, xxvii
*Blow-Up*, 10
Blues music, 61
*Bonanza*, 47
Bond Films (1962–1969), 4
*Bonnie and Clyde*, 10–11
Boston Celtics, 161–162
Bra Burning, 237
Brautigan, Richard, 132–136
   *A Confederate General from Big Sur*, 135–136
   *The Pill versus the Springhill Mine Disaster*, 135
   *The Springhill Mine Disaster*, 136
   *Trout Fishing in America*, 133–135
*Breakfast at Tiffany's*, 3
The Brill Building, 72
British Invasion, 61–62
Broadway and Off-Broadway musicals, 62–63
Brown, James, 77
Bukowski, Charles, 144–146
   association with Black Sparrow Press, 145
   *Notes of a Dirty Old Man*, 145

*Bullitt*, 16
Burroughs, William S., 121–125
   fatal shooting of Joan Vollmer, 122
   *Junky*, 122
   *The Last Words of Dutch Schultz*, 125
   *Naked Lunch*, 122–124
   *The Nova Trilogy*, 124–125
Burton, Richard, 23
*Butch Cassidy and the Sundance Kid*, 17

Cage, John, 64
Capone, Al, 238
Capote, Truman, 95–98
   *Answered Prayers*, 97
   *Breakfast at Tiffany's*, 95–96
   films about Capote, 98
   *In Cold Blood*, 96–97
   *Other Voices, Other Rooms*, 95
Carlos, Juan, 168
Carmichael, Stokely, 261
*The Carol Burnett Show*, 33
Cartoons on television, 50–51
Castaneda, Carlos, 128–131
   issues of genre related to his books, 130–131
   *The Teachings of Don Juan: The Yaqui Way of Knowledge*, 128–129
Celebrity, xxx
   books authored by celebrities, 91
   product endorsements, 171
Chamberlain, Wilt, NBA records set, 163
Charles, Ray, 77
Chicago race riots in 1968, 218–219
Chicago Seven, 249–250
Clark, Dick, 72
Classical music, 63–64
*Cleopatra*, 5
Cleveland, James, 68
Cline, Patsy, 81
Cold War, xvii
   Korean War, parallels to Vietnam War, xx
College football broadcasts, 55
Coltrane, John, 68
*Combat*, 46
Comics and cartoons, 92–95
Concept albums, 83, 278
Conceptual art, 178
Connery, Sean, 23

Controversies, 205–248
  assassinations, 205–213
  "Boston Strangler" murders, 241–243
  Manson "family," 234–236
  Miss America pageant protests, bra burning, and the mainstreaming of radical feminism, 236–237
  organized crime, 237–241
  racial unrest, 213–220
  Richard Speck's murder of eight nurses, 243–244
  the Summer of Love and the Woodstock Music Festival, 231–234
  Vietnam War, 220–231
  Whitman, Charles, and the Texas tower mass murder, 244–245
Cooke, Sam, 81
*Cool Hand Luke*, 11
Corporate culture, xvii
Country music, 64–65
Cuban Missile Crisis, 253
Cunningham, Merce, 65

Dale, Dick, 77
Dance, 65
Dance crazes, 65
Darin, Bobby, 24, 73
*The Dating Game*, 52
Day, Doris, 24
DC Comics, 93
*Death Valley Days*, 47
Dee, Sandra, 24
*The Defenders*, 43
DeSalvo, Albert, and the "Boston Strangler" murders, 241–243
Detective series on television, 40–43
Detroit race riots in 1967, 217–218
Diem, Ngo Dinh, 221–222
The Diggers, 232–233
*The Dirty Dozen*, 11
Division Street race riots in Chicago in 1967, 216–217
The Doors, 60–61
*Dr. Kildare*, 46
*Dr. Strangelove Or: How I Learned to Stop Worrying and Love the Bomb*, 6
Dylan, Bob, 66, 79–80
  *Blonde on Blonde*, 80
  *Highway 61 Revisited*, 80
  *John Wesley Harding*, 80

Earth or land art, 180–181
Eastwood, Clint, 24
*Easy Rider*, 17
*The Ed Sullivan Show*, 31–32, 77
8-track cassette recordings, 82
Eisenhower, Dwight D., presidency, xxiii
Environment Movement
  environmental legacy of the hippies, 287
  roots in Conservation Movement, xxix–xxx
Espionage series, 44–45
Evers, Medger, 208
Exley, Frederick, 107–108
  *A Fan's Notes*, and its impact, 107–108

Fabian, 24–25
Family programming, 49–50
Fantasy situation comedies, 38–39
Farina, Richard, 81, 131–132
  *Been Down So Long It Looks Like Up to Me*, 131–132
Fashion, 187–193
  bell-bottoms, 189
  the bikini, 187–188
  miniskirts, minidresses, and microminis, 188–189
  mod clothing and psychedelic prints, 190
Fast food, 199–201
Feiffer, Jules, 94
Ferlinghetti, Lawrence, 136–139
  influence of Walt Whitman, 137
  influence of William Carlos Williams, 137–138
  integration of music into his poetry readings, 136
  political poems and the poet's public role, 138–139
Film, 3–30
  animated movies, 94–95
  Bond films (1962–1969), 4
  Iconic stars of the 1960s, 22–30
  teen movies, 18–22
  younger stars of 1950s, xxiii
"Five Families," 238, 240
Flatt, Lester, and Earl Scruggs, 65
Fleming, Ian, 89
Fleming, Peggy, 167
*Flipper*, 49
Flower Children, 232

Fluxus, 178–179
Folk music, 66–67
Fonda, Jane, 25
Fonda, Peter, 25
Food advertising, 196–199
Food packaging, 199
Football, 156–161
    AFL's all-time team, 160
    AFL championship games, 158
    college football, 160–161
    formation of the American Football League, 157
    NFL championship games, 157–158
    NFL's all-decade team, 159–160
    notable college football broadcasts, 161
    notable college football coaches, 160
    racial integration of college football, 161
    Super Bowls, 158–159
Fosbury, Dick, 167
Franklin, Aretha, 76, 77
Frazier, Joe, 166
Freed, Alan, 72
*The Fugitive*, 43–44
Funicello, Annette, 25, 78

*The Gallant Men*, 46
Game-changers, 249–285
Game shows, 51–52
Garage bands, 75
*Gentle Ben*, 49–50
*Get Smart*, 38
Ginsberg, Allen, 121–122, 125–128
    *Howl and Other Poems*, 125–126
    *Kaddish and Other Poems, 1958–1960*, 126–127
    *Planet News*, 127
    *Reality Sandwiches*, 127
    *The Yage Letters*, 128
Glass, Philip, 64
Gordy, Barry, 70
*The Graduate*, 11–15
Graffiti, 181
Graham, Billy, 261
Graham, Martha, 65
*The Great Escape*, 5
Great Migration, xxiv
Green Bay Packers, 157–158
*Guess Who's Coming to Dinner*, 15

*The Guns of Will Sonnett*, 49
*Gunsmoke*, 47
Guthrie, Woody, and influence, 66

Haight-Ashbury, 232–233
Hamilton, Richard, 172
Hammarskjöld, Dag, 92
Hampton, Fred, and Mark Clark, 209–210
Happenings, 179
Harlem race riots in 1964, 215
*Hawaii Five-O*, 41–42
*Hawaiian Eye*, 42
Hayes, Bob, 166
Heller, Joseph, 109–111
    *Catch-22*, 109–111
Hendrix, Jimi, 60
Hepburn, Audrey, 25–26
Hoffman, Dustin, 26
Hudson, Rock, 26

*I Spy*, 45
Iconic stars of the 1960s, 22–30
Immigration and nativism, xxvi–
*In the Heat of the Night*, 16, 264
*Ironside*, 41
*It Takes a Thief*, 45
Italian American Civil Rights League, 241

*The Jackie Gleason Show*, 33
Jackson, Mahalia, 67
Jan and Dean, 77
Jazz, xviii, 68–69
Jazz Age, xxvii–xxviii
    parallels to the 1950s and 1960s, xxviii
Johns, Jaspar, 181–182
Johnson, Lyndon, 253–255
Johnson, Rafer, 165
Jones, Tommie, 168
*Judd for the Defense*, 43
*Julia*, 37
Junk or trash art, 180

Kaepernick, Colin, 293–294
Kaufman, Murray (aka Murray the K), 85
Kaufman, Sue, 117–118
    *Diary of a Mad Housewife*, 117–118
Kefauver hearings, 239
Kennedy, Jaqueline, 190–192, 251–252

Kennedy, John F., 90, 205–207, 210–213, 250–255
  assassination, 205–207
  books about Kennedy and his administration, 90
  Camelot and the mythologizing of Kennedy presidency, 250, 252
  and the Civil Rights Movement, 253, 254
  and conduct of the Vietnam War, 253–255
  Cuban Missile Crisis, 253
  films related to the assassination released in the 1960s, 210–212
  novels related to the assassination published in the 1960s, 212–213
  rhetoric and ability to inspire, 252–253
Kennedy, Robert F., 207–208, 255–258
  assassination, 207–208
  presidential candidacy, 256–257
  ruthlessness and idealism, 255
  wit, 258
Kerouac, Jack, and *On the Road*, 121
Kesey, Ken, 142–144
  notoriety from promotion of psychedelic drug use, 142
  *One Flew over the Cuckoo's Nest*, 142–143
  *Sometimes a Great Notion*, 142–144
    comparison to Faulkner's *As I Lay Dying*, 142–143
Killy, Jean-Claude, 167
King, Martin Luther, Jr., 207–208, 260–264
  assassination, 207–208
  "I Have a Dream" speech, 263–264
  "I Have Been to the Mountaintop" speech, 264
  "Letter from Birmingham Jail," 263
  riots in response to the King assassination, 218–220
Kirby, Jack, 93
Kirschner, Don, 73
Klu Klux Klan, xxvi
Korean War, parallels to Vietnam War, xx
Kosuth, Joseph, 178

Labor unions, xvi–xvii
Lambert, Dave, 81
*Land of the Giants*, 50
*Lassie*, 49
Latin music, 69
*The Lawrence Welk Show*, 32–33
LeCarre, John, 89
Lee, Stan, 93
Legacy, 286–296
  appropriation of hippie values by the political Right, 288
  continuing impact of the Civil Rights Movement, 292–294
  continuing impact of student protests, 294–295
  continuing impact of the Women's Movement, 292–293
  digital media and individual privacy, 290
  distrust of the deep State on both the Far Right and the Far Left, 288–289
  environmental legacy of the hippies, 287
  link between the protest music and underground 'zines of the 1960s and social media, 295
  political values associated with the hippies, 286–290
  prevalence of conspiracy theories, 289
  resurgence of support for labor unions, 292
  skepticism about corporate values, 290–292
Legal dramas on television, 43
Lehrer, Tom, 71
*The Leslie Uggams Show*, 34
*Let's Make a Deal*, 52
Lewis, Jerry, 26
Lichtenstein, Roy, 175–176
  most well-known works, 176
Literature, 87
  best sellers
    fiction, 87–90
    nonfiction, 90–92
  comics and cartoons, 92–95
  novels of the First and Second World Wars, xxviii–xxix
Live music, 69–70
"The Long, Hot Summer," 217–218
*The Longest Day*, 4
Loren, Sophia, 27
Los Angeles Lakers, 162
*Lost in Space*, 50

Index 307

LP recordings, 83
Lymon, Frankie, 81
Lyrical abstraction, 178

MAD magazine, 94
Mailer, Norman, 98–102
   *Advertisements for Myself*, 99
   *An American Dream*, 100
   *The Armies of the Night*, 101, 226
   *Barbary Shore*, 99
   *Cannibals and Christians*, 102
   *The Deer Park*, 99
   experimental filmmaking, 103
   *The Idol and the Octopus*, 102
   *Miami and the Siege of Chicago*, 102
   *The Naked and the Dead*, 98
   *The Presidential Papers*, 102
   stabbing of Adele Morales, 100
   *Why Are We in Vietnam?*, 101
Malcolm X, 208, 261
*The Manchurian Candidate*, 210–212
*Mannix*, 43
Manson, Charles, and the Manson "family," 132, 234–236
*Marcus Welby, M.D.*, 46
Marshall, Catherine, 90
Marvel comics, 93
Marvin, Lee, 27
Max, Peter, 177
McKuen, Rod, 92
McLuhan, Marshall, 56–58
   *The Gutenberg Galaxy: The Making of Typographic Man*, 56–57
   *The Mechanical Bride: Folklore of Industrial Man*, 56
   *The Medium Is the Message: An Inventory of Effects*, 57
   *Understanding Media: The Extensions of Man*, 57
   *War and Peace in the Global Village*, 57
McQueen, Steve, 27
Media and advertising, 194–204
   advertising in the media, 194–196
   fast food, 199–201
   food advertising, 196–199
   food packaging, 199
   tobacco and advertising, 201–203
Medical dramas on television, 46
*Medium Cool*, 18
Merry Pranksters, 142
Metafictionists, 105, 123, 133

Michener, James, 89
*Midnight Cowboy*, 18
Military series on television,
Military situation comedies, 38
Miller, Roger, 71
Mills, Billy, 166
Minimalism, 177–178
Miniskirts, minidresses, and microminis, 188–189
*The Misfits*, 3
Miss America Pageant protests, 236–237
*Mission Impossible*, 45
Mod clothing, 190
*The Mod Squad*, 41
Modernist art, 170
The Monkees, 79
Motorcycle clubs, xviii
Motown, 70
Music, 60–86
   acid rock, 60–61
   blues, 61
   the British Invasion, 61–62
   Broadway and Off-Broadway musicals, 62–63
   classical music, 63–64
   country music, 64–65
   dance, 65
   folk music, 66–67
   gospel music, 67–68
   jazz, 68–69
   Latin music, 69
   live music, 69–70
   Motown, 70
   novelty music, 71–72
   payola, 72
   pop music, 72–73
   protest music, 74
   radio, 83–86
   records and cassettes, 82–83
   rock and roll, 75
   rock music, 74–75
   San Francisco sound, 75, 233
   soul music/rhythm and blues, 76–77
   surfer and hot rod music, 78
   teen idols, 78–79
   television musical and variety shows, 77–78
   tragedies in music, 80–81
Music festivals, 69–70
Music meccas, 70

Namath, Joe, 159
NBA broadcasts, 55–56
Nelson, Ricky, 78
New Journalism, 97
New York Mets, 154–155
New York Radical Women, 236–237
New York Yankees, 152–154
Newark race riots in 1967, 217
*The Newlywed Game*, 52
Newman, Paul, 27
Newspaper comics, 94
NFL broadcasts, 54–55
Nick Carter, 212–213
Novelty music, 71–72
Novelty songs, controversial, 71–72

O'Connor, Edwin, 88
Oerter, Al, 167
O'Hara, John, 87
Olympic Games, 165–168
   1960 Summer Olympics, 165
   1960 Winter Olympics, 165
   1964 Summer Olympics, 166–167
   1964 Winter Olympics, 165–166
   1968 Summer Olympics, 167–168
   1968 Winter Olympics, 167
   tragedy involving U.S. figure skating team, 166
*Once Upon a Time in the West*, 5–6
Organized crime, 237–241
   Apalachin conference, 239
   the "Bananas Wars," 240
   the "Five Families" and the Commission, 238, 240
   Italian American Civil Rights League, 241
   Kefauver hearings, 239
   and Prohibition, 237
   the Syndicate, 238
   Valachi hearings, 237, 239–240
O'Toole, Peter, 27–28

Paolozzi, Eduardo, 172
Parks, Rosa, 261
Payola, 72
*Peanuts*, 92, 94
Peck, Gregory, 28
Performance art, 179
Perkins, Anthony, 28
*Perry Mason*, 43
*Planet of the Apes*, 17

Poitier, Sidney, 28
Political parties, shifting composition of the major parties, xxiv–xxv
Pop art, 170–173
Pop music, 72–73
Postmodern novelists, 105, 133, 144
Presidential election of 1960, xxiii
Presley, Elvis, 73, 271–275
   the Elvis stamps issued by the U.S. Postal Service, 272
   films, 272–273
   impact on music and popular culture in the 1950s, 271–272
   Las Vegas act, 274
   posthumous popularity, 274–275
   *'68 Comeback Special*, 274
   soundtrack albums of the 1960s, 273
   tabloid interest in his life and death, 274
Pre-teen comics, 93
Previn, Andre, 63
*The Price Is Right*, 51
Process art, 180
*The Producers*, 16
Protest music, 74
Psychedelic art, 176–177
Psychedelic clothing, 190
Psychedelic music, 233
Puzo, Mario, and *The Godfather*, 238, 241
Pynchon, Thomas, 105–107
   *The Crying of Lot 49*, 106–107
   reclusiveness, 105–106
   *V*, 106
Pyne, Joe, 85

Quant, Mary, 189

Radio, 83–87
   AM radio, 83–84
      impact of television on AM radio, 84
      integration of news and music programming, 84
   FM radio, 83–85
      development of FM stations, 83
      formats, 84–85
   radio personalities, 85–87
*The Rat Patrol*, 46
Records and cassettes, 82–83
*The Red Skelton Show*, 32
Redding, Otis, 76, 77, 81

# Index

Rock and roll, 75
Rock music, 74–75
    development of rock and roll music in 1950s, xxii
Rockwell, George Lincoln, 208–209
*Rosemary's Baby*, 17
Roth, Philip, 114–116
    *Goodbye, Columbus*, 114
    *Letting Go*, 114
    *Portnoy's Complaint*, 115–116
    *When She Was Good*, 114–115
*Route 66*, 44–45
*Rowan and Martin's Laugh-In*, 34
Rudolph, Wilma, 165
*Run for Your Life*, 44
Rural situation comedies, 37

*The Saint*, 45
Salinger, J. D., 104–105
    *Catcher in the Rye*, 104–105
    *Franny and Zooey*, 105
    *Hapworth 16, 1924*, 105
    *Nine Stories*, 105
    *Raise High the Roofbeam, Carpenters*, 105
    reclusiveness, 105
    *Seymour: An Introduction*, 105
San Francisco sound, 75
Schollander, Don, 166–167
Schulz, Charles, 92, 94
Second World War, xiii–xvii
    GDP impact, xv–xvi
    G.I. Bill of Rights, xvi
    human cost, xiii–xiv
    Lend Lease Act, xiv–xv
    manufacturing production, xiv–xv
Self-aware thrillers on television, 43–44
Sellers, Peter, 28
Sergio Leone's trilogy, 5–6
Serial killers, 241–242
*77 Sunset Strip*, 42–43
Sexual revolution,
    books about, 91
Sharif, Omar, 28–29
Sherman, Allan, 71
Sinatra, Frank, 29, 73, 269–271
    films of the 1950s, 270
    films of the 1960s, 271
    founding of Reprise Records, 270
    kidnapping of Frank Sinatra, Jr., 270
    *The Manchurian Candidate*, 270
    musical recordings of the 1950s, 270
    musical recordings of the 1960s, 270
    organized crime associations, 270
    the Rat Pack, 270
    shifting relationship with the Kennedys, 270–271
Situation comedies, 35–40
    fantasy situation comedies, 38–39
    military situation comedies, 38
    rural situation comedies, 37
    Western situation comedies, 37–38
Smith, Robert Weston (aka Wolfman Jack), 86
*The Smothers Brothers Comedy Hour*, 33–34, 78
Snyder, Gary, 139–142
    *The Back Country*, 140–141
    *Myths and Texts*, 140
    *Regarding Wave*, 141–142
    *Six Sections from Mountains and Rivers without End*, 140
Soul music/rhythm and blues, 76–77
*The Sound of Music*, 6–10
Southern Christian Leadership Conference, 261–262
Speck, Richard, 243–244
Spector, Phil, 72–73
Spock, Benjamin, 226
Sports, 151–169
    baseball, 151–156
    basketball, 161–165
    Black Power advocacy, 168
    football, 156–161
    gender disparities on Olympic teams, 165–168
    Winter and Summer Olympic Games, 165–168
Sports programming on television, 53–56
    *ABC's Wide World of Sports*, 55
    Arledge, Roone, 55
    college football broadcasts, 55
    history of sports programming before 1960, 53–55
    racial integration and sports broadcasts, 56
    MLB television broadcasts, 53, 55, 56
    NBA television broadcasts, 55–56
    NFL television broadcasts, 54–55
    Olympic Games television broadcasts, 165–168

Stevens, Ray, 71
Student protests, 225–226, 230–231, 249–250
　continuing impact of student protests, 294–295
Subcultures, xvii–xviii
Suburbs and suburban culture
　growth of, xvi
　women in, xviii–xix
The Summer of Love, 231–233
Surfer and hot rod music, 78
Sutton, Henry, 90, 117

Talk radio, 83, 87
Taylor, Elizabeth, 29
Teen idols, 78–79
Teen movies, 18–22
　beach movies, 19–20
　teen-rebellion movies, 20–22
Television, 31–58
　action adventure series, 40–46
　cartoons, 50–51
　family programming, 49–50
　game shows, 51–52
　McLuhan, Marshall, 56–58
　rapid increase in popularity in the 1950s, xxi–xxii
　situation comedies, 35–40
　sports programming, 53–56
　variety shows, 31–35
　Westerns on television, 46–49
*That Girl*, 36–37
Tie-dyed t-shirts, 190
Till, Emmett, murder of, 260–261
*To Kill a Mockingbird*, 4
Tobacco use and advertising, 201–203
Toole, John Kennedy, 108–109
　*A Confederacy of Dunces*, 108–109
Tragedies in music, 80–81
Twiggy, 192–193
*2001: A Space Odyssey*, 16

UCLA basketball teams, coached by John Wooden, 164
Underground comics, 95
United States and world affairs, xxv–xxvi
Updike, John, 116–117
　*The Centaur*, 116
　*Couples*, 116–117
　*Of the Farm*, 116
　*The Poorhouse Fair*, 116
　*Rabbit Run*, 116

Valachi, Joe, and *The Valachi Papers*, 237, 239–240
Variety shows, 31–35, 77–78
Vidal, Gore, 102–104
　*The City and the Pillar*, 102
　conflicts with Norman Mailer, 103
　conflicts with Truman Capote, 103
　conflicts with William F. Buckley, 103
　detective novels written under pseudonym Edgar Box, 102
　*Julian*, 103
　*Myra Breckinridge*, 104
　*Reflections upon a Sinking Ship*, 103
　*Rocking the Boat*, 103
　*Washington, DC*, 103
　*Williwaw*, 102
Video art, 179
Vietnam War, U.S. involvement, xx–xxi, 220–231
　Diem regime, 221–222
　erosion of military morale, 228–229
　effect of war on 1968 presidential election, 229–231
　escalation of American military involvement, 222–224
　French defeat by the Viet Minh, xx–xxi, 220
　Khe Sahn, 227–228
　My Lai massacre, 229
　parallels to Korean War, xx
　POWs, 223
　protests against conduct of the war, 225–226, 230–231, 249–250
　search-and-destroy strategy, 227
　strategic bombing campaigns, 223–224
　Strategic Hamlet Program, 222
　Tet offensive, 227
　undermining of U.S. military, 228
　war crimes, 229
Vonnegut, Kurt, 111–114
　*Cat's Cradle*, 111–112
　*Slaughterhouse-Five*, 112–113
*Voyage to the Bottom of the Sea*, 50

Wallace, George, 258–260
  ardent defense of segregation, 259
  synthesis of racism and populism, 259
  third-party presidential campaign in 1968, 259–260
*Walt Disney's Wonderful World of Color*, 49
Warhol, Andy, 82, 173–175, 210
  Campbell's soup cans series, 175
  the "Factory," 173
  shooting by Valerie Solanas, 173
  work in other media, 174
  works sold at high prices, 175
Washington, DC, race riots in 1968, 219–220
Waters, Muddy, 61
Watts race riots in 1965, 215–216
Wayne, John, 29–30, 222, 265–269
  *The Alamo*, 267
  as a box office draw, 268
  as a controversial public figure, 269
  *The Conqueror*, 267
  *The Green Berets*, 222, 268–269
  *The Longest Day*, 268
  *The Man Who Shot Liberty Valance*, 267
  *The Searchers*, 268
  *The Shootist*, 268, 269
  *Stagecoach*, 266
  *True Grit*, 268
  war films, 266
  Westerns directed by John Ford and starring Wayne, 266
Welch, Raquel, 30, 187–188
*West Side Story*, 3
Western situation comedies, 37–38
Westerns on television, 46–49
Whitman, Charles, and the Texas tower mass murder, 244–245
*Who's Afraid of Virginia Woolf*, 10
*The Wild Bunch*, 18
*The Wild, Wild West*, 48
Williams, Robert F., 261
Wolfe, Tm, 142
  *The Electric Kool-Aid Acid Test*, 142
Women's movement, xviii–xix, xxix, 236–237
  continuing impact of the Women's Movement, 292–293
  employment, xviii–xix
  suffragette and abolitionist movements, xxix
  suburban life, xviii–xix
Wood, Natalie, 30
Woodstock Music Festival, 233–234
World War II in fiction, 109
The Wrecking Crew, 72

Z, 212
Zappa, Frank, 71

## About the Authors

**Martin Kich**, PhD, is a professor of English at Wright State University. He is the author of *Western American Novelists* (Garland, 1995) and coeditor of *Postcolonial Theory in the Global Age: Interdisciplinary Essays* (McFarland, 2013). In 2000, he received Wright State's Trustees' Award, recognizing sustained excellence in teaching, scholarship, and service, and he has also received service awards from AAUP and from the Association for the University Regional Campuses of Ohio.

**Aaron Barlow**, PhD, is a professor of English at New York City College of Technology (CUNY). His published works include Praeger's *The Cult of Individualism: A History of an Enduring American Myth* and *Beyond the Blogosphere: Information and Its Children*, as well as Greenwood's *The Depression Era: A Historical Exploration of Literature*. Barlow holds a doctorate in English from the University of Iowa and has worked extensively with research of primary source documents.

www.ingramcontent.com/pod-product-compliance
Lightning Source LLC
Chambersburg PA
CBHW082029300426
44117CB00015B/2410